AUSTRALIA & NEW ZEALAND

PUBLISHED BY LipCORP Publishing

PUBLISHER/EDITOR-IN-CHIEF David Lipman

ART DIRECTOR & PRE PRESS Lucy Glover Design, © LipCORP Publishing

CONCEPT LipCORP Publishing

COVER, LOGO & AD DESIGN Matt Burns Design, © LipCORP Publishing

SUB EDITORS Tamarah Pinaar, Chris Leese

EDITOR-AT-LARGE (NZ) Neil Miller

COMMISSIONING EDITOR Tim Baker

TITLE
Ultimate Beer Guide Australia & New Zealand.

ISBN
978-0-6465-5359-7 (paperback).

RRP
Australia $24.99 incl. GST.
New Zealand $34.99 incl. GST.

AUTHOR
Various, Edited by *Beer & Brewer* magazine.

CATEGORY
Beer, Cider, Distilling, Drink, Food & Wine, Travel & Holiday, Guidebook.

PRINTER
KHL, Singapore.

CONTRIBUTORS
Helen Alexander, Roger Allnutt, Neal Cameron, Chris Canty, Winsor Dobbin, Paul Edwards, Sandy Guy, Vanessa Hayden, Jo Hegerty, Julie Holland, Bruce Holmes, Pammy Kokoras, John Kruger, Chris Leese, Liz Lewis, Victoria Mackey, Laura MacIntosh, Greig McGill, Monica Mead, Neil Miller, Paul Murrell, Jeremy Sambrooks, Linda Smith, Sadhbh Warren Samantha Wight, Anthony Williams.

IMAGES
Copyright © select images to iStockphoto.com (cover), Tourism ACT, NSW, NZ, NT, Qld, SA, Tas, Visions of Victoria, WA, Destination Great Lake Taupo Tourism Department, Tourism Dunedin, photographers and venues as supplied.

PHOTOGRAPHERS
Daniel Allan, Ben Allerton, Rick Besserdin, Brett Boardman, Brian Rogers Photographics, C.J.R Photography, David Cann, Mark Chipperfield, Chris Canty, Glenn Cormier, Nic Crilly-Hargrave, Sean Fennessy, Gecko Photographics, Richard Hatherly, Sam Highley, John Kruger, Chris Leese, Liz Lewis, Steve Lovegrove, Hamilton Lund, Chris McNamara, Monica Mead, Geoff Murray, Damien Naidoo, Cheyne Tillier-Daly, Rob Fox photography, Donald Y Tong, Ilona Schneider.

ACKNOWLEDGEMENTS
To our contributors and photographers far and wide, the production team, Tourism ACT, NSW, NZ, NT, Qld, SA, Tas, Vic, WA, Tourism NZ, John Stallwood from Nail Brewing Australia, Martin Bennett from The Twisted Hop Christchurch, Emma McCashin from McCashin's Brewery Stoke, Rachael Lipman, Karyn Watson, Marcin Weiss.

COPYRIGHT
© LipCORP Publishing 2011.
PO Box 474 Balgowlah NSW 2093. Tel: 61 415 081 285, www.beerandbrewer.com
All rights reserved. No part of this publication may be reproduced, stored in a retrieval system, or transmitted in any form or by any means, electronic, mechanical, photocopying, recording, or otherwise, without the permission of both the copyright owner and the publisher.

EDITORIAL SUBMISSIONS
If your venue, beer or cider has been missed in this edition of Ultimate Beer Guide, or you are interested in contributing, or we have used your photo without permission/credit, please contact the editor@beerandbrewer.com to ensure inclusion/credit in the 2012 edition. We apologise for any omissions, as we have made every effort to source information to be as comprehensive and correct as possible.

DISTRIBUTION & ORDERING
To order this book to sell in your outlet, please contact:

Bookstores (Aus & NZ)
Woodslane Pty Ltd,
www.woodslane.com.au,
Tel: 61 2 9970 5111

Breweries & Liquor stores (Aus & NZ)
david@beerandbrewer.com
Tel: 61 415 081 285

Home Brew Shops (Aus)
BREW Cellar Distribution,
www.brewcellar.com.au
Tel: 61 7 3209 7574

Home Brew Shops (NZ)
Brewers Coop,
www.brewerscoop.co.nz
Tel: 64 9 525 2448

ONLINE ORDERS AVAILABLE AT
www.beerandbrewer.com/books

To subscribe to or advertise in *Beer & Brewer* magazine Please go to www.beerandbrewer.com

Foreword

"It's known as the culture dodge. Every beer tourist has done it. Or, at least, every beer tourist in a long-term relationship..." So says Pete Brown, a world-renowned beer writer based in the UK, in his travel story about Copenhagen in Issue 17 of *Beer & Brewer* magazine.

Pete's sentiment sets the scene for the *Ultimate Beer Guide* Australia & New Zealand. Let's face it, not everyone drinks beer, and our partners may be more inclined to visit a winery than a brewery, or a shopping mall over a beer festival. The trick is to make the holiday, road trip or getaway seem like it's all about your partner and the kids, and there is so much to see or do, or how relaxing it's going to be.

When you can rattle off a list of day spas, shopping, wineries, zoos and theme parks for the kids, museums, beaches, waterfalls and so on, you won't even need to mention that there is a brewery at the end of the road or a beer festival in town. Since you've selflessly made sure your partner and family have so much to do to enjoy their holiday, stopping by said beer festival is surely your just reward...

To help you create this win-win situation, we created the *Ultimate Beer Guide*. Every article in the 33 regions that follow lists all the breweries, cider producers, distilleries, beer bars, bottle shops and events for the beer enthusiasts, as well as the things to see and do along the way for the family and non-beer drinkers.

We've tried to leave no stone unturned in showcasing all things beer travel across Australia & New Zealand. If you would like to share an experience, weird and wonderful beer or destination we should include in future editions of the *Ultimate Beer Guide*, please email editor@beerandbrewer.com.

One final note to the designated driver, or Skipper as they are known in WA: be sure to check the alcohol level of all drinks prior even trying them, or hopefully have your partner drive for a day (or four)!

Happy and safe travels from the team at *Ultimate Beer Guide* and *Beer & Brewer* magazine.

Contributors

■ **BRUCE HOLMES (NSW)**

Bruce is a freelance travel writer and photographer who lives in the Hunter Valley, NSW. A member of the Australian Society of Travel Writers, his travel articles and photographs have appeared in a range of publications around the world, details of which can be seen at www.bruceholmestravel.com

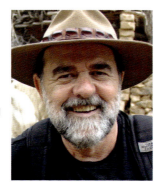

■ **CHRIS CANTY (VIC)**

Chris has been a travel journalist for over 12 years, writing for over 30 publications (including *Beer & Brewer* magazine) worldwide and focusing on travel related topics from business travel to budget guidebooks. His real passion is discovering and sharing craft beers throughout the world, which is why he founded beer tours in Hanoi and Buenos Aires.

■ **JEREMY SAMBROOKS (WA)**

Freelance writer, teacher and keen homebrewer, Jeremy has been writing about beer since 2009. He has spent recent years travelling through the world's most renowned beer regions in the UK, Belgium, Germany and Czech Republic. He now teaches part time, works as a barman for Mash Brewing and writes for *B&B*.

■ **JO HEGERTY (QLD)**

Travel writer, journalist and beer drinker, Jo is based on a sunny peninsula north of Brisbane. Her words regularly appear in *The Sun-Herald* and other newspapers and magazines. To Jo, a good beer means a (yes, warmish) pint of ale at the end of a long walk in Dorset, England.

■ **ANTHONY WILLIAMS (WA)**

There's a beer for every occasion and, as Anthony has discovered, there's also a beer vocation for every minute of the working day. During business hours, he's a beer writer (including for *Beer & Brewer* magazine), seller (retail and wholesale) and ambassador at Perth's BEERtasters events. After hours, he enjoys a beer.

■ **JOHN KRUGER (SA)**

John is a South Australian professional photographer and writer with a passion for all-grain brewing and cooking. His work offers him the opportunity to rub shoulders with some of Australia's best brewers, winemakers and chefs, picking up as many tricks of the trade as possible. www.johnkruger.com.au

in profile

■ **MONICA MEAD (NZ)**

Nelson-based, ex-pat Californian Monica has a penchant for lush, hopped-up American ale. When not tasting her partner's delectable homebrews and wrangling two pet lambs, she tackles food, beer, and wine for regional magazine, *Wild Tomato*, as well as bits and bobs for *Dish*, *Next*, and *North & South*.

■ **NEAL CAMERON (NSW)**

A corporate escapee & a life-long lover and writer of all things beer, Neal retrained as a brewer in 2005. Making a spectacular start in the industry in starting up William Bull Brewery for wine giant De Bortoli Wines, Neal currently heads up The Australian Brewery in Sydney as well as regularly contributing to *B&B*.

■ **NEIL MILLER (NZ)**

Neil is a beer writer who combines a strong knowledge of beer with extensive research, interview skills, a passable palate, pop culture references and a dry wit. In addition to his work as Editor-at-Large for *Beer & Brewer* magazine, Neil's work has appeared in publications such as *Cuisine*, *The Dominion Post*, *Dish*, *BEER* and *The Wellingtonian*.

■ **VANESSA HAYDEN (WA)**

Vanessa has lived in the Kimberley region for 20 years, currently residing in Kununurra. She works within the tourism industry and operates her own marketing company. She has visited many iconic destinations in the region and for the past 10 years has enjoyed writing about her experiences for various travel magazines.

■ **LINDA SMITH (TAS)**

Linda is a news and features writer, who has an affinity for all things beer-related. A recent round-world trip, which included a stopover at Oktoberfest, provided plenty of opportunity for her to sample beers from across the globe and indulge her passion for travel writing.

■ **VICTORIA MACKEY (NSW)**

Travel Writer, Photographer, Producer, with features published in the UK and Australia, Victoria celebrates every destination visited, by eating and drinking with the locals, and gathering stories and images along the way. Victoria also writes and produces television at home.

Contents

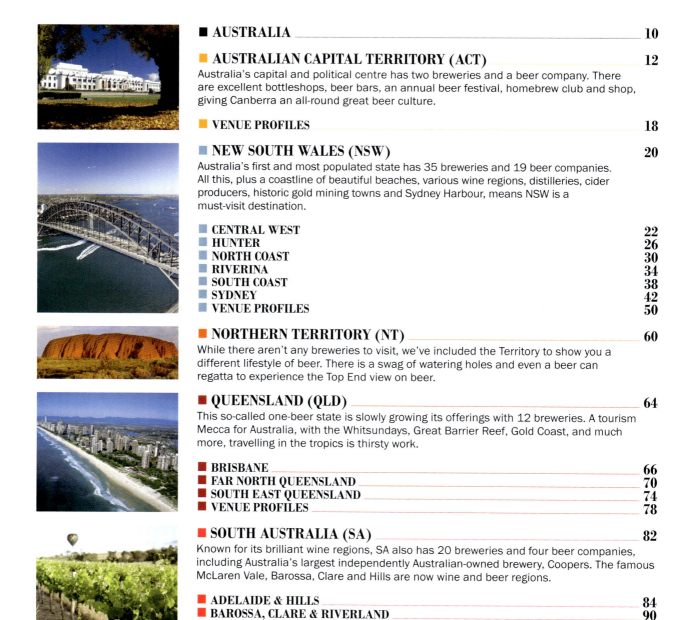

- **AUSTRALIA** — 10
- **AUSTRALIAN CAPITAL TERRITORY (ACT)** — 12

  Australia's capital and political centre has two breweries and a beer company. There are excellent bottleshops, beer bars, an annual beer festival, homebrew club and shop, giving Canberra an all-round great beer culture.

  - **VENUE PROFILES** — 18

- **NEW SOUTH WALES (NSW)** — 20

  Australia's first and most populated state has 35 breweries and 19 beer companies. All this, plus a coastline of beautiful beaches, various wine regions, distilleries, cider producers, historic gold mining towns and Sydney Harbour, means NSW is a must-visit destination.

  - **CENTRAL WEST** — 22
  - **HUNTER** — 26
  - **NORTH COAST** — 30
  - **RIVERINA** — 34
  - **SOUTH COAST** — 38
  - **SYDNEY** — 42
  - **VENUE PROFILES** — 50

- **NORTHERN TERRITORY (NT)** — 60

  While there aren't any breweries to visit, we've included the Territory to show you a different lifestyle of beer. There is a swag of watering holes and even a beer can regatta to experience the Top End view on beer.

- **QUEENSLAND (QLD)** — 64

  This so-called one-beer state is slowly growing its offerings with 12 breweries. A tourism Mecca for Australia, with the Whitsundays, Great Barrier Reef, Gold Coast, and much more, travelling in the tropics is thirsty work.

  - **BRISBANE** — 66
  - **FAR NORTH QUEENSLAND** — 70
  - **SOUTH EAST QUEENSLAND** — 74
  - **VENUE PROFILES** — 78

- **SOUTH AUSTRALIA (SA)** — 82

  Known for its brilliant wine regions, SA also has 20 breweries and four beer companies, including Australia's largest independently Australian-owned brewery, Coopers. The famous McLaren Vale, Barossa, Clare and Hills are now wine and beer regions.

  - **ADELAIDE & HILLS** — 84
  - **BAROSSA, CLARE & RIVERLAND** — 90
  - **FLEURIEU PENINSULA** — 94
  - **VENUE PROFILES** — 98

■ TASMANIA (TAS) — 102

Home to eight breweries and two beer companies, including Australia's oldest brewery, Cascade. With such beautiful scenery, natural produce and historic buildings, the Apple Isle is a haven for getting back to nature and enjoying the simple things in life.

- ■ NORTH TASMANIA — 104
- ■ SOUTH TASMANIA — 108
- ■ VENUE PROFILES — 114

■ VICTORIA (VIC) — 118

The craft beer capital of Australia, with 42 breweries and 13 beer companies. With double these numbers for good beer venues, Melbourne alone is a buzz of hospitality and events, with regional Victoria having many beautiful attractions to also visit.

- ■ MELBOURNE — 120
- ■ MORNINGTON PENINSULA & PHILLIP ISLAND — 128
- ■ NORTH EAST — 130
- ■ NORTH WEST — 134
- ■ SOUTH EAST — 138
- ■ SOUTH WEST — 142
- ■ YARRA VALLEY — 146
- ■ VENUE PROFILES — 150

■ WESTERN AUSTRALIA (WA) — 158

Australia's largest state is recognized with the birth of craft beer in Fremantle, at the Sail and Anchor Hotel. With 33 breweries and one beer company, WA produces world class beers, in a varied landscape that even offers camel trekking.

- ■ MARGARET RIVER — 160
- ■ NORTH WA — 164
- ■ PERTH & FREMANTLE — 166
- ■ SOUTH WA — 174
- ■ SWAN VALLEY — 178
- ■ VENUE PROFILES — 182

■ NEW ZEALAND (NZ) — 192

Kia ora Aotearoa (welcome to NZ in Māori), an island country, with the most breweries per capita in Australasia. The North Island has 35 breweries and five beer companies and South Island has 38 breweries and two beer companies.

- ■ NORTH ISLAND CENTRAL — 196
- ■ NORTH ISLAND LOWER — 200
- ■ NORTH ISLAND TOP — 204
- ■ SOUTH ISLAND BOTTOM — 208
- ■ SOUTH ISLAND TOP — 212
- ■ VENUE PROFILES — 220

■ DIRECTORY OF BEER & CIDER — 224

A comprehensive listing of 1800+ local and imported beers and ciders available in Australia &/or New Zealand. Listings are sorted by country, then alphabetically by brewery or brand, including name, style, ABV and unit size.

■ INDEX — 244

Alphabetical listing of venues mentioned in the *Ultimate Beer Guide*.

LEGEND

 NATIONAL/REGIONAL BREWERY
 BREW PUB
 MICROBREWERY
 BREW ON PREMISE
 (BC) BREWING COMPANY

AUSTRALIA BREWING DIRECTORY

AUSTRALIAN CAPITAL TERRITORY
1. Wig and Pen, CBD
2. Zierholz, Fyshwick
3. U-Brew It
(BC) 1842 Beer, Fyshwick

NEW SOUTH WALES
1. Lion-Nathan, Tooheys, Lidcombe
2. Lord Nelson, The Rocks
3. Scharer's, Picton (BC)
4. Malt Shovel, Camperdown
5. Old Goulburn Brewery
6. Ironbark, Tamworth
7. St Peters Brewery
8. Paddy's, Flemington
9. Bluetongue, Warnervale
10. Hunter Beer Co., Nulkaba
11. Redoak, CBD
12. King St Brewhouse
13. Steel River, Mayfield
14. Australian Independent Brewers, Smeaton Grange
15. Schwartz Brewery Hotel, CBD
16. Murray's, Port Stephens
17. Five Islands, North Wollongong
18. Happy Goblin, Mt Kuringai
19. William Bull, Bilbul
20. Little Brewing Co. Port Macquarie
(BC) Akuna, Mona Vale
22. Mudgee Brewing Co.
23. Infusion Bar & Bistro
24. Stone & Wood, Byron Bay
25. 4 Pines, Manly
26. Byron Bay Premium Brewery
27. Dalgety Brewing Company, Dalgety
28. Mountain Ridge Brewery, Shoalhaven Heads
29. Australian Hotel & Brewery Rouse Hill
30. Kosciuszko Brewing Company, Jindabyne
31. Fishrock Brewery, Mittagong
32. U-Brew It, Tweed Heads
33. U-Brew It, West Gosford
34. U-Brew It , Wollongong
35. U-Brew It, Wyong
36. U-Brew It, Hunter
37. The Beer Factory, Seven Hills
38. The Beer Factory, Wollongong
39. Thirsty Crow, Wagga
40. Black Duck Brewery, Herons Creek
42. Underground Brewing
43. Badlands Brewery (BC)
44. Rocks Brewing, The Rocks (BC)
45. Bluetongue Brewery Café, Pokolbin
46. Murray's At Manly
(BC) Balmain Brewing Company
(BC) Snowy Mountains Brewery
(BC) Fusion Brewing
(BC) Brewtopia
(BC) Bowral Brewing Company
(BC) Barons Brewing Company
(BC) Brothers Ink
(BC) Longboard Brewing Company
(BC) Lovells
(BC) Endeavour True Vintage Beer
(BC) Ekim Brewing Co.
(BC) Koala Beer/Burragumbilli
(BC) St Arnou

QUEENSLAND
1. Lion, Milton
2. CUB, Yatala
3. Sunshine Coast, Kunda Park
4. International Hotel
5. The Brewery, Townsville
6. Burleigh Brewing Co.
7. Blue Sky, Cairns
8. Mt Tamborine Brewing Co.
9. Brewhouse Brisbane, Woolloongabba
10. Castle Glen Brewery
11. U-Brew It, Varsity Lakes
12. U-Brew It, Portsmith
13. U-Brew It, Warana
14. U-Brew It, Nerang
15. Brew By U, Underwood
16. Brew By U, Brendale
17. Brew By U, Labrodoor
18. Brew By U, Clontarf
19. Brew By U, Townsville
20. Brew4U, Boondall
21. Brew4U, Wacol
22. Brew4U, Deception Bay
23. Brew4U, Toowoomba
24. Brew4U, Woolloongabba
25. Brew4U, Cleveland

SOUTH AUSTRALIA
1. Coopers, Regency Park
2. Lion Nathan, Southwark
3. Port Dock, Port Adelaide
4. Grumpy's Brewhaus, Verdun
5. Holdfast Hotel, Glenelg
6. Lovely Valley Beverage Factory, Myponga
7. Barossa Brewing, Greenock
8. Gulf, Hackham
9. Knappstein Enterprise, Clare
10. Steam Exchange, Goolwa
11. Campus Brewery, Regency Park TAFE
12. Lobethal Bierhaus
13. Woolshed Brewery Renmark
14. Brewboys Croydon Park
15. McLaren Vale Beer Company (BC)
16. Goodieson Brewery McLaren Vale
17. Beard & Brau
18. Yorke Brewing, Warooka
19. Boars Rock Winery
20. Pikes Beer Company
21. Pepperjack of Barossa
22. U-Brew It, Parra Hills
23. U Brew Here, Lonsdale
24. Barossa Valley Brewing, Lyndoch
(BC) Swell Brewing Company
(BC) Boar's Rock Beer
(BC) Swanky Beer
(BC) Island Brew

TASMANIA
1. Cascade, South Hobart
2. James Boag's, Launceston
3. Moorilla, Berridale
4. Two Metre Tall, New Norfolk
5. Iron House, White Sands Estate
6. Seven Sheds, Railton
7. Van Dieman Brewing, Evandale
8. Tavener's Brewery Launceston
9. The Squires Bounty
(BC) Wine Glass Bay Brewing
(BC) Tasmanian Chilli Beer Company

VICTORIA
1. CUB, Abbotsford
2. Grand Ridge, Mirboo North
3. Southern Bay, Moolap
5. Buffalo, Boorhaman
6. Holgate Brewhouse, Woodend
7. Jamieson Brewery, Jamieson
8. James Squire Brewhouse, Portland Hotel, CBD
9. Ballarat University Brewery
10. Matilda Bay Garage Brewery, Dandenong South
11. Buckley's Beers, Healesville
12. Independent Distillers, Laverton
13. Three Ravens, Thornbury
14. Lone Hand, Cassilis
15. Mildura Theatre Brewery
16. Mountain Goat, Richmond
18. Bridge Road Brewers, Beechworth
19. Red Hill Brewery
20. Bright Brewery
21. O'Briens Brewery, Ballarat
22. 2 Brothers, Moorabbin
23. Otway Estate, Barongarook
24. Coldstream Brewery
26. The Flying Horse, Warrnambool
27. Sweetwater, Mt Beauty
28. White Rabbit, Healesville
29. Savaraln Brewery, Sale
30. Arctic Fox, Dandenong
31. Tooborac Hotel, Heathcote
32. Hargreaves Hill Brewing Company, Yarra Glen
33. True South, Black Rock
34. Coldwater Creek Tavern & Microbrewery, Doveton
(BC) Beacon Brewing Company
36. Hickinbotham Winery and Brewery
37. Red Duck Provedore
38. Avonmore Estate
39. Bellarine Brewing Company
40. Echuca Brewing Company
41. Harcourt Valley Brewing Company (BC)
42. U-Brew It, Keilor Park
43. U-Brew It, Wodonga
44. The Brew Barn
45. Brew 4 U, Geelong South
46. BarleyCorn Brewers
47. Forrest Brewing, Forrest
48. Kooinda Boutique Brewery
49. Mornington Peninsula Brewery
50. Thunder Road Brewing Company
51. Bullant Brewery, Bruthan
(BC) Broo Bee
(BC) Three Troupers Brewery
(BC) Hawthorn Brewing Company
(BC) Boatrocker Brewing Company
(BC) Temple Brewing Company, Brunswick
(BC) PI55 Brew Company
(BC) Effen Enterprises
(BC) Sundance Brewing International
(BC) Bitch Brewing
(BC) Two Birds Brewing, Melbourne

WESTERN AUSTRALIA
1. Swan Brewery, Perth
3. Last Drop, Canning Vale
4. Bootleg Brewery, Wilyabrup
5. Matso's, Broome
6. Bush Shack, Yallingup
7. Little Creatures, Fremantle
8. Edith Cowan University
9. Feral, Baskerville
10. Ironbark, Caversham
11. Blackwood Valley & The Cidery, Bridgetown
12. Colonial, Margaret River
13. Elmar's, Henley Brook
14. Gage Roads, Palmyra
16. Tanglehead, Albany
17. Occy's, Vasse
18. Mash, Henley Brook
19. Indian Ocean, Mindarie
20. Cowaramup Brewing
21. Billabong, Myaree
22. The Monk, Fremantle
23. Wild Bull Brewery, Ferguson
24. Brew 42, Allanson
25. Duckstein, Wilyabrup
26. The Old Brewery, Perth
27. Mash, Bunbury
28. Old Coast Road, Myalup
29. Duckstein Brewery, Swan Valley
30. Blacksalt Brewery North Fremantle
32. Moody Cow Brewery Ferguson Valley
34. U-Brew It, Canningvale
35. U-Brew It, Joondalup
36. U-Brew It, Malaga
37. U-Brew It, Midvale
38. U-Brew It, Osborne Park
39. U-Brew It, Rockingham
40. U-Brew It, Webberton
41. Brews R Us
42. Eagle Bay Brewing Company, Eagle
43. Brew 'N' Bottle
44. Cheeky Monkey, Marg River
45. The Grove Vineyard Brewery, Willyabrup
(BC) Nail Brewing Company

PROUDLY SUPPORTED BY

BINTANI
Premium ingredients sourced and supplied globally. www.bintani.com.au

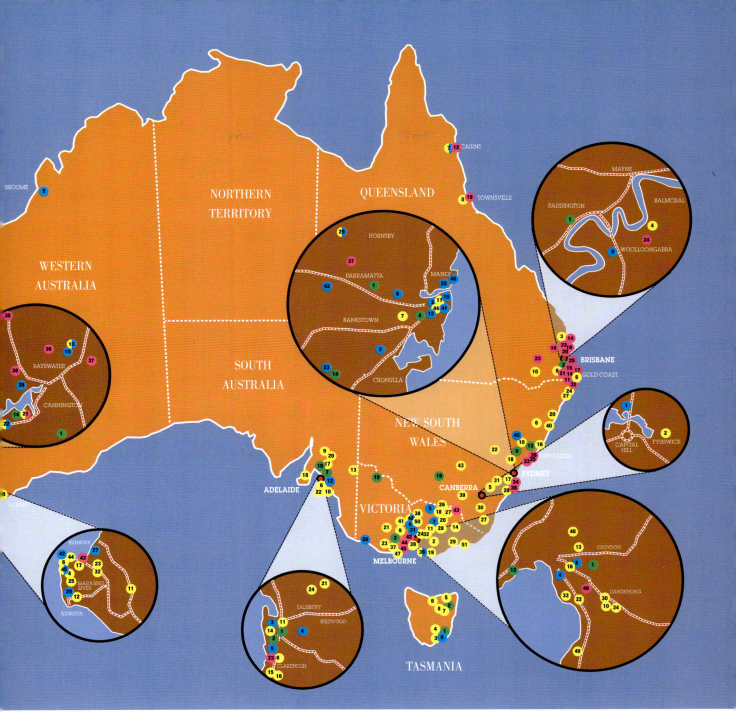

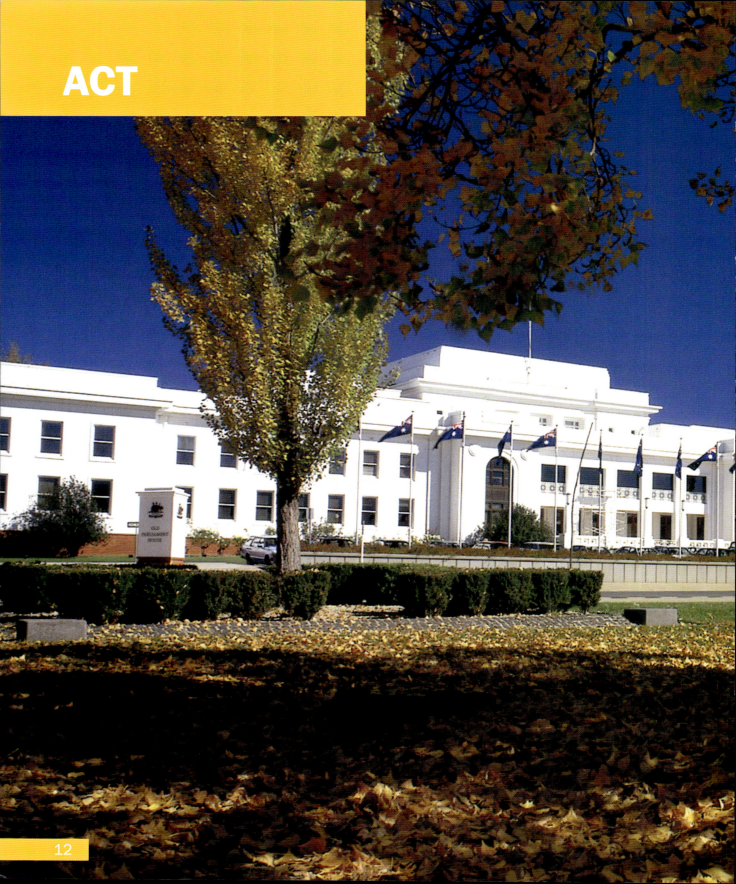

ACT

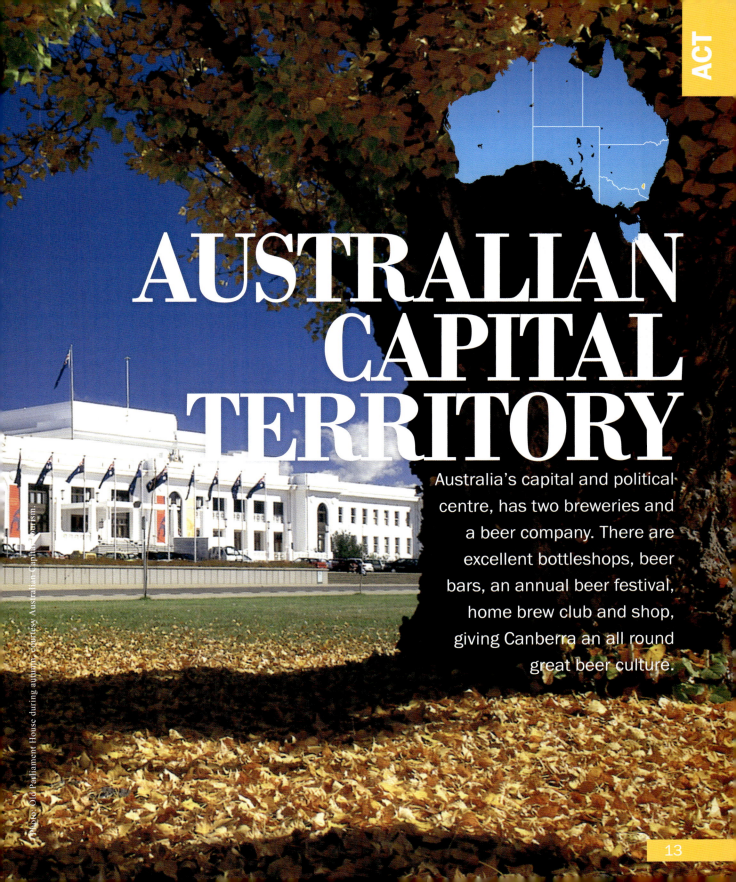

AUSTRALIAN CAPITAL TERRITORY

Australia's capital and political centre, has two breweries and a beer company. There are excellent bottleshops, beer bars, an annual beer festival, home brew club and shop, giving Canberra an all round great beer culture.

ACT

Canberra: home to the world's most elaborate flagpole

AUSTRALIAN CAPITAL TERRITORY

Is Canberra really just a city of fly-in, fly-out latte-sipping bureaucrats out of touch with ordinary Australians, or is there life in our nation's capital beyond five o'clock? If the relatively relaxed local liquor laws are anything to go by, this is one city that takes its social scene very seriously.

By Roger Allnutt

As in most other parts of Australia, Canberrans like to unwind with a beer or a glass of wine after a hard day's work. The local liquor laws make it very easy for locals to buy their favourite tipple, with supermarkets and corner stores allowed to sell liquor seven days a week. And there is a proliferation of excellent liquor outlets.

There are fewer traditional pubs in Canberra, but many people belong to and support sporting and social clubs that have bars, restaurants and cafes, though these places tend to sell only the major brands of beer.

■ BREWERIES

Canberra is home to two breweries: Zierholz Premium Brewery and the Wig & Pen.

Located in Fyshwick, Zierholz Premium Brewery is the brainchild of Christoph Zierholz, who emigrated to Australia with his family from Germany aged 15. After becoming a soil and water scientist, he started making beer. His Bavarian Wheat Beer not only pleased his father with its nod to the motherland, but won him the title of Grand Champion Brewer two years in a row at the Australian Amateur Brewing Championships.

From here, Zierholz established his own full-scale commercial brewery with copper-clad JV Northwest equipment bought and shipped to Australia from the Wild

The Modus Hoperandus (the mode of using hops), at the bar at the Wig & Pen, which was pioneered in Australia by Richard Watkins

Christoph Zierholz mashing in, in the Zierholz Premium Brewery

Richard Watkins on a tour in the brewery at the Wig & Pen

Duck Brewery in Oregon, USA, including a steam-jacketed mash tun, boiler and hot liquor tank, glycol-jacketed stainless-steel conical primary fermenters, cold-conditioning tanks in a custom-designed chiller room and a state-of-the-art filtering and keg-transfer system. Tours of the brewery are available, but it is highly recommended that you telephone ahead.

Zierholz Premium Brewery uses the finest ingredients and traditional German brewing techniques to create a range of handcrafted, European-style beers sure to tantalise any palate. Currently available year round are Amber Ale, German Ale, Hopmeister, Pilsner, Porter, Schankbier and Weizen, along with seasonal and special-occasion brews such as Zierholz Belgian Ale. All are available onsite in the brewery's excellent cafe.

Zierholz beers are also available on tap at various cafes, clubs, bars and restaurants around the city, including the Canberra Labour Club at Belconnen, the Hellenic Club at Woden and Civic, The Lobby restaurant and Pork Barrel Café near Old Parliament House, as well as the Soul Bar at Woden and Rydges Lakeside.

The Wig & Pen microbrewery was established by microbiologist Lachie McOmishin in 1993 with equipment purchased from the defunct Craig Brewery in Sydney, then augmented to create the full-mash brewhouse currently under the charge of brewer Richard Watkins.

A large variety of beers are produced at the Wig & Pen, including six regular brews, ranging from a delicious, rich, creamy Stout to a thirst-quenching Light Ale. Brews on tap and pump include Kembery Ale, Rumpole's Belgian Blonde, Ballyragget Irish Red, Wig & Pen Pale Ale and Kiandra Gold – a pale, golden Pilsner in the Czech style. There are also seasonal brews, including a Wheat Beer and a Bavarian-style Doppelbock. Tours of the brewery can be arranged if you call ahead.

To complement this range of fine beers, the restaurant at the Wig & Pen provides great meals and regular live music to accompany it. On Sunday afternoons you can take part in (or just listen to) the Wig & Pen's Muso's Jam Session. The food is traditional pub fare, and the mains come in generous servings with a recommendation from the brewer on the best brew to match.

■ 1842 BEER

Though contract-brewed in Geelong, 1842 beers are available by the bottle or keg from the company's Fyshwick premises and on tap at All Bar Nun, The Lobby and Pork Belly Café in Canberra.

■ SPECIALIST BARS

Canberra also has three specialist bars with restaurants that specialise in serving unusual local and overseas beers on tap or by the bottle.

Debacle in Lonsdale Street, a cafe strip in Braddon on the edge of the CBD, has a fantastic range including 12 beers on tap and over 100 by the bottle.

Among the beers on tap are Old Speckled Hen (UK), Hoegaarden Wit (Belgium), Pilsner Urquell (Czech Republic), Trumer Pils (Austria) and Franziskaner Dunkel (Germany). Beers by the bottle include many unusual offerings from around Australia and a fascinating selection sourced from far and wide by owner Vladimir Hatala.

Debacle in Braddon also serves great food and holds a beer-matching degustation dinner about four times a year.

Photography by Sam Highley, Steve Lovegrove (select images), Australian Capital Tourism (select images).

Belgian Beer Cafe, Kingston

The extensive selection at Plonk, Fyshwick

All Bar Nun, located in the suburban O'Connor shopping centre close to the Australian National University, has been a popular venue for people from all walks of life since it opened in 1996. Major sporting events are regularly broadcast on the big screen, which always draws a crowd, and the quality menu is complemented by one of Canberra's largest arrays of international and domestic beers. Among the beers available on tap and by the bottle are a number from Coopers, James Squire, Little Creatures, White Rabbit, Mad Brewers, McLaren Vale Beer Company and 1842.

The Belgian Beer Café in Kingston offers around 38 Belgian brews on tap or by the bottle, and the adjoining cafe, Brasserie Little Brussels, offers both traditional Belgian and Australian fare.

■ SPECIALIST BEER (AND WINE) OUTLET

If you are after a really unusual beverage, be it made from grape or grain, then make your way to Plonk, open Thursdays to Sundays at the Fyshwick Fresh Food Market. As well as an extensive range of hard-to-get wines, Plonk stocks more than 900 Australian and imported craft beers, as well as more than 140 ciders – Australia's largest range.

■ HOMEBREWING

There are a couple of places in Canberra specialising in homebrewing, offering materials, products, recipes, brewing advice and so on. Brew Your Own at Home in Kambah Village and U-Brew It in Hume are well with the trip for DIY beer enthusiasts.

■ OTHER ATTRACTIONS IN CANBERRA

Many visitors to Canberra are surprised at the number and variety of its tourist attractions.

As you would expect in a national capital, Canberra is home to many national institutions and monuments, and entry to many of these is free.

Must-visits on an ACT itinerary include the Australian War Memorial, the new and old Parliament House complexes, the National Museum of Australia, National Library of Australia, National Gallery and adjacent National Portrait Gallery, and Questacon (the National Science and Technology Centre) – the latter is always a big hit with the kids. Animal lovers will enjoy a leisurely stroll through the National Zoo and Aquarium (www.visitcanberra.com.au).

Lake Burley Griffin is the centrepiece of Canberra and walks and bike rides around the lake foreshore are rewarding. The National Botanic Gardens are a peaceful retreat and there are great views of Canberra from Black Mountain, Mount Ainslie and Red Hill.

■ PLACES TO STAY

Canberra has accommodation options to suit all budgets. At the top of the range are the historic Hyatt Hotel Canberra, Diamant Hotel, Hotel Realm, Rydges Capital Hill, Novotel and Crowne Plaza Canberra. Serviced apartments are growing in popularity and Waldorf Apartment Hotel, Breakfree Capital Tower Apartments, Quality Suites Clifton on Northbourne and Medina are great options if this is your preference.

There are also many excellent but more modestly priced options located around the city, including All Seasons Olims Hotel, Hotel Heritage, Yowani Country Club and Manuka Park Serviced Apartments.

National Capital Craft Beer Festival, Olims Hotel, Braddon

EVENTS

APRIL
The National Capital Craft Beer Festival
Annual festival held in Canberra during April with 80+ craft beers, food stalls, entertainment and brewer talks. www.canberrabeerfest.com

Canberra District Wine Harvest Festival
www.canberrawines.com.au

SEPTEMBER
14-16 Canberra Regional Wine Show
www.rncas.org.au

28-2 Floriade NightFest
Live entertainment, bars and markets in the park. www.floriadeaustralia.com

OCTOBER
29 Stonefest
All-ages music festival. www.stonefest.com.au

NOVEMBER
Wine, Roses and all that Jazz Festival
Entertainment, food and wine tastings. www.canberrawines.com.au

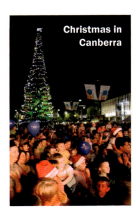

Christmas in Canberra

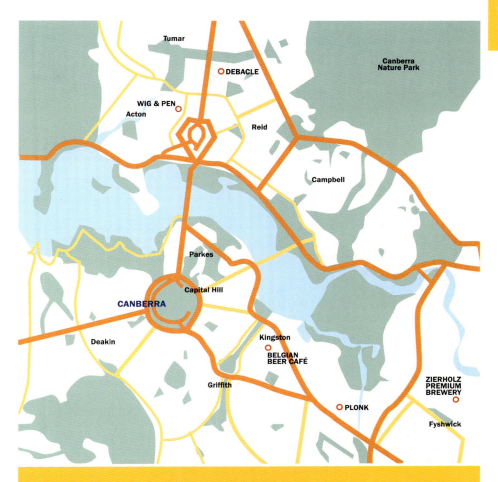

BREWERIES, BEER COMPANY, PLACES TO DRINK

All Bar Nun
O'Connor Shops, St, O'Connor. (02) 6257 9191, www.allbarnun.com.au

Belgian Beer Cafe
Tel 29 Jardine St, Kingston. (02) 62606511

Dan Murphy's
1300 72 33 88
www.danmurphys.com.au

Debacle
30 Lonsdale St, Braddon. (02) 6247 1314, www.debacle.com.au

Plonk Beer Store
Fyshwick Markets, Fyshwick. (02) 6260 6336, www.plonk.net.au

Stricklands Beer Group
www.1842beer.com.au

Wig & Pen Tavern & Brewery
Canberra House Arcade, Canberra City. (02) 6248 0171, www.wigandpen.com.au

Zierholz Premium Brewery
Unit 7/19-25 Kembla St, Fyshwick. Tel: (02) 6162 0523, www.zierholz.com.au

OTHER INTERESTING PUBS

King O'Malleys City Walk, Canberra City, (02) 6257 0111 **PJ O'Reilly's** cnr Alinga St and West Row, Canberra City, (02) 6230 4752 **O'Neills of Dickson** 30 Woolley St, Dickson, (02) 6262 8253 **Durham Castle Inn** Green Square, Kingston, (02) 6295 1769 **The George Harcourt Inn** 3 Gold Creek Rd, Nicholls, (02) 6230 2484 **Tongue and Groove** 1 Bunda St, Canberra City, (02) 6230 4455

Beer & Brewer promotion

AUSTRALIAN CAPITAL TERITORY

WIG & PEN TAVERN & BREWERY

Best Beer Venue in ACT, 2010 Beer & Brewer magazine Awards, along with multiple international award winning beers.

The Wig & Pen is a traditional brewpub and has been part of the Canberra social scene since 1994. The pub offers 16 beers which includes 4 hand pumped real ales, 2 hand pressed ciders and several barrel aged Belgium styles. From the balanced fruitiness of the Kembery Ale to the delightfully robust chocolate and coffee extravaganza, the Velvet Cream Stout and numerous one off batches that really push the boundaries of flavour, there's always something interesting and unique to drink at the Wig.

The Wig is open Monday through Friday 11:30am till late and Saturday and Sunday from 2pm.

Canberra House Arcade
Cnr West Row and Alinga St
Canberra
Tel: (02) 6248 0171
www.wigandpen.com.au

Opening hours:
7 days a week

ZIERHOLZ BREWERY

Christoph Zierholz, owner and Brewmaster at Zierholz Brewery was a former Scientist and Australian Amateur Brewing Champion. He founded the brewery to supply the Canberra Region with its own local beer, as a genuine alternative to local and imported premium brands for the ACT area.

Zierholz is dedicated to creating the freshest and most flavoursome beer for its local region. The beer, mostly traditional German styles but also others, is available on draught at selected cafes, bars, clubs and restaurants in and around Canberra as well as at the Brewery. The brewery restaurant menu showcases locally sourced fresh produce and their own beer to satisfy and inspire the taster.

U6-7/19-25 Kembla St
Fyshwick
Tel: (02) 6162 0523
Zierholz @ Brewery Restaurant and Bar
Tel: (02) 6162 0710
www.zierholz.com.au

Opening hours:
Wed, Sun 11:30am – 3:30pm.
Thu-Sat 11:30am – 9pm or later.

Coming soon: Zierholz @ UC – a new Zierholz Bar and Eatery with its own brewery at Canberra University.

DAN MURPHY'S

Many people think of Dan Murphy's as an incredible wine store, however their passion for liquor runs to beer as well. Even Mr. Murphy himself was known to enjoy a beer or two.

Every Dan Murphy's store sells at least 250 different beers. These range from local favourites to exceptional Craft and premium International beers.

At last count, Dan Murphy's had beers from over 30 countries. And the joy of it all is not just the sheer quantity but the price. You see just like their wines and spirits, every beer in every store is backed by their unique lowest price guarantee.*

There are over 140 Dan Murphy's stores nationwide.

For store locations or trading hours, simply SMS the postcode or suburb and state that you are in to 0487 723 388†, or visit their website.

Tel:1300 723 388
www.danmurphys.com.au

*Conditions apply, visit www.danmurphys.com.au for details. †Standard SMS charges apply

Beer & Brewer promotion　　　　　　　　　　　　　　　　　　　　　　　　　**AUSTRALIAN CAPITAL TERITORY**

PLONK BEER STORE

At Plonk Beer Store they love their beer, stocking more than 800 beers from craft breweries throughout Australia and around the world.

Plonk carries the largest range of Belgian beers in the country. Their weekly educational course, 'Plonk's Beerology Journey' is based on the Beer Judging Certification Programme (BJCP) and is out booked in advance. Over 13 weeks, they cover all the styles of beer that are found on their shelves, delving into the history of each style, food matching combinations and more.

At their weekly beer expression sessions, on Saturday and Sunday afternoon's, they offer free tastings of beer that is stocked in the shop. Their knowledgable staff will answer any question you have to do with beers of the world.

10% discounts on mixed 6 buys and bigger discounts on mixed case buys, offering something that no other beer store can.

All beers are displayed by their style. So, Australian Pale Ales are all together, Belgian Blonde's are all together, German Wheat beers are all together etc etc. This allows customers to try other beers of a style that they enjoy.

Plonk could easliy be called 'Plonk Cider Store' with the largest range of cider in the country, with more than 140 ciders to choose from. Ciders from England, Wales, Belgium, France, New Zealand, Sweden and all over Australia. Dry to sweet, still to sparkling. Plonk have them a plenty.

Their on-line purchasing web page is now up and running. Great deals are on offer if you can't make it into Plonk, Canberra. Delivered anywhere in Australia.

Plonk Beer Store has a wonderful selection of gifts and accessories. Their hampers can be made to order from over 800 beers, 140 ciders or their eclectic hand selected Australian, international and local Canberra district wines. Delivered anywhere in Australia.

Fyshwick Markets
Fyshwick, Canberra
Tel: (02) 6260 6336
info@plonk.net.au
www.plonk.net.au

Opening hours;
Thurs-Sun 8.00am – 5.30pm

NSW

NEW SOUTH WALES

Australia's first and most populated state has 35 breweries and 19 beer companies. All this, plus a coastline of beautiful beaches, various wine regions, distilleries, cider producers, historic gold mining towns and Sydney Harbour, means NSW is a must-visit destination.

NSW

NSW

CENTRAL WEST

A few hours west of Sydney, everything – the air, the vegetation, the land – is that much drier. A cleansing ale is the ideal tonic when checking out the attractions of NSW's central west.

By Bruce Holmes

Sure, Australia's coastal areas may have sophisticated cities, azure sea and white sand – all well and good if you like that sort of thing. And granted, many people do. But there's another side to this beautiful land – vast sweeping plains, blue skies as far as the eye can see... This is the stuff of Aussie literary legend.

■ **MUDGEE AND SURROUNDS**
Mudgee is famous as the place where storyteller Henry Lawson grew up. Along Henry Lawson Drive can be seen the remains of a homestead where Lawson once lived.

Gary and Debbie Leonard of Mudgee Brewing Co

Mudgee is also well known for its vineyards, such as Robert Stein, with very good ports, and di Lusso, featuring Italian grape varieties.

Beer aficionados should head straight for Mudgee Brewing Co in Church Street. Mudgee Brewing brews in a 100-year-old former wool store, where visitors can see all the magic happening and smell the malt and hops as it is transformed into nectar of the Gods. There's a restaurant that serves breakfast, lunch and dinner, plus live music on Thursdays and Sundays.

There are seven beers on tap here, including a Pale Ale, Wheat Beer and Chocolate Porter. Brewer Gary Leonard's favourite among the seasonal beers is the India Pale Ale, which is amber in colour and packed with hops.

Another place where you can enjoy a Mudgee Brewing Co beer is at the Wineglass Bar and Grill in the Cobb & Co Court Boutique Hotel.

Nearby, the old gold-mining town of Gulgong has a Henry Lawson Centre with books and memorabilia, the Pioneers Museum and a main street that time forgot. There's also Hill End, where you can fossick for gold, and Sofala, whose main street featured in a Russell Drysdale painting.

Heading toward Dubbo, a stop at Wellington's caves complex is worthwhile, with guided tours of the Gaden and Cathedral caves, as well as the adjacent phosphate mine notable for the many bone fragments and fossils as old as 300,000 years found there.

Ballooning in Canowindra

Taronga Western Plains Zoo

■ DUBBO

Dubbo's attractions include Old Dubbo Gaol, a 19th-century prison used right up until 1966. The site of eight hangings, it offers themed tours led by characters such as an unforgiving warden or devious prisoner.

Taronga Western Plains Zoo is a brilliant activity for the whole family, and it's so vast that you'll feel like you own the place. Something special is the Wild Africa Encounter, a behind-the-scenes opportunity to get up close with zebras, cheetahs and giraffes and hand feed endangered black rhinos.

When you're worn out from all that activity, head to the Commercial Hotel, established in 1862 and popular for its food, or to the contemporary surrounds of Monkey Bar, Dubbo's newest bar, restaurant and cafe serving a range of craft beers.

■ PARKES

On the Newell Highway is the CSIRO Parkes Observatory. It has been used by astronomers for almost 50 years and was featured in the movie *The Dish* (2000).

Parkes Observatory

A more down to earth attraction is the Parkes Car Museum, with a display that's refreshed every six months. Maybe you'll see the last Cadillac (a 1976 Seville) purchased by Elvis Presley – a sure-fire hit with the fans and impersonators who flock here every January for the Countrylink Parkes Elvis Festival.

■ FORBES

Southwest of Parkes lies Forbes, which boomed in the 1860s gold rush and was targeted by bushrangers Ben Hall and Frank Gardiner. Hall was shot by police at Billabong Creek in 1865 and lies buried at Forbes Cemetery, as does Ned Kelly's sister, Kate. Visit Forbes Historical Museum for the full story.

There's also McFeeters Motor Museum, with a collection said to range from veterans to custom cars, rare, common and just downright bizarre.

■ COWRA AND CANOWINDRA

On the southern edge of the district is Cowra, which features vineyards with beautiful views of the Lachlan River Valley, where visitors will also find the Lachlan Valley Railway preservation society's steam and diesel locomotives and the Cowra War Museum's collection of wartime and rural memorabilia. There's also the award-winning Japanese Garden and Cultural Centre with its traditional Edo Cottage and tea house.

Nearby Canowindra features guesthouses, art galleries and cafes as well as the Age of Fishes Museum, which contains a collection of 360-million-year-old freshwater fish fossils discovered nearby in 1955.

Canowindra also bills itself as Australia's capital of hot-air ballooning – a peaceful way to spend an early morning.

■ ORANGE

The Orange district's parks and reserves make it ever so green. There's Banjo Paterson Memorial Park, site of the poet's birthplace, walks in Cook Park and the reserve at Mount Canobolas, the ancient volcano standing 1395 metres above sea level.

On the town's outskirts is local produce store Totally Local, selling meats, vegetables, jams, bread, local wines and Badlands Brewery beer.

Badlands Brewery's Jon Shiner (back right) at Coolroom Cafe

Orange local Jon Shiner is the man behind Badlands and while the brewing takes place in Sydney at present, he hopes to have his own brewery on the Totally Local site up and running early in 2012. But in the Cool Room Cafe @ Totally Local, four of his beers are on tap already.

His flagship Badlands Pale Ale, an English-style Golden Ale, brewed using English Maris Otter malted barley, English yeast and Whitbread Goldings hops, is what Jon calls his "homage to the beer I missed most from the UK when I arrived in Australia 16 years ago – Archers Golden from Swindon".

Just outside Orange, on the way in from Canowindra, is Small Acres Cyder, where Gail and James Kendell's business has thrived since opening in 2007.

Small Acres claims to be the first to release a dessert-style cider, Pomona Ice, and James believes the brewery's Cidre Rouge, made using Methode Champenoise for a dry, savoury finish, is one of a kind in Australia.

At Millthorpe, mid-way between Orange and Bathurst, is Basalt@The Commercial Hotel. A busy restaurant and bar, it offers an excellent range of beer, cider and spirits from around the region, plus a range of local wines.

■ BATHURST

Top Bathurst attractions include Abercrombie House, an 1870s Tudor Gothic/Scottish mansion, Chifley Dam for watersports and, 70 kilometres south of town via Trunkey Creek, the Abercrombie Caves, which includes a bushranger's hideout.

Another place once associated with bushrangers Ben Hall and Johnnie Vane is the historic homestead of

Central Ranges Brewing Co

Merembra. Today, it's not the spirits of the bushrangers lingering here but spirits of the drinking kind. In 2008, Bev and Ian Glen established Stone Pine Distillery. Stone Pine's flagship product is a dry gin, made with five native botanicals, and other offerings include Founder's Rum, Wild Lime Vodka, a peach schnapps, a grappa and a summer berry liqueur.

Among the places stocking the Stone Pine and Small Acres products is the Beekeeper's Inn at Vittoria, west of Bathurst, a licensed cafe where they've just begun brewing their first ale. They'll be trading as the Central Ranges Brewing Company and, proud of their history, an image of the 1859 Cobb and Co. cottage will feature on the bottles.

Bathurst, of course, has one annual obsession – the Supercheap Auto Bathurst 1000, held every October. Get in the mood before getting in on the action at the National Motor Racing Museum on Mount Panorama, which includes motorcycles, cars and racing memorabilia.

Some of the fare on offer at Small Acres Cyder, near Orange (left) The Stone Pine Distillery (right)

Underground Abercrombie Caves and cavern, Trunkey Creek

BEER, CIDER, DISTILLERY

Badlands
426 Mitchell Hwy, Orange
0411 025 437
www.badlandsbrewery.com.au

Central Ranges Brewing Co.
2319 Mitchell Highway
Vittoria
(02) 6368 7382
www.beekeepersinn.com

Dan Murphy's
1300 72 33 88
www.danmurphys.com.au

Mudgee Brewing Co
4 Church St, Mudgee
(02) 6372 6726
www.mudgeebrewing.com.au

Small Acres Cyder
12 Akhurst Rd, Borenore
(02) 6365 2286
www.smallacrescyder.com.au

Stone Pine Distillery
Merembra
218 Gormans Hill Rd
Bathurst
(02) 6332 1517
www.stonepinedistillery.com.au

NSW

EVENTS

JANUARY
Countrylink Parkes Elvis Festival
www.parkeselvisfestival.com.au

MARCH
Mudgee International Short Film Festival
www.mudfest.com.au
Canowindra Balloon Festival
www.canowindra.org

APRIL
Annual Orange Show
www.orange-nsw.com
Orange F.O.O.D. Week
www.orangefoodweek.com.au
Annual Dubbo Show
www.dubbotourism.com.au
Forbes Camel Races
www.forbes-nsw.com

SEPTEMBER
Mudgee Wine Festival
www.mudgeewine.com.au

OCTOBER
Supercheap Auto Bathurst 1000
www.bathurst.v8supercars.com.au
Blue Mountains Craft Beer Festival
Though not quite in the Central West, on 15 October 2011 the Fairmont Resort at Leura will host the inaugural Blue Mountains Craft Beer Festival, an initiative of Schwartz Brewery, founders of the National Capital Craft Beer Festival.
Orange Wine Week
www.orange-nsw.com

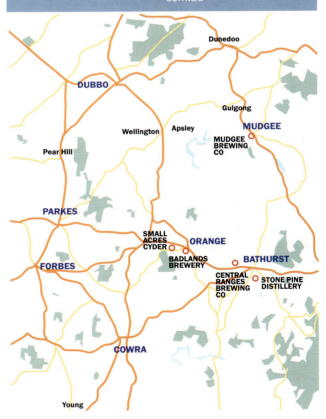

Photos: Gecko Photographics, Tourism NSW

TOURISM INFORMATION

Mudgee Region www.visitmudgeeregion.com.au **Wellington** www.visitwellington.com.au **Dubbo** www.dubbotourism.com.au **Parkes** www.parkes.nsw.gov.au **Forbes** www.forbes-nsw.gov.au **Cowra and Canowindra** www.cowratourism.com.au **Orange** www.orange-nsw.com **Bathurst** www.visitbathurst.com.au

NSW

HUNTER

The fertile farmlands of the Hunter have given rise to a wealth of world-class wines, olives and some sweet, sweet brews. If you love the finer things in life, the Valley and surrounds are the place to be. **By Bruce Holmes**

The Hunter region's 120-plus wineries with cellar door operations may be its best-known tourist drawcard, but there are several breweries and a host of things to do apart from visiting vineyards.

■ POKOLBIN-CESSNOCK AREA

Potters Hotel Brewery Resort is built on the site of a 1920s pottery business at Nulkaba near Cessnock. Hunter Beer Co's microbrewery is right next to the hotel and head brewer, Keith Grice, leads public tours (daily at 12pm, 2pm, 4pm; $10) of the facility. Keith explains the brewing process and guides the tasting of selected brews, then lets you get hands-on with the brewing process – crushing hops between your fingers to release the aromatic oil and tasting different malts. You'll never look at a beer the same way again.

Hunter Beer offers a German-styled Kolsch, a crisp Golden Ale, the hoppy and bitter Pale Ale, the Belgian-inspired Wit Bier (an unfiltered Wheat Beer), an alcoholic Ginger Beer and more. The beers are on tap in the restaurant and in the new bar next to the brewing area.

The enthusiasm for making something different saw Hunter win a number of awards at Melbourne's 2009 Australian International Beer Awards and the Champion Porter Trophy in the 2010 Awards for its Chocolate Porter.

Aerial view of Hunter Valley Gardens, Hunter

Hunter Beer Co's beers on tap at Potters Hotel Brewery Resort

Brewer Jess Herman giving a tour at Hunter Beer Co

Potters offers accommodation from spa suites to group rooms, and the restaurant's lamb shanks and beer and beef pie are most welcome after a day's driving or touring.

A short drive to Pokolbin takes you to the Hunter Resort, where the Bluetongue Brewery Cafe is situated. The original Bluetongue Brewery was founded by four Hunter entrepreneurs in 2003, but success and the need for expansion saw them sell a part share to John Singleton and the remainder to Pacific Beverages, which built a new $120 million brewery at Warnervale on the Central Coast.

At the Bluetongue Brewery Cafe, beer lovers can try the Tasting Paddle of six brews (with accompanying notes), ranging from alcoholic Ginger Beer, brewed from a 300-year-old recipe with green Thai ginger, to the hoppy Traditional Pilsener and a Premium Black Ale with roasted chocolate characteristics for lovers of dark beer.

The Pokolbin area is famous for its wineries, and it's worth trying some large and some small. Among the bigger ventures, a visit to Petersons Champagne House is worthwhile. Renowned for its sparkling wines made by Methode Champenoise, its dessert wines are also excellent. The restaurant and Hunter Valley Chocolate Company outlet on site make this a good place to stop.

Another of the big boys to visit is McGuigan Wines; be sure to sample the cheeses at the Hunter Valley Cheese Company next door while you're there. Pick up some antipasto and bread to go with the cheese and a bottle of McGuigan's – you can make lunch on the outdoor tables more economically than eating in a restaurant.

Smaller cellar doors have an ambience all their own. Consider Windsor's Edge (adjacent to top Hunter restaurant Amanda's on the Edge), the relaxed Honeytree Estate and the Small Winemakers Centre, which represents several different vineyards.

When you've eaten and drunk your fill, work off the excesses with a stroll around Hunter Valley Gardens. Eight kilometres of pathways meander through 10 themed gardens, such as the Sunken Garden with waterfall feature, Rose Garden (with 8000 plants!) and the Storybook Garden, where you can see Jack and Jill tumble down the hill or join Alice in Wonderland at the Mad Hatter's Tea Party.

The village here has shops that sell all sorts of things. There's even a British Lolly Shop. Close by is Harrigan's Irish Pub which stocks a considerable variety of boutique and imported beers, with names like Old Fart, Black Sheep and Hob Goblin among them. There's accommodation here too.

Other activities include horse and carriage rides, hot-air ballooning, a zoo, golf, cycling, day spas and a cooking school.

MAITLAND AREA

Centrally located between the vineyards and Newcastle and Port Stephens, the Maitland area has attractions of its own.

Maitland Gaol will thrill history buffs and ghost-seekers, and offers tours led by ex-inmates, ex-warders and psychics. Established in 1844, the prison saw 16 hangings and several escapes before its closure in 1998. In 2011 (5-6 November), the gaol will be the venue for the Bitter & Twisted International Boutique Beer Festival.

Steamfest, held annually in April, sees Maitland revert to yesteryear with steam locomotives taking passengers to Newcastle, Branxton and Paterson, while all sorts of steam-driven machinery is on display in a field adjacent to the station.

The historic river port village of Morpeth is popular, with many craft shops, boutiques, galleries and cafes. Themed weekends are a feature here, from jazz to novelty teapots.

Good pubs in the area include The Imperial in Maitland and the Windsor Castle at East Maitland, while for anyone needing to stock up there's a Dan Murphy's liquor outlet at the Greenhills shopping mall.

NEWCASTLE

There are many reasons to visit Newcastle – its beaches, revamped foreshore precinct, historic Fort Scratchley, art gallery and eat streets – notably Darby St in town (if you love Vietnamese, make a beeline for Le Dynasty) and Beaumont St in nearby Hamilton (The Grain does to-die for Thai).

The Bluetongue Brewery Cafe at the Hunter Resort, Pokolbin

Ian Partland, Steel River Brewery

Head Brewer Shawn Sherlock (right) taking a group tour at Murray's Brewery

By the harbour, in Honeysuckle Drive, is Silo Restaurant & Lounge, winner of the *Beer & Brewer* Best Beer Venue award for Best Restaurant/Cafe. Here there are many Australian boutique beers as well as a massive range of imported beers. For $20, you can even lift a stein of Löwenbräu Original Lager. Stay tuned to the Silo website for monthly beer degustation dinners and the seasonally updated beer list.

The former steel city has a lively pub scene. The Clarendon Hotel in the CBD has 24 bottled Australian craft beers and three rotating guest taps for local craft beers and one tap dedicated to imported beer. The Albion Hotel 'opposite the marina' has seven of its 10 taps with local and imported craft beers, around 60 Aussie craft and fully imported bottled beers and bi-monthly beer degustation dinners recently including Coopers, James Squire and Stone & Wood. Others worth a mention are Finnegans Irish Pub in Darby Street, the Beach Hotel Merewether overlooking the ocean and Queens Wharf Brewery by the harbour.

Growler machine at Warners at the Bay Bottleshop

Nearer to Lake Macquarie is Warners at the Bay. The hotel is hosting its 4th Annual Boutique Beer Festival on 28 November, 2011, while the on-site bottleshop stocks more than 900 beers from 50 countries and now offers growlers (2L glass bottles) for takeaway sales.

Situated at Mayfield West, the Steel River Brewery produces Virgin Blonde, an organic low-carb Lager made from lightly roasted barley that has been grown in virgin soil, without the use of pesticides or herbicides. There are no public tours or tastings however.

A locally owned beer company, Koala Beer, contract brews three beers that are readily available in the Newcastle area, plus nationally on Virgin Australia domestic and V Australia international flights. Look out for Burragum billi Organic Lager and the soon-to-be-released Wilde Organic Golden Lager and Wilde Gluten-Free Lager.

■ PORT STEPHENS AREA

In the area north of Newcastle harbour, visitors can take a 4WD tour of the Stockton sand dunes, the largest in the southern hemisphere. This includes sandboarding as well as visits to the historic Sygna shipwreck and the shacks of Tin City where part of the first *Mad Max* movie was filmed.

The bay at Port Stephens is 2½ times the size of Sydney Harbour. Cruise all year and catch the resident bottlenose dolphins at play; from late May to early November, you might see migrating humpback whales as well.

Close to Nelson Bay on the road from Newcastle is Oakvale Farm, a magic place for children and the young-at-heart to feed kangaroos, goats and emus, pat koalas and see the reptile exhibit.

While the children are having fun with the animals, just up the road there's more brewery action.

Murray's Brewery is located on Nelson Bay Road at Bobs Farm. Take the tour (daily at 2pm, $5) and learn how hops are imported from New Zealand as pressed pellets and how grain from Belgium is preferred for sugar extraction.

Murray's makes 30 beers, and the bottling plant here can handle 2000 bottles an hour. Just like your spag bol improves in flavour in the fridge, so too Murray's beers get two weeks of bottle conditioning before they're released to the discerning drinking public.

Murray's deserves points for creative naming, with beers like Punch and Judy, Retro Rocket and Dark Knight gracing the shelves. But that's how it is with these microbrewers – they just can't help but get creative.

Silo Restaurant & Lounge

EVENTS

FEBRUARY
Taste of the World Beer Festival
Newcastle Harness Racing Club
www.tasteoftheworld.com.au

FEBRUARY/MARCH
Hamilton Food & Wine Festival
Beaumont St, Hamilton

MARCH
Karuah Oyster & Timber Festival
www.portstephens.nsw.gov.au

APRIL
Steamfest Maitland

JUNE
Blue Water Country Music Festival www.bluewatercountrymusic.com.au
Hunter Valley Food & Wine Month

SEPTEMBER
Shoal Bay Jazz, Wine & Food Festival
www.shoalbayresort.com
Spring Festival of Flowers
Hunter Valley Gardens

OCTOBER
Jazz in the Vines
Tyrell's Vineyard
Opera in the Vineyards
Wyndham Estate Winery
Rose Spectacular
Hunter Valley Gardens

NOVEMBER
Bitter & Twisted International Boutique Beer Festival
Maitland Gaol, www.bitterandtwisted.com.au
Tastes at the Bay
Nelson Bay
www.tastesatthebay.com.au

Warners at the Bay Boutique Beer Festival
Warners Bay, www.warnersatthebay.com.au

MARKETS
Nelson Bay Craft Markets at Neil Carroll Park, 1st, 3rd and 5th Sundays every month, alternating with **Tomaree Craft Markets** at Tomaree Sports Complex, 2nd and 4th Sundays.

BREWERIES BEER CO. & PLACES TO DRINK

Bluetongue Brewery Cafe
917 Hermitage Rd, Pokolbin
(02) 4998 7777
www.hunterresort.com.au/bluetongue

Harrigan's Cellars
Hunter Valley Gardens, Pokolbin
Tel (02) 4998 4300
www.hvg.com.au

Hotel Delany
134 Darby St, Cooks Hill
(02) 4929 1627
www.thedelany.com

Hunter Beer Company
Wine Country Drv, Nulkaba
(02) 4991 7922
www.pottershbr.com.au
www.hunterbeer.com.au

Koala Beer
www.koalabeer.com.au

Mary Ellen Hotel
57 Railway St, Merewether
(02) 4963 1100
www.maryellen.com.au

Murray's Craft Brewing Co
3443 Nelson Bay Rd, Bobs Farm; (02) 4982 6411
www.murraysbrewingco.com.au

Silo Restaurant & Lounge
18/1 Honeysuckle Drive
Newcastle; (02) 4926 2828
www.silolounge.com.au

Steel River Brewery
4 Laurio Pl, Steel River Industrial Estate, Mayfield West
(02) 4960 0000
www.steelriverbrewery.com

The Albion Hotel
72 Hannell St, Wickham
(02) 4962 2411
www.thealbion.com.au

The Clarendon Hotel
347 Hunter St, Newcastle
(02) 4927 0966
www.clarendonhotel.com.au

Warners at the Bay
320 Hillsborough Rd, Warners Bay
(02) 4956 6066
www.warnersatthebay.com.au

TOURISM INFORMATION

Hunter Valley Wine Country www.winecountry.com.au **Maitland** www.maitlandhuntervalley.com.au
Newcastle www.visitnewcastle.com.au **Port Stephens** www.portstephens.org.au

NSW
NORTH COAST

From beer to beaches to bush, NSW's North Coast has it all

Just four hours' drive north of Sydney is a holiday trail full of craft breweries, world-class scenery and enough leisurely activities to fill a three- or four-day getaway. **By Samantha Wight**

Sydneysiders are a fortunate lot. When they've had their fill of the city, they can just pack up the car and drive to Paradise, also known as the NSW North Coast.

■ PORT MACQUARIE AND SURROUNDS

Nestled between the Pacific Ocean and the Hastings River, Port Macquarie is the perfect place to begin a beer lovers' journey north to the surfing Mecca of the Northern Rivers.

Just before you drive into Port, detour off the Pacific Highway to Herons Creek, home to Black Duck Brewery owned by Al and Kate Owen. "Our mainstay is our Proper Bitter," says Al, which he describes as being in the style of English Bitter. "It is not overly bitter, with a good balance of UK hops and Aussie malts," he says, "and at 4% ABV and lower carbonation, it's a sensational beer."

Black Duck also has a Dark Beer in the testing phase. "At this stage it's not very dark – certainly not as dark as I expected – but it still has a good chocolate-malt flavour," says Al. The working title for this beer is Daylight Savings, and it weighs in at about 5% ABV. Stay tuned to *Beer & Brewer* for the outcome.

Black Duck doesn't offer tours of its brewery due to zoning restrictions but Al says by year's end, tours by appointment may be available. He and Kate suggest a visit to Bago Vineyards (in nearby Wauchope), which serves Proper Bitter on tap at its monthly Sunday Jazz afternoon. Or, for those heading into Port Macquarie, Lighthouse Beach Flavours and The Breakwall Restaurant both have Proper Bitter on tap.

On the road into Port Macquarie is The Little

Al Owen, Black Duck Brewery

The Little Brewing Company is a boutique brewery with a big following

Brewing Company. Launched in 2007 by Kylie and Warwick Little, it produces small-batch beer with quality ingredients. The Littles open their cellar door at selected times from Monday to Saturday, offering tastings and sales of their brews, which are bottled under the Wicked Elf and Mad Abbot labels.

Wicked Elf Pale Ale and Witbier are now known to some as 'Oprah's beer' after being consumed at the television host's glitzy cocktail event on Sydney Harbour in 2010. Kylie describes the Witbier as having "low bitterness and subtler flavour", and often wins over non-beer drinkers.

The Mad Abbot label encompasses limited-release beers, including a Belgian-style Dubbel and 9.5% ABV Tripel – which rules out the driver tasting too much.

Wicked Elf Pale Ale is on tap at Zebu Bar+Grill, located right on the waterfront in Port Macquarie's CBD. Flame on the Water, has Wicked Elf Pale Ale, Wicked Elf Witbier and Mad Abbot Dubbel on tap. If you're heading to the hinterlands, Kylie and Warwick recommend sampling some of their beer at Blue Poles in Byabarra.

For those flying into Port Macquarie and renting a car for the journey north, the first brew of the holiday can be had at the Airport Cafe & Bar, where The Little Brewing Company's beer is available in bottles.

When you've had your fill of food and beer, send Mum to the Port Macquarie Day Spa for a soothing massage, while Dad and the kids take a tour of the Koala Hospital. And on the way out of town the next day, don't forget to stop at Ricardoes Tomatoes & Strawberries to pick your own fruit.

■ THE COFFS COAST AND WATERFALL WAY

Back on the beer trail, it's full-steam north. South West Rocks, north-east of Kempsey, is a great place to extend the long weekend by a day or two. This area is home to the ruins of historic Trial Bay Gaol and Smoky Cape Lighthouse, both worth exploring. There are relaxed eateries such as Pizza on the Rocks, and great local pubs like the Seabreeze Beach Hotel and The Heritage Hotel of Gladstone.

The Koala Hospital

Next, head north to the Coffs Coast, a breathtaking drive through World Heritage Listed rainforests. The Waterfall Way takes in Bellingen and Dorrigo. Rich volcanic soils provide the perfect growing conditions for macadamias, coffee, tea, dairy and wine. In the charming town of Bellingen, stop into the Federal Hotel and try a schooner of the local Bellingen Darkwood Ale (brewed by local homebrewer Richard Jennings). Morning tea should include macadamia bread from the Hearth Fire Bakery.

Half an hour up the Waterfall Way is the Dorrigo Plateau. The Dorrigo Rainforest Centre, with a 70-metre suspended walkway over the rainforest canopy, is a must. Lunch afterwards at Lick the Spoon in the Red Dirt Distillery – Australia's only potato vodka manufacturer – in Dorrigo.

Back on the coast, pick up a picnic for dinner from the Fisherman's Co-op on Marina Drive in Coffs Harbour, with takeaway beer from The Jetty Cellars. Stay at Novotel Pacific Bay Resort and let the kids join the circus. Yep, they can learn to fly the trapeze or juggle like a clown while you kick back and relax. Darlington Beach Holiday Park, nestled in 44.5 hectares of forest, is a nature lover's option.

■ THE BYRON COAST AND HINTERLAND

A few hours' drive from the Coffs region and about 10 hours' out of Sydney, paradise continues – and so does the beer. Hang-gliders ride the thermals over endless beaches and rolling hinterlands. Byron Bay bustles with tourists and a growing number of artists, writers and tree-changers.

First stop must be Stone & Wood, on the outskirts of town. Established in 2008, it was started by three mates, brewer Brad Rogers, Jamie Cook and Ross Jurisich.

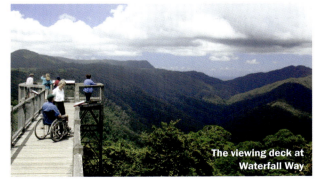

The viewing deck at Waterfall Way

Master distiller David Scott at the Red Dirt Distillery

The dramatic Byron Coast

Stone & Wood's handcrafted Lager is Germanic in style. "It's brewed from pure German malt, which adds both a softness to the palate and a full-bodied malt character," says Jamie. "We add the German hops Tettnang and Spalt to provide a subtle bitterness that is in perfect harmony with the malt at 4.7% ABV."

In tribute to the brewing practices of Middle Ages, the boys brew a Stone Beer by "adding wood-fired stones to the kettle to rouse the boil and intensify the malt characters of the brew," says Jamie. "The brewing stones also caramelise the wort to create subtle but rich toffee-like flavours."

Visitors are welcome to pop into the brewery for a taste and a chat. Jamie and co also take group bookings – drop them an email to ensure they are home when you arrive.

You can pick your preferred Stone & Wood beverage at the brewery or in one of many bottle shops and pubs in town, such as The Beach Hotel. "The Beach Hotel in Byron is an icon of a pub, and our Pacific Ale was designed with lazy, schooner-filled afternoons in mind," says Jamie.

Stone & Wood Brewery

Next stop is Byron Bay Premium Brewery. It hosts tours and allows guests to sit in the working brewery while enjoying lunch from the Buddha Bar Restaurant. Or sit in the beer garden and soak up sunshine while enjoying a brew like Billy Goat Dark Lager or Broken Head Bitter. After lunch, stroll along Cape Byron Walking track or visit stunning Broken Head Reserve.

■ NEED A PLACE TO STAY?

Those feeling cashed up and in need of a world-class pamper can head to hip Rae's on Wategos, host to rock stars, royalty and the über-traveller. For families, the villas of East on Byron are a swank option. If you want to get out of town, head to the Byron Bay Rainforest Resort, which offers budget-style accommodation in coastal rainforest and ti-tree wetlands.

Don't forget a trip to the lush hinterlands. The historic Bangalow Hotel is nestled into the picturesque village of Bangalow, just 15 minutes' drive out of Byron. And enjoy a relaxing afternoon on the wide verandahs of the beautifully restored Middle Pub in the laidback town of Mullumbimby.

Takeaway beer and wine is available from The Cellar chain of bottleshops in Lawson Street, Byron Bay, and all over the Northern Rivers district.

In Byron Bay, eat fish and chips at Fishmongers Café for dinner with a cold Lager, and as the sun dips low, visit the famous Cape Byron lighthouse, Australia's most easterly point. From here, the north coast stretches onwards towards Tweed Coast to the Queensland border where more beer awaits the thirsty traveller.

Byron Bay Premium Brewery and Buddha Bar

EVENTS

COFFS COAST
Coffs Coast Growers Markets Every Thursday, 8am-4pm Coffs Harbour City Square, Harbour Drv (02) 6648 4084
Bellingen Growers' Market Every 2nd and 4th Saturday of the month, 8am-1pm Bellingen Showground, Black St (02) 6653 5288
Woolgoolga Beach Markets Every 2nd Saturday of the month, Woolgoolga Beach Reserve (02) 6654 1785
Coffs Jetty Markets Every Sun, 8am-2pm Jetty Shopping Village (02) 6651 1151
JANUARY Festival of Sails www.coffscoast.com.au
APRIL NRMA Woolgoolga Curryfest www.curryfest.com.au
JULY Sawtell Chilli Festival www.sawtellchillifestival.com.au
Janison Short Sharp Film Festival www.shortsharpfilmfest.com
AUGUST Bellingen Jazz Festival www.bellingenjazzfestival.com.au
OCTOBER Coffs Coast International Buskers & Comedy Festival www.coffsharbourbuskers.com

PORT MACQUARIE
Hastings Farmers Market, Every 4th Saturday of the month, 9am-1pm. Various locations (02) 6581 8633. www.hastingsfarmersmarket.org
The Foreshore Market Every 2nd Saturday of the month, 8am-1pm Westport Park 0414 376 868
Laurieton Riverwalk Market Every 3rd Sunday, 8am-1pm Cnr Tunis & Short Sts, Laurieton 0428 695 084
JANUARY Annual Golden Lure Game Fishing Tournament www.portmacquarieinfo.com.au
MARCH Ironman Australia Triathlon www.ironmanoz.com
APRIL Camden Haven Music Festival www.camdenhavenmusicfestival.org.au
AUGUST Country Energy Australian Surf Festival www.portmacquarieinfo.com.au
NOVEMBER Tastings of the Hastings www.tastingsofthehastings.com.au
DECEMBER NSW Touch Football Association State Cup www.portmacquarieinfo.com.au
Festival of the Sun www.portmacquarieinfo.com.au
Slice of Haven Food and Wine Festival www.sliceofhaven.com.au

BYRON
Byron Bay Farmers Market Every Thursday, 8-11am Butler Street Reserve (02) 6687 1137. www.byronfarmersmarket.com.au
FEBRUARY/MARCH Byron Bay Film Festival www.bbff.com.au
APRIL The East Coast Blues and Roots Festival www.bluesfest.com.au
JULY The Byron Bay Writers Festival www.byronbaywritersfestival.com.au
JULY/AUGUST Splendour in the Grass www.splendourinthegrass.com
SEPTEMBER A Taste of Byron (02) 6685 7591

OTHER PLACES
Koala Hospital Macquarie Nature Reserve, Lord St, Port Macquarie. (02) 6584 1522 or www.koalahospital.org.au **Dorrigo Rainforest Centre** Dome Rd, Dorrigo. (02) 6657 2309 or www.nationalparks.nsw.gov.au **The Big Banana** 351 Pacific Hwy, Coffs Harbour. (02) 6652 4355 or www.bigbanana.com

Select images courtesy Tourism NSW

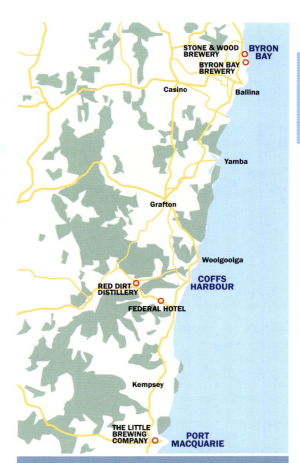

PLACES TO DRINK

Black Duck Brewery
Herons Creek
www.blackduckbrewery.com.au

Byron Bay Premium Brewery and Buddha Bar
1 Skinners Shoot Rd,
Byron Bay
(02) 6685 5833
www.byronbaybrewery.com.au

The Little Brewing Company
Unit 1, 58 Uralla Rd
Port Macquarie
(02) 6581 3949
www.thelittlebrewingcompany.com.au

Stone & Wood
4 Boronia Pl,
Byron Bay
(02) 6685 5173
www.stoneandwood.com.au

Red Dirt Distillery & Lick the Spoon
51-53 Hickory St
Dorrigo
(02) 6657 1373
www.reddirtdistillery.com.au

Federal Hotel
77 Hyde St,
Bellingen
(02) 6655 1003
www.federalhotel.com.au

NSW

RIVERINA

The Riverina region is the beating heart of NSW agriculture, a hugely rich and vibrant food bowl fed by the extraordinary Snowy Mountains Scheme. **By Neal Cameron**

A traveller to the Riverina requires two things: a long-legged travelling ethic and an understanding that the region is a real and working environment offering much to the tourist without pandering to them. That said, the history, food and wine of the region is extraordinary, but, as when visiting any regional area, a little planning will be well rewarded. The best times to visit the area are late spring to early autumn. The summers can be intimidatingly fierce.

■ TUMUT

Tumut is a holiday destination in its own right. Sitting on the Tumut River in the foothills of the Snowy Mountains, it's a delightfully pretty town with a long history that encompasses gold rushes and hydro-electric schemes, and it's still prosperous today thanks to a thriving timber industry and proximity to Kosciuszko National Park – a favourite with campers and hikers.

To fully understand the Riverina's prosperity, a tour of the Snowy Mountains hydro-electric operation is essential. The scale of what was achieved post-WWII is simply mind-boggling, with 16 dams and seven power stations built to harness melt-water from the Snowys. The water is then diverted inland into the Murray and Murrumbidgee rivers, creating an essential source of water and power for a significant portion of Australia.

Driving out of the town past the mighty (and thankfully now fairly full) Blowering Dam to the Talbingo Visitor Display Centre is a great start, as is a tour of one of the power stations.

Further up the mountains, visit the Yarrangobilly Caves and discover some subterranean wonders. Take your swimmers for a dip in the slightly freaky warm outdoor pool fed from a natural warm spring. Keep going up this dramatic road and you will enter Kosciuszko National Park from a side that few experience. The park is a whole chapter in itself.

After such an eventful day, visitors to the region might seek well-earned refreshment in one or more of Tumut's six hotels. Most date back to the late 1800s, with the highlights being the Royal, the Oriental and the Commercial. And while the beer in these establishments may be at the mass-market end of the spectrum, the surroundings more than make up for it.

On your way out of Tumut, visit Adelong, a small but perfectly formed gold rush town. Take a trip to Adelong Falls Reserve for a stroll, and some gold fossicking should keep the kids happy for an hour or so.

If you have a designated driver, try the exceptionally hearty cuisine – the local trout is fantastic – washed down with a variety of imported German beers, at the Coat of Arms Kaffeehaus Restaurant.

De Bortoli vineyards, Griffith

Thirsty Crow

Taps at the Thirsty Crow

Fourship at Temora Aviation Museum

■ WAGGA WAGGA

Wagga Wagga (so nice they named it twice) is a true outback town on the banks of the Murrumbidgee, made vibrant by the large student population at Charles Sturt University. A keen nose here will sniff out some great wines, olive oil and even craft beer.

Experienced brewer Craig Wealands returned to his home town last year to set up the Thirsty Crow brew-pub. Craig is producing a truly interesting range of beers from his 500L system, brews that are in such fierce demand that he's struggling to keep them in stock.

If it's available, try the Vanilla Milk Stout, winner of the Champion Hybrid Beer trophy at the 2011 Australian International Beer Awards, or the popular Pale Ale and a house pizza. Brewery tours are held twice a week on Saturdays and Sundays at 12pm, costing $13 per person.

On a hot day, a swim in the river is refreshing and, once suitably exercised, visitors might visit one of two distinctly different highlights of the Wagga (never Wagga Wagga) dining scene.

A little way out of town is The Magpie's Nest, run by the intensely likeable and passionate Chris Whyte, a fervent advocate of local produce.

At the top of Bayliss Street is Zen X, a Japanese sushi and teppanyaki bar. The food is excellent if you stick to the authentic offerings, and the reasonably priced bottles of Sapporo are cold and fresh and match the cuisine perfectly.

A wine tour of the area is a must. Being an irrigated area, there are many 'fruit-driven' wines, so the opportunity to try before you buy is a good one. Charles Sturt University Winery, Harefield Ridge and Borambola make a good start.

■ NARRANDERA

An hour down the road takes travellers to the once highly prosperous town of Narrandera. Tagged as the city of trees, the wide open avenues over-arched with stunning European trees and historic houses make it a pretty town to visit.

An hour wandering around the koala sanctuary on the banks of the Murrumbidgee, spotting an animal cleverly designed to move as little as possible, is more fun than it rightly should be. In April you can join in the annual koala count.

For one weekend in March you can't move in the town for bush poets due to the John O'Brien Festival. If you like that sort of thing, of course.

The world's largest playable guitar is essential viewing, though you'll need three or more people to play *Smoke on the Water*. And the golf course in Narrandera is rated one of the best in country NSW, although many years of drought have taken their toll of late.

■ LEETON

Leeton was made prosperous by irrigated crops such as rice, with nearly two million tonnes of the stuff being grown prior to the last decade of drought. Leeton rice mill has its own SunRice visitors centre, and a tour around the mill is briefly diverting. The annual SunRice Festival is a rather curious affair, with all things rice celebrated every Easter.

If you choose to spend the evening here, staying in the magnificent old Historic Hydro Motor Inn, recently restored with great care, is a must. The Hydro also has a lovely bar, with a verandah out the front and a fair choice of beer for the more discerning drinker. Over the road, the Roxy Theatre is an Art Deco delight, albeit without any heating or cooling, so choose a mild evening.

Restaurant Pages on Pine in the main street is exceptional and a rare treasure in a country town. There are a couple of wineries in town, with the pick being Lillypilly. Red Velvet aside, a tour through Robert Fiurama's sweet wines is a joy.

■ GRIFFITH

Griffith has one the highest GDPs of any city in the country thanks to agriculture, wine and more wine. The area produces nearly 20 per cent of Australia's wine and, while much of it hits the shelves priced at the lower end of the market, there are some great wines to be had.

National icons including De Bortoli, McWilliams and Casella are based here, with acres of enormous stainless-steel tanks holding millions upon millions of litres of wine – a wonder to behold.

Joe, Marcello and John Casella

At De Bortoli in Bilbul you'll also find the William Bull Brewery. Though tours are not available, super-fresh Red Angus Pilsener and Williams Pale Ale are.

Casella Wines in Yenda doesn't have a cellar door but a rather large brewery is currently under construction. Daniel Casella, commercial manager at Casella Wines, says the brewery operation will be export-focused, however product will be available in selected local retailers late 2011.

Cuisine-wise, there are a few pearls. For a totally authentic Italian experience head to La Scala on Banna Avenue. The food is good and the wine list is excellent. The Clock is also excellent. Chef Michelle Armstrong's menu of local produce recently earned the restaurant a *SMH Good Food Guide* hat and there's a fair range of beers to boot.

Easter time is festival time in Griffith, with La Festa offering entertainment and food for the whole weekend, with buses to take visitors around the wineries.

■ TEMORA

After a few days in Griffith, a leisurely drive home cross-country via Temora is a must. The aviation museum there is extraordinary, with great events and a couple of Spitfires, which even the non-aeroplane enthusiasts seem to love. Major air shows are held here every November, but planes fly most weekends.

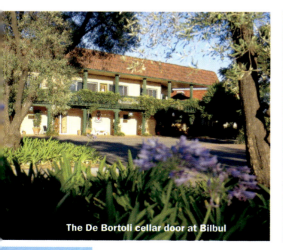

The De Bortoli cellar door at Bilbul

Amanda Oades of William Bull Brewery

Tanks at William Bull Brewery

Tanks of [yellow tail], Casella Wines

EVENTS

MARCH
John O'Brien Festival
www.johnobrien.org.au

APRIL
La Festa
www.lafesta.org.au

SunRice Festival
www.leetontourism.com.au

JUNE
UnWINEd
www.unwined-riverina.com

SEPTEMBER
Jazz and Blues Festival
www.waggajazz.org.au

NOVEMBER
Temora Air Festival
www.aviationmuseum.com.au

NSW

BREWERIES

Casella Wines
Wakley Rd,
Yenda
(02) 6961 3000
www.casellawines.com.au

Thirsty Crow Brewery
31 Kincaid St,
Wagga Wagga
(02) 6921 7470
www.thirstycrow.com.au

William Bull Brewery and De Bortoli Wines
De Bortoli Rd,
Bilbul
(02) 6966 0100
www.williambull.com.au

Photo courtesy Rob Fox photography (select image).

37

Stanwell Park – a hanglider's paradise

NSW

SOUTH COAST

See golden sands and snow-capped mountains – enjoying the delights of breweries along the way – all within easy reach of both Sydney and Melbourne. **By Victoria Mackey**

You don't have to go far to experience South Coast brews. Just 50 minutes on the M5 from Sydney lands you at the Infusion Restaurant, Bar and Brewery at Campbelltown, where three beers are brewed and very much enjoyed: Appin Ale, Macarthur Wheat and Fisher's Ghost (the latter named after the town's resident spook. Tours and brewing master-classes are available by appointment, and there's accommodation on site, too.

Toast the town ghost, then hunt him down! Supernatural tours run by day or night. Or, for adrenaline minus anxiety, take your mates to Delta Force Paintball or Battlefun Laser Skirmish, then cool off with a friendly lap around the track at FastLane Karting.

■ PICTON

Continue south along the M5 and in an hour you'll hit Scharer's Little Brewery at the George IV Inn. Scharer's Lager is popular with the locals but, if you fancy something darker, Scharer's Bock comes in at the sweeter end of the scale with hints of bitterness from hopping at the end of the brew. Brewing is no longer done on site, but you can look in on the historic facilities.

If you're seeking thrills while in Picton, try sky-diving with Skydiving Sydney for an exhilarating view of the town.

For family fun back on terra firma, the New South Wales Rail Transport Museum is just the ticket. The kids can meet Thomas the Tank Engine and everyone can ride a steam engine further south along the coast.

■ WOLLONGONG

Whether steaming in by train or driving down from Picton, the surf and breweries of Wollongong are less than an hour away.

Duck into Five Islands Brewery, where the bar overlooks South Beach. Before you choose a pint to settle in with,

The George IV Inn in Picton

Broughton Pale Ale by Mountain Ridge Brewery in Shoalhaven Heads

sample the selection. Tasting trays offer three 200ml samples, one of the more popular being the Rust Amber Ale, with a roasted flavour and fresh hops for easy drinking. There are seasonal brews available, too.

There's plenty to do in the 'Gong. Ask at Five Islands for a tour of the brewing operation or make the most of the beaches. Swim, surf, fish or take in the scenery over a hit at the Wollongong Golf Club.

If dining is your fancy, book in to the local hatted restaurant Caveau, or simply celebrate all the city has to offer with cultural events such as the annual Tutti In Piazza or Viva La Gong Festival.

Also calling the Illawarra region home is The Longboard Brewing Company. Its Australian Pale Ale is popular with locals and day-trippers alike, and it's on tap in such fine watering holes as the Figtree Hotel, the North Wollongong Hotel and the picturesque Scarborough Hotel. It's competitively priced, too, so there's no forking out extra for a taste.

■ SHOALHAVEN

Shoalhaven beckons next, with more beaches and more breweries. Less than an hour further south is Nowra. Be one of the first to experience HopDog BeerWorks, where the beer is fresh, unadulterated and naturally carbonated.

The HopDog cellar door is open Fridays to Sundays (10am to 4pm), with four original brews to taste: The Pale, a crisp, clean American Pale Ale; the intensely hopped Horns Up; an oatmeal Stout called Black Sunshine; and The Midgee, a mid-strength Red Ale. Take home a two-litre growler of your favourite or enjoy it there. Brewery tours are available on request.

Head inland to Berry and the Mountain Ridge Brewery, a family-run operation offering a full farm-to-table experience, making beer, wine, liqueurs and growing a range of produce. Mountain Ridge even has a wind turbine to generate its own power.

This hive of activity has something for everyone, including live entertainment. Try the Broughton Pale Ale, matched so perfectly with local Asian cuisine. Or the Bolong Black, so good with steak, and with rich chocolate flavours to finish. The hint of sweetness makes it a hit with the ladies, too.

Berry is a beautiful historic town full of charming shops selling handmade creations and artisan fare such as the Berry Woodfired Sourdough Bakery, famous for, well, it's in the name! And if you're up for a spot of antiquing, prepare to empty those pockets at one of the many auction houses or vintage stores and fill those display cases.

Kosciuszko Brewing Co at the Banjo Paterson Inn

The Five Islands range

■ BOWRAL

Keep satisfying the shopaholic, foodie and culture lover in you as you head into the Highlands – a place where the local beer label reads 'Anything Is Possible'.

Head to Bowral to sample the Pigs Fly range of beers made by the Bowral Brewing Company, including a Pale Ale and a Pilsener.

And while you're enjoying an autumnal day at the Tulip Festival or honing your cricket trivia at the Bradman Museum, stop at the Bowral Hotel to grab a six-pack of Pigs Fly or stock your cellar with locally produced wines.

Old Goulburn Brewery

■ GOULBURN

Driving on from Bowral, grazier's territory is another hour away. See the Big Merino, then bone up on traditional brewing practices with a tour of The Old Goulburn Brewery.

Taste the Fine Sparkling Ale, Goulburn Gold and the Goulburn Stout, and then stay for lunch or a snack. Brews here are made with the holy trinity of ingredients: barley malt, ale yeast and local water.

Note: if you love your blues music, time your visit to coincide with the Australian Blues Music Festival, held in Goulburn every February.

Keep heading south and in around three hours you'll reach the Dalgety Brewing Company. Dalgety's five beers are kegged, bottled and packaged by hand. The brewery grows its own hops and uses water pumped from the Snowy Mountains, making the brews unique. The popularity of the beers peaks in snow season; the Strong Ale is often referred to as 'dinner in a glass'.

Make a weekend of your visit by staying and brewing your own. Bookings are essential and bottles are ready to take away the next morning.

The Dalgety Brewing Company, AKA Snowy Vineyard & Microbrewery

Kevin O'Neill, Snowy Mountains Brewery

Brumby Schnapps Distillery

■ JINDABYNE

Climb higher for the Snowy Mountains and, on entering Jindabyne, look out for Banjo Paterson Inn.

This is the home of Kosciuszko Brewing Company, where Chuck Hahn and his team craft the refreshing Kosciuszko Pale Ale. The brewery is in open view and you can stop in for lunch, dinner or overnight stays.

Ever had that schnappy feeling the mountains bring? Well, you're in for a treat at the Wildbrumby Schnapps Distillery. It's off the Alpine Way, about 11 kilometres from Jindabyne.

The cellar door and café open daily until 5 pm and there are myriad flavours to try and take home, including the newly released Kosciuszko Vodka.

Equally good as a winter warmer is Razorback Red Ale, a rich, malty offering from the Snowy Mountains Brewery that is widely available in the region. Their Crackenback Pale Ale, Bullocks Pilsener and Charlotte's Hefeweizen are also worth a go.

So, next time you decide to go coastal, but can't leave the city, ask your local bar or bottle shop for a taste of the south, and drink in those pleasant memories.

EVENTS

JANUARY
Illawarra Folk Festival
www.illawarrafolkfestival.com.au

FEBRUARY
Berry Food & Wine Show
www.berry.org.au
Australian Blues Music Festival
www.australianbluesfestival.com.au

JUNE
Shoalhaven Winter Food & Wine Festival
www.shoalhavencoastwine.com.au

JULY
Bundanoon Winterfest
www.bundanoon.nsw.gov.au

SEPTEMBER
Kiama Regional Wine Show
www.kiamawineshow.org.au
Tulip Time
www.southern-highlands.com.au

OCTOBER
Snowy Mountains Trout Festival
www.troutfestival.com

NOVEMBER
Wine, Arts and Roses
www.southern-highlands.com.au

DECEMBER
Southern Highlands Christmas Fair
www.visitnsw.com

Photography from Tourism NSW (select images)

BREWERIES AND DISTILLERY

Brumby Schnapps Distillery
Thredbo Valley Distillery
Cnr Wollondibby Rd and
The Alpine Way, Jindabyne
(02) 6457 1447
www.wildbrumby.com

Five Islands Brewery
Cnr Crown & Harbour Sts,
Wollongong
(02) 4220 2854
www.fiveislandsbrew.wordpress.com

HopDog BeerWorks
Unit 2/175 Princes Hwy,
South Nowra
0428 293 132

Infusion Bar and Brewery
15 Old Menangle Rd,
Campbelltown
(02) 4645 0557

Kosciuszko Brewing Company
1 Kosciuszko Rd,
Jindabyne
1800 046 275,
www.banjopatersoninn.com.au

Longboard Beer
www.longboardbeer.com

Mountain Ridge Brewery
11 Coolangatta Rd,
Shoalhaven Heads
(02) 4448 5825
www.mountainridgewines.com

Scharer's Brewery at George IV Inn
180 Argyle St, Picton
(02) 4677 1415
www.scharers.com.au

Snowy Mountains Brewery
www.snowybeer.com.au

The Dalgety Brewing Company
Snowy Vineyard Estate
Werralong Rd (via Rockwell Rd, Berridale)
Dalgety
1300 766 608

The Old Goulburn Brewery
23 Bungonia Rd
Goulburn
(02) 4821 6071

TRAVEL INFO

Picton and Wollondilly tourism info www.visitwollondilly.com.au
Tourism Wollongong www.tourismwollongong.com
Viva La Gong vivalagongfestival.blogspot.com **Tourism Berridale** www.berridale.org
Snowy Mountains tourism info www.snowymountains.com.au
Southern Highlands information www.southern-highlands.com.au/home
Southern Highlands Wine www.shw.com.au

NSW

SYDNEY

Scratch the history and attractions of Sydney and you'll never find a beer far away. And in a city that never sleeps, it's always a good time to sample them.

By Sadhbh Warren

You'd think four tonnes of beer would be enough. But in September 1768, just a month after the *Endeavour* set sail for Sydney, Captain Cook's vessel was nearly dry. He noted, "Served wine to the ship's company, the beer being all expended to two casks which I wanted to keep some time longer."

Sydney seems determined to ensure the beer never runs out again. The city's passion for brewing is as inexhaustible as it seems inescapable when you realise the sheer scale that even quite a small sampling of local breweries will get to. But, with planning, it's possible to design a visit that samples Sydney's many delights and many of its brews.

Start where the city started, in The Rocks. This is the oldest part of Sydney; originally a warren of laneways where criminality and debauchery would abound. These days, the criminality has gone – although a glance at some of the prices may make you think otherwise – but up-market debauchery remains with many restaurants and bars serving up sumptuous indulgences.

The Rocks is home to some of Sydney's most noted attractions: the weekend markets, the Sydney Observatory and the infamous but expensive bridge climb. If your budget or vertigo won't allow for that, an alternative is the nearby Pylon Lookout, which gets a family of four almost as high over The Rocks for less than $30. The Rocks has it all: shopping, eating, culture and, of course, lots and lots of beer.

■ LORDS, BOXERS AND BUTCHERS

A natural starting point for beer historians is The Rocks' oldest licensed hotel and Australia's oldest brew-pub, Lord

Sydney Harbour, at dawn

Enjoying a beer at the Australian Hotel

Lord Nelson Brewery Hotel

The bar at the Lord Nelson

Nelson Brewery Hotel, voted best brew-bar in the 2010 *Beer & Brewer* Awards. This stately pub combines colonial grandeur with a no-nonsense attitude to serving up great beer. You can contemplate the fermenting brews through the glass walls before requesting some of the finished product through the taps. The Lord brews six mainstay Ales, including the deliciously dry Australian Pale Ale Three Sheets, and occasional seasonals.

Try not to get too Three Sheeted yourself, however, for this is just the first stop in The Rocks. Down the road is the Belgian Beer Café – Heritage and the excellent Harts Pub, which narrowly missed out on a People's Choice Award in the 2010 *Beer & Brewer* Awards. This cosy but contemporary heritage-listed pub is the home of Rocks Brewing Co. Rocks Brewing kegged its first brew, an Irish-style Red Ale called The Boxer, in September 2008 and, according to director Mark Fethers, it was no quick process. "It took 16 versions to get it quite right, unlike our Porter, The Butcher, which took two versions. We knew exactly what we were after for the Porter, which definitely helps!"

The Rocks Brewing Co. now makes four brews and you'll often find Mark sampling them – and those of other local craft brewers, such as 4 Pines, Brothers Ink, Doctor's Orders and Schwartz – through Harts' 12 taps. An apple cider and a Lager are also coming along very nicely, says Mark. "It's difficult to wow with a Lager, but we are very happy with what we've got."

In the meantime, you can sample the beers on a tasting paddle or incorporated in Harts' excellent food menu. If you're after a real feast of food and beer, the $100 'beergustation' dinner, held on the third Wednesday of every month is guaranteed to satisfy (book ahead).

■ ACROSS AUSTRALIA ON A BARSTOOL

Just up the road is another pub that combines local beer and food to great effect – the Australian Heritage Hotel. Outdoor tables and an extensive but reasonably priced menu make this a popular stop for visitors looking for a breather.

While not a brewery, it has an admirably stocked fridge that is Tardis-like in the boundless wealth of craft beer it holds. Watch out for the excellent Endeavour Reserves – 'vintage' beers so good you wouldn't blame Cook if he had kept all four tonnes to himself. If you are eating, pick up a Fusion brew. The Prime Beer is an Amber Ale designed to go

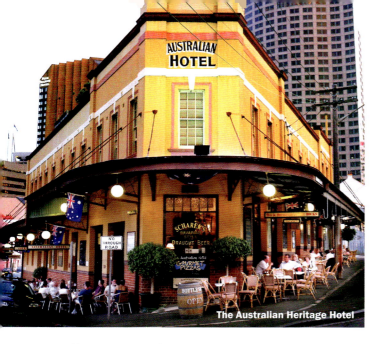
The Australian Heritage Hotel

Redoak Boutique Beer Cafe

with meat, the Firefly with spicy food and the Bluebottle Lager goes with seafood. This might seem straight-forward enough, but the Australian's eclectic menu can throw a spanner in works. Entertaining arguments about whether the crocodile and lime pizza counts as spicy, seafood or meat await, and can clearly be solved only by sampling with each of the brews.

An easy roll downhill is Redoak Boutique Beer Café, Australia's most awarded brewery and no slouch in the food stakes itself. It brews more than 40 premium beers, including the velvety smooth Belgian Chocolate Stout, of which 20 are available at any one time.

A highlight is the tasting platters, matching four beers with mouth-watering cheese, meat, seafood or vegetarian offerings. Redoak also runs beer-appreciation classes, serving a four-course degustation with six matching beers. Chef Chris Beard isn't afraid to push the envelope on what food goes with a brew or even contains a brew. Take the time to sample the beer chocolate truffles or the fruit-based beer sorbets and ice-creams if you can fit them in.

The kitchen is open for lunch from Mondays to Saturdays and beer-appreciation classes are held on the first Saturday of the month ($75 per person). Bookings essential.

■ THE FIRST BEER – OR WAS IT?

It's doubtful that Sydney's first colonists enjoyed such salubrious treats or excellent selection of beer. If you decide on a postprandial stroll (or, realistically, waddle) swing through the Domain and the Botanic Gardens. You'll find free outdoor events in the area in summer, from Opera in the Domain to Tropfest, but the gardens are well worth visiting all year round.

And you're still not that far from a beer. Watch out for the plaque near the Rose Garden Pavilion that marks the spot where John Boston is claimed to have brewed Sydney's first beer. (We say 'claimed' because we know that Boston and the infamous James Squire were both brewing in 1796, but we don't know who was first.) John Boston's name adorns a brew created by Bruce Peachy of Bluetongue Premium Lager, but there's no doubt that Squire's name is more recognisable, thanks to the Malt Shovel Brewery, which immortalised his chicken-stealing, lothario lifestyle with six excellent beers.

Once a year, the Malt Shovel Brewery in Camperdown opens for members of the James Squire Beer Club. Malt Shovel also makes seasonal brews under the aptly-named Mad Brewers label, such as the winter 2011 release, Stout Noir, which is available along with other Malt Shovel brews at the brewers' recommended venue, the Marly Bar in Newtown.

If you're out that way, be sure to try the local St Peters Brewery's beers. St Peters has been serving Sydney's inner-west with environmentally friendly, no-drama brews, including a tasty Blonde (Wheat Beer) and the delicious Killagh Irish Dry Stout, since 1996.

St Peters doesn't have a website, tours or on-site sales, as owner and brewer Matt Donelan prefers to keep it low-

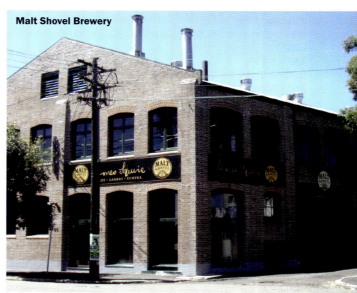
Malt Shovel Brewery

King Street Brewhouse

key so he can focus on what he does best – brewing. Matt has been known to show people around his operation occasionally but recommends punters pop into the Union Hotel on King Street in Newtown to sample his beers.

■ SYDNEY'S DARLINGS

Darling Harbour brings in visitors in droves and knows how to amuse them. It has fireworks every Saturday night at 8.30pm and events year-round. You'll also find the Chinese Garden of Friendship, the Maritime Museum and Sydney Aquarium here.

Down on King Street Wharf, the King Street Brewhouse serves 17 local craft and imported beers on tap, along with the products of the 8hL microbrewery on site, and excellent food, making this one of the most pleasant outdoor venues in Sydney.

Nearby, The Pumphouse stocks more than 100 local and imported beers, plus its own house beers, including the tasty Thunderbolt Strong Ale.

■ INSIDE SYDNEY'S BEERS

Brewery tours in Sydney can be hard to find. The old Carlton United Brewery at Broadway is being redeveloped and the Tooheys Brewery in Lidcombe, where the country gets its vast supplies of Tooheys and Hahn, has suspended tours due to upgrading work.

The unpretentious Schwartz Brewery Hotel, previously known as the Macquarie Hotel, in Surry Hills, is one of the few spots where you can get a guided look around.

Brewery tours are held each Wednesday from 2pm and cost $15, finishing with a sample of the beers.

The front bar at Schwartz Brewery Hotel

You'll need to book in advance for the tour, but if you miss it, you can still take in a brew or three and peer in at the microbrewery and bottling plant through the glass walls of the lounge. The Schwartz Dark Bier alone is worth the trip downtown, and the Summer Time Ale is a crisply fruited salute to the warmer months.

Also in Surry Hills is an unassuming beer bar on Crown Street called Yulli's. The team there really know their beer, so drop in and experience the selection.

Since you are out that way, you may as well stop by the Bavarian Bier Café. It would also be a shame not to call by the Cricketer's Arms for a Lovell's Lager or into the Local Taphouse in Darlinghurst, which boasts 20 beer taps with a changing selection and some great grub. They're the perfect spots for post-game analysis after visiting the Sydney Cricket Ground or Sydney Football Stadium.

Two good beer bars in Potts Point, close to the famous Coca Cola sign in Kings Cross, include Prague Beer Restaurant and Doma Bohemian Beer Café. Both venues are Czech-themed in beer and food.

A visit to Sydney for beer lovers wouldn't be complete without a visit to the numerous pubs in Balmain and Rozelle, only 10 minutes' drive from the CBD. Stand out pubs and restaurants include the 3 Weeds, Welcome Hotel, Town Hall, La Boheme, Pizza E Birra, The Riverview and The London. Balmain is, of course, also home to Balmain Brewing Co. Drop into The Royal Oak for a taste of the Balmain Bock and Balmain Pale Ale.

Nearby Glebe has a new beer bar called Tommy's European Beer Café on Glebe Point Road. Drop by for some Bernard, Budvar, Paulaner or Delirium Tremens, to name a

Head Brewer Michael Capaldo, Schwartz Brewery Hotel

few of the beers on offer, with some hearty and filling European food. The well-known Glebe Markets are also just a block away, running every Saturday from 10am to 4pm.

Other notable beer bars and restaurants in Sydney include Belgian Beer Café – Epoque in Cammeray, Löwenbräu Keller in The Rocks, Essen Restaurant in Ultimo, Bazaar Beer Café in St Leonards, Jackson's on George in the CBD and the Woolloomooloo Bay Hotel.

Some stand-out bottleshops in Sydney include Platinum Liquor, winner of the Best Bottleshop award (under 300 beers) in the 2010 *Beer & Brewer* Awards, which has shops in Bellevue Hill and Strathfield. Amato's in Leichhardt has a great selection and Broadway Liquor in Glebe, Porter's Liquor in Balgowlah, Oak Barrel in the city, Northmead Cellars and Dan Murphy's and 1st Choice all have good selections of local craft and imported beers and ciders.

■ A BEER WORTH THE BOAT TRIP

If it's a typical Sydney experience you want, you'll need to get out on the harbour. There are plenty of options for visitors: take a cruise, catch the ferry from Circular Quay to Taronga Zoo, or to Manly – a very popular destination since the first ferry ran in 1855.

Manly is known for surfing and beaches, but even if the weather isn't warm, it's still worth the ferry trip. You can fill your stomach at the Manly Food and Wine Festival in June, or fill your ears at the Manly Jazz Festival in October.

And all year round you'll find it worthwhile visiting the Bavarian Beer Café (one of seven venues across Sydney) or the 4 Pines Brewery.

Just minutes from the wharf, 4 Pines has rapidly become a local favourite with its tasty menu, cosy atmosphere and regular live entertainment. There are five mainstays on tap, plus a cider, a rotating specialty range and a real ale hand pump. And there's one brew in particular that you could say is out of this world – literally.

In conjunction with Saber Astronautics, 4 Pines is working on Vostok, the world's first beer tailored to the emerging space-tourism industry.

So, by raising a glass, you are not merely enjoying a drink but donating to vital research in the quest for a beer that tastes superb on Earth and in orbit.

In May 2011, Manly welcomed another great beer venue, called Murray's at Manly and located on the beachside, a block up from the iconic Steyne Hotel.

Murray's is owned by Murray's Craft Brewing Co and is expecting to have 24 taps and a hand pump for its regular beers, plus seasonals and single-keg limited releases. Guest ciders and beers are also available on tap with a limited imported beer selection. The restaurant has a menu of good honest Australian food to match with your favourite glass of Murray's beers.

Going into orbit might seem a bit extreme, but if you manage to make it out of the city, you'll be well rewarded. One of the suburbs' best finds is Paddy's Brewery in Flemington, next to the famous markets. Try Paddy's award-winning Pilsner called, obviously enough, the Paddy's Award Winning Pilsner, or take on the Fat Arsed Bastard. It's well worth the trip out, but if you're worried that you may not want to leave, Paddy's even does accommodation.

Murray's At Manly

Three for the road at the Bavarian Beer Cafe

4 Pines Brewery

BEER BARS

30 Knots
Level 1, The Grand Hotel
30 Hunter St, Sydney
30knots@merivale.com

3 Weeds
193 Evans St, Rozelle
(02) 9818 2788
www.3weeds.com.au

Bavarian Bier Café
Entertainment Quarter, 212 Bent St, Sydney
(02) 9361 3833
Shop 2-5 Manly Wharf
(02) 9977 8088
2-8 Phillip St, Parramatta
(02) 8836 1400
16 O'Connell St, Sydney
(02) 9221 0100
24 York St, Sydney
(02) 8297 4111
108 Campbell Pde, Bondi Beach
(02) 8988 5935
Shops 4-6, Chatswood Central Precinct,
1-5 Railway St, Chatswood
(02) 8922 8100
www.bavarianbiercafe.com.au

Bazaar Beer Café
1 Albany St, St Leonards
(02) 9438 1999
www.bazaarbeercafe.com.au

Belgian Beer Café
429 Miller St, Cammeray
(02) 9954 3811
135 Harrington St, The Rocks
(02) 9241 1775
www.belgian-beer-cafe.com.au

Coogee Cafe After Dark
221 Coogee Bay Rd, Coogee
(02) 9665 5779

Doma Bohemian Beer Café
29 Orwell St, Potts Point
(02) 9331 0022
www.unasdoma.com.au

Essen Restaurant
133-135 Broadway, Ultimo
(02) 9211 3805
www.essenrestaurant.com.au

Jackson's on George
176 George St, Sydney
(02) 9247 2727
www.jacksonsongeorge.com.au

King St Brewhouse & Restaurant
Kings St Wharf
(02) 8270 7901
www.kingstbrewhouse.com.au

La Boheme Restaurant & Café
332 Darling St, Balmain
(02) 9810 0829
www.laboheme.net.au

Löwenbräu Keller
Cnr Playfair and Argyle Sts, The Rocks
(02) 9247 7785
www.lowenbrau.com.au

MuMu Grill
70 Alexander St, Crows Nest
(02) 8999 7027
www.mumugrill.com.au

Murray's at Manly
49 North Steyne, Manly
(02) 9977 0999
www.murraysbrewingco.com.au

Opera Bar
Lower Concourse Level, Sydney Opera House
(02) 9247 1666
www.operabar.com.au

Bavarian Beer Cafe

Pizza e Birra
Shop 1, 332 Darling St, Balmain
(02) 9810 5333
500 Crown St, Surry Hills
(02) 9332 2510

Prague Beer Restaurant
42 Kellett St, Potts Point
(02) 9368 0898
www.prague-restaurant.com.au

Pumphouse Bar
17 Little Pier St, Darling Harbour
(02) 8217 4100
www.pumphousebar.com.au

Royal Oak Hotel
36 College St, Balmain
(02) 9810 2311
www.royaloakbalmain.com.au

The Australian Hotel
100 Cumberland St, The Rocks
(02) 9247 2229
www.australianheritagehotel.com

The Local Taphouse
122 Flinders St, Darlinghurst
(02) 9360 0088
www.thelocal.com.au

The London Hotel
234 Darling St, Balmain
(02) 9555 1377
www.londonhotel.com.au

The Riverview Hotel
29 Birchgrove Rd, Balmain
(02) 9810 1151
www.theriverviewhotel.com.au

The Town Hall Hotel
Cnr Montague and Darling Sts, Balmain
(02) 9818 8950
www.townhallhotel.com.au

The Welcome Hotel
91 Evans St, Rozelle
(02) 9810 1323
www.thewelcomehotel.com

Tommy's European Beer Café
123 Glebe Point Rd, Glebe
(02) 9660 6870
www.tommysbeercafe.com.au

Union Hotel
576 King St, Newtown
(02) 9557 2989
www.unionnewtown.com.au

Woolloomooloo Bay Hotel
2 Bourke St, Woolloomooloo
(02) 9357 1177
www.woolloomooloobayhotel.com.au

Yulli's
417 Crown St, Surry Hills
(02) 9319 6609
www.yullis.com.au

In Rouse Hill you'll find the Australian Hotel & Brewery, which opened in 2009 with the aim of providing both great beers and a spot to socialise. The Australian's best offerings are the AB Pale Ale and the excellent Dark Saaz Lager with a smooth but spiced-up finish.

Neal Cameron & Dan Shaw from The Australian Brewery

If you are out that far, consider heading to the Happy Goblin in Mt Kuringai. Just don't expect brewer Colin Larter to stand on ceremony. "We don't really do tours unless people arrange to come up when we're there," he says. "Normally a tour involves me shoving a beer in your hand, telling you to find a bottle opener yourself then running around swearing while things overflow."

Wherever you end up in Sydney, raising a glass is not just a pleasure, or even research, it's an authentic way to experience the history of the city, as exemplified by Sydneysiders since the colony was first founded.

In 1848, Reverend J. Byrne noted in his memoir, *Twelve Years Wandering in the British Colonies*, "[f]rom high to low, the [Sydney] merchant, mechanic, and labourer, all are alike a thirsty community. Drink, drink, drink, seems to be the universal motto, and the quantity that is consumed is incredible; from early morning to dark night, it is the same – Bacchus being constantly sacrificed to."

Well, with beers this good, can you blame them?

BOTTLESHOPS

1st Choice
www.1stchoice.com.au

Amato's Liquor Mart
Shop 2, 267-277
Norton St, Leichhardt
(02) 9560 7628
www.amatos.com.au

Balmain Village Cellars
263 Darling Street
Balmain
(02) 9810 7277

Broadway Liquor (Little Bottler)
96 Glebe Point Rd, Glebe
(02) 9660 2193
www.broadwayliquor.com.au

Dan Murphy's
www.danmurphys.com.au

IGA Plus Liquor
Shop 1, 25-27 Ralston Ave, Belrose
(02) 9957 6978
www.iga.net.au

Liquor Stax (Unique Liquor)
483 Elizabeth Dr, Bonnyrigg
(02) 9823 1922
www.liquorstax.com.au

Little Bottler
Shop 1, 282 Victoria Avenue, Chatswood
(02) 9411 4038
www.mylittlebottler.com.au

Northmead Cellars (Little Bottler)
Cnr Briens and Kleins Rds, Northmead
(02) 9630 7316
www.mylittlebottler.com.au

Platinum Liquor
169 Concord Road, North Stratfield
Tel: (02) 9743 1572
25A Bellevue Road, Bellevue Hill
Tel: (02) 9389 3875
www.platinumliquor.blogspot.com

Porter's Liquor
404 Sydney Rd, Balgowlah
(02) 9948 0745
201 High St, Willoughby
(02) 9958 8408
www.portersliquor.com.au

The Oak Barrel
152 Elizabeth St, Sydney
(02) 9264 3022
www.oakbarrel.com.au

The Sackville Hotel
599 Darling St, Rozelle
(02) 9555 7788
www.sackvillehotel.com.au

EVENTS

FEBRUARY
Chinese New Year www.cityofsydney.nsw.gov.au

AUTUMN
Rosemount Australian Fashion Week Circular Quay
www.sydney.com

MARCH
Mardi Gras
www.mardigras.org.au
Taste of Sydney
Centennial Park
www.tasteofsydney.com.au

APRIL
Sydney Royal Easter Show
Olympic Park
www.eastershow.com.au

JUNE
Sydney Film Festival
www.sff.org.au

JULY
Good Food and Wine Show
Darling Harbour
www.goodfoodshow.com.au

JULY
The Rocks Aroma Festival,
www.therocks.com

Brewer's Feast The Rocks
www.hartspub.com

AUGUST
Sun Herald City2Surf
www.city2surf.com.au

SEPTEMBER/OCTOBER
Oktoberfest Frenchs Forest
www.austrianclubsydney.com
Oktoberfest Cabramatta
www.germanaustriansoc.com.au

OCTOBER
Crave Sydney Food Festival/Good Food Month
www.cravesydney.com
Australian Beer Festival The Rocks www.australianheritagehotel.com

DECEMBER
New Year's Eve Extravaganza
www.newyearseve.com.au

SUMMER
Sydney Festival, Symphony and Jazz in the Domain
www.sydneyfestival.org.au

BREWERIES & BEER COMPANIES

4 Pines Brewing Company
29/43-45 East Esplanade, Manly
(02) 9976 2300
www.4pinesbeer.com.au

Balmain Brewing Company
www.balmainbrewingcompany.com.au

Barons Brewing
www.baronsbrewing.com

Brewtopia
www.brewtopia.com.au

Brothers Ink
www.skinnyblonde.com.au

Doctor's Orders Brewing
www.doctorsordersbrewing.com

Fusion Brewing
www.fusionbrewing.com.au

Ekim Brewing Co
www.ekimbrewing.com.au

Endeavour True Vintage Beer
www.endeavourbeer.com

Happy Goblin Brewery
11/1 Marina Cl, Mt Kuringai
www.happygoblin.com.au

Harts Pub (Rocks Brewing Co.)
176 Cumberland St, The Rocks
(02) 9251 6030
www.hartspub.com

John Boston Premium Beverages
www.johnboston.com.au

**Malt Shovel Brewery
(James Squire and Mad Brewers)**
Pyrmont Bridge Rd, Camperdown
(02) 9519 3579
www.malt-shovel.com.au

**Paddy's Brewery
at the Markets Hotel**
268 Parramatta Rd, Flemington
(02) 9764 3500
www.paddysbrewery.com

Redoak Boutique Beer Café
201 Clarence St, Sydney
(02) 9262 3303
www.redoak.com.au

Schwartz Brewery Hotel
40/44 Wentworth Ave, Sydney
(02) 8262 8877
www.schwartzbrewery.com

St Arnou
www.st-arnou.com.au

St Peters Brewery
15 May St, St Peters
(02) 9519 0191

**The Australian Hotel
& Brewery**
350 Annangrove Rd,
Rouse Hill
(02) 9679 4555
www.australianhotelandbrewery.com.au

The Lord Nelson Brewery Hotel
19 Kent St, The Rocks
(02) 9251 4044
www.lordnelsonbrewery.com

Tooheys Brewery
29 Nyrang Ave, Lidcombe
www.lion-nathan.com.au

Underground Brewing
Gottie's Woodfired
Pizzeria and Restaurant
Erskine Park Shopping Centre
Swallow Drive, Erskine Park
(02) 9670 1800

NSW

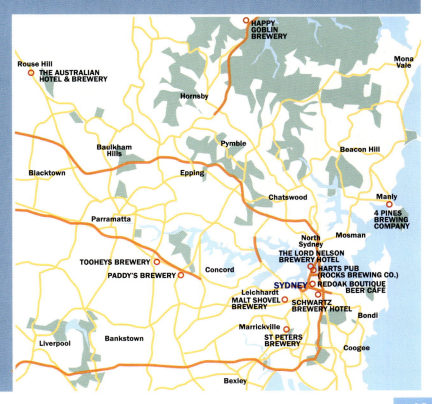

Beer & Brewer promotion   NEW SOUTH WALES – CENTRAL WEST

BADLANDS BREWERY

You can taste all of the Badlands Brewery beers on tap at the Badlands Brewery Bar, within the Coolroom Cafe Restaurant, Orange. The last stop as you head out of town on the Dubbo Road.

Brewer Jon Shiner, who is currently making his beers in Sydney while waiting for final council approval to start building a brewery on-site, is often hanging out at the bar ready to pour tasters and chat about his beers. There are currently five beers on tap, including a traditional English handpump pouring one of the range.

A must-visit stop on any Central West trip as apart from beer tasting you can also stock up on all-locally grown produce at the award winning "Totally Local" shop on the same site. Here you will find all sorts of regional produce - oilve oils and meats, jams and the current seasonal veggies as well of one of the regions finest local wine selections.

The restaurant offers fine dining in a casual and relaxed setting. With a focus on local produce, hearty portions and great beer- food combinations all beer tourists will not leave wanting - bookings essential.

426 Mitchell Highway
Orange
Totally Local number for restaurant bookings - (02) 6360 4604
www.badlandsbrewery.com.au
www.totallylocal.com.au

Opening hours:
Restaurant - Thursday, Friday and Saturday evenings. Café - 7 days a week for breakfast and lunch

MUDGEE BREWING COMPANY

Mudgee has a long history of brewing with the first brewery established in 1858. Mudgee breweries produced export quality beers, sending beer as far as Darwin and several Pacific Islands during World War II.

During this period the legend of Mudgee Mud was born. Due to a change in water quality a number of brews of questionable quality were produced and the term Mudgee Mud was coined. Fortunately the beer improved but the name lived on.

The establishment of the Mudgee Brewery in 2007 has brought back the legend of Mudgee Mud. Located in a 100 year old wool store, the brewery produces a range of quality boutique beers ranging from crisp clear Pale Ale to a chocolate Porter and a hop laden IPA.

The brewery also boasts an exceptional restaurant and Mudgee's finest live music venue featuring local artists on Thursday nights and jazz every Sunday afternoon.

4 Church St
Mudgee
Tel: (02) 63 726 726
info@mudgeebrewing.com.au
www.mudgeebrewing.com.au

Opening hours:
Mon-Wed 8:30am – 5:30pm
Thurs-Sat 8:30am – Late
Sun 8:30am – 6:00pm

Beer & Brewer promotion   NEW SOUTH WALES – HUNTER

BLUETONGUE BREWERY CAFE

The Bluetongue Brewery Cafe, located within Hunter Resort, is the original site of the first boutique brewery in the Hunter Valley. It is where the Bluetongue story began in 2001, when four Hunter-based mates came together to brew a Premium Australian beer from the local Hunter region, with Australian tastes in mind. A glass wall is all that separates you at the bar and the original brewery.

Try the unique Beer Tasting Paddle with accompanying tasting notes for each of the brews. All Bluetongue beers are triple hopped for great taste, meaning they use three different hops to achieve the perfect balance of flavour, aroma and clean finish which results in a great taste that will keep you coming back for more.

There are many styles of beer available including the great tasting Bluetongue Premium Lager and Bluetongue Premium Light, the unique Bluetongue Alcoholic Ginger Beer and the malty Bluetongue Traditional Pilsener. Laze away the afternoon at the Bluetongue Brewery Cafe listening to great music over a beer, accompanied by a meal from the delicious Cafe menu.

Also onsite at Hunter Resort is the Hunter Wine Theatre, Wine School, San Martino Restaurant, the Hermitage Road Winetasting Cellars, horse riding, and Sally Margan's Heavenly Hunter Massage Centre.

Hunter Resort
Hermitage Rd, Pokolbin
Tel: (02) 4998 7777
sales@hunterresort.com.au
Group reservations: functions@hunterresort.com.au

Opening hours:
Cafe 12.00pm – 5.00pm
7 days

Beer & Brewer promotion

NEW SOUTH WALES – HUNTER

DAN MURPHY'S

Many people think of Dan Murphy's as an incredible wine store, however their passion for liquor runs to beer as well. Even Mr. Murphy himself was known to enjoy a beer or two.

Every Dan Murphy's store sells at least 250 different beers. These range from local favourites to exceptional Craft and premium International beers.

At last count, Dan Murphy's had beers from over 30 countries. And the joy of it all is not just the sheer quantity but the price. You see just like their wines and spirits, every beer in every store is backed by their unique lowest price guarantee.*

There are over 140 Dan Murphy's stores nationwide.

For store locations or trading hours, simply SMS the postcode or suburb and state that you are in to 0487 723 388†, or visit their website.

Tel: 1300 723 388
www.danmurphys.com.au

*Conditions apply, visit www.danmurphys.com.au for details.
†Standard SMS charges apply

MURRAY'S CRAFT BREWING CO.

Welcome to Bobs Farm – funny little name and a funny little place to discover a craft beer company.

Murray's Craft Brewing Co. is Australia's most extreme brewer, and proudly a 100% Australian owned craft beer business. Based at Port Stephens, just north of Sydney, Murray's 24HL Brewery brews unconventional, often unique and always full-flavoured handcrafted beers. Murray's Brewery shares its home with Port Stephens Winery, the peninsula's oldest and most successful vineyard. Set on 35 acres of natural bushland and vineyards, the destination is the region's only working brewery, winery and licensed restaurant all at one location. Murray's Craft Brewing Co. has now also opened its first Sydney venue, Murray's At Manly.

3443 Nelson Bay Rd
Bobs Farm Port Stephens
Tel: (02) 4982 6411
www.murraysbrewingco.com.au

NEW – Murray's At Manly
49 North Steyne, Manly
Tel: (02) 9977 0999

Opening hours:
7 days from 10am (closed Christmas Day). Public Brewery Tour daily at 2pm. Private Brewery Tours by appointment only.

BITTER & TWISTED INTERNATIONAL BOUTIQUE BEER FESTIVAL

"First Weekend in November"

From housing inmates notorious for their crimes to brews notorious for their quality, the former maximum security prison of Maitland Gaol will swing open its heavy gates to unlock an experience not to be missed by any discerning beer drinker ... centre stage there's nationally recognised entertainment, seriously twisted performers in the Beer Hall, international food, arts and regional produce stalls, Food and Beer Matching lunches, Home Brew and Meet the Brewer Master Classes and tastings of over 50 boutique beers from around the globe.

Maitland Gaol
John Street, East Maitland
Tel: (02) 4931 2888
www.bitterandtwisted.com.au

When:
First Weekend in November

Beer & Brewer promotion

NEW SOUTH WALES – HUNTER

THE ALBION HOTEL

If you are a lover of real beer, than The Albion is your place in Newcastle.

They have hand selected a fine array of fine ales from Australia's best craft breweries & some interesting fully imported beers that are sure to please the beer connoisseur.

Their draught beer selection is focused on showcasing Australia's best craft beers - 7 out of 10 taps are dedicated to craft beer, featuring beers from Stone & Wood, Vale Ale, Mountain Goat, Lord Nelson, Mad Brewer's & promoting local brewers Murray's & Hunter Beer Co. Their beer tasting tray consists of 4 x 200ml serves of craft beer for $10 that is a great way for people to go outside their usual choice of beer.

The Albion is committed to pushing the beer & food message. Bistro Albion was awarded the equal highest rating in NSW's first edition of the Good Pub Food Guide 2011 and regular Beer Degustation Dinners are extremely popular and always sell out. They have recently hosted Dr Tim Cooper, James Squire's & Mad Brewers where attendee's received a pre-launch taste of the latest Squire family member 150 lashes Pale. The latest dinner they have hosted was Stone & Wood Brewery & Little World Beverages White Rabbit combined.

Located opposite the marina
72 Hannell St
Wickham
Tel: (02) 49622 411
info@thealbion.com.au
www.thealbion.com.au

Opening hours:
Hotel 7 days from 11.00am – late
Bistro Albion 7 Days for lunch (12.00pm – 2.30pm) & dinner (6.00pm – 8.30pm).

HUNTER BEER CO.

A Beer Experience. We Love Our Beer!

The Hunter Beer Co. has created a Beer Experience for you to enjoy.

Try a tasting paddle, chat to the brewers, watch the team make a brew, join a brewery tour or just kick back, relax & enjoy a pint of your favourite.

There are ten hand crafted beers to try! All brewed using traditional techniques and the finest ingredients sourced from around the world. There is a diverse range: Golden Ale, Witbier, Ginger, Pilsner, Pale and Bock. You also need to keep an eye open for the seasonal releases: Hopmonster, Oyster Stout, Crankypants IPA, Chocolate Porter – there's always something different on tap!

The Hunter Beer Co. is located at Potters Hotel Brewery Resort at the Gateway to the Hunter Vineyards. You can choose to stay on site in accommodation ranging from standard motel style through to luxurious spa suites. The site has a family friendly playground, brasserie, public bar with gaming, function facilities and many other attractions.

Wine Country Drive
Nulkaba
Tel: (02) 4991 7922
www.pottershbr.com.au
www.hunterbeer.com.au

Opening hours:
Tours are conducted 7 days a week at 12 noon, 2pm & 4pm. The brewery is open to the public from 10am - 5pm and all beers are available in the main bar till late.

Beer & Brewer promotion   NEW SOUTH WALES – HUNTER

WARNERS AT THE BAY

Warners at the Bay is your complete entertainment venue.

Boasting a 50 room 4 Star Motel, award winning 220 seat Bistro, live entertainment 5 nights a week and New South Wales No 1 Bottle-Shop.

The hotel has just entered its' 7th year of trading. The Motel is a haven for business men and women alike looking for a comfortable stopover. The award winning bistro offers more than just value for money meals, they have Blackboard specials 7 days a week as well as regular nightly dinner deals that range from the freshest local seafood delicacy to spicy Asian dishes.

Entertainment is second to none locally, with top line artists performing every weekend as well as Trivia and Karaoke and the largest T.V screen in Lake Macquarie. The back bars offer a quieter option and are often booked out for functions, whether it be a special occasion or just a regular meeting for your local club.

The huge Bottle-shop was recently named the Best Craft Beer store in New South Wales, in the 2010 Beer & Brewer Awards. The store boasts over 1000 beers from over 50 countries, more than 70 ciders and a comprehensive range of wines from all of Australia's best grape growing regions.

The latest inclusion to the store is the "Growler Machine" a purpose built beer dispensing system which was put into action in late April 2011 and has proven to be a hit with Beer Geeks and regular drinkers alike. It offers 6 different beers to choose from at any given time which is poured into a 2L "Growler" (glass bottle) for the consumer to take home and consume then (hopefully) return to the store and pick out a new one to try. Another way to try some new beers is to attend their annual Beer Festival which is held on the last Sunday of November each year, with 2011 being the 5th year. There is usually between 25 and 30 suppliers from Australia and overseas that attend with up to 80 different beers and ciders available for tasting.

So if you have an hour or so to spare come and find the drop of your dreams in the bottle-shop or if you have a couple of days why don't you Come, Stay and Play at Warners at the Bay, you won't be disappointed.

320 Hillsborough Road
Warners Bay
Tel: (02) 4956 6066
www.warnersatthebay.com.au

Opening hours:
Open 7 days.
Hotel Sun-Wed 11am – 10pm, Thu - Sat 10am – late
Bottle-shop Mon-Wed 9am – 8pm, Thu 9am – 9pm
Fri-Sat 9am-10pm, Sun 9am - 6pm

Beer & Brewer promotion　　　　　　　　　　　　　　　　　　　　　　　　　　　　　　　NEW SOUTH WALES

4 PINES BREWING COMPANY

Overlooking Manly Wharf sits international award winning 4 Pines. It's easy to sit back, relax, enjoy a meal & sip on a beer as the brewer works his magic right in front of you. The delicious all day menu boasts generous meals that match the beers perfectly. They have become known as one of Sydney's friendliest venues and a proud Manly icon.

4 Pines unpretentiously serves one of the largest specialty rotations of different beer styles in Australia, through the taps in the venue, with up to 30 unique styles per year... AND GROWING!!

43 East Esplanade
Manly
Tel: (02) 9976 2300
www.4pinesbeer.com.au

Opening hours:
Every day 11am – midnight
(all day menu).

THE CLARENDON HOTEL

The Clarendon Hotel is a classic Australian Art Deco pub that prides itself on its wide selection of that great Australian classic beverage: beer. Boasting 7 taps dedicated to the finest in Australian Craft Beer plus another 26 by the bottle, this is the largest range of boutique Aussie beer available in Newcastle.

Four of the 7 taps are rotating "guest" taps, featuring limited edition and seasonal brews. Some of the notable breweries that appear on their extensive beer list include: Little Creatures (WA), Moo Brew (TAS), Burleigh Brewing Co. (QLD), Coopers (SA), Mountain Goat (VIC), 4 Pines (NSW) and Lord Nelson (NSW) – just to name a few!

347 Hunter St
Newcastle
Tel: (02) 4927 0966
www.clarendonhotel.com.au

Opening hours:
6 days Mon-Sat
Restaurant from 7.00am
Bar 11:30am – late

 The Clarendon Hotel

PLATINUM LIQUOR

Awarded Best Bottleshop (less than 300 beers) in 2010 Beer & Brewer Awards.

Adam is a 4th generation independent liquor merchant. His family has been providing the public with quality wines & ales almost since the dawn of time. Purveyors of the most commodified of liquor products to the specialisations of each brother. Toni, wine. Adam, Beer. You can regularly find Toni or Adam providing the knowledgeable service that is often considered dying in the digital age, pontificating, being charming, displaying their strong opinions about the Wine/Beer industry & occasionally working hard.

Consider them if you want an old fashioned experience with plenty of soul, character and the best selection.

169 Concord Rd
Nth Strathfield
Tel: (02) 9743 1572

25A Bellevue Rd
Bellevue Hill
Tel: (02) 9389 3875

www.platinumliquor.blogspot.com

Opening hours:
Bellevue Hill
Mon-Sat 10.30am – 8.00pm
Sun 11.00am – 6.30pm

North Strathfield
Mon-Tue 11.00am – 8.00pm
Wed-Sat 10.30am – 8.30pm
Sun 10.30am – 7.30pm

SILO RESTAURANT LOUNGE

Newcastle's Premier Craft Beer Venue – Winner Best Restaurant/Café, 2010 Beer & Brewer Awards.

40 local and imported beers and ciders, including eight beers on tap, which are always changing based on the season and regularly updated on their web site.

Monthly beer (and wine) degustation dinners are themed such as Murray's, all Australian craft beer, Coopers, Oktoberfest and Spanish.

Located on the waterfront of the picturesque marina, Silo has an award winning list of cocktails to indulge your taste buds, along with great food, which is modern Australian with a French twist.

The Boardwalk
1 Honeysuckle Dr
Newcastle Harbour
Tel: (02) 4926 2828
silo@silolounge.com.au

Opening hours:
Open 7days 9am – 11pm
Bar Food All Day
Happy Hour Daily 4pm – 6pm

Join The Silo Social Club, $30 and receive 10% off your entire bill*.

*4 or less, 5% off for groups 5 or more.

Beer & Brewer promotion   NEW SOUTH WALES – SYDNEY

SCHWARTZ BREWERY HOTEL

Schwartz Brewery is a Micro Brewery in the historic Macquarie Hotel (recently renamed Schwartz Brewery Hotel) and has been pumping out quality craft beer for over 6 years.

The site has been occupied by a hotel since at least 1888, and had been known as the Macquarie Hotel since 1908.

In the belly of the hotel you'll find the Schwartz Brewery, a state of the art 8hl microbrewery on show for all to see. Our core range of beers includes Dr Schwartz Pils, Pale Ale, Schwarz Bier and Bavarian Red, along with seasonal specialties such as Hefeweizen, Belgian Strong Ale and Porter. We also produce Sydney Summertime and Sydney Cider, which along with the Schwartz Brewery products are all made with natural ingredients under the strictest guidelines. The passion of the brewers and staff is evident for all to see and makes drinking at Schwartz Brewery a unique Sydney experience!

You can experience all the processes from grain to glass and watch our brewers bottle our finest brew in a purpose built bottling plant.

Our multiple award winning beers are handcrafted in small batches from the finest natural ingredients, have no additives or preservatives and are brewed without compromise. With monthly 'Beer of the Month' and daily 'Happy Hours', we can offer you the ultimate in craft beer appreciation at the most affordable prices!

Also within the Schwartz Brewery Hotel you will find 'The Mac' live music venue, 'Bill and Toni's Pub Life' for great pub food and 'Econolodge' for affordable boutique accommodation.

42 Wentworth Avenue
Surry Hills
Tel: (02) 8262 8888
www.schwartzbrewery.com

Opening hours:
Mon-Thurs 10.00am – 4.00am
Fri 10.00am – 5.00am
Sat 10.00am – 5.00am
Sun 10.00am – 12 midnight

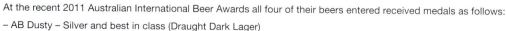

AUSTRALIAN HOTEL & BREWERY

The Australian Hotel and Brewery is an exciting new venue located in Sydney's Hills district. With a state-of-the-art micro brewery and well regarded brewer Neal Cameron at the helm, they have already produced four award winning boutique beers with many more on the way.

At the recent 2011 Australian International Beer Awards all four of their beers entered received medals as follows:

– AB Dusty – Silver and best in class (Draught Dark Lager)
– AB Pale Ale – Bronze (Draught Australian Style Ale)
– AB 3.3 – Silver (Reduced Alcohol Draught)
– AB Sunshine – Bronze (Lager Draught Other).

All beers are already on tap in a variety of venues around Sydney and have quickly led sales within their own Hotel.

The Australian Hotel & Brewery always provides an exciting dining experience. The menu caters for everybody with aged steaks through to classic Australian dishes & gourmet pizzas all rounded off with wonderful desserts and coffee made from specially selected beans roasted on site.

With a full Seven day forecast of entertainment and specials the venue has something to offer everyone.

350 Annangrove Road
Rouse Hill
Tel: (02) 9679-4555
www.australianhotelandbrewery.com.au

Opening hours:
Mon-Sat 10.00am – 3.00am
Sun 10.00am – 12.00am

Beer & Brewer promotion　　　NEW SOUTH WALES – SYDNEY

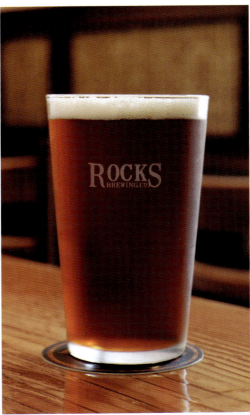

HARTS PUB

Bar, restaurant, functions

Harts Pub is quickly becoming one of Sydney's most popular gastro pubs recently awarded "One Schooner" by the Sydney Morning Herald Good Pub Food Guide. Best known for its rotating menu of Australian craft beer, restaurant quality menu and its friendly, knowledgeable staff, one would struggle to find a better place to relax with mates, colleagues or family. Its award winning beers unveil the story of beer evolution from the early settlement of the Rocks.

Set within a heritage protected building, wandering downstairs you can view the local area history through the black and white photographs decorating the walls. As you head up the stairs one is struck by the life-size characters that bring the beer history to life. Scan the walls upstairs to be entertained by quotes from famous (or infamous) lovers of the golden, amber or dark liquid including Winston Churchill, Benjamin Franklin and even Plato! Read them whilst you enjoy your appropriately beer-matched meal, with a heaven sent pint of ale or simply catch up on the latest sporting events from the seven plasmas located throughout the pub.

No Sydney pub is complete without a beer garden, and Harts will not disappoint. It is surrounded by beautiful sandstone and is regularly filled with patrons enjoying a sunny afternoon or one of the many hosted events like quarterly Brewers Feasts, Australia Day spit roasts, ANZAC Day two-up and of course St Patrick's' Day and 4th of July celebrations for ex-pats and tourists alike!

Harts is where you will find a great overall pub, delivering new craft beers perfectly matched to its seasonal menu. The staff are highly knowledgeable and will happily introduce newcomers with one of the sample paddles. Of course on offer are also Australian wines, champagne and bottled beers from across the globe. So grab colleagues, friends or family and head to the "Hart" of the Rocks and fulfill that soft spot in all beer lovers.

Corner of Essex & Gloucester St
The Rocks
Tel: (02) 9251 6030
www.hartspub.com
www.facebook.com/hartspub

Opening hours:
Sun-Wed 11.00am – 12midnight
Thurs-Sat 11.00am – 1.00am

Beer & Brewer promotion   NEW SOUTH WALES – SYDNEY

THE AUSTRALIAN HOTEL

The Award winning Australian Hotel has long been a top destination to go in Sydney. The Australian Hotel was originally located on George Street, next to where the Museum of Contemporary Art now stands. The Sydney Gazette announced that the Australian was open for business on 12th August 1824, making it the oldest continuously licensed pub in the City of Sydney. When the plague hit Sydney in 1900, many of the buildings were pulled down to prevent further outbreaks, including the Australian Hotel.

In 1913 the present building was constructed and remains to this day, one of the most intact pubs in Sydney, still retaining its original features and unique split level bars. The Australian today looks much the same as it did when soldiers drank there after the First World War in 1918, during the Great Depression of the 1930's or when patrons witnessed the gangland-style murder of John William Manners outside the hotel in 1956.

The friendly and charming atmosphere adds to the rustic feel throughout the Rocks village. The Australian offers true Aussie hospitality with a quaint Australiana theme throughout. The incredible range of over 100 Australian beers and the Annual Australian Beer Festival has established the Australian Hotel as one of Australia's most famous beer specialist venues, but it's also renowned for its gourmet pizzas - Kangaroo, Crocodile and Roast Duck to name a few. Scharers Lager, a Bavarian style lager continues to be the house beer, as it was when Geoffrey Scharer ran the hotel in the 90's and brewed it in Picton.

The Australian Hotel is the home to the Annual Australian Beer Festival which takes place every October. It brings together an array of Australian beers in the one place for everyone to see. It's not just a weekend for beer enthusiasts, but rather the beer curious. For those who might be too intimidated to take the plunge into the exciting world of Aussie boutique beers, this is exactly the push they need to become a true blue fan and giving the Australian Craft industry the recognition it so rightly deserves.

100 Cumberland Street
The Rocks
Tel: (02) 9247 2229
www.australianheritagehotel.com

Opening hours:
Mon-Sat 10:30am – Midnight
Sun 10:30am – 10.00pm

Beer & Brewer promotion NEW SOUTH WALES – SYDNEY

REDOAK BOUTIQUE BEER

Enjoy Australia's most awarded name in beer!

With aspirations of being a pilot, by 14 yrs David Hollyoak had received his pilot license before he was old enough to drive a car. Thank goodness, in a harsh sort of way of course, a football injury - a burst ear drum, saw him have to stop flying and so he took up his 'other' hobby at the time ... making ginger beer (non alcoholic of course).

Since opening Redoak in 2004, David, along with sister Janet, have created Australia's most awarded Brewery. Brewing an extensive array of beer with a litany of national and international beer awards, it is often said 'Redoak is showcasing the amber ale and raising beer to its rightful place on the pedestal of beverages'.

Redoak brews over 30 beer styles and a new range of apple ciders and perry. All brewed without preservatives/additives. Brewed both to age old traditional methods and recipes but also David's own unique styles, he is often called the Willie Wonka of Beer in Australia, brewing with some unique ingredients such as Belgian chocolate, cherries, blackberries, raspberries, lemon myrtle and other Australian spices and leatherwood honey to name but a few!

At the café, Redoak takes pride in teaching the finer qualities of beer appreciation, the meticulous matching of beer and food. Redoak's signature tasting boards take you through a taste bud wonderland, not to mention their own range of beer ice creams/sorbets and chocolate truffles.

Be sure to visit and enjoy their premium range of boutique beers, modern Australian food and friendly/knowledgeable staff.

201 Clarence St
Sydney
Tel: (02) 9262 3303
www.redoak.com.au

Opening hours:
Mon-Sat (lunch & dinner), 11.00am till late

NT

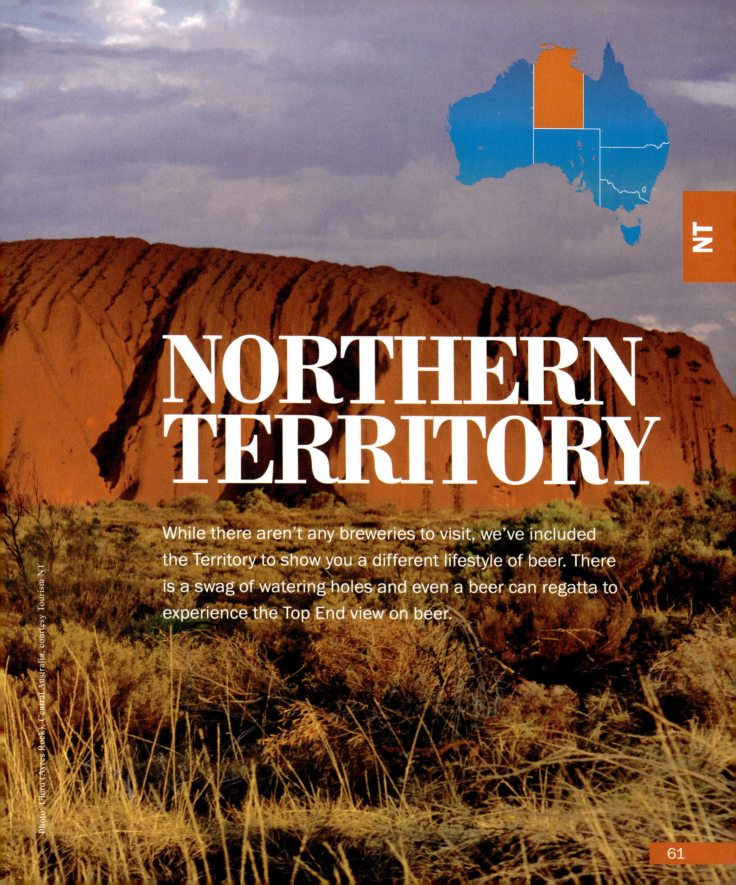

NORTHERN TERRITORY

While there aren't any breweries to visit, we've included the Territory to show you a different lifestyle of beer. There is a swag of watering holes and even a beer can regatta to experience the Top End view on beer.

NT

NORTHERN TERRITORY

Finding a great watering hole in the Top End can mean being prepared to go the distance, or even take to the air. **By Lee Mylne**

It comes as a bit of a surprise to find that the Northern Territory, a place where beer is the thirst-slaker of choice, doesn't have even a solitary brewery.

Even the famous 'Darwin stubbie', that tallest of tallies, is now – according to the locals – only ever ordered by tourists. Unlike most of the states, the Territory doesn't have its own namesake brew, and moves a couple of years ago to establish a microbrewery have so far come to nothing.

But while you might not be able to find anything new or different to taste, beer drinkers are spoilt for choice when it comes to venues.

In Darwin, one of the most interesting places to enjoy a beer is the Victoria Hotel on Smith Street Mall. The old stone pub, which has weathered several cyclones since it was built in 1890 (largely rebuilt after Cyclone Tracy in 1974), is a real treasure. Head there during the quieter daytime sessions – it can be pretty rowdy at night, especially in the Dry when tourist (ie backpacker) numbers soar.

In the former cellar, there are barrel tables and stools and an interesting display about the history of Darwin and the pub itself. One of its more recent owners was Alec Lim, who ran it for 19 years from the late 1940s and was later a popular Lord Mayor of Darwin.

Other good places to quench your thirst and meet the locals are the clubs that dot the harbour foreshore. The Darwin Ski Club, which has been around for about 45 years, offers the revamped outdoor Bali Bar along with two swimming pools (one for toddlers), and a happy hour from 4.30pm, Monday to Thursday. Not far away are the Darwin Sailing Club and the Darwin Trailer Boat Club, both of similar vintage. The latter has a bottle shop that offers regular specials.

■ DROP IN FOR A DRINK

A new way of getting to a few pubs – and covering a lot of territory – in a short time has been devised by Darwin-based helicopter company Airborne Solutions.

Chief pilot Dave Paech has launched what he calls the Historic Hotels Heli Tour, which drops in at five pubs in a day-long trip that will set you back $990 per person.

The tour has you in the air for around two hours, with time on the ground at Goat Island Lodge on the Adelaide River, the Humpty Doo Hotel, Crab Claw Island, the Dundee Hotel and Mandorah Beach Hotel.

All but Goat Island can also be reached by road (Crab Claw is an island only at very high tides) and you can also jump on a ferry at Darwin's Cullen Bay for the 15-minute trip across to Mandorah Beach. There's plenty to do for families, from dropping a line in from a jetty or a tinny to exploring the resort at Crab Claw.

Darwin Lions Beer Can Regatta

Danish publican Kai Hansen presides over Casey's Bar at Goat Island Lodge, the only building on the 10-hectare island. The bar – named for the resident crocodile who comes up to feed on the river bank most evenings – is adorned with hand-carved furniture and entertainment is provided by Hansen's pooch Hot Dog who 'sings' to Hansen's harmonica.

■ OUTBACK ICONS

Beyond the reach of the helicopter tour, there are several good outback pubs to be discovered on the Stuart Highway, heading south from Darwin.

The Adelaide River Inn, built in 1942 and now next to a Commonwealth war cemetery, gives pride of place in the bar to Charlie, the buffalo that starred in *Crocodile Dundee* (after the attentions of a taxidermist).

The Lazy Lizard Tavern at Pine Creek, 220 kilometres south of Darwin, is built of mud bricks formed from termite mounds similar to those you'll see as you drive along the highway. The tavern, built 15 years ago, is a welcoming spot with a swimming pool, lots of Aboriginal artwork, a French cook at work in the kitchen and homemade ice-cream on the menu. There's no beer on tap, and the most popular order is XXXX Gold, but owner Bruce Jenkins keeps it all on ice.

One of Australia's best-known outback watering holes is the Daly Waters pub, about 600 kilometres south of Darwin, and a good stop if you're doing a through-the-centre road trip or fancy a weekend excursion.

Thirsty travellers have been calling in here since the 1930s and Daly Waters was also a stopover point for early aviators and war-time bombers and fighter squadrons. Take a quick drive out to the old World War II aircraft hanger, which is heritage-listed and has some somewhat neglected displays of the wartime history of the place.

On the way, detour slightly to the Stuart Tree, where explorer John McDouall Stuart carved his initial in the trunk on his third attempt to cross the centre.

And the great thing is that all these places have affordable (if a bit basic) accommodation – either rooms in the pub, cabins, or camping areas – so if the thirst really takes you it's easy to stay overnight.

Photography from Tourism NT.

DRINKING HOLES

Adelaide River Inn
106 Stuart Highway,
Adelaide River
(08) 8976 7047
www.adelaideriverinn.com.au

Crab Claw Island
(08) 8978 2313
www.crabclawisland.com.au

Daly Waters Historic Pub
Stuart Street, Daly Waters
(08) 8975 9927
www.dalywaterspub.com

Darwin Sailing Club
Aitkins Drive,
Vesteys Beach
(08) 8981 1700
www.dwnsail.com.au

Darwin Ski Club
Conacher Street,
Fannie Bay
(08) 8981 6630
www.darwinskiclub.com.au

Darwin Trailer Boat Club
Atkins Drive, Fannie Bay
(08) 8981 6749
www.dtbc.com.au

Goat Island Lodge
Virginia
(08) 8978 8803
www.goatisland.com.au

Humpty Doo Hotel
Arnhem Higway,
Humpty Doo
(08) 8988 1372

Mandorah Beach Hotel
Parap
(08) 8978 5044
www.mandorahbeachhotel.bigpondhosting.com

The Lazy Lizard Tavern
299 Millar Terrace,
Pine Creek
(08) 8976 1019
www.lazylizardpinecreek.com.au

EVENTS

AUGUST
Darwin Festival
www.darwinfestival.org.au

EASTER
Family Fishing Competition
Dundee Social and Recreation Club
www.dundeesrc.org.au

MAY-OCTOBER
Mindil Beach Sunset Markets every Thursday and Saturday night.

JUNE
Daly Waters Rodeo and Campdraft
www.dalywaters.net.au

The Adelaide River Show
www.arss.org.au

Darwin Blues Festival
Darwin Ski Club
www.darwinbluesfestival.com

JULY
Darwin Lions Beer Can Regatta
www.beercanregatta.org.au

Airborne Solutions (08) 8972 2345 or 0437 254121; www.airbornesolutions.com.au **For more information** on the Top End, contact the Northern Territory Tourist Commission, www.visitnt.com

QLD

This so-called one-beer state is slowly growing its offerings with 12 breweries. A tourism Mecca for Australia, with the Whitsundays, Great Barrier Reef, Gold Coast, and much more, makes travelling in the tropics thirsty work.

QUEENSLAND

QLD

BRISBANE

The capital of the Sunshine State has long been derided as a one-beer town. Scratch the surface, however, and you'll find a crew of dedicated beer lovers that are keen to make Brisvegas the craft-beer capital of the world. **By Jo Hegerty**

Barry Humphries once quipped that Australia was the Brisbane of the world, the implication being that we're an over-grown country town where rugby league is considered a cultural pursuit. These days, Brisbane has has generated its own sense of laidback style and nabbed some of the best cultural and culinary talent in the country – something Australians can be proud of on the world stage. And while it once may have been a one-beer town, there is a small but dedicated crew of beer lovers in Brisbane worth checking out.

First, let's deal with the elephant in the bottle-o. Think Queensland, think XXXX. But whatever you think of the beer itself, a trip to the XXXX Ale House is a worthwhile excursion. The tour is a little rough around the edges, but

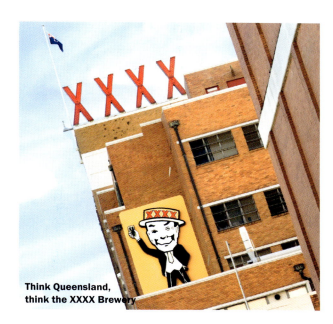

Think Queensland, think the XXXX Brewery

The Bowery

Nectar Beer & Wine Specialists

it's interesting to see how this iconic brewery, in the trendy suburb of Milton, has weathered 130 years since it was moved from Transpose '(yes it's true)' and Victoria. The brewery still produces 23 wooden barrels of beer per week, three for its Ale House (open weekends only) and the rest for another Brisbane icon, The Breakfast Creek Hotel. These are the only two places you can try XXXX "off the wood".

Once the Lion Nathan behemoth is ticked off the list, it's time to turn your attention to the new Brisbane.

Microbreweries may be few and far between in the River City, but a number of establishments are demonstrating a real passion for craft beers. The standout of these is Archive Beer Boutique & Bistro, a finalist in two categories of the 2010 *Beer & Brewer* People's Choice Awards. Located in funky West End, this place is heaving of an evening, with trendy Brisvegans lounging on battered sofas in the spacious newspaper-lined bar. The selection of brews is staggering: in addition to 14 taps (rotated daily), there are more than 200 Australian craft beers in the fridge, with a further 60 or so in the import bar next door. Takeaways are available from Archive's Next Door Cellars and Nectar Beer & Wine Specialists (across the road), which is stacked to the ceiling with boutique beers, wine and cider.

More intimate than Archive, but no less groovy, is The Gunshop Café. Within this petite heritage building, creative types muse and hungry types hone in on the busy kitchen serving breakfast, lunch and dinner. Gunshop offers a small but well-thought out beer list, with boutique brews from every state.

The West End is lively at all times – especially Saturday mornings with the weekly market – but it comes into its own at night. Try Uber (above Archive) or Hi Fi for clubbing, Lychee Lounge for chilling or Musik Kafe for low-key live acts, all on Boundary Street. Another good area for nightlife is Fortitude Valley with its range of megaclubs. Before heading to the likes of Family or Cloudland, enjoy quality aperitifs at The Bowery, a laneway cocktail bar/speakeasy with its own bottled beer and a good range of others, or try Kerbside, an emerging talent on the boutique bar scene. Cru Bar & Cellars is also a good bet, a sophisticated watering hole with an insightful range of craft beers behind the bar and on the shelves.

If you're looking for handcrafted beers on tap and an Aussie pub feel, the Brewhouse Brisbane has staged a comeback at Woolloongabba. So far, there are six beers available from the Brewhouse's microbrewery in Albion, including Sunshine Honey Wheat, which promises that "everyone will think the sun shines out of your glass". This place has everything a good pub should offer – trivia nights, bar meals and a beer garden, plus fresh craft beer.

While you're in the area, check out Brews Brothers, a self-brew operation that welcomes visitors with $3 samples. These guys brew for The Bowery and you'll find their beers in restaurants and bottleshops around town.

Brisbane's last pub to brew beer on site is the International Hotel. The decor's a bit confused, but the beer travels just 10 metres from brewery to bar, which makes it all worthwhile. Veteran master brewer Rudi Herget has been here for more than 10 years and is always on hand to prescribe the exact beer for your needs and to discuss his four beers. His Indian Chief Wheat Beer, Irish Red Ale, Noble Pilsener, and Belgian Gold Mid-Strength are all made in accordance with the German Purity Law.

Germans are well represented in Brisbane. As well as The Black Forest German Café at Highgate Hill, traditionalists

The tap beers at Archive are rotated daily

Grand Central Hotel, home of Platform Bar

will love the Brisbane German Club, housed in a suitably formidable hall and serving the finest German brews just opposite the 'Gabba. On the menu are all your favourite dishes, from schnitzel to sauerkraut, pork knuckle to potato dumplings. This is a great place to watch an AFL match or partake in *frühschoppen*, a traditional morning pint.

For a taste of the Black Forest with a modern twist head to the city's chic Bavarian Bier Café. Choose a three- or five-bier flight, matched with the Munich Brewers Platter and enjoy the view over Storey Bridge.

Just around the corner, you'll find the recently refurbished Belgian Beer Café Brussels, which features the city's only beer garden. Buckets of mussels, big Belgian beers and Art Nouveau decor cater to a rowdy city crowd during the week, with a more relaxed vibe on the weekend. Also in the CBD is one of Brisbane's standout bottleshops, Festival Cellars. This wine emporium and deli is independently owned and supports similar small businesses such as clever Aussie breweries. Tucked away underneath Central Station, Grand Central Hotel is full of surprises, including whimsical train-themed bars and a selection of boutique beers in the fridge behind Platform Bar. You'll find a more extensive range in the attached bottleshop, and if something there really takes your fancy, you can ask to drink it in the bar.

From Central, you could visit Roma Street Parklands with its collection of public art and guided walks. From the city, it's an easy stroll to the Botanic Gardens, then across the Goodwill Bridge to South Bank, where you can cool off at Streets Beach, enjoy the weekend markets, have an inner-city barbecue at the riverside parklands or hit the cultural precinct. The Queensland Performing Arts Centre, Queensland Museum and Maritime Museum are all here, and kids are invited to get creative at the Gallery of Modern Art Children's Centre.

There also just happens to be another of Brisbane's great beer venues in South Bank – 5th Element. This slick wine bar offers plates to share, plus a massive list of craft beers, including Stone & Wood from Byron Bay. A little further back from the river, you'll find Era Bistro, a casual bar, bistro, restaurant serving fine food and exquisite drinks. Be sure to visit the adjacent wine store, which has a monumental range of wines and beers.

Don't think it's only the central areas serving quality beers, the Brisbane 'burbs are also hungry for quality. In the trendy suburb of Bulimba, east of the city, Scales & Ales is a tiny restaurant offers fish dishes matched with Australia's national drink. The fish and chips here is the best you'll ever taste, and the beer list is outstanding, including rare brews from owner and chef Frank Correnti's private cellar.

Further afield, Drinx Cellars at Shorncliffe and Woody Point and Dan Murphy's in Albany Creek to the city's north maintain good standards in beer. If you want to see the best the southside has to offer, head to Bacchus Brewing Co at Capalaba, an all-grain on-premises brewery that welcomes visitors to try something from their 20 taps or take a six-pack home. This will no doubt help you recover from Brisbane's family favourites such as the Lone Pine Koala Sanctuary, Alma Park Zoo or the planetarium at the Botanical Gardens, Mount Coot-tha.

Wherever you find yourself in the River City be assured you will never be far from a quality craft beer. So kick back and relax – Brisvegas style.

■ MADE IN QUEENSLAND

Australia's second-largest malt producer now has a presence in Brisbane. Barrett Burston Malting at Pinkenba, near the airport, is a sparking new facility with the capacity to turn out 86,000 tonnes of malt a year. While much of this is gobbled up by the mammoth Carlton United Brewery at Yalata, the remainder is distributed around the country and overseas, meaning there's a little bit of Queensland sunshine in more of the world's beer.

Making merry at Oktoberfest Brisbane

Brews Brothers

International Hotel

EVENTS

MARCH
Brisbane Comedy Festival
www.briscomfest.com
Future Music Festival
www.futureentertainment.com.au

MAY
Cootha Classic
www.coothaclassic.com.au
(date subject to change)

JUNE
Brisbane Cheese Awards
www.brisbanecheeseawards.com.au

AUGUST
Royal Queensland Show (The Ekka),
www.ekka.com.au
Brisbane Boat Show,
www.brisbaneboatshow.com.au

SEPTEMBER
Brisbane Festival & Riverfire www.brisbanefestival.com.au

OCTOBER
Oktoberfest Brisbane www.oktoberfestbrisbane.com.au

NOVEMBER
Brisbane Good Food & Wine Show www.goodfoodshow.com.au

NOVEMBER
Brisbane International Film Festival
www.biff.com.au

BREWERIES

XXXX Ale House
Cnr Black & Paten Sts, Milton
(07) 3361 7597
www.xxxxbrewerytour.com.au

Bacchus Brewing Co
Unit 1, 2 Christine Pl, Capalaba
(07) 3823 5252
www.bacchusbrewing.com.au

Brews Brothers
31 Wellington Rd, Woolloongabba
(07) 3891 3050
www.brewsbrothers.com.au

Brewhouse Brisbane
601 Stanley St, Woolloongabba
(07) 3891 1011
www.brewhouse.com.au

International Hotel
525 Boundary St, Spring Hill
(07) 3227 1999
www.internationalhotel.com.au

BEER BARS

Archive Beer Boutique & Bistro 100 Boundary St, West End; (07) 3844 3419

Bavarian Bier Café
Level 1, 45 Eagle St, Eagle St Pier; (07) 3339 0900

Belgian Beer Café Brussels
Cnr Mary & Edward Sts, Brisbane; (07) 3221 0199

Black Forest German Café
196 Gladstone Rd, Highgate Hill; (07) 3217 2180

Brisbane German Club
416 Vulture St, East Brisbane; (07) 3391 2434

Scales & Ales 5 Wambool St, Bulimba (07) 3899 4001

Breakfast Creek Hotel
2 Kingsford Smith Dr, Albion
(07) 3262 5988

5th Element
1b/188 Grey St, South Brisbane; (07) 3846 5584

Kerbside
Constance St, Fortitude Valley; (07) 3252 9833

The Gunshop Café
53 Mollison St, West End
(07) 3844 2241

Cru Bar & Cellars
1/22 James St, Fortitude Valley; (07) 3252 2400

The Bowery
676 Ann St, Fortitude Valley; (07) 3252 0202

BOTTLESHOPS

Dan Murphy's Albany Creek 1300 723 388

Drinx Shorncliffe
(07) 3269 8193

Drinx Woody Point
(07) 3284 2245

Era Bistro & Wine Store
(07) 3255 2033

Festival Cellars
(07) 3012 9880

Grand Central Hotel & Cellars (07) 3220 2061

Nectar Beer & Wine Specialists
(07) 3846 4655

QLD

FAR NORTH

Beautiful Cairns

Some people travel to the pointy end of Queensland for the Great Barrier Reef, others for the fishing. Some are looking for that easygoing vibe or for adventures such as Australia's last bungee jump or jungle surfing at Cape Tribulation. But you, dear reader, should visit for the beer.
By Jo Hegerty

In Cairns, among the backpackers and stinger suits, you'll find a highly awarded craft-beer producer. Surprised? Since the demise of its last brewery in 1993, Far North Queensland has occasionally been described as a "beer wasteland". But in 2005, the Newman family strolled into the void and founded Blue Sky Brewery.

It was an inspired idea, and the locals took to Blue Sky's brews like crocs to water. Within a few years, the brewery's restaurant and bar was one of the most popular venues in town, and another was opened in 2010 at Cairns' domestic

The Hotel Cairns

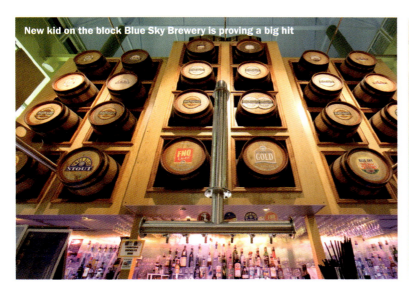
New kid on the block Blue Sky Brewery is proving a big hit

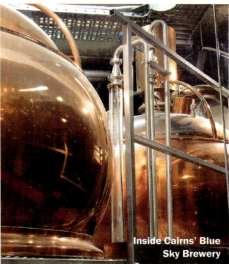
Inside Cairns' Blue Sky Brewery

airport. The reputation of brewery's Blonde, Stout and Cider and particularly Cairns Gold, Blue Sky Pilsner and FNQ Lager ("so good you have to FNQ for it"), has spread like cane toads as far afield as Vietnam.

Visit the source of this greatness in the heart of Cairns city, making time for a brewery tour and a meal (rest assured, beer sorbet tastes better than it sounds!). You'll find Blue Sky beers in more than 60 restaurants in Cairns; for incredible seafood, try Tha Fish or Pesci's, Italian at Villa Romana or modern Australian at Ochre.

You could go all out and rest your head at the Shangri-La Hotel at the Marina where you'll find Blue Sky beers in the mini-bar. The Hotel Cairns also makes a great base, with stylish colonial-style decor and a winning location just a block back from the Esplanade. Best of all, guests are invited to borrow a Mercedes Smart Car to explore the region – at no charge.

There are world-class attractions within an hour's drive north of Cairns, including the Daintree Rainforest, Kuranda Scenic Skyrail and Cairns Tropical Zoo. Pop into the Shannonvale Tropical Fruit Winery for kaffir lime, mangosteen and pineapple wines, or try the wattleseed or soursop flavours at The Daintree Ice Cream Company.

Just 20 minutes' drive gets you to Palm Cove and Apres Beach Bar & Grill. This is a fun place to ease into the evening, with a range of more than 100 beers from around the world, live entertainment and hearty meals.

■ PORT DOUGLAS

This is the point where the "rainforest meets the reef". Visit in May for Port Douglas Carnivale, a mammoth celebration of the flavours of the tropics. Events include the Sheraton Mirage Longest Lunch and a Food Fight Battle of the Chefs. Stay at Thala Beach Lodge on a picture-perfect private headland with five-star service and six-star views.

An unforgettable dining experience is 10 minutes inland at Flames of the Forest, an indigenous adventure by candlelight in a secret location in the rainforest. You can also taste the rainforest at Julaymba restaurant, located at Australia's first eco-retreat and award-winning pamper palace, the Daintree Eco-Lodge & Spa.

If you can bear to turn your back on the coast, head to the Atherton Tablelands. Scattered among rainforest and savannah around the 100-year-old town of Mareeba is a whole new range of culinary experiences, from tropical-fruit wines to bush tucker.

Get off to a good start with Skybury Coffee Estate, Australia's oldest coffee plantation set high on the Great

Nestled in the trees, Thala Beach Lodge is the ideal holiday hideaway

You're spoilt for choice at the Townsville Brewing Company

Townsville Brewing Company

Dividing Range. Housed in an airy timber structure is The Australian Coffee Centre, with restaurant, coffee lab and "coffee cinema", all overlooking the 145-hectare plantation. Another caffeinated experience not to miss is Bruno Maloberti's tour of his NQ Gold Coffee Plantation. Here you get the passion of Italy in the tropics and very possibly the best cappuccino in Queensland.

For something a little harder but no less fruity, stop in at de Brueys Boutique Wines where there's not a grape in sight. Instead, Bob and Elaine create their award-winning wines, liqueurs and ports from mangoes, lychees, native bush cherry and other exotic fruits. Things get even wilder at the Mt Uncle Distillery. Located at the fertile foot of Mt Uncle (next to Mt Aunty, of course), North Queensland's only distillery produces SexyCat marshmallow liqueur, Anjea Vodka and Premium Rum. With the contemporary yet rustic Bridges Café and Tearoom onsite and more than 50 styles of tea to try, this is a great place to take a load off.

Cheese lovers will be in a steamy version of heaven up here, with a number of dairies producing a vast range of cheeses, plus chocolates and yoghurt. Gallo Dairyland produces traditional European-style cheeses such as brie, Gruyère and gorgonzola, plus a few Aussie specials such as macadamia cheese. Also stop in at Out of the Whey Cheesery & Teahouse at Mungalli Creek Dairy, producers of biodynamic fromage, yoghurt and milk.

All these foodie attractions and more can be found on the Mountain Tablelands and Savannah Tablelands food trails, visit www.tasteparadise.com.au for maps and information.

Cairns isn't the only place up north clinging onto good beer like it's a life raft, the Townsville Brewing Company, which opened The Brewery in 2001, is a firm local favourite spreading craft-beer joy throughout North Queensland. Head brewer Mitch Bradey produces seven unpasteurised beers, including Townsville Bitter Premium, Belgian Blonde Wit and internationally awarded Flanagans Dry Irish Stout. The Brewery is housed in a magnificent heritage-listed building with its very own clock tower, plus chandeliers, topnotch restaurant and a state-of-the-art polished brewery in the middle of the ground floor.

Tourists and locals of all persuasions rub shoulders at this sophisticated venue, all sharing a love of fresh, local beer. Townsville Brewing Company beers can be found in a number of restaurants around town, including C Bar on The Strand and A Touch of Salt. If you're out to impress, try The Saltcellar, a fine-dining restaurant with Townsville's best wine cellar and a good selection of Australian and international craft beers.

Catch your own dinner at the Townsville Barra Fishing Farm or, if you're game, hand-feed a crocodile at the Billabong Sanctuary. For a tasty local attraction that doesn't bite, visit Frosty Mango orchards and try delights such as mango trifle, mango cheesecake, muffins, ice-cream and more.

Townsville is a slip, slop and a slap from Maggie, as the locals call Magnetic Island, with all its gorgeous beaches and outdoor fun ranging from Harley Davidson tours to sea kayaking. Be sure to check out the chilled ambience of Barefoot Art Food Wine at Horseshoe Bay, offering casual gourmet dining and a gallery onsite.

Head north for your next holiday and savour the flavours of the tropics. It may be so far, bit it's definitely so good.

Flames of the Forest - Indigenous performers

EVENTS

MAY
Cairns Blues Festival
www.cairnsbluesfestival.com.au
Port Douglas Carnivale
www.carnivale.com.au

MAY TO DECEMBER
QCCU Strand Night Markets (first Friday of the month), Townsville.
www.willowsrotarymarkets.com.au

JUNE
Cairns Home Show and Caravan, Camping & Boating Expo www.australianevents.com.au

AUGUST
Townsville Cultural Fest
www.culturalfest.org;
(07) 4772 4800

AUGUST/SEPTEMBER
Cairns Festival
www.cairnsfest.com.au

SEPTEMBER
Sunferries Magnetic Island Race Week
www.magneticislandraceweek.com.au
Cairns Buskers Festival
www.cairnsstreetbuskersfestival.com

OCTOBER
Tablelands Folk Festival http://tablelandsfolkfestival.org
Taste of the Tablelands Festival
www.tastesofthetablelands.com

Dates are subject to change. Photos courtesy Tourism Qld (select images).

BREWERIES & DISTILLERY

Blue Sky Brewery
34-42 Lake St, Cairns
(07) 4057 0500
www.blueskybrewery.com.au

Mt Uncle Distillery
1819 Chewko Rd, Walkamin
(07) 4086 8008
www.mtuncle.com

Townsville Brewing Company
252 Flinders St, Townsville
(07) 4724 2999
www.townsvillebrewery.com.au

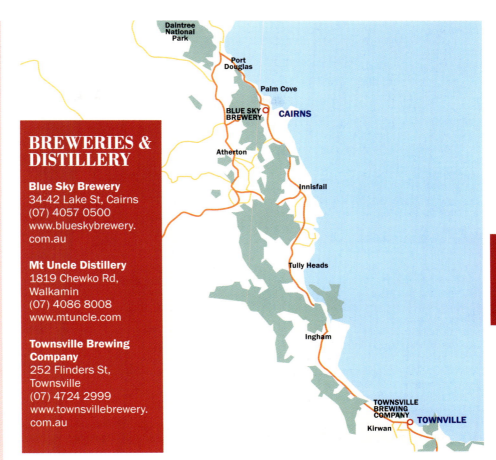

THINGS TO SEE AND DO

Tha Fish Cairns, (07) 4041 5350; www.thafish.com.au **Pesci's Mediterranean and Seafood Restaurant** Cairns, (07) 4041 1133; www.pescis.com.au **Villa Romana Trattoria** Cairns, (07) 4051 9000; www.villaromana.com.au/cairns **Ochre Restaurant & Catering** Cairns, (07) 4051 0100; www.ochrerestaurant.com.au **Shangri-La Hotel** Cairns, (07) 4031 1411; www.shangri-la.com **The Hotel Cairns** Cairns, (07) 4051 6188; www.thehotelcairns.com **Shannonvale Tropical Fruit Winery** Mossman, (07) 4098 4000; www.shannonvalewine.com **The Daintree Ice-cream Company** Cape Tribulation, (07) 4098 9114 **Apres Beach Bar & Grill** Palm Cove, (07) 4059 2000; www.apresbeachbar.com.au **Thala Beach Lodge** Port Douglas, (07) 4098 5700; www.thalabeach.com.au **Flames of the Forest** Port Douglas, (07) 4099 5983; www.flamesoftheforest.com.au **Daintree Eco Lodge & Spa** Daintree, (07) 4098 6100; www.daintree-ecolodge.com.au **Skybury Coffee Estate** Mareeba, (07) 4093 2190; www.skybury.com.au **NQ Gold Coffee Plantation** Dimbulah Rd (via Mareeba), (07) 4093 2269; www.nqgoldcoffee.com.au **de Brueys Boutique Wines** Mareeba, (07) 4092 4515; www.debrueys.com.au **Gallo Dairyland** Atherton, (07) 4095 2388; www.gallodairyland.com.au **Out of the Whey Cheesery & Teahouse** Millaa Millaa, (07) 4097 2232; www.mungallicreekdairy.com.au **Eden Retreat & Mountain Spa** Yungaburra, (07) 4089 7000; www.edenhouse.com.au **Jabiru Safari Lodge** Biboohra (via Mareeba), 1800 788 755; www.jabirusafarilodge.com.au **C Bar** Townsville, (07) 4724 0333; www.cbar.com.au **A Touch of Salt** Townsville, (07) 4724 4441; www.atouchofsalt.com.au **The SaltCellar** Townsville, (07) 4724 5866; www.atouchofsalt.com.au **Townsville Barra Fishing Farm** Kelso, (07) 4789 3093; www.barrafishing.net **Billabong Sanctuary** Townsville, (07) 4778 8344; www.billabongsanctuary.com.au **Frosty Mango** Mutarnee, (07) 4770 8184; www.frostymango.com.au **Barefoot Art Food Wine** Horseshoe Bay, Magnetic Island, (07) 4758 1170; www.barefootartfoodwine.com.au

QLD

SOUTH EAST

Broadbeach, Surfers Paradise

It's hardly surprising visitors to South-east Queensland keep coming back for another round. From the NSW border to Noosa and inland to Toowoomba, this region has beaches, mountain chalets, sandy islands and dense rainforest – and all within a few hours of each other. **By Jo Hegerty**

You can fly into Brisbane or the Sunshine Coast, but for many, the real destination is the Gold Coast. Tell the kids that Dreamworld, Movieworld and Wet'n'Wild are closed and head straight for Burleigh Brewing Co, home of fresh-as-a-daisy Duke beers, Black Giraffe, My Wife's Bitter and Fanny Gertrude's, plus whatever else takes these surfer dudes' fancy. Take a tour of the brewery the first Saturday of every month with master brewer Brennan Fielding, or meet like-minded beer nuts at the monthly Brewhouse Bash. (Plans are afoot to open the Tap Room & Brewery Lounge a couple of nights a week – check the website for updates.) Being freshness fanatics, the crew only distributes Duke within four hours of the brewery; you'll find them in most quality bottleshops and restaurants nearby. Burleigh Brewing Co occasionally releases limited-edition beers, such as The Hef, for the rest of the country.

For another evening well spent, take in a show at Jupiters Hotel & Casino. Here you'll also find one of the state's best beer venues, The PA, which feels like a traditional Aussie pub and serves a fantastic range of Australian and international craft brews.

As hard as it is to turn away from the

Burleigh Brewing Co

The Brewhouse Bash at Burleigh Brewing Co is a popular event

The PA at Jupiters Hotel & Casino

MT Brewery

The Spotted Cow

beaches and glitz of the strip, a trip into the hinterland is a must. Your destination: Mt Tamborine.

Anglophiles and homesick Poms will dissolve into tepid pools of joy when they discover the Fox & Hounds Inn at the foot of the mountain. This traditional Irish/British pub comes complete with rose garden, ploughman's lunches and smooth Ales on tap, including Foxy Bitter.

Next, make a beer-line to MT Brewery at Mt Tamborine. Beer Monster Andre Morris has created a venue that feels like a winery, but produces quality craft beers such as Yippy IPA and Czech Mate Pils. The brewery is at the rear of an open compound that also houses Witches Chase cheese and mod-Oz restaurant Liquid Amber. The atmosphere in this eco-friendly space is so chilled that your cheese plate and four-beer taster could easily turn into a long afternoon or evening out. On the weekends, live music has the place jumping until late.

The brewery is at the end of Gallery Walk, a street of esoteric and gourmet delights ranging from fairies to art galleries to cellar doors. There are 10 or so wineries close by, notably Witches Falls and Cedar Creek Estate, which also has glow-worm caves.

Be sure to visit Tamborine Mountain Distillery too. Here, in a Tudor-style chalet, you'll find Alla and Michael Ward's fine liqueurs, spirits and schnapps pot-stilled from local fruits. Another Mt Tamborine institution is The Polish Place, serving heart-warming Polish meals on the western escarpment of the mountain. If the view across the ranges isn't enough to make you dizzy, the big, rich Polish beers certainly will. The Polish Place has six cosy chalets – and you'll need that wood fire during the cooler months.

Committed beer lovers should consider two pilgrimages while in this area. The first is to The Spotted Cow in Toowoomba, arguably Queensland's best pub. It has a long and distinguished reputation as a craft-beer mecca, attracting pilgrims from far and wide. There are three taps dedicated to "beer of the month" boutique brews, and some 70 more in the fridge. MT Brewery, Burleigh Brewery, Stone & Wood, Fat Yak... they're all waiting for you in the Oropa European Beer Cafe.

Ninety minutes south of Toowoomba (or three hours from Brisbane) is Stanthorpe and the Castle Glen distillery and now brewery. Housed in an actual castle, this spirit house has been here for 21 years and produces a mammoth range of wines, liqueurs and now beers. There are currently 15 preservative-free, bottle-aged beers ranging from traditional Ales to fruit beers. Surprisingly popular are Castle Glen's wine beers, which owner Cedric Miller says were originally brewed as a bit of a joke during the drought, when they had more wine than water.

If you take the motorway up to the Sunshine Coast, you'll drive right past one of Australia's biggest breweries, the Carlton Brewhouse. The scale of this operation is impressive and the hourly tours take you right into the heart of the process.

Michael Ward at the Tamborine Mountain Distillery

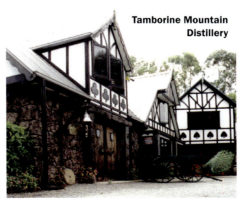
Tamborine Mountain Distillery

Past Brisbane, a worthy deviation is into the Glasshouse Mountains area behind Caloundra. If you have a spare day, visit Australia Zoo; otherwise, head to Maleny, stopping in for a tasting at Maleny Mountain Wines, housed in a giant wine barrel, and Maleny Cheese. For the best view of the Glasshouse Mountains, plenty of warm hospitality and German beers, enjoy a meal at King Ludwig's Restaurant, a long-time favourite of locals and visitors alike. Continue on to quaint Montville for Devonshire tea or to poke around the boutiques.

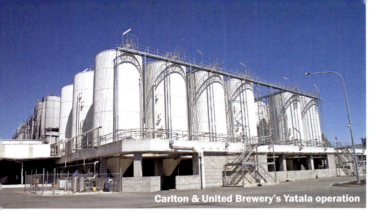
Carlton & United Brewery's Yatala operation

A couple of famous brands on the packaging line at CUB's Yatala Brewery

The Sunshine Coast's Brewery Bar & Restaurant

Greg Curran, The Sunshine Coast Brewery

Back on the Sunny Coast, in Maroochydore to be precise, you'll find Brewery Bar, the new front for the Sunshine Coast Brewery. Owner Greg Curran is on a mission to improve the palate of Queenslanders and show them that Aussie handcrafted beers are as good as – if not better than – imported. Brewery Bar has 10 beers on tap, ranging from mid-strength Summer Ale to the chocolatey Porter, which appears in a number of dishes on the restaurant's clever menu devised by Russell Crowe's former chef Brent Cressey. The beers are brewed 10 minutes away at Kunda Park, and the brewery itself is only open for functions.

The Brewery Bar is one of the venues visited by Thirsty Critters, which operates an upmarket booze bus covering Brisbane, the Sunshine Coast, the Gold Coast and northern NSW. This is a great way to sample south-east Queensland's finest brews without worrying about driving.

■ THE SUNSHINE COAST

Sunny Coast beaches offer surf, sheltered bays and estuaries. At Yandina (inland from Coolum), you'll find a theme park with spice, The Ginger Factory. Take the steam train tour to see how Buderim Ginger is made into sauce, sweets, side dishes and ginger beer. Nearby is the spectacular Spirit House, a Thai restaurant that offers daily cooking classes (often booked out months in advance).

Don't miss the Eumundi markets on a Wednesday or Saturday morning, where you'll find local produce, crafts, jewellery and clothing all with that Noosa *je ne sais quoi*. Noosa is jammed with fantastic restaurants and cafes, but if you want to escape the crowds, check out the offerings at Noosaville. The beaches and walks on the Noosa Headland are a must too.

Noosa now has its own beer thanks to the people behind Laguna Jacks Cellar & Bar. Brewed by their buddies down at Burleigh Brewing, Hastings Premium Lager has just been launched and is available on tap at Laguna Jacks.

The Audi Noosa Food & Wine Festival takes place in May, a three-day extravaganza celebrating Aussie producers and attracting just about every celebrity foodie in the country.

Finally, dedicated drinkers of the Bundaberg variety – be it ginger beer or rum – might want to consider a visit to the source. Bundaberg is about three hours north of Noosa, past World Heritage-listed Fraser Island, and here you can visit The Bundaberg Barrel, showroom of the creators of Bundaberg Ginger Beer and other brewed soft drinks, or take a tour of the Bundaberg Distillery where Australia's favourite rum has been brewed since 1888. This is also the only place you can try Bundaberg's Rum Liqueur, which will win over even the harshest rum critic. A tilt-train operates between Brisbane and Bundaberg, visit www.queenslandrail.com.au for information.

It's thirsty work exploring south-east Queensland, but rest assured you'll be well catered for, with plenty of options to while away a day or three, or four.

Barbara Lutze at King Ludwig's Restaurant

Bundaberg Distilling Co

EVENTS

JANUARY
Magic Millions Carnival & Race Day Gold Coast, www.magicmillionscarnival.com.au

FEBRUARY
Good Vibrations Gold Coast, www.goodvibrationsfestival.com.au

FEBRUARY/MARCH
ASP World Tour, Gold Coast, www.aspworldtour.com

MAY
Ipswich Show www.ipswichshow.com.au
Sanctuary Cove International Boat Show, www.sanctuarycoveboatshow.com.au
Audi Noosa Food & Wine Festival www.celebrationofaustralianfoodandwine.com.au

JULY
Gympie Ultimate Steam Festival www.gympieultimatesteam.com

AUGUST
Optus Gympie Music Muster www.muster.com.au

SEPTEMBER
Sunshine Coast Real Food Festival www.realfoodfestival.com.au

OCTOBER
Armor All Gold Coast 600 www.goldcoast600.com.au
Tamborine Mountain Scarecrow Festival www.tamborinemtncc.org.au

NOVEMBER TO MARCH
Turtle hatching Mon Repos Conservation Park, Bundaberg, www.bookbundabergregion.com.au

DECEMBER
Australian PGA Championship, Coolum, www.championship.pga.org.au

BEER BARS

Fox & Hounds Country Inn
Cnr Oxenford Tamborine Rd & Elevation Dr, Wongawallan
(07) 5665 7582
www.foxandhounds.net.au

King Ludwig's German Restaurant & Bar
401 Mountain View Rd, Maleny
(07) 5499 9377
www.kingludwigs.com.au

Laguna Jacks Cellar & Bar
50 Hastings St, Noosa
(07) 5474 9555
www.lagunajacks.com.au

The PA, Jupiters Hotel & Casino
Broadbeach Island, Gold Coast
(07) 5592 8100
www.jupitersgoldcoast.com.au

The Spotted Cow
296 Ruthven St, Toowoomba
(07) 4639 3264
www.spottedcow.com.au

BREWERIES & DISTILLERIES

Bundaberg Distilling Co
Avenue St, Bundaberg East
www.bundabergrum.com.au

Burleigh Brewing Co.
17A Ern Harley Dr, Burleigh Heads
(07) 5593 6000
www.burleighbrewing.com.au

Brewery Bar & Restaurant
20/22 Ocean St, Maroochydore
(07) 5443 3884
www.sunshinecoast-brewery.com

Carlton BrewHouse
Cuthbert Drive, Yatala
(07) 3826 5858
www.carltonbrewhouse.com.au

Castle Glen Liqueurs
3184 Amiens Rd, The Summit
(07) 4683 2363 or
(07) 4131 2999
www.castleglenliqueurs.com

MT Brewery
165-185 Long Road, North Tamborine
(07) 5545 2032
www.mtbeer.com

Tamborine Mountain Distillery
87-91 Beacon Road North Tamborine
(07) 5545 3452
www.tamborinemountaindistillery.com

Brewery Tours: Thirsty Critters
0449 784 610
www.thirstycritters.com.au

Beer & Brewer promotion   QUEENSLAND

SUNSHINE COAST BREWERY

Their new bar & restaurant at Maroochydore is a beer lover's heaven, with a choice of 10 craft beers on tap and a theme A World of Beers – brewed locally; the variety and quality on offer is extensive.

As well as outstanding beers, they have put together a great food menu that complements their beers. The choice ranges from gourmet items enjoyed as starters shared with friends, through to mains and a selection of desserts, as well as a separate lunch menu and daily specials.

The focus in the restaurant is on beer – both using beer in the preparation of dishes and also on matching the food with the various beers available.

13 Endeavour Drive
Kunda Park
Tel: (07)5476 6666

Sunshine Coast Brewery Bar & Restaurant
Cnr Ocean St & Horton Pde
Maroochydore
Tel: (07)5443 3884
www.sunshinecoastbrewery.com

Opening hours:
Bar: Mon-Sun 11.30am – late
Brewery: Cellar door sales
Mon-Fri 10.00am – 3.00pm

XXXX ALE HOUSE & BREWERY TOURS

A XXXX Alehouse tour is an unbeatable way to experience an Australian icon up close and discover its proud legend.

The Castlemaine Perkins Brewery was established at Milton, just west of Brisbane city, way back in 1878. Flash forward 130 years or so and a visit to the brewery is your ticket to a rich taste of the science, art and heritage behind these truly great beers.

The tour takes about an hour and a quarter and you'll cover a millennia of history in that time – from the beginnings of beer, through 130 years of XXXX heritage and finally to the cold fresh glass of XXXX in front of you.

Cnr Black and Paten St
Milton
(just down from Milton Road)
Tel: (07) 33617585
www.xxxxalehouse.com.au
www.xxxxbrewerytour.com.au

Opening hours:
Tours start from 11.00am
Mon – Sun

BREWHOUSE BRISBANE

Brisbane's home of craft-made beer - Restaurant / Bar / Beer Garden / Functions / Gaming

Brewhouse Brisbane's Grill offers you a blend of traditional and modern cuisine inspired by the best of Queensland's fresh produce; grain-fed steaks, locally-caught seafood and more.

To compliment an impressive a la carte menu, the award-winning brewery offers a choice of up to six beers brewed fresh at their nearby brewery. Sourcing inspiration from every corner of the globe, but with a particular focus on locally-derived ingredients, the regular favourites are "Starlager" Classic Pilsner, "Dog's Bollocks" ESB, "BPA" Brisbane Pale Ale, "Sunshine" Honey Wheat, "Up Yer Kilt" Scottish Ale, and "Midnight" Extra Stout.

Right on the fringe of Woolloongabba and South Brisbane, Brewhouse Brisbane occupies a prime corner opposite the Mater Hospital and the Mater Hill Bus Station. And only 2 minutes from the CBD makes it ideal for commuters to get to via car, bus or train.

The multi-faceted venue oozes character that dates back to 1889. Spread out over two levels is two bars, a restaurant, a fabulous big beer garden, gaming room, bottle shop and oodles of function space. The hotel is currently being sensitively restored to its former glory with a particular focus on melding 'traditional beer venue' with a 'modern craft beer Mecca'.

601 Stanley Street
Woolloongabba
Tel: (07) 3891 1011
www.brewhouse.com.au

Opening hours:
Daily 10.00am to 1.00am
Lunch, Dinner, Late

ARCHIVE BEER BOUTIQUE

Nestled in the heart of West End's busy restaurant and bar district, Archive Beer Boutique is truly one of a kind. With the most comprehensive and eclectic beer list in Brisbane, Archive is a haven for any beer lover. Dedicated to promoting craft beers, Archive stocks its fridges from boutique breweries all over Australia and the world; from Byron Bay to Bavaria. Archive opened its doors as an Australian craft beer bar, stocking over 140 bottled beers from craft breweries in every state of Australia; but it wasn't long until Archive's customers' palates demanded international offerings. With fridges now boasting over 200 different bottled beers as well as 14 constantly rotating draught beers on tap; Archive is now Australia's premier beer bar and an essential stop for any beer enthusiast.

Not content with beer alone, Archive's bistro offers a modern seasonal menu, with light meals and mains 7 days a week. Using only the best local produce, Archive's menu offers to please everyone, from vegetarians to steak lovers. Never forgetting the venue's true passion - Archive's head chef expertly matches all of the bistro's offerings with hand selected beers; so every one of Archive's visitors can enjoy their meal with a perfectly matched beer.

With charm not limited to the food and drink, Archive's décor is affectionately renowned throughout Brisbane. From the bar made almost entirely of Reader's Digest spines, to the quirky and eclectic mix of over-stuffed couches and comfortable retro lounges; to its much used pool tables and off-beat custom made light fittings, Archive quickly becomes a place to relax and enjoy yourself for hours on end.

From the beer connoisseur to a brew beginner, Archive doesn't shy away from the promise of delivering the perfect beer. With a beer list that would daunt many, the friendly bar staff act as beer encyclopaedias; and are always eager to help their guests navigate the library of beers, providing recommendations, tasting advice and personal favourites. While Archive only opened in 2010, it has quickly become the destination for beer lovers and experts and continues to expand and improve its selection of craft beers from all over Australia and around the world.

100 Boundary St
West End, Brisbane
Tel: (07) 3844 3419
www.archivebeerboutique.com.au

Opening hours:
11.00am - Late 7 days

Beer & Brewer promotion   QUEENSLAND

BLUE SKY BREWERY

Blue Sky Brewery's located in Cairns, Tropical North Queensland, which is a beautiful place to brew beer. They have a great history of using only the purest ingredients with the purest water. So, it is only natural that they created premium award winning handcrafted beers brewed onsite giving you a full flavoured, preservative free, naturally brewed 100% Cairns beer.

As their brewery is located onsite, customers will experience beer at its freshest, coming straight to the bar taps from the tanks. All of Blue Sky's handcrafted beers are unpasteurised and brewed naturally, giving a distinct depth of flavour and fresh taste not found in mass-produced beers made by larger commercial breweries.

Choose from a variety of beers, including seasonal specialty brews and local's favorites, with alcohol ranging from 3% to 6%. They source the finest malts, yeast and hops from around the world and combine with pristine Cairns water to produce truly premium beers that compete with the world's best.

You can now buy Blue Sky beers in major retail chains and independents, Australia wide.

34-42 Lake Street
Cairns
Tel: (07) 4057 0500
www.blueskybrewery.com.au

Opening hours:
7 days 11:00am – Late
Tour Times: Daily

BURLEIGH BREWING COMPANY

Burleigh Brewing is the Gold Coast's only brewery and Queensland's largest independent brewer.

They have a respect for tradition, yet a thirst for innovation. Their beers are a family of diverse styles but brewed to identical standards. All brews are different, to satisfy a broad range of tastes, but they all share the same DNA. All distinctly different. All distinctly Burleigh. From traditional European lagers, to flavour-filled ales, to creative beers that defy style definitions.

There is an overriding commitment to authenticity – of ingredients, processes and approach to life. They pride themselves on using local ingredients and raw materials. If it's available in Australia, they buy it here - bottles, cartons, 6 packs, labels, malted barley – you name it!

Their beers are made without compromise, respecting century old brewing processes and traditions. No accelerated brewing, no additives, no preservatives. Drop in and enjoy a beer with the team in their Tap Room and Brewery Lounge, or if you want to hear more about how it's all done, join their Brewmaster for his monthly tour and tasting session.

Events:
Brewhouse Bash (live music and German sausage BBQ) – first Friday night of every month from 5pm.

Tanks, Tales and Tastings (Brewmaster-led tour and beer tasting session) – first Saturday of every month at 2pm. Book online or via the brewery contacts listed.

17A Ern Harley Dr
Burleigh Heads
Tel: (07) 5593 6000
www.burleighbrewing.com.au

Opening Hours:
Tap Room and Brewery Lounge – check website for current opening times.

Beer & Brewer promotion   QUEENSLAND – SEQ

MT TAMBORINE BREWERY

Beer, Cheese and Food

With the open and easy atmosphere and stunning views over Mount Tamborine, this venue is where the three best things in life are at your ready hands.

MT BREWERY

MT love Beer… Real Beer. All of their beers use traditional brewing procedures avoiding pasteurization, artificial colouring, additives and over filtration. MT Brewery was voted Best Brew Bar/Pub in Queensland from the 2010 Beer & Brewer Awards. MT Brewery offers the general public the opportunity to view the brewing and bottling processes, while sampling a taster tray of beer, and lunch from the bar menu. Their beer range varies from a 2.8% ABV Moderation Golden Ale (APA) to a big and smooth Belgian ST Bridget (Dubbel) at 7.2% ABV. Currently they are producing eight beers on tap and in bottles.

WITCHES CHASE CHEESE CO

Opening its doors in 2004, this artisanal, family owned boutique cheese factory has been hand crafting multi-award winning cheeses using traditional recipes, the finest French cultures, vegetarian rennet and locally farmed jersey and goat's milk. View the cheese making process through the glass walled factory, then head up and visit the cheese shop to sample the award winning cheeses. Best Cheese in Queensland 2 years in a row. Ice cream, yoghurts and coffee's are also available in the cheese shop.

LIQUID AMBER BISTRO AND GRILL

Awarded "Best Restaurant in a Brewery" by Gold Coast People's Choice, this modern eco friendly Bistro designed to bring the outside in is a perfect location to relax and enjoy some unique fresh quality foods. Local produce, MT beer and cheese are utilised to make your dining an experience.

Liquid Amber and MT Brewery are quickly becoming a leading choice as a function and wedding venue on the Gold Coast. The relaxed atmosphere and unique surroundings are sure to impress every guest, and create memories that last a lifetime. MT Brewery and Liquid Amber provides the perfect backdrop for any wedding or function experience, utilising their function room and restaurant, all while enjoying the beautiful surroundings, exquisite food and outstanding service.

165-185 Long Road
Eagle Heights
(Southern End of Gallery Walk)
Tel: (07) 5545 2032
www.mtbeer.com

Opening hours:
MT Brewery
Open 7 days.
Mon-Thurs 10.00am – 5.00pm
Fri-Sun 9:30am – until late

Liquid Amber Bistro & Grill is also open 7 days for lunch from 11.30am.

Open for dinner Friday, Saturday & Sunday evenings

$15 Buffet Breakfast Saturday and Sunday 8.00am – 11.00am

Witches Chase Cheese
Open 7 days
Mon-Fri 10.00am – 4:00pm
Sat-Sun 9.00am – 5.00pm

SA

SOUTH AUSTRALIA

Known for its brilliant wine regions, SA also has 20 breweries and four beer companies, including Australia's largest independently Australian-owned brewery, Coopers. The famous McLaren Vale, Barossa, Clare and Hills are now wine and beer regions.

SA

SA

ADELAIDE

Thanks to a wealth of innovative small breweries and brew-pubs within its easy-to-navigate city limits, a day on the beer trail in Adelaide is a day very well spent. **By Paul Murrell**

In most large cities, traffic, congestion and sheer geography limit the number of breweries you can visit in a day. But Adelaide is just about perfect for a one- or two-day ramble, and there's plenty to keep the whole family amused while you sample some fine brews.

■ FIRST, ENTERTAIN THE FAMILY

Start your journey of discovery in the historic port district northwest of Adelaide. The drive along Port Road from the CBD isn't very inspiring although you'll pass lots of interesting old pubs. Focus – you don't want to peak too early!

When you reach the Port, entrust the family to the Visitor Information Centre where they'll discover a wide range of activities including the Maritime Museum Trail, Dolphin Trail, Aviation Museum, Railway Museum, various guided Port walks and Port Adelaide River Cruises along the Port

Coopers Brewery, Regency Park

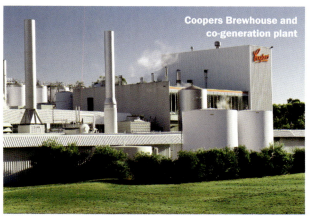

Coopers Brewhouse and co-generation plant

River. Nearby is the Sunday Market, art galleries and the wharf district. Not far away is Semaphore, the Enfield heritage trail and Garden Island. That frees you up to indulge in the Port Dock Hotel, a Port Adelaide institution that's been slaking dockworkers' thirsts since 1855 and still pours a great brew. Relax in the old public bar (the refurbed bars have nowhere near as much character) and tuck into The Brewers' Paddle – a tasting treat of six beers served in 100ml portions, ranked from bitterest to sweetest and accompanied by a bitterness chart and tasting notes. Be sure to try the smooth Black Bart Milk Stout and the Dock's famous Dark Strong Ale, Old Preacher.

■ ANY PORT IN A STORM

Leave the family to their exploring while you reacquaint yourself with one of South Australia's great gifts to Australia and the world: Coopers Brewery.

Coopers is one of South Australia's best-loved exports. In 1862, jack-of-many-trades Thomas Cooper created a batch of beer as a tonic for his ailing wife. Sensing an opportunity, he gave up his career as a stonemason and became a full-time brewer. Today, his descendants still own and run the brewery, and stay true to his principles. No visit to Adelaide is complete without at least one refreshing glass of Coopers Sparkling Ale but while you're here, be sure to also try Extra Strong Vintage Ale. Coopers Clear and Coopers 62 Pilsner are something different for the Coopers family but demonstrate there's more to this lot than the traditional cloudy brews most people associate with the name. You'll need to book in advance for a tour – they're held Tuesday to Friday at 1pm and cost $22 per person, with $20 donated to the Coopers Foundation supporting many charities – wear closed toe shoes.

■ SEEING DOUBLE ALREADY

If it's a Thursday, Friday or Saturday, head less than a kilometre west along Regency Road to Croydon Park,

Beard and Brau Brewery

Simon Sellick (right), Brewboys

Earl of Leicester – Liars Bar

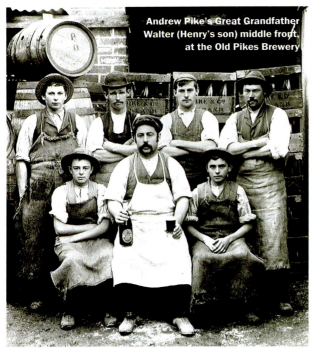
Andrew Pike's Great Grandfather Walter (Henry's son) middle front, at the Old Pikes Brewery

The Wheatsheaf Hotel

Grumpy's Brewery Bar

location of the well-loved Brewboys. Simon Sellick is committed to using proven principles and traditional values to create beers as they used to be, with real character rather than artificial consistency. An hour or so in the Brewboys' tasting room will be a learning experience for even the most ardent brew fan. Highly recommended are Seeing Double (the name should be sufficient warning), a "Scottish wee heavy" best drunk at room temperature, and a trio for muscle car fans to work their way through – Charger Lager, GT Lager and GTS Pale Ale. Just don't jump behind the wheel afterwards!

A few metres further to the west is a TAFE college with a fully functioning brewery that you can view through windows inside the college. TAFE runs short courses on brewing and you can assess the work of brewer Kai Cook by buying some to take home. Try his Summer Ale, Nut Brown Ale and Irish brew. Campus open daily 9am-5pm, shop open Tuesday to Friday 10am-4pm.

Another worthwhile place to visit and close by is the Beard and Brau brewery in Para Hills West. Brewers Chris Herring and Tanya Harlow craft beers that are balanced, lace the glass and retain a good head. A must-try is Bon Chiens French farmhouse ale. If you are planning a visit, call ahead so Chris and Tanya can have a range of well-chilled samples ready for you. And that odd name? Put it down to their pet dogs... Cute. (If you don't get it, take a look at a photo of a schnauzer.)

■ HEAD FOR THE HILLS

Now might be a good time to swing back to Port Adelaide and collect the family before heading back along Port Road towards town. On your right, you'll soon see the imposing edifice that houses Adelaide's West End Brewery. Tours are held for groups of 10 to 35 and you'll need to book well in advance. There is a charge (currently $12 per person) for the 1¼ hour tour and there are appropriate refreshments at the end.

Just off Port Road is one of Australia's best pubs. The Wheatsheaf (affectionately called "The Wheaty" is a beer lover's nirvana and Best Beer Venue in SA in the 2010 *Beer & Brewer* Awards. The Wheaty's motto is "no crap on tap", and the place is true to its word. The 12 regular taps, one hand pump and the intriguing "GlassHopper" on the bar dispense beers to keep the most dedicated beer buff happy and the brews change up to 10 times daily. Publican Jade really knows her stuff – ask for The Book for a full listing or, even better, just take her advice.

Now carry on towards Adelaide's famed Hills. Make your way to the South Eastern Freeway and a few minutes later, you'll crest Mount Lofty at Stirling and in another few kilometres reach the Hahndorf exit. Drop the family off in the main street of this thoroughly German village, then retrace your path back to the roundabout and the road to Verdun. On your right is Grumpy's Brewhaus. The name is misleading – it's a brew house but not at all grumpy: there's a warm and friendly welcome from proprietor and brewer Andrew Schultz, and some impressive brews. There are up to six beers on tap – be sure to try some of the British-style

Bitters and Old Speckled Chook, a strong English Ale. You can take your time at Grumpy's because the partner and kids will have plenty to amuse them in Hahndorf. After sampling some traditional German cakes, they might like to pick their own strawberries at Beerenberg Farm or explore Misty Hollow Fantasy Cave near the Council Chambers.

Now follow the Onkaparinga tourist drive to Balhannah (did you remember to collect the family from Hahndorf?) through to the racecourse town of Oakbank, location of the famous Great Eastern Steeplechase every Easter. Here you'll find the original home of another old SA family beer company with a long history. Henry Pike migrated to South Australia in 1878 and established a family brewery in this sleepy Hills town. The Pike brothers (Henry's great-great-grandsons, Andrew and Neil of Pikes Wines in the Clare Valley of SA) brought Pikes beer back to life with the help of another old family beer company (Coopers) back in 1996. More recently, Andrew and Neil enlisted the help of Nick Button who is Head Brewer at Australian Independent Brewery in NSW, which is where Pikes Pilsener is still brewed. Call into the pub and savour the traditional Pilsener-style Pikes Oakbank beer made from super premium hops. It has a clean, malty finish with just the right hint of bitterness – perfect on a hot summer's day. To see the original Pikes Brewery, turn right into Elizabeth Street.

Lobethal Bierhaus

■ RACING MEMORIES

Back on the road, continue for a few more kilometres before taking a left turn towards Lobethal. You are now driving along a grand prix circuit. The Lobethal Australian Grand Prix was held here in 1939 on a 14-kilometre course that went right up the main street. It's a challenging track, and racing continued there until 1948. Once you turn right past the Old Woollen Mills into the main street, on your left you'll find the Lobethal Bierhaus and a suitable amber reward. Have a chat to the enthusiastic Alistair Turnbull who gave up a career as a merchant banker to follow his dream of brewing. You'll be glad he did, too, because the Bierhaus has won many awards for its various brews. Highlights on tap include a German Wheat Beer, an American-style Pale Ale and a just-released Pilsener. Another beer not to be missed is Devil's Choice, a Belgian-style strong Golden Ale. If the sun is shining, sit at one of the outdoor tables and chat with Alistair about his newest passion, historic motor racing (he bought an old race car to participate in the Lobethal Grand Carnival, a festival that recalls the great Lobethal motor races of the past). Open Friday and Saturday, 12-10pm, Sunday 12-6pm.

If you're still not sated, call in to the Holdfast Hotel at Glenelg, also an ideal stop-off on your way to the airport. Ask for a tasting when you arrive. If it's cold outside, a warming Chocolate Porter (made with Haigh's chocolate liquor) is a real winter favourite with the locals or try The Dominator, an extra hoppy Pale Ale and a White Pointer with a hint of lemon spiciness.

■ TAKE IT AWAY

If any of the brews have really taken your fancy (and they will!), Adelaide is well supplied with some excellent bottle shops. The Ed (Edinburgh Hotel and Cellars) is well stocked and the staff really know their stuff. It's a similar story at Melbourne Street Cellars and Goodwood Cellars. Dan Murphy stores are all over town.

■ CHOCOLATE HEAVEN

How about letting the kids do some tasting, as well? Not of the beer, of course, but some of the yummy sweets on offer at Melba's Chocolate and Confectionery

Goodwood Cellars

Belgian Beer Cafe – Oostende

Factory at Woodside (between Oakbank and Lobethal on your tour). Entry to the factory is free and you're more than welcome to watch sweets and chocolates being made using the heritage equipment. Open 7 days, 9am-4.30pm.

■ BERRY GOOD FUN

Beerenberg Farm is famous around the world for its jams, chutneys, sauces, marinades and salad dressings. Pick your own strawberries and then buy something else to take home. Open 7 days, 9am-5pm; strawberry picking 9am-4.15pm.

BOTTLESHOPS

Bar on Gouger
123 Gouger St, Adelaide
(08) 8410 0042

Belair Fine Wines
9 Russell St, Belair
(08) 8278 5222r
www.belairfinewines.com.au

Dan Murphy's
1300 723 388
www.danmurphys.com.au

Edinburgh Hotel & Cellars
7 High St, Mitcham
(08) 8373 2700
www.edinburgh.com.au

Goodwood Cellars
125 Goodwood Rd, Goodwood
(08) 8271 7481
www.goodwoodcellars.com

Melbourne Street Fine Wine Cellars
93 Melbourne St, North Adelaide
(08) 8267 1533
www.wine.com.au/melbourne-st-wine-cellars

EVENTS

JANUARY
Harvest Festival Fleurieu Peninsula
Santos Tour Down Under Adelaide and Regions
Freshwater Classic Yacht Race Fleurieu Peninsula
Port Lincoln Tunarama, Eyre Peninsula
Crush 12 – Adelaide Hills Wine & Food Festival Adelaide Hills
50th Australian Sprint car Championships Adelaide

FEBRUARY
Coopers Kangaroo Island Cup Carnival, Kangaroo Island
Natuzzi The Parade Food, Wine & Music Festival Adelaide
Specialised Australian Mountain Bike Championships Adelaide Hills
Cellar Door Festival Adelaide

FEBRUARY-MARCH
Adelaide Fringe Adelaide

MARCH
Clipsal 500 Adelaide
Adelaide Festival Adelaide
WOMADelaide Adelaide
Clare Film Festival Clare Valley

APRIL
Oakbank Easter Racing Carnival Adelaide Hills
Port Pirie Pura Light Start State Masters Games Flinders and Outback
Rock n Roll Rendezvous Adelaide Hills
National BMX Championships Limestone Coast
Yorke Peninsula Saltwater Classic Yorke Peninsula

APRIL-MAY
Tasting Australia Adelaide
World Croquet Championships Adelaide

AUGUST
SALA Festival Visual-arts festival involving 3000 artists and 500 venues statewide.
Langhorne Creek Cellar Treasures Weekend Fleurieu Peninsula

SEPTEMBER
Royal Adelaide Show
OzAsia Festival, Adelaide
Knights Beach Pro World Tour Bodyboarding, Fleurieu Peninsula
Classic Targa Adelaide Adelaide and regions
Toop & Toop Rock 'n' Roll Festival Fleurieu Peninsula
City to Bay Fun Run Adelaide
Australian Trampoline Sport Championships Adelaide
Bay to Birdwood Adelaide and Adelaide Hills

SEPTEMBER-OCTOBER
Kangaroo Island Art Feast Kangaroo Island

OCTOBER
Australian Masters Games Adelaide
Adelaide Festival of Ideas, Adelaide
Port Festival Adelaide
Coonawarra Cabernet Celebrations Limestone Coast
Kapunda Celtic Festival, Clare Valley

CheeseFest 2011 Adelaide
World Solar Challenge & World Eco Challenge Darwin to Adelaide
Earth Station Adelaide
Fleurieu Folk Festival, Fleurieu Peninsula
Barossa Ranges Music Festival Barossa Valley
Riverland Wine & Food Festival Riverland
Semaphore Music Festival Adelaide

NOVEMBER-DECEMBER
Fleurieu Art Prize Fleurieu Peninsula

NOVEMBER
Credit Union Christmas Pageant Adelaide
Feast Festival Adelaide
Gorgeous Festival McLaren Vale

DECEMBER 2011
Lights of Lobethal, Adelaide Hills
Ceduna Christmas Race Day, Eyre Peninsula
Bay Sheffield Gift Adelaide
SeaRay Aquapalooza Fleurieu Peninsula

BEER BARS

Belgian Beer Café – Oostende
27-29 Ebenezer Pl, Adelaide
(08) 8359 3400
www.oostende.com.au

Coopers Alehouse at the Earl
316 Pulteney St, Adelaide
(08) 8223 6433
www.coopersalehouse.net

Gilbert St Hotel
88 Gilbert St, Adelaide
(08) 8231 9909
www.gilbertshotel.com.au

Hahndorf Inn
35 Main Street, Hahndorf
(08) 8388 7063
www.hahndorfinn.com.au

Oakbank Hotel
Main St, Oakbank, (08) 8388 4267
www.hoteloakbank.com.au

The Austral Hotel
205 Rundle St, Adelaide
(08) 8223 4660
www.theaustral.com.au

The Colonist
44 The Parade, Norwood
(08) 8362 3736, www.colonist.com.au

The Crown & Sceptre
308 King William Street, Adelaide
(08) 8212 4159, www.sceptre.com.au

The Earl of Leicester Hotel
85 Leicester St, Parkside
(08) 8271 5700, www.earl.com.au

The Kings
357 King Wiliam Rd, Adelaide
(08) 8212 6657
www.thekingsbardining.com

The Lion Hotel
161 Melbourne St, North Adelaide
(08) 8367 0222
www.thelionhotel.com

The Wheatsheaf Hotel
39 George St, Thebarton
(08) 8443 4546
www.wheatsheafhotel.com.au

BREWERIES

Beard and Brau Brewery
Para Hills West
0420 962 952 or
0410 417 882
www.beardandbrau.com.au

Brewboys Tasting Room
151 Regency Rd,
Croydon Park
(08) 8346 5200
www.brewboys.com.au

Coopers Brewery
461 South Rd,
Regency Park
(08) 8440 1800
www.coopers.com.au

Grumpy's Brewhaus
115 Mount Barker Rd,
Verdun
(08) 8188 1133
www.grumpys.com.au

Holdfast Bay Brewing Company
83 Brighton Rd,
Glenelg
(08) 8295 2051
www.holdfasthotel.com.au

Lobethal Bierhaus
3 Main St, Lobethal
(08) 8389 5570
www.ahcb.com.au

Port Dock Brewery Hotel
10 Todd St, Port Adelaide
(08) 8240 0187
www.portdockbreweryhotel.com.au

TAFE Regency Campus
137 Days Rd,
Regency Park
(08) 8348 4444
www.tafe.sa.edu.au

West End Brewery
107 Port Rd,
Thebarton
(08) 8354 8744
www.westenddraught.com.au

THINGS TO SEE AND DO

Beerenberg Strawberry Farm Mount Barker Rd, Hahndorf, (08) 9399 7272, www.beerenberg.com.au. **Cocolat,** 83 Main Road, Balhannah; (08) 8388 4666 or www.cocolat.com.au. **Melba's Chocolates** 22 Henry St, Woodside, (08) 8389 7868 or www.melbaschocolates.com. **Port Adelaide Visitor Information Centre** 66 Commercial Rd, Port Adelaide, (08) 8405 6560, www.portenf.sa.gov.au.

SA

BAROSSA, CLARE AND RIVERLAND

SA's fertile Barossa Valley.

If it's beer that floats your boat, you might have crossed the wine regions of South Australia off your itinerary. But where there's fine wine, there's bloody good beer. **By John Kruger**

South Australia is blessed with some of the best wine regions in Australia, but it's a little-known fact that there are plenty of good beer destinations to visit in the Barossa and Clare Valleys too.

■ THE BAROSSA

Thanks to the newly completed Northern Expressway, the Barossa Valley is only an hour away from Adelaide. There's loads to see and do in the Barossa, and it's a good base for day trips to Clare, Burra or the Riverland.

First port of call is the German-settled town of Tanunda and the recently relocated Barossa Valley Brewing brewery and brasserie. Previously in Lyndoch, the new operation boasts a great selection of beers, all the snacks you'd need and a chance to see the brewery in action as well. Head brewer Mark Prior is a passionate bloke who's keen to keep a few staples like the Bee Sting Honey Wheat Beer and Organic Ale on tap, but is also free to play around with Russian Imperial Stouts, English Bitters and the like. In fact, Barossa Valley Brewing has seven beers on tap, with the eighth dedicated to a non-alcoholic brew for kids or designated drivers. A pizza and tapas menu provides a wide range of choices to match the beers, and there's an excellent selection of local wines to peruse as well.

In the centre of Tanunda is acclaimed restaurant 1918 Bistro & Grill, in the grand old home of a long-gone local mayor. The restaurant not only has a reputation for quality dining, roaring log fires and relaxed outdoor settings but also serves local bottled beers along with its extensive wine list. Head chef and owner Christian Fletcher serves fresh, seasonally inspired modern Australian cuisine with inspiration from Asia and the Middle-East.

On the western side of the Barossa Valley is the charming hamlet of Greenock. The impressive Murray Street Vineyards winery stands on the hill approaching Greenock,

Barossa Valley Brewing Company brewer Mark Prior (left) and founder Denham D'Silva

Barossa Brewing Company

and the cellar door is just at the edge of town on the main road. A good range of wines is available, along with regional platters, and the outdoor area is a great spot to relax with the kids and take in the views.

Further into Greenock is the Barossa Brewing Company. Situated in the 1860s Wheat Store, owner Darryl Trinne opens the tasting room on weekends for beer aficionados and other interested parties. Darryl's operation is particularly unusual: the brews are mashed and boiled in Mildura, then immediately brought back to Greenock to be fermented, conditioned and bottled or kegged. Darryl is happy to show inquisitive visitors through the facility, which uses an eclectic mix of new custom-made stainless steel and classic German machinery. The Barossa Brewing Company produces regular beers – the Millers Lager, Greenock Dark Ale and Wheat Store Hefeweizen, which are complemented with occasional appearances of a hoppy American-style Pale Ale called Victorville, and the Bunawunda Blonde – definitely not a low-carb excuse for a beer. The Barossa Brewing Company beers are becoming so popular that they've been known to sell out after a big event such as the Barossa Vintage Festival (a week-long wine event held annually in April), so it's worth calling ahead. Second only to having a beer with Darryl in the Wheat Store is trying one of his beers on tap just around the corner at the Greenock Tavern. It's not unusual to see him wheel a keg into the pub on a sack truck direct from the cold room in cellar door so the beer is guaranteed fresh.

On the eastern side of the Barossa is the quaint town of Angaston, and just before the town is Saltram Cellar Door & Restaurant. Saltram is well known for its wines, restaurant and wood-fired pizzas, but it's also the home of Saltram's Pepperjack Ale. Pepperjack Ale is the only beer in the valley to use local Shiraz juice to add fermentables, a hint of colour and the unmistakable Shiraz aroma to this tidy Ale. Only open for lunch, it's a great place to relax with a few beers (or wine, if you prefer). There's toe-tapping live music on Sundays too.

Saltram's unique Pepperjack Ale

Further into Angaston is another Barossa pizza institution, 40's Café. Among the delights on the menu is the Smokey Pizza, winner of the 2009 Dairy Farmers Best of the Best Pizza Challenge. The Café offers a modest beer selection as well as wines and spirits.

If a few days of enjoying the local beers and wines have taken their toll, drop into Blond Coffee in Angaston for the best coffee in the Valley, along with excellent breakfast and lunch options. Saturday mornings are particularly busy with many locals making Blond part of their Saturday routine. There's also a toy box and small play area for the kids.

If early mornings aren't too much of a strain, the Vintners Farmers Markets just out of Angaston behind the Vintners Bar & Grill is one of the best farmer's markets in the state. Fresh coffee and smokey bacon and egg rolls are available from 7.30am Saturdays, and the range of fresh produce is amazing. Many locals drop in to purchase a good percentage of their fresh supplies for the week so the biggest range is available early.

■ CLARE

The drive from the Barossa Valley to Clare is only 90 minutes through rolling countryside. The Clare Valley actually encompasses a string of towns running through the valley, rather than just the area around the large town of Clare itself so there's plenty to see. The Rising Sun Hotel in the picturesque town of Auburn offers a good range of beers, good honest pub food as well as accommodation with ensuites. A perfect spot to sit out under the veranda sipping on a few beers and watching the world go by.

Travelling towards Clare along the Main North Road, there are plenty of regular little towns ready to explore, each with a different little hotel and more winery cellar doors than you can poke a stick at.

A somewhat under-rated little town is Watervale. The area is famous for Watervale Riesling and up on the hill behind the pub is Crabtree Wines' cellar door. It's rustic, charming, and boasts some of the best wines in the Clare Valley. The popular 35 kilometre walking and cycling track that weaves through the Clare Valley – known as the Riesling Trail – runs right past Crabtree and the Watervale Hotel, so don't be surprised if there are more bicycles than cars in the car parks.

Pikes may have started brewing in the Adelaide Hills town of Oakbank back in 1886, but these days the Pike family calls the Clare Valley home. The Pikes continue their family history of fine beverages concentrating on excellent wines including their massively popular Riesling and Sauvignon Blanc/Semillon blend. Sadly, the Pikes don't make their eponymous Pikes Oakbank beer anymore, but the brew was resurrected in 1996 and is now contract-brewed in Sydney. The beer and an outstanding range of wines are available at their family-friendly cellar door situated at Polish Hill River near Sevenhill. There's also an art gallery incorporated within the cellar door.

In the main township of Clare is the renowned beer destination, Knappstein Enterprise Winery & Brewery. Established in 1878, the grand cellar door boasts the only place in Australia to try the renowned Knappstein Reserve Lager on tap. Guaranteed to really get those Nelson hop aromas wafting out of the glass, there's nothing better than fresh draught beer. For those beer geeks who like their brewery bling, there's a big glass window viewing area where brewing and bottling can be seen if the timing's right. More organised people can call ahead and book a brewery tour to get closer to the action.

Another of the grand old hotels in Clare is Bentley's Hotel Motel in the main street. It offers local Knappstein Reserve stubbies and an extensive range of other beers, plus great pub meals. There's even a play area with toys to keep the kids occupied while you take some time out. It's the kind of pub that's large and comfortable enough to stay for most of the day relaxing with good food and plenty of drink options. Bentley's is also popular with travellers who are just after a quick counter meal and a drink on the way through town.

■ DAY TRIPS

Moonta – Yorke Peninsula

Moonta is situated on the western coast of Yorke Peninsula, and the area known as the Copper Coast – encompassing Moonta, Kadina and Wallaroo – has a strong history of Cornish copper mining. So it will come as little surprise to discover that Moonta is home to the biennial Kernewek Lowender, the world's largest Cornish festival, which runs for five days in the middle of May (the next festival is scheduled for May 2013). Every two years, a batch of beer known as Copper Coast Swanky is made by Brew Boys in Adelaide strictly for the festival and available only at the Moonta Bay Patio Motel and Restaurant as well as a small quantity available to guests at the Adelaide Caravan Park. Six different labels are produced and beer fans are encouraged to buy a six-pack to collect the different labels.

Yorke Brewing is a relatively new operation with its heart at the small town of Warooka in southern Yorke Peninsula.

Justin Murdock of Yorke Brewing

The Yorke Peninsula is a well-loved holiday destination for many South Australians with beautiful scenery, a thriving local gourmet scene and – just between you and me – some of the best fishing spots around. Justin Murdock is a proud local and Company Director of Yorke Brewing who currently brews his own beers at a facility in Adelaide, but he's keen to eventually move the operation completely back to Warooka. He's pleased to maintain the regional authenticity by adding locally grown wheat to his White Sands Wheat Beer. Justin has carefully selected a few local hotels that meet his requirements of no pokies and good service and is in negotiations now to have his beers on tap at these local pubs. Keep an eye on the Yorke Brewing website and he'll announce where the beers will be available. Along with the White Sands, his English-style ale called Shipwrecked will be welcome on a winter's day at 6% ABV and has become very popular with those lucky punters who have tried it.

Renmark

Renmark is situated in the South Australian Riverland along the banks of the Murray River. A two-and-a-half hour drive from the Barossa, it's completely different scenery. Long flat roads that occasionally cross the banks of the Murray, banks of deep red soil and, often, clear blue skies. One minute the roads are surrounded by orange groves and the next, vineyards that stretch on as far as the eye can see. An old shearing shed has been transformed into the Woolshed Brewery, where partners Tom Freeman and Sarah Dowdell currently produce their first beer, the Amazon Ale. Named after the nearby Amazon creek, Amazon Ale is described as an Australian-style Pale Ale. The brewery is open for tours by appointment. Tom and Sarah are keen to cash in on the fact that Woolshed is possibly the only brewery in South Australia that can be visited via the river, and plan to offer activities such as kayaking in the future. Tourists travelling

The rustic cellar door at Pikes Premium Wines & Oakbank Beer

Susan and Tony Thorogood of Thorogoods

Woolshed Brewery has its heritage on display

along the Murray River will be able to moor their houseboat or tinny at the brewery and enjoy the day there.

Burra

Burra is less than 90 minutes from the Barossa and only 30 minutes from Clare. It's another area of South Australia that rose to fame and fortune in 1845 when copper was discovered. In its heyday, the town was a thriving community with its own brewery, Unicorn Brewery, established in 1873. You can tour the remains of Unicorn – contact the Burra Information Centre for details.

One operation that is still thriving in Burra is Thorogoods cidery. Tony Thorogood and his wife Susan have worked hard to plant orchards of a variety of classic cider apples and still use an old Italian basket press to press their own estate-grown organic apples, making traditional ciders with wild yeasts native to the area. The result is a range of mouthwatering ciders, liqueurs and even a dark and golden apple beer (both beers weigh in at hefty 12% ABV). The Thorogoods cellar door is open to the public for sales and tastings pretty much every day of the year.

Burra still has four operational hotels, one of which, the Kooringa Hotel, is directly across the street from the historic Paxton Square Cottages. The Kooringa is a beautiful old hotel with polished wooden floors and a cozy little front bar. It's known for good value meals and a modest selection of beers on tap. It's the perfect spot for a pint of Kilkenny and a filling counter meal.

EVENTS

APRIL/MAY
Barossa Vintage Festival www.barossavintagefestival.com.au (next event is 2013)

MAY
Kernewek Lowender (biannual) www.kernewek.org
Clare Valley Gourmet Weekend www.clarevalleywinemakers.com.au

NOVEMBER
Barossa Airshow www.barossaairshow.com.au

TBC
Riverland Balloon Fiesta Renmark (08) 8586 6704

The Rotary Farm Shed Markets Kadina. Last Saturday of every month. 0458 368 419

BEER & CIDER

Barossa Valley Brewing
(08) 8563 0997
www.bvbeer.com.au

Barossa Brewing Company
(08) 8563 4041
www.barossabrewingcompany.com

Knappstein Enterprise Winery & Brewery
(08) 8841 2100
www.knappstein.com.au

Thorogoods
(08) 8892 2669
www.thorogoods.com.au

Saltram (08) 8561 0200
www.saltramwines.com.au

Swanky (08) 8825 247
www.swankybeer.com.au

Pikes Oakbank Beer
(08) 8843 4370
www.pikeswines.com.au

Yorke Brewing
0439 890 006
www.yorkebrewing.com

Woolshed Brewery
(08) 8595 8037
www.woolshedbrewery.com.au

THINGS TO SEE AND DO

Barossa Farmers Markets, Angaston, 0402 026 882. **Wineries: Crabtree**, Watervale, www.crabtreewines.com.au. **Murray Street Vineyards**, Greenock, (08) 8562 8373. **Cafes/restaurants: 40's Café**, Angaston, www.40scafe.com.au. **1918 Bistro & Grill**, Tanunda, www.1918.com.au. **Blond Coffee**, Angaston, www.blondcoffee.com.au. **The Rising Sun Hotel**, Auburn, (08) 8849 2015. **The Bentley's Hotel Motel**, Clare, (08) 8842 1700. **Kooringa Hotel**, Burra, (08) 8892 2013.

SA

FLEURIEU PENINSULA

SA's Fleurieu Peninsula is renowned for its wineries. Now, a host of craft breweries are making a name for themselves too. **By Chris Leese**

The descent into McLaren Vale on Victor Harbor Road greets visitors with row after row of vines and, following the turn onto Main Road, signs pointing to the many prominent wineries in the area line both sides of the road like runway lights leading travellers to the visitors centre.

■ McLAREN VALE

McLaren Vale is home to more than 65 cellar doors, including some of the best-known wineries in Australia. Just 40 minutes' drive from Adelaide, it enjoys the regular company of day-trippers and a healthy share of high-profile events, such as the cycling Tour Down Under, which showcase its wine and varied produce

Vineyards in McLaren Vale

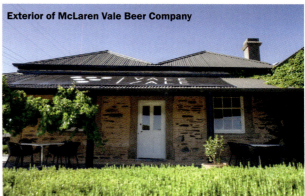
Exterior of McLaren Vale Beer Company

Taps at McLaren Vale Beer Company

as well as its summertime beauty to visitors and TV viewers overseas.

It was this combination of rural splendour and proximity to the city which attracted Jeff and Mary Goodieson. Goodieson Brewery has now been operational for a year, producing a well-received range including a Pale Ale, a Pilsner, a Wheat and a Stout. Tastings are available at the cellar door.

On the other side of McLaren Vale is the Salopian Inn, the oldest inn in the region and, since 2009, the home of the McLaren Vale Beer Company, which gained the attention of many on the east coast earlier this year when its flagship product, Vale Ale, took first place in The Local Taphouse's Hottest 100 Craft Beers of 2010.

In the tasting room, visitors can sample Vale Ale and Vale Dry, along with seasonal brews and a range of local wines. The restaurant offers a first-class dining experience, complemented by a range of quality craft brews and a cellar range selected by master of wine David LeMire.

With the completion of a new brewery in nearby Willunga in late 2011, the McLaren Vale Beer Company aims to bring home production of Vale Ale and Vale Dry, begin production of two new brews under the Vale label and kick off a range of more adventurous craft brews under a new label.

A little further along Main Road, turn off onto Branson Road and arrive at an uncharacteristically modern building housing Producers of McLaren Vale. Producers is an initiative of David Arbon and Tori Moreton, biological farmers who, like many others in the region, grow grapes and olives, but offer visitors an interactive experience.

Tori says vineyard walks are very popular with wine drinkers looking to learn more about their vino. "We don't run wine appreciation courses, as such, but people do say they appreciate their wine more knowing where it's come from and what's gone into making it." Visitors can stay in apartments on site and join hands-on workshops on making sparkling wine, olive oil or cheese.

From McLaren Vale, follow Main South Road along the south-west coast to Myponga and the Lovely Valley Beverage Factory, a microbrewery producing a small range of beers and soft drinks made with the local coral base water. Stop for a dip at nearby Aldinga and Myponga beaches; further down the road at Yankalilla Bay, divers can explore the wreck of the HMAS *Hobart*.

The drive east brings you to the most populated town on the peninsula, Victor Harbor. Once the site of two whaling stations, the town now relies heavily on tourism, including many who come to watch southern wright whales frolic in Encounter Bay and the colony of fairy penguins that return from the sea to their burrows on Granite Island daily at dusk.

■ PORT ELLIOT AND MIDDLETON

Heading north-east along the coast, the road passes through Port Elliot, home to culinary icon The Flying Fish Cafe, where you can break for fish and chips in a paper cone or something more refined in the restaurant overlooking the beach in Horseshoe Bay.

In nearby Middleton, set back from one of the region's favourite surfing beaches is the Beach Huts Bed and Breakfast. Proprietors Haylie and Dave Palmer have built a row of individually styled, self-contained huts, all situated within a short stroll of the shore. And at the end of a long day spent on the sand and in the sea, or visiting the local attractions, you can indulge in local produce, beer and wine at award-winning restaurant Blues, which is situated onsite and just a few metres' walk back to your cabin when it's time to retire.

Mary Goodieson

McLaren Vale Beer Company

The Steam Exchange Brewery

■ GOOLWA

The next stop, Goolwa, is also the last on the Victor Harbor-to-Goolwa rail line, and it has a significant place in South Australian history. Goolwa was the centre of a bustling river trade in the latter half of the 19th century. Sea-bound goods freighted down the Murray on paddle-steamers were transferred between Goolwa and Port Elliot on Australia's first steel railway, built in 1854 and later extended to Victor Harbor.

The port was considered so important to South Australia that it was proposed as the state's capital. Advances in rail transport, however, eventually made the once-innovative transport network obsolete, taking with it the town's lofty ambitions.

Goolwa Wharf is home to The Steam Exchange Brewery nowadays, which occupies an original railway goods shed. The shed's National Trust listing demands that it remain a functional railway platform should one be required, so the cool room is a refrigerated shipping container on a train carriage that sits on the existing rails. The Steam team's range has achieved considerable recognition at the Australian International Beer Awards, including Steam Ale, Southerly Buster Dark Ale, a Stout, and an always-adventurous range of seasonal offerings.

Next, turn inland to Langhorne Creek, a prosperous wine region that is home to seven cellar doors including Bleasdale Wines, a National Trust-listed winery established by Frank Potts, who planted the first grapes in the region in the 1860s.

From there, it's just a one-hour drive back to Adelaide through the leafy Adelaide Hills, no doubt with a bootful of world-class wine, beer and produce.

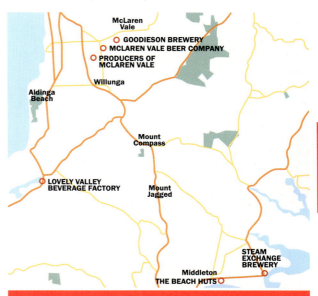

Vines aplenty in McLaren Vale

EVENTS

OCTOBER
Fiesta! Food Festival
www.fleurieufood.com.au

FEBRUARY
Port Elliott Film Festival
www.portelliot.net.au

APRIL
Leafy Seadragon Festival
www.leafyseadragon festival.com.au

JUNE
Sea & Vines Festival
www.mclarenvale.info

BREWERIES & BEER COMPANIES

Boar's Rock Beer
McLaren Vale
(08) 8323 6100
www.boarsrock.com.au

Goodieson Brewery
194 Sand Road,
McLaren Vale
0409 676 542
www.goodiesonbrewery.com.au

Lovely Valley Beverage Factory
Myponga
(08) 8558 6166
www.lovelyvalley.websyte.com.au

McLaren Vale Beer Company
5 McMurtrie Road,
McLaren Vale
(08) 8323 8769
www.mvbeer.com

Swell Brewing Co
McLaren Vale
0448 288 822
www.swellbeer.com.au

The Steam Exchange
Brewery, Goolwa
(08) 8555 3406
www.steamexchange.com.au

Beer & Brewer promotion   SOUTH AUSTRALIA

DAN MURPHY'S

Many people think of Dan Murphy's as an incredible wine store, however their passion for liquor runs to beer as well. Even Mr. Murphy himself was known to enjoy a beer or two.

Every Dan Murphy's store sells at least 250 different beers. These range from local favourites to exceptional Craft and premium International beers.

At last count, Dan Murphy's had beers from over 30 countries. And the joy of it all is not just the sheer quantity but the price. You see just like their wines and spirits, every beer in every store is backed by their unique lowest price guarantee.*

There are over 140 Dan Murphy's stores nationwide.

For store locations or trading hours, simply SMS the postcode or suburb and state that you are in to 0487 723 388†, or visit their website.

Tel: 1300 723 388
www.danmurphys.com.au

*Conditions apply, visit www.danmurphys.com.au for details. †Standard SMS charges apply

Beer & Brewer promotion

SOUTH AUSTRALIA – ADELAIDE & HILLS

COOPERS BREWERY

Brewery, museum, tours

In 1862, Thomas Cooper entered into a career in brewing. Following a family recipe, Thomas brewed a restorative beverage for his ailing wife. Locals in the fledgling colony of South Australia quickly caught on, and came to appreciate his Sparkling Ale and Best Extra Stout.

Through the Great Depression and two World Wars, successive generations of the Cooper family have continued the tradition of brewing fine ales and stouts. Each generation either applied their knowledge of science to brewing, or devoted themselves to the commercial success of the business.

Coopers Brewery is Australia's sole remaining family-owned brewery of stature, and although much has changed since brewing in wooden barrels in Thomas Cooper's day, the family name remains synonymous with exceptional quality beers. Coopers Ales and Stouts are lauded the world over for consistent, traditional quality, unaffected by the hand of progress. Fourth generation Coopers oversaw the introduction of Lager beer into the range of products. Maxwell Cooper, as brewer, improved the process of natural conditioning to provide consistent ales and stouts. Bill Cooper injected a strong marketing effort into promoting Coopers beers nationally and internationally.

By 1990, Bill and Maxwell were joined in the business by fifth generation Coopers; Glenn, Tim and Melanie. Glenn Cooper has elevated brand awareness with innovative marketing strategies, while Tim Cooper, as chief brewer, has worked on improving the brewing process and equipment.

461 South Rd
Regency Park
Tel: (08)8440 1800
www.coopers.com.au

Tour times:
Tues-Fri 1.00pm
Bookings are essential

Beer & Brewer promotion   SOUTH AUSTRALIA

BEARD AND BRAU BREWERY

The Beard and Brau team respect the vast history and knowledge behind brewing the perfect beer. They look at sustainable ways of producing consistent and high quality libations made only from local malts. A traditional mash system is used of relatively small size to allow the brewery to produce continual fresh batches, seasonal and speciality brews.

The brews are available around the country and can always be found at the brewery's home – The Earl of Leicester Hotel (Parkside, South Australia). Enjoy a freshly brewed real ale or even try a small run speciality that pops up from time to time, with a plate of sensational fare.

Para Hills West
Tel: 0420 962 952 /
0410 417 882
beer@beardandbrau.com.au
www.beardandbrau.com.au

Open by appointment only

GOODWOOD CELLARS

Goodwood Cellars is a small, independently owned bottleshop specialising in the unique, hard to find and premium quality beers, wines and spirits. With over 120 beers in stock at any time and the range adjusting regularly to reflect new releases and changing seasons, you're sure to find something to tempt your palate.

Highly knowledgeable and friendly staff are always on hand to assist you with your choice and if you're out to sample the weird and the wonderful, take advantage of their mixed 6-pack offer in-store. They also offer free delivery to the local area as well as corporate accounts.

125 Goodwood Rd
Goodwood
Tel: (08) 8271 7481
www.goodwoodcellars.com

Opening hours:
Mon-Wed 9.00am – 8.00pm
Thurs-Sat 9.00am – 9.00pm
Sun/Public holidays
10.00am – 8.00pm

Polish Hill River Rd
Sevenhill via Clare
Tel: (08) 8843 4353
www.pikeswines.com

Opening hours:
10.00am – 4.00pm 7 days a week
(except Xmas day and New Years day)

Pike's Oakbank Beer

First brewed in 1886 by Henry Pike.

Henry's great, great grandsons, Andrew and Neil Pike established Pikes Wines in the Clare Valley of S.A. in 1985. The brothers had long held a desire to see a Pikes beer back on the market and with the help of another longstanding S.A. brewing family (Coopers), Pikes Sparkling Ale was re-launched in 1996.

Today, the style has changed, but the integrity behind the label has not. Pikes Pilsener is hand crafted using the finest hops and malt and is sold throughout Australia in 330 ml bottles, and in selected venues in Sydney, Melbourne and Adelaide on tap. A family tradition continues.

Beer & Brewer promotion SOUTH AUSTRALIA – FLEURIEU PENINSULA

MCLAREN VALE BEER COMPANY

McLaren Vale is home to the oldest Australian vineyard, but well before the first wineries opened, the Vale was home to a thriving brewing trade.

To satisfy thirsty travellers, their Inn opened its doors in 1851, originally called Gumprs after its original owner.

In 2009 McLaren Vale Beer Company purchased the Inn as its home and returned the hostelry to its original purpose - to provide thirsty travellers and hard working locals with the finest refreshments.

This purpose feeds into their passion for brewing good beers. Their award winning beers, VALE ALE, VALE DRY and VALE DRK are lovingly crafted by the Artisans of McLaren Vale Beer Company for your pleasure. Beers can be enjoyed at the bar, with your meal or taken away by the case through their cellar door.

Boasting a world-class kitchen, an unparalleled selection of craft beer, local, interstate and overseas wines, McLaren Vale Beer Company's Inn exudes the quality of the beer that calls it home.

Cnr. McMurtrie & Main Rd
McLaren Vale
Tel: (08) 8323 8769
www.facebook.com/mvbeer

Cellar door case sales available

Opening hours:
Lunch Thurs-Mon
Dinner Thurs-Sat

TAS

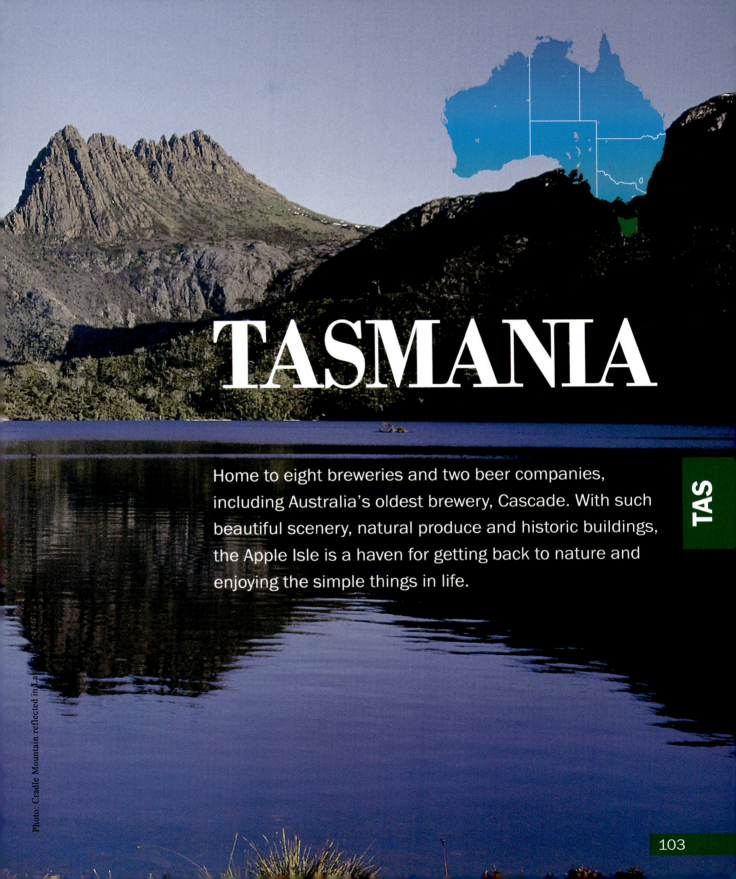

TASMANIA

Home to eight breweries and two beer companies, including Australia's oldest brewery, Cascade. With such beautiful scenery, natural produce and historic buildings, the Apple Isle is a haven for getting back to nature and enjoying the simple things in life.

TAS

TAS

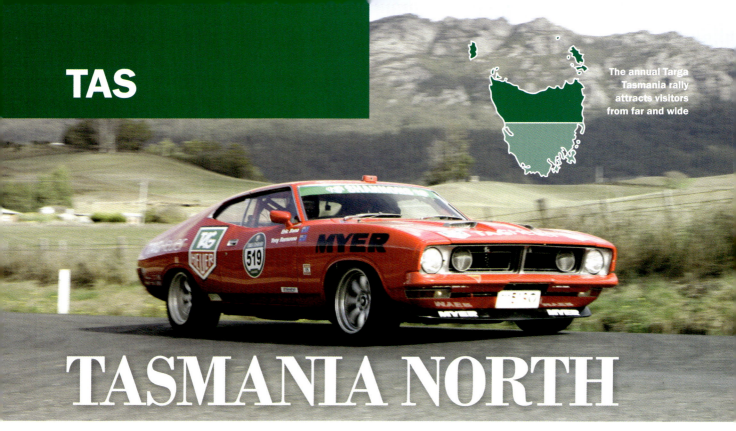

The annual Targa Tasmania rally attracts visitors from far and wide

TASMANIA NORTH

When it comes to beer and sightseeing, Tasmania's north has plenty to offer. As well as breathtaking scenery, there's Boag's and beaut microbreweries all over the place. Must be something in the water... **By Linda Smith**

Launceston is often thought of as Hobart's poor cousin. But when you consider that this northern city is home to the iconic Boag's Brewery, plus offers easy access to the stunning wilderness Tasmania is famous for, Launceston looks more like a hidden gem.

You can visit Cataract Gorge and ride the world's longest single-span chairlift, hang out with the resident monkeys in City Park or sample Tasmania's cool-climate wines on a leisurely drive through the Tamar Valley wine region. Launceston is also the perfect base for exploring Tasmania's many beaches, national parks and other natural wonders, as well as the state's quaint historic towns. Best of all, the state's north is a haven for beer lovers, with plenty of pubs, bars and breweries waiting to be discovered. And the best way to start your beer experience is to visit James Boag's Brewery.

Scotsman James Boag and his son James Boag II have been brewing beer in Launceston since 1881. There is much parochial banter among Tasmanians about whether Boag's beer (brewed in the north) is better than rival Cascade beer (brewed in the south), so the best way to find out is to sample them both yourself.

■ THE BOAG'S CENTRE FOR BEER LOVERS

First stop is The Boag's Centre for Beer Lovers. Housed in the Tamar Hotel (which started serving beer in the 1830s), the centre is open Monday to Saturday. Here, you can learn about the history of the establishment, buy Boag's merchandise and book tours of the brewery.

A one-hour Discovery Tour takes visitors through how Boag's beers are brewed and packaged, and includes tasting. The tours are open for ages 5 and above (under 18s to be accompanied by an adult).

Boag's Brewery

The Discovery Tour is a great introduction for tourists, but *Beer & Brewer* readers would be better catered for by the 90-minute Beer Lovers' Tour, an in-depth tour that includes tastings of some award-winning beers accompanied by a selection of Tasmanian cheeses.

Tours don't run on weekends, but Saturday visitors can purchase an Amber Tasting Ticket. This golden ticket gives beer aficionados 40 minutes with an expert staff member, who will guide you through the individual taste, appearance, aroma and character of each Boag's beer.

■ TAVERNER'S BREWERY

For a boutique experience, visit Launceston's Taverner's Brewery. Beekeeper/entrepreneur Lindsay Bourke brews Taverner's Mead Ales and offers visitors tastings and beer sales from a former maternity hospital.

Where once babies entered the world, Lindsay brings to life his Honey Porter, Honey Mead Ale, Strong Mead Ale and signature beer the Honey Pale Ale, using his own award-winning honey, malt extract and Tasmanian hops. To say he makes a good honey mead is an understatement – it won the gold medal in the World Honey Show 2009.

Launceston has a population of about 100,000, and there are plenty of pubs to ensure residents and visitors do not go thirsty.

Be sure to visit European pub The Cock 'N' Bull in the CBD, which has a superb range of British, Irish and local draught beers on tap, and is also home to the Launceston Guinness Appreciation Society. The Kings Meadows Hotel is also worth a visit – it was voted in the top five Tassie beer venues in the 2010 *Beer & Brewer* Awards. Homebrewers should check out Northern Home Brewing, a one-stop shop for brewing needs, while chocolate lovers shouldn't miss Cocobean Chocolate, which serves delectable organic, fair-trade coffee and hot chocolate as well as boutique chocolates handcrafted on the premises.

For a contemporary drinking experience, visit the Mud Bar and Restaurant, a waterfront eatery at the Old Launceston Seaport. Stop and browse the assortment of shops on the marina, or visit the day spa at Peppers Seaport Hotel. A great place to enjoy boutique beers, woodfired pizza and delectable desserts is Blue Café Bar at Launceston's vibrant Inveresk Precinct, once a former railyard, which is also home to Queen Victoria Museum and Art Gallery.

■ CATARACT GEORGE

A visit to Launceston wouldn't be complete without a trip to Cataract George, just a 15-minute walk from the city centre.

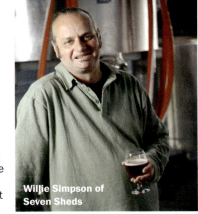
Willie Simpson of Seven Sheds

Here you'll find walking/hiking trails, a swimming pool, suspension bridge, lookouts and the aforementioned chairlift. Enjoy lunch or an ice cream in the expansive gardens while watching the resident peacocks roam.

Launceston's City Park, in the heart of the city, is worth a wander too. The gardens and conservatory are magnificent, and kids of all ages will love to feed the ducks and be entertained by the Japanese Macaque monkeys who live in an enclosure in the park, or just burn off some energy in the playground. City Park is also home to Festivale – a food, beer, wine, arts and entertainment festival held annually on the second weekend of February.

This year, Launceston also played host to a two-day Tamar Valley Beer Festival; the event is expected to be held again in the future. AFL fans should catch a footy match at York Park, where Hawthorn play a few times each year.

When it comes time to leave Launceston, there are plenty of options on the roads heading west, east or south.

■ SEVEN SHEDS BREWERY, MEADERY AND HOP GARDEN

In Railton, just over an hour's drive west on the Bass Highway, you'll find Seven Sheds Brewery, Meadery and Hop Garden, which is famous for beers such as the Willie Warmer.

The microbrewery is run by author Willie Simpson, who wrote the *Beer Bible* in 2006 before turning his hand to brewing handcrafted beers, using fresh local produce, in small commercial batches in his Railton backyard.

The brewery opened in May 2008 and visitors can enjoy tours and tastings of beers including the flagship Seven Sheds Kentish Ale and the strong Willie Warmer Dark Ale, from Wednesday to Sunday and most public holidays. Best of all, Seven Sheds sells its brews online and will ship directly to your home, which means there's no need to worry about excess baggage.

■ HELLYERS ROAD DISTILLERY

Continue north west to Burnie and stop at Hellyers Road Distillery, one

Lindsay Bourke, Taverner's Brewery – award winning honey makes good beer

Freycinet Vineyard, Bicheno

of Australia's largest single-malt whisky distilleries. Open seven days a week, the distillery produces fine, single-malt whisky and a premium-grain Southern Lights vodka, both made from Tasmanian-grown barley and pure Tasmanian rainwater. Take a guided Whisky Walk to learn the history of the distillery and the finer points of whisky-making. You can even bottle and wax seal your own bottle of Hellyers Road, complete with a signed Certificate of Authenticity. Visit the Visitor Interpretation Centre and relax with a drink in the tasting bar and lounge, or indulge in fine Tasmanian cuisine in the restaurant.

While in Burnie, drop into the Club Hotel Bottleshop (Big Bargain) on Mount Street and stock up on quality local craft and imported beers. Nearby attractions include Anvers chocolate factory, Ashgrove Cheese, Christmas Hills Raspberry Farm Cafe, The Honey Farm, and several vineyards. Car enthusiasts should watch out for stages of the annual Targa Tasmania rally, which are run in the area each April.

If your itinerary takes you south from Launceston, a mere 15-minute drive finds you in the historic town of Evandale, where brewer Will Tatchell creates brews like Ragged Jack Pale Ale, Little Hell ESB, and Giblin Imperial Stout at Van Dieman Brewing.

■ VAN DIEMAN BREWING

Van Dieman Brewing is a microbrewery is nestled among century-old English oak trees on a family farming property just outside Evandale, a town famous for hosting the National Penny Farthing Championship every February, and for its Sunday market with more than 100 art, craft, food and bric-a-brac stalls. The brewery isn't yet open for tours or tastings, but there are plans to do so in the future.

In the meantime, you can test the entire Van Dieman range at Evandale's Ingleside Bakery. Nearby, the Josef Chromy Vineyard also has the beer available for drinking at its cellar door.

■ BEER-SWILLING PET PIGS

Van Dieman Brewing

East of Launceston, there are plenty of delights awaiting beer lovers, including a remote pub at Pyengana that is famous for its beer-swilling pet pigs.

Known as the Pub in the Paddock (because it is in the middle of nowhere), the Pyengana pub is about two hours north-east of Launceston and offers cold beer on tap and country-style fare. For $1, you can buy a special stubby for seven-year-old swine Priscilla Babe and her apprentice Little Pinky, who wait expectantly by the fence. Animal welfare activists shouldn't be alarmed – their beer intake is strictly limited to ensure the animals' wellbeing.

Pyengana is also famous for its award-winning cheddar cheese at Pyengana Dairy Company and for spectacular St Columba Falls, an easily accessible landmark that cascades 90 metres over the Mt Victoria foothills.

■ IRONHOUSE BREWERY

Next stop for the thirsty traveller is Ironhouse Point, an hour south-east of Pyengana, for a beer at the White Sands Resort and IronHouse Brewery.

The brewery began operating in 2007 and visitors can sample many beers including a cloudy Bavarian-style Wheat Beer with a hint of banana and cloves, or Paddy's Head Stout, double fermented with bitterness from dark roasted barley and coffee plus liquorice and pepper flavours.

IronHouse also offers an Australian Lager, which is lightly hopped and pale straw in colour with flowery aromas; for a more worldly taste, try the Czech-style Pilsener, brewed with European malts and Czech saaz hops to create a malty beer with an aromatic nose.

Tastings and sales available from the White Sands Restaurant every day during lunch from noon onwards and dinner from 5pm (except Sundays). Orders can be placed directly with Iron House and brewery tours are available by appointment so be sure to call ahead and book a time to see how its beer is made.

As more of these microbreweries pop up around the state, Tasmanians continue to debate the age-old question about whether Cascade or Boag's is a better drop. But one thing is for certain, whichever beer you prefer, be it a big-name brand or a boutique brew, northern Tasmania has plenty to offer.

Discover the delights of single-malt whisky at Hellyers Road Distillery

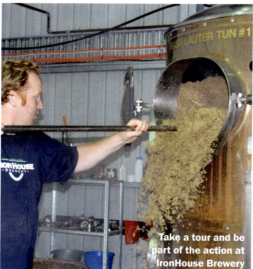

Take a tour and be part of the action at IronHouse Brewery

BREWERIES

Boag's Centre for Beer Lovers
39 William St, Launceston
(03) 6332 6300
www.boags.com.au

Seven Sheds
22 Crockers St, Railton
(03) 6496 1139
www.sevensheds.com

IronHouse Brewery
21554 Tasman Hwy, Ironhouse Point
(03) 6372 2228
www.ironhouse.com.au
www.white-sands.com.au

Taverner's Brewery
11 High St, Launceston
(03) 6331 0888
www.ozhoney.com.au

Van Dieman Brewing
537 White Hills Rd, Evandale
(03) 6391 9035
www.vandiemanbrewing.com.au

DISTILLERIES

Hellyers Road Distillery
153 Old Surrey Rd, Burnie
(03) 6433 0439
www.hellyersroaddistillery.com.au

Small Concern Whisky Distillery
(03) 6429 1208
www.tasmanianwhisky.com.au

BOTTLESHOPS

Club Hotel Bottleshop (Big Bargain)
22 Mount St, Burnie
(03) 6432 3666

Crown Cellars (Thirsty Camel)
152 Elizabeth St, Launceston
(03) 6331 4137

Original Pizza Pub Bottleshop (Big Bargain)
111 Wellington St, Launceston
(03) 6334 2322

BARS

Blue Café Bar
Inveresk Railyards, Launceston
(03) 6334 3133
www.bluecafebar.com.au

Cock 'N' Bull
Cnr Wellington & Elizabeth Sts, Launceston
(03) 6331 0844

Kings Meadows Hotel
117 Hobart Rd, Launceston
(03) 6344 4722

Mud Bar & Restaurant
28 Seaport Blvd, Launceston
(03) 6334 5066
www.mudbar.com.au

Pub in the Paddock
250 St Columba Falls Rd, Pyengana
(03) 6373 6121

HOMEBREW SHOP

Northern Home Brewing
7/2 Elphin Rd, Launceston
(03) 6334 0081

EVENTS

FEBRUARY
Festivale City Park, Launceston
www.festivale.com.au

Evandale Village Fair and National Penny Farthing Championship
www.evandalevillagefair.com

Launceston Cup Launceston,
www.tsrc.com.au

MARCH
Tamar Valley Beer Festival Launceston,
www.tamarvalleybeerfestival.com.au

APRIL
Targa Tasmania Rally
www.targa.org.au

JUNE
Suncoast Jazz Festival
St Helens
www.tasjazz.iinet.net.au

JULY
Chocolate Winterfest
Latrobe, www.chocolatewinterfest.com.au

AUGUST
Taste of the Tamar
Launceston,
www.tasteofthetamar.com.au

OCTOBER
Royal Launceston Show
http://launcestonshowground.com.au

NOVEMBER
Tasmanian Craft Fair
Deloraine
www.tascraftfair.com.au

THINGS TO SEE AND DO Cataract Gorge, City Park, **Old Launceston Seaport**, Inveresk precinct, **Tamar Valley**, St Columba Falls, **Mt Victoria foothills**. Cocobean Chocolate (03) 6331 7016. Peppers Seaport Mud Urban Day Spa (03) 6334 0033. Queen Victoria Museum and Art Gallery (03) 6323 3777. Anvers (03) 6426 2958. Ashgrove Cheese (03) 6368 1105. **Christmas Hills Raspberry Farm Cafe** (03) 6362 2186. The Honey Farm (03) 6363 6160. Pyengana Dairy Company (03) 6363 6160.

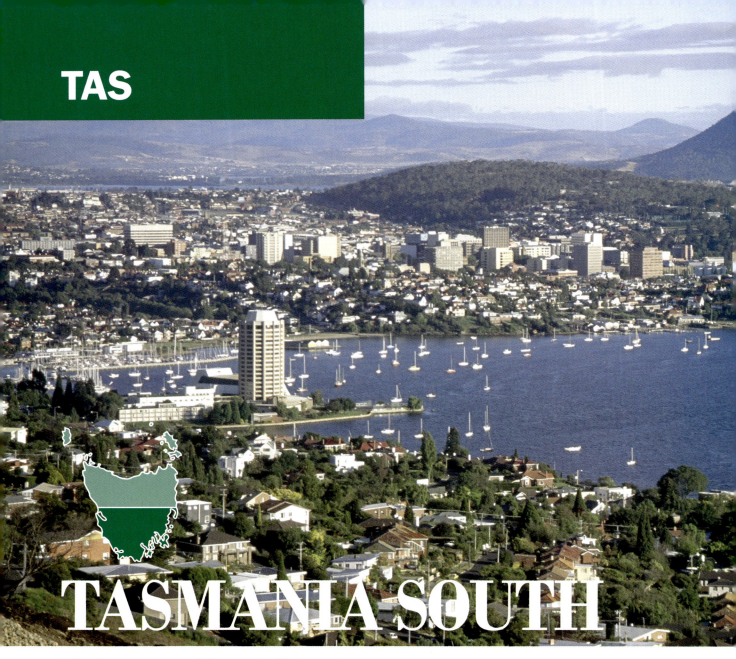

TAS

TASMANIA SOUTH

Whether you're a history buff, love the outdoors or simply enjoy fine food, wine and beer, the Tasmanian capital and surrounds are deservedly popular destinations to escape for a few days.

By Winsor Dobbin

Visitors to Hobart have always enjoyed its lively waterfront, many historic buildings and rich colonial heritage, but the city is increasingly popular with gourmands, drawn by its fresh seafood, superb local produce and the many boutique wineries nearby.

There's also plenty to keep beer lovers happy, from brewery tours of Cascade (Australia's oldest operating brewery) to visits and tastings at boutique producers such as Moo Brew and Two Metre Tall and a range of traditional local pubs with atmosphere in spades.

Tassie's once-sleepy capital has experienced a renaissance over the past decade, with stylish restaurants, wine bars, delis, patisseries and cafes popping up all over the place.

Hobart

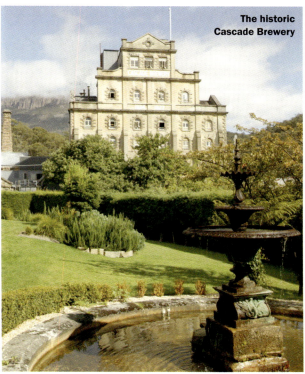
The historic Cascade Brewery

Two Metre Tall's farm-based brewery in the heart of the Derwent Valley

■ SOUTH HOBART

First stop for beer aficionados should be Cascade Brewery in South Hobart. Founded in 1824, Cascade offers regular daily tours and tastings with the chance to see how several different styles are brewed. Two different tours and beer and food matching sessions are among the highlights.

You can also enjoy the full range – including the annual First Harvest release – in the Visitor Centre overlooking the Woodstock Gardens. Be sure to check out the new Cascade walking track, too, for the best views of the lower slopes of Mt Wellington.

At The Two Metre Tall Company in the Derwent Valley, owner Ashley Huntington, a former winemaker, is committed to brewing by traditional methods and grows most of his ingredients on his own farm. Real Ales and ciders are the specialities here, and are made in what was originally the St Ives Brewery (established in Hobart in the late 1980s). Moved upriver in 2008, the 15-hectolitre brewhouse now sits in a converted shearing shed on Huntington family farm. Tastings are offered on Fridays (3pm 'til late) from early October until mid April only, but are available by appointment at other times. Ashley also produces Two Metre Tall 'beer-fed' beef, raised on a free-range pasture diet, supplemented with the spent grain and hop waste, as well as ale and cider waste. Picnic and barbecue facilities are available, should you want to make a day of it.

See Australia's largest hop plantings at Bushy Park Estates.

■ BUSHY PARK ESTATES

Visitors to nearby Bushy Park can, in March, see some of Australia's biggest hop plantings. Sited along the banks of the Styx and Derwent Rivers, Bushy Park Estates have grown hops continually since the 1860s, making these hopfields as old as those of Tettnang in Bavaria. Managed by Hop Products Australia, Bushy Park is the Tasmanian source of flavour hops such as Galaxy, Topaz, Summer, Southern Hallertau, Southern Saaz, Pride of Ringwood, as well as Australian-grown Cascade.

Hops can be seen growing from the roadside as you enter or exit the township of Bushy Park, or you can turn off the Glenora Road onto the Uxbridge Road and follow the signs to the cemetery for a panoramic perspective from the top of the hill. While much of the crop is exported, don't forget to seek out local breweries to sample Bushy Park hops in Tasmanian beer.

The Squires Bounty in Hobart, opened in late 2009, is Tasmania's first James Squire concept bar and the fifth in Australia. Beers from the James Squire range are matched with appropriate dishes and this lively bar is right in the centre of the action on Salamanca Square. Think dishes like freshly-shucked oysters, fish and chips or a beef cheek ragu served with tagliatelle and a rich tomato sauce. Restaurant open daily for lunch and dinner.

■ EAT, DRINK AND BE MERRY

Back in Hobart, the area around Salamanca Place is dotted with terrific eating and drinking spots include Smolt, Monty's On Montpelier and the Battery Point Steak House; for a laidback option, try fish and chips from Fish Frenzy or pizzas and a glass of wine or beer at Cargo Bar or The Grape. On a sunny day, enjoy the passing parade over a cold one at Knopwoods Retreat or the Customs House Hotel.

There is a great selection of beers at the cosy New Sydney Hotel, where there's a roaring fire in winter and sometimes live entertainment as well. Beers on tap here can include Burleigh Brewing Black Giraffe, Brewdog Hardcore IPA, New Sydney Brown Ale, Kilkenny and Stone & Wood Pacific Ale. Alternatively, head to atmospheric old seafarer's haunt Shipwright's Arms in Battery Point. If you like a joint that's jumping, try Bar Celona, Mobius Lounge Bar (a late-night venue with DJs) or The Brisbane Hotel, all in Hobart, or The Alley Cat and Republic Bar & Cafe (live entertainment nightly), both in North Hobart. T42, on Queen Elizabeth Pier, is popular with tourists.

In town, Garagistes and Ethos Eat Drink are two exciting restaurant newcomers. Stefano Lubiana, Moorilla Estate, Frogmore Creek, Pooley, Pressing Matters, Domaine A and Home Hill are just a handful of the many local wineries producing superb cool-climate wines for their wine lists.

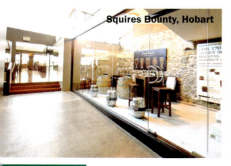

Squires Bounty, Hobart

Great produce

The areas surrounding the city, to the north, east and south are paradise for a wine lover, with dozens of boutique cellar doors within a short drive of the city and three distinct grape growing regions: the Derwent Valley, Coal River Valley and the Huon Valley.

Moorilla, a 10-minute drive north of the city on the Derwent River, is also home to The Source restaurant, where chef Philippe Leban cooks up a storm, as well as the Moo mini-brewery and the hugely successful $175 million Museum of Old and New Art, usually referred to as MONA.

This is among the "must visit" cellar doors – particularly given the chance to also sample some of the four Moo Brews: an American Pale Ale, an American Dark Ale, a German-style Cloudy Wheat Beer and a Pilsner. It's open daily for tastings and there are brewery tours every Friday at 4pm. Bookings recommended.

The Tasmanian Chilli Beer Company hand brews naturally fermented and unfiltered non-alcoholic beverages from its purpose-built micro-brewery in Southern Tasmania. You can find these marvels at several retail outlets, as well as at Salamanca Market in the city on Saturdays.

Wineglass Bay Brewing, on the east coast, produces just one beer, Hazards Ale, which can be purchased at local hotels and bars, as well as at Hobart outlets including 9/11 and Larks Distillery.

In the Huon Valley, standout cellar doors include Home Hill (with a fine restaurant that's open daily for lunch), Panorama and Hartzview. Pop into the pretty hamlet of Cygnet for lunch at acclaimed local eateries the Red Velvet Lounge (where you'll find Two Metre Tall on the list) or The Lotus Eaters' Café (where you can BYO). You can stay overnight at the snug Old Bank B&B.

Lark Distillery

The south's premier cider producer is Tasmanian Inn Cider at Margate, where local apples from the Huon Valley are used to produce ciders styled on those of Normandy, while Captain Blighs is soon to launch a new range of ciders, also made from Huon Valley apples.

■ DISTILLERIES

Pop into the Lark Distillery to sample a range of local whiskies and brandies in a relaxed atmosphere. The good people at Lark offer a range of fully escorted tours, including one- and two-day tours and the four-day Ultimate Whisky Experience.

Alternatively, drive an hour out of town to the Nant Distillery in the hamlet of Bothwell, where The Priory Country Lodge is a delightful spot to stay if you fancy extending your visit. Nant is open daily (except Christmas Day and Good Friday) 10am-4pm and offers tastings and tours.

The Tasmania Distillery at Cambridge, not far from Hobart Airport, produces three Sullivan's Cove malt whiskies. While not a tourist facility, interested visitors are welcome to see the distillery operations, taste and purchase. Appointments are recommended (Mon-Fri only) or order online.

■ STAY AND PLAY

Hobart and its surrounds play host to several food and wine festivals each year, including the annual Taste festival (late December to early January) and Savour Tasmania, a statewide food and wine festival that runs from late May to early July. There are also several local events, such as Taste of the Huon, which is held every March.

Beer lovers would be well advised to plan their trip to coincide with one of Australia's largest beer events, Tasmanian Beerfest, which this year will be held at Princes Wharf on November 18-19.

The Henry Jones Art Hotel, home to the IXL Long Bar.

Tasmanian Distillery

Void bar at MONA

Tasmanian Beerfest, our favourite of Tassie's festivals.

Inside the old brewery at Moo Brew.

Back in the capital, there has been a huge leap in the quality of accommodation in Hobart with the Henry Jones Art Hotel (home to the very popular IXL Long Bar) and Islington top of the pile along with the MONA Pavilions overlooking the Derwent River at the Moorilla Estate facility. Smaller hostelries like Gattonside Heritage Accommodation and the new Hotel Collins downtown are good value for money.

Salamanca Market, just across the road from Constitution Dock (where the Sydney to Hobart yacht race fleet finishes), is the best place to sample a range of Tasmanian produce every Saturday from 8.30am-3pm.

Cruise boats leave nearby Watermans Dock heading to destinations including Wrest Point Casino and the D'Entrecasteaux Channel. The trip to Peppermint Bay, home to a spectacular restaurant and a bar with great water views, is particularly popular. You can also catch a ferry to MONA from Watermans Dock and enjoy a Moo Brew or two en route.

Cool Wine is considered one of Hobart's best wine shops with The Grape and the Wursthaus Kitchen and 9/11 bottle stores offering wide selections of local beers and wines, while Tasmanian Home Brewing Supplies in the city caters for the do-it-yourself brewer, open 9am-5.30pm Monday to Friday and 9am-1pm on Saturdays.

For those who prefer a non-alcoholic beverage, Chado: The Way of Tea, a traditional Japanese tea house, is operated by Brian Ritchie, a founder member of US rock band the Violent Femmes. That's Hobart for you – a place to expect the unexpected.

BARS

Bar Celona
23 Salamanca Sq, Hobart
(03) 6224 7557

Customs House Hotel
1 Murray St, Hobart
(03) 6234 6645
www.customshouse
hotel.com

Knopwoods Retreat
39 Salamanca Pl, Hobart
(03) 6223 5808

Mobius Lounge Bar
Despard St, Hobart
(03) 6224 4411

The Brisbane Hotel
3 Brisbane St, Hobart
(03) 6234 4920

Republic Bar
299 Elizabeth St,
North Hobart
(03) 6234 6954
www.republicbar.com

Shipwright's Arms
29 Trumpeter St,
Battery Point
(03) 6223 5551
www.shipwrights
arms.com.au

The Alley Cat
381 Elizabeth St,
North Hobart
(03) 6231 2299

MONA Wine Bar
Moorilla Estate
655 Main Rd, Berriedale
(03) 6277 9900
www.moobrew.com.au

The New Sydney Hotel
87 Bathurst St, Hobart
(03) 6234 4516
www.newsydney
hotel.com.au

The Squires Bounty
55 Salamanca Pl, Hobart
(03) 6224 3667
www.thesquiresbounty.
com.au

The IXL Long Bar
The Henry Jones Art Hotel
25 Hunter St, Hobart
(03) 6210 7700
www.thehenryjones.com

BOTTLE SHOPS

9/11
403-405 Brooker Hwy,
Lutana
(03) 6214 7911

Big Bargain Bottleshop
Various locations
(03) 6424 0600
www.goodstone.com.au

Channel Court Cellars
Shop 17-18, Channel Court
Shopping Centre, Kingston
(03) 6229 2999

Cool Wine
Cnr Mid City Arcade &
Criterion St, Hobart
(03) 6231 4000
www.coolwine.com.au

Grape Bar & Bottleshop
55 Salamanca Pl, Hobart
(03) 6224 0611
www.grape.net.au

Thirsty Camel
Various locations
(03) 9915 0600
www.thirstycamel.com.au

Wursthaus Kitchen
1 Montpelier Retreat,
South Hobart
(03) 6224 0644
www.wursthauskitchen.
com.au

BREWERIES AND BEER COMPANIES

Cascade Brewery
140 Cascade Rd,
South Hobart
(03) 6224 1117
www.cascadebreweryco.com.au

Moo Brew
Moorilla Estate,
655 Main Rd, Berriedale
(03) 6277 9900
www.moobrew.com.au

The Tasmanian Chilli Beer Company
www.tasmanianchillibeercompany.com.au

The Two Metre Tall Company
2862 Lyell Hwy, Hayes
(03) 6261 1930
www.2mt.com.au

Wineglass Bay Brewing
www.wineglassbaybrewing.com.au
www.freycinetvineyard.com.au

CIDER

Tasmanian Inn Cider
North West Bay Cider
16 Waterworth Dr,
Gemalla Rd, Margate
0419 309 589
www.inncider.com.au

HOMEBREW SHOP

Tasmanian Home Brewing Supplies
222 Liverpool St, Hobart
(03) 6234 6230
www.thbs.intas.net

DISTILLERIES

Lark Distillery
14 Davey St, Hobart
(03) 6231 9088
www.larkdistillery.com.au

Nant Distillery
The Nant Estate,
Nant Lane, Bothwell
(03) 6259 5790
www.nantdistillery.com.au

The Tasmania Distillery
1/14 Lamb Pl, Cambridge
(03) 6248 5399
www.tasmaniadistillery.com

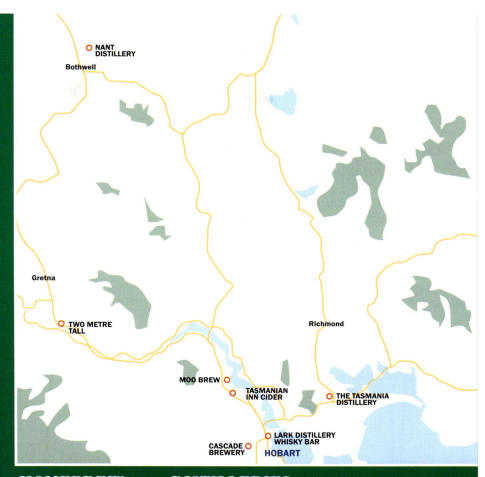

EVENTS

MARCH
Taste of the Huon
www.tasteofthehuon.com

MAY
Savour Tasmania
www.savourtasmania.com.au

NOVEMBER
Tasmanian Beerfest
www.tasmanianbeerfest.com.au

DEC-JAN
The Taste Festival
www.hobartsummerfestival.com.au

THINGS TO SEE AND DO

Bushy Park Estates Derwent Valley, www.hops.com.au.
Salamanca Market Salamanca Place, Hobart. Every Saturday, 8.30am-3pm. (03) 6238 2843; www.salamanca.com.au.
Wrest Point Casino Sandy Bay, 1800 703 006; www.wrestpoint.com.au. **D'Entrecasteaux Channel**, **Peppermint Bay Huon Valley wineries** – Panorama, Hartzview, Bruny Island Premium Wines, Home Hill Winery and Restaurant. **Chado: The Way of Tea** Hobart. (03) 6231 6411.

Photography from Tourism Tasmania, Damien Naidoo, Chris McNamara, Brett Boardman, Sean Fennessy, MONA (select images)

Beer & Brewer promotion   TASMANIA – NORTH

AUSTRALIAN HONEY PRODUCTS

Award winning honey makes good beer.

Located on the Tamar Valley wine route, a café is on-site which displays a huge range of honey, including White Clover, Organic Manuka and Tasmanian Leatherwood and many more.

Their mead is a Dessert Honey Mead (16%), aged & fortified, made from Prickly Box/Christmas Bush honey – known as the true nectar of the Gods.

Taverner's beers include a Honey Porter (6%), Honey Pale Ale (5.5%) and Strong Honey Ale (8%).

Honey and beer can be purchased online at www.ozhoney.com.au.

11/11 High St
Launceston
Tel: (03) 6331 0888
www.ozhoney.com.au

Opening hours:
5 days
Mon-Fri 8.00am – 6.00pm

Van Dieman Brewing

Van Dieman Brewing is dedicated to delivering fresh, progressive and unique beers directly to the public, unveiling some of the world's classic beer styles. Brewer Will Tatchell trained in the UK, and now brings that experience and imparts his knowledge into each individual brew, with beer flavour, quality and enjoyment at the forefront of Van Dieman Brewing's philosophy. They let the beers do the talking.

A White Ale, Pale Ale, Amber Ale and Oatmeal Stout are available all year round, as well as seasonal limited releases, including Hedgerow, an autumn Berry Ale which is matured on a blend of rose hips, sloe & hawthorn berries, all of which are hand-picked from hedgerows on the brewery farm.

537 White Hills Road
Evandale
Tel: (03) 63 91 90 35
Fax: (03) 63 91 90 38
info@vandiemanbrewing.com.au
www.vandiemanbrewing.com.au

Not open to public.
See the web site for where to buy Van Dieman Brewing beer.

Beer & Brewer promotion　　　　　　　　　　　　　　　　　　　　　　　　　　TASMANIA – SOUTH

MOO BREW

Before there was MONA there was Moo Brew

In case you have been living under a rock for the last few months, MONA is the Museum of Old and New Art. It's north of Hobart on the banks of the beautiful Derwent River and it's where Moo Brew was born.

Moo Brew comes is an understated bottle but there's nothing understated about the contents. Their bottles have real art on the labels, rather than real art without labels.

Their architecturally designed brewery sits on top of the hill rather than under it. They like to say that Moo Brew isn't suitable for bogans and they have the price point to prove it, versus MONA that says its egalitarian.

Every Friday afternoon at 4pm the guys offer a brewery tour, trotting out all their old jokes and favourite beer stories. Visit them on-site, then you can judge if they are self-deluded or if they just make damn good beers.

Brewery Tours every Friday at 4pm

Moo Brew

655 Main Road Berriedale TAS 7011
Ph: (03) 6277 9900
www.moobrew.com.au
info@moobrew.com.au

Then check out:

Wine Bar

Oysters, charcuterie, cheese, dessert, and a view of the vineyard.

Moorilla wine, Moo Brew and other craft wines and beers. Try a flight: four samples of wine or beer with self-guided tasting notes.

Open 10am until late.

Getting There:
FERRY
35 minutes from the MONA Brooke Street Ferry Terminal (Hobart)
$15 return pp.
Bookings 03 6223 6064 or www.mona.net.au/visit

Beer & Brewer magazine

Beer & Brewer magazine is a highly awarded quarterly consumer title that celebrates all things beer in Australia & New Zealand. Beer & Brewer was established in May 2007, with each issue serving up:

- Latest beer news
- Lifestyle of beer, with celebrity interviews
- History & collecting
- Travel ideas
- Beer & food matching
- Homebrewing tips & recipes (in a flip cover magazine entitled Homebrewer)
- Tasting notes on local and imported beer, cider and whisk(e)y.

JOIN OUR MAILING LIST
KEEP UP-TO-DATE ON ALL THINGS BEER IN AUSTRALIA & NEW ZEALAND

BEER & BREWER IS NOW AVAILABLE ON ITUNES WITH AN APP FOR IPAD AND IPHONE

Search for Beer & Brewer in the App Store. You can purchase the App for AUD$3.99 which comes with one free issue of your choice, or subscribe for AUD$24.99 for 1 year (5 issues), which can be used up with back issues or upcoming issues.

4 easy ways to subscribe or renew

1 ONLINE www.beerandbrewer.com **2 CALL** (02) 8877 0371 **3 FAX** (02) 8877 0340
4 MAIL Beer & Brewer, c/o DCA, Suite 2, L3, 201 Miller St, North Sydney NSW 2060

	AUSTRALIA	NEW ZEALAND	OTHER INTERN.
3 YEARS (15 ISSUES)	$92.99 SAVE $41.26	AUD96.99	AUD$214.99
2 YEARS (10 ISSUES)	$64.99 SAVE $24.51	AUD66.99	AUD$145.99
1 YEARS (5 ISSUES)	$32.99 SAVE $11.76	AUD33.99	AUD$75.99

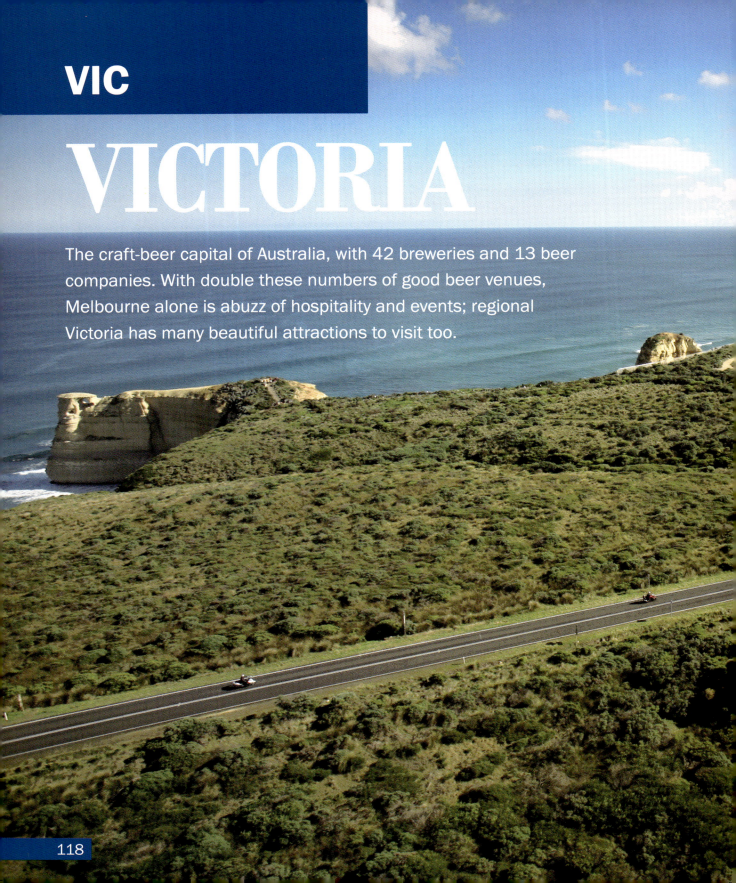

VIC

VICTORIA

The craft-beer capital of Australia, with 42 breweries and 13 beer companies. With double these numbers of good beer venues, Melbourne alone is abuzz of hospitality and events; regional Victoria has many beautiful attractions to visit too.

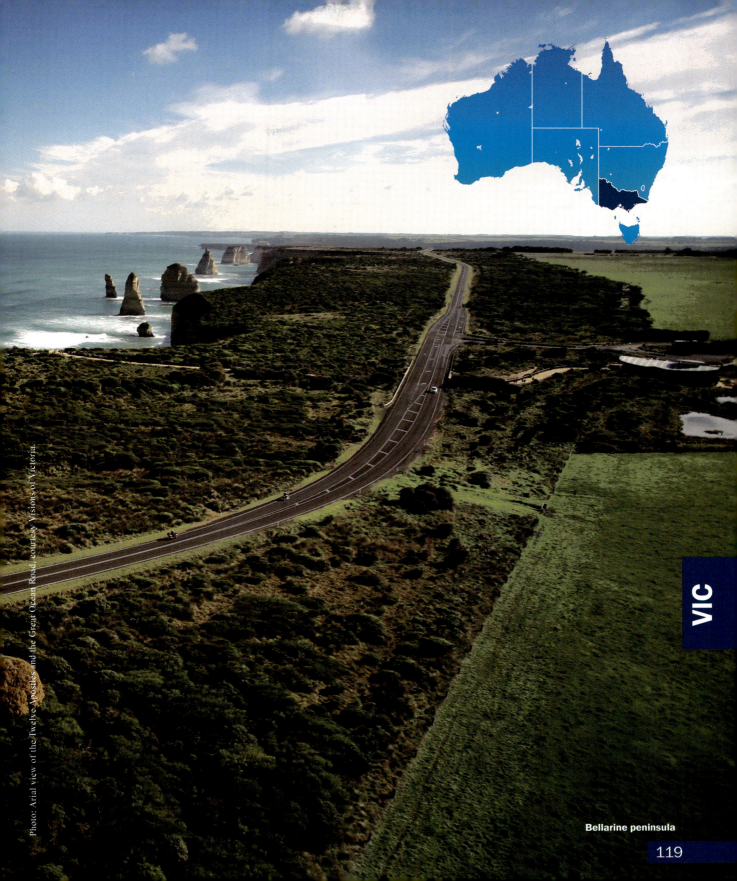

Photo: Arial view of the Twelve Apostles and the Great Ocean Road, courtesy Visions of Victoria.

VIC

Bellarine peninsula

VIC

MELBOURNE

Melburnians are justifiably proud of their beautiful and eventful city

The resident herders at Mountain Goat Brewery.

With inner-city breweries, excellent bars and an active beer-appreciation scene, Melbourne is arguably the country's craft-beer capital. We tend to agree. **By Chris Canty**

Melbourne is heaven for beer lovers. There are breweries open to the public dotted around the city, dedicated beer bars, and plenty of pubs and bottle shops just itching to give their customers something new. What more could you want?

■ BREWERIES TO VISIT

The Mountain Goat Brewery was one of the first of its kind in Melbourne and has remained a quintessential inner-city

James Squire Brewhouse at the Portland Hotel

3 Ravens Brewery

Andrew and Dave Ong, 2 Brothers Brewery

Brewing in full swing at 3 Ravens

True South Brewery

experience. Located in the heart of Richmond's industrial district, the former tannery is open to the public every Wednesday and Friday (from 5pm), with tastings on offer. Free tours are also available.

In the CBD, the James Squire Brewhouse is a favourite with local office workers, who flock there when the 5 o'clock whistle blows. The tanks are visible to the public and the food menu is better than the average pub fare.

The 2 Brothers Brewery is a great place to try sample the bros' brews, including the hard-to-find seasonal drop. The brewing equipment comes from the Times Square Brewery in New York and was shipped over under the cover of darkness. Special events and live music often add to the fun here. Open Thursdays (4pm until late) and Fridays (midday to late).

Also in the southern suburbs is the True South Brewery, a respectable restaurant/brewery venue. It is located just metres from the waters of Port Phillip Bay. Open daily midday-11pm.

The highly respected 3 Ravens Brewery in Thornbury looks just like the office block it is, but visitors will not be disappointed as the brewers are always on hand to offer answers to any questions asked. The brewery door is open Fridays 2-8pm.

Helping make the inner northern suburb of Brunswick the new beer centre of Melbourne, two new breweries have emerged and both are open to the public. The Temple Brewery & Brasserie (expecting to open late 2011) and Thunder Road Brewing Company offer an exciting range of brews and comfortable surrounds in which to taste them.

Also worth visiting is the iconic Carlton & United Brewery, which conducts tours (Visitor Centre open daily 9am–4pm) giving an insight into how a large brewery operates. The on-site bar also serves "brewery fresh" beers to the public.

In the shadows of CUB, the Moon Dog Craft Brewery, despite its youth, is building a reputation for producing some monster beers. Moon Dog isn't generally open to the

High-volume bottling at the Carlton & United Brewery, Abbotsford

Moon Dog Craft Brewery

CUB's iconic draught horses

Josie Bones, owned by *MasterChef* finalists Chris Badenoch and Julia Jenkins

public but folks are more than welcome to swing by and taste what's in the tanks.

While the brewery itself is not open to the public, hunting down beers from Kooinda Brewery is certainly worth the effort. Arctic Fox Brewery, too, has some tasty brews ideal for all-year drinking.

■ WHERE TO DRINK

The emergence of craft beers has seen the rise of quality bars and pubs that specialise in serving tasty brews. Many pride themselves in tapping one-off and seasonal kegs.

Leading the way is The Local Taphouse in St Kilda, which, thanks to 20 taps and regular beer events, has become *the* place to go for quality beer. The monthly Ale Stars sessions (third Tuesday of the month) are increasing in popularity and are a great way to meet like-minded people.

Also south of the CBD, the Belgian Beer Café is one of Melbourne's go-to places in warm weather. Its huge beer garden and live jazz performances are reason enough to visit, though the long beer list is an even better excuse. Beer courses are available throughout the year for those who want to increase their knowledge.

In the backstreets of Richmond, opposite the Mountain Goat Brewery, The Royston Hotel was one of the first pubs in Melbourne to embrace craft beer. With nine revolving taps, including a UK-style hand pump, it's a great venue to discover the best craft beers Victoria has to offer.

New on the block is Biero Bar (Little Lonsdale Street), which has invented world first beer-dispensing technology in order to showcase beers from around the world. It also features seasonal and one-off brews from local breweries. (Tip: beers are half price on Wendesday nights.)

Also in the heart of the city, within Federation Square, Beer Delux offers a beer list that exceeds 17 pages. The friendly and knowledgeable staff are always on hand for those daunted by what's on offer. Special beer-related events run regularly – check the website for details.

Nearby, the iconic Young & Jackson is worth a visit for more than the history lesson, as it often showcases craft brews (including cider) from around Victoria. Also close at hand is the European Bier Café, which has a wealth of European labels on hand.

In Collingwood, the Fox Hotel has won Melburnians over with its rooftop deck, tasty menu and arm-long beer list. It also has one of the largest collections of beer cans and bottles in the country. In the backstreets of Fitzroy, The Rainbow Hotel's impressive beer list is popular with locals. Together with its new beer garden and free live music most nights of the week, it is fast becoming one of the best beer pubs in Melbourne.

Nearby, Josie Bones (owned by Chris Badenoch and Julia Jenkins, both of *MasterChef* fame), has arguably the city's most detailed and interesting beer list. Food is matched to the brews, and a Beer & Food feast is held monthly.

The Local Taphouse – you'll think you've died and gone to beer heaven

The Fox Hotel

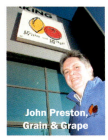
John Preston, Grain & Grape

Fiona and Mel, Mrs Parma's

Belgian Bier Café Bluestone

Biero Bar

Carlton's Bar Fred does two things particularly well: great pizza and incredible beers. It slips under the radar of the masses, but it's a favourite with locals and beer connoisseurs.

Oscar's Ale House in Belgrave might be a long way from the city, but it remains a beacon of quality for those who live out in the outer eastern suburbs and enjoy craft beer. Along with speciality beer nights and tastings, Oscar's is also a big supporter of local music.

■ WHERE TO BUY

If you want to find that rare beer or have a casual chat about the latest craft beers on offer, pop into Purvis Beer (and Purvis Cellars), Slow Beer or Blackhearts & Sparrows Wine Purveyors. These establishments are absolute industry leaders with their collective fingers on the pulse of the local craft-beer scene. They also offer very educational beer nights, often with brewers in attendance to talk about their creations. Acland Cellars, Smith St Cellars and Prince Wine Store have a great range of local and imported beers.

Chapel St Cellars is unique in that it doubles as a bar, so that you can pick a beer off the shelf, then choose to drink it there. Tap beers are also available.

Dan Murphy's outlets are located across Melbourne and have a huge array of craft beers from throughout the world.

Homebrewers should head to Grain & Grape, Australia's most-awarded homebrew shop, where you'll find beer for sale, plus educational sessions and expert advice.

■ CONTRACT KINGS

These Melbourne-based brews are made under contract and are worth seeking out. Hawthorn Brewing, Sundance Brewing, Piss Beer Co (Piss Beer and Piss Weak can be found at the Great Britain Hotel in Richmond). BROO Beer, Bitch Brewing, Effen Enterprises, Boat Rocker Brewing Company.

Thunder Road Brewing Company

The front bar of the historic Young & Jackson Hotel

■ WHERE TO STAY

For those on a budget, the award-winning Melbourne Metro YHA is one of the new breed of "flashpacker" hostels – that is, it more closely resembles a four-star hotel than traditional backpacker's accommodation. Offering great value for money, it is located just a few minutes from the CBD, and has a full tour desk, daily activities, clean rooms and a great rooftop barbecue area.

For those craving a measure of nature, the Amora Hotel Riverwalk gives you that and lets you stay where the action is. The hotel sits serenely on the riverbanks of the Yarra in Richmond, but is only moments away from bustling Bridge Road (and the Mountain Goat Brewery).

If it's luxury you want, make a beeline for the Langham Hotel. Located in the middle of Southbank, across the river from the CBD, the hotel is well known for its spa treatment centre and in-house restaurant, which serves an incredible buffet lunch.

■ WHERE TO EAT

Melbourne is an incredibly diverse city, populated by all manner of cultures. As such, there is a myriad of cuisines on offer, yet certain streets and suburbs tend to concentrate on one. Victoria Street in Richmond is the Vietnamese hub, whereas Lygon Street in Carlton could be considered "Little Italy". In Footscray, a hotbed of African food is on offer, while little Chinatown in the CBD is the place to sample Chinese cuisine. Personal favourites include Binh Minh in Richmond for Vietnamese, Café Lalibela in Footscray for Ethiopian, Tiamo on Lygon Street for Italian and the HuTong Dumpling Bar (city and Prahran) for Chinese.

But for those who want to blend the best beer with some of the best food, the following are certainly worth a visit.

Mrs Parma's cooks up a ravishing chook, with many varieties of the classic pub parmigiana (with all-you-can-eat salad and chips). The bar offers nine taps, often including one-off seasonal specials. Just down the road, Cookie's expansive beer list, is matched with what many regard as some of the best Thai cuisine in the city. In the summer months, be sure to venture out to the rooftop area (beer in hand, naturally) where an open-air cinema screens both cult films and modern classics.

Fitzroy's Napier Hotel is an old-school corner pub, well-known for its mammoth meals, including the Bogan Burger. It also has a range of good local craft beers on tap and is an ideal retreat if you want to get a true sense of the suburb. A mere minute away, Little Creatures Dining Hall is your upmarket option in this area. The food is designed to match the full list of excellent Little Creatures beers. Housed in an old warehouse, it is ideal for groups.

One of the first gastro pubs in Melbourne, The Courthouse offers great beers and quality fare in a casual yet elegant atmosphere. Knowledgeable staff are always on hand to recommend the brew that will perfectly complement your meal.

The highly regarded Great Northern Hotel has won national competitions for its juicy steaks, but the real reason punters flock to this pub is the interesting tap list (it's one of

Luna Park

Transport Hotel

BEER BARS

Bar Fred
797 Nicholson St, Carlton
(03) 9381 0501
www.barfred.com.au

Beer DeLuxe
Federation Square,
Melbourne
(03) 9663 0166
www.beerdeluxe.com.au

Belgian Beer Café Bluestone
557 St Kilda Rd,
Melbourne
(03) 9529 2899
www.bbcmelb.com

Belgian Bier Café Eureka
5 Riverside Quay,
Southbank
(03) 9646 4450
www.bbcmelb.com

Bertha Brown's
562 Flinders St,
Melbourne
(03) 9629 1207
www.berthabrown.com.au

Biero Bar
525 Little Lonsdale St,
Melbourne
(03) 9600 0940
www.bierobar.com.au

Big Mouth
168 Acland St, St Kilda
(03) 9534 4611
www.bigmouthstkilda.com.au

Bimbo Deluxe
376 Brunswick St, Fitzroy
(03) 9419 8600
www.bimbodeluxe.com.au

Campari House
23-25 Hardware Ln,
Melbourne
(03) 9600 1574
www.camparihouse.com.au

Charlie's Bar
Basement,
71 Hardware Ln,
Melbourne
(03) 9600 1454
www.charliesbar.com.au

Collins Quarter
86A Collins St,
Melbourne
(03) 9650 8500
www.collinsquarter.com

Cocoon Bar
Swanston Hotel,
195 Swanston St,
Melbourne
(03) 8662 1341
www.cocoonbar.com.au

European Bier Café
120 Exhibition St,
Melbourne
(03) 9663 1222
www.europeanbiercafe.com.au

Hell's Kitchen
20 Centre Pl, Melbourne
(03) 9654 5755

Hofbräuhaus
18-24 Market Ln,
Melbourne
(03) 9663 3361
www.hofbrauhaus.com.au

Josie Bones
98 Smith St,
Collingwood
(03) 9417 1878
www.josiebones.wordpress.com

Lucky Coq
179 Chapel St, Windsor
(03) 9525 1288
www.luckycoq.com.au

Mitre Tavern
5 Bank Pl, Melbourne
(03) 9670 5644
www.mitretavern.com.au

Oscar's Ale House
7 Bayview Rd, Belgrave
(03) 9754 8002

Penny Blue
2 Driver Ln, Melbourne
(03) 9639 3020

Rainbow Hotel
27 St David St, Fitzroy
(03) 9419 4193
www.therainbow.com.au

Saint & Rogue
582 Little Collins St,
Melbourne
(03) 9620 9720
www.saintandrogue.com.au

Tazio Birraria, Pizzeria, Cucina
66 Flinders Ln, Melbourne
(03) 9654 9119
www.tazio.com.au

The Albert Park Hotel
Cnr Montague St &
Dundas Pl, Albert Park
(03) 9690 5459
www.thealbertpark.com.au

The Aviary
271 Victoria St, Abbotsford
(03) 9428 7727
www.theaviary.com.au

The Cherry Tree Hotel
53 Balmain St, Richmond
(03) 9428 5743
www.thecherrytree.com.au

The Fox Hotel
351 Wellington St,
Collingwood
(03) 9416 4957
www.thefoxhotel.com.au

The Local Taphouse
184 Carlisle St,
St Kilda East
(03) 9537 2633
www.thelocal.com.au

The Retreat Hotel
280 Sydney Rd, Brunswick
(03) 9380 4090

The Royston
12 River St, Richmond
(03) 9421 5000
www.roystonhotel.com.au

The Terminus Hotel
492 Queens Pde,
North Fitzroy
(03) 9481 3182
www.terminus.com.au

Three Degrees Bar
1 QV Square
Cnr Swanston
& Lonsdale Sts, Melbourne
(03) 9639 6766
www.3degrees.com.au

Transport Hotel
Federation Square,
Melbourne
(03) 9654 8808
www.transporthotel.com.au

World Restaurant & Bar
Shop 4, Building 2,
Riverside Quay, Southbank
(03) 9690 6999
www.worldrestaurantbar.com.au

Young & Jackson Hotel
1 Swanston St, Melbourne
(03) 9650 3884
www.youngandjacksons.com.au

the only places in Victoria that Feral beer is available) and huge beer garden.

■ THINGS TO SEE AND DO

Just minutes from the CBD, the Melbourne Zoo is Australia's oldest zoological park and generally regarded as one of the country's best. Encounter more than 320 animal species just by wandering around, or join in one of a variety of tours and hands-on experiences. For more animal fun, head to Collingwood Children's Farm, where city kids can get up close and personal with animals usually found in rural settings such as sheep, pigs and cows. The monthly farmers' market held here is also worth visiting.

No trip to Melbourne can be complete without a visit to Luna Park, on the St Kilda foreshore. This historic amusement park was built in 1912 and offers a fun day for the family with a mixture of modern and historic rides.

The Melbourne Museum has a range of activities for all ages, however the Children's Gallery is aimed at three to eight year olds and includes the Big Box exhibition gallery, The Learning Environment and the Children's Garden.

For a family shopping excursion, there is no better choice than Chapel Street, which offers an array of designer stores and boutiques. There are also many restaurants and cafes on the strip to break up a day of shopping.

WHERE TO EAT

Binh Minh
Richmond (03) 9421 3802

Café Lalibela
Footscray (03) 9687 0300
www.cafelalibela.com.au,

Cookie
Melbourne
(03) 9663 7660
www.cookie.net.au

Great Northern Hotel
North Carlton
(03) 9380 9569
www.gnh.net.au

HuTong Dumpling Bar
Melbourne
(03) 9650 8128

Little Creatures Dining Hall
Fitzroy (03) 9415 1590
www.littlecreatures.com.au

Mrs Parma's
Melbourne
(03) 9639 2269
www.mrsparmas.com.au

Napier Hotel
Fitzroy (03) 9419 4240
www.thenapierhotel.com

The Courthouse
North Melbourne
(03) 9329 5394
www.thecourthouse.net.au

Tiamo
Carlton (03) 9347 5759
www.tiamo.com.au

BOTTLE SHOPS

1st Choice
1300 308 833
www.1stchoice.com.au

Acland Cellars
187 Acland St, St Kilda
(03) 9525 3818

Australian Wine Clearance Centre
317 St Georges Rd, Fitzroy North
(03) 9486 8788
www.awcc.com.au

Blackhearts & Sparrows Wine Purveyors
115 Scotchmer St, North Fitzroy
(03) 9486 8046
www.blackheartsandsparrows.com.au

Carwyn Cellars
829a High St, Thornbury
(03) 9484 1820

Chapel St Cellars
89 Chapel St, Windsor
(03) 9533 7769
www.chapelstcellars.com.au

Cloudwine
317 Clarendon St, South Melbourne
(03) 9699 6700
www.cloudwine.com.au

Dan Murphy's
1300 723 388
www.danmurphys.com.au

Grain & Grape (Home Brew Shop)
5/280 Whitehall St, Yarraville
(03) 9687 0061
www.grainandgrape.com.au

Prince Wine Store
2a Acland St, St Kilda
(03) 9536 1155
80 Primrose St, Essendon
(03) 9686 3033
www.princewinestore.com.au

Purvis Beer
292 Bridge Rd, Richmond
(03) 9078 2779
www.purvisbeer.com.au

Purvis Cellars
615-617 Whitehorse Rd, Surrey Hills
(03) 9888 6644
www.purviscellars.com.au

Slowbeer
63 Burwood Rd, Hawthorn
(03) 9078 7995
www.slowbeer.com.au

Smith Street Cellars
195 Smith St, Fitzroy
(03) 9419 6962
www.smithstreetcellars.com

Speakeasy Cellars
211 Upper Heidelberg Rd, Ivanhoe
(03) 9499 9493
www.speakeasycellars.com

Swords Select
South Melbourne, North Melbourne, Prahran, Clifton Hill
(03) 9348 9333
www.swordsselect.com.au

The Local Bottle Store & Provisions
186 Carlisle St, St Kilda East
(03) 9537 3300
www.thelocal.com.au

THINGS TO SEE AND DO

Melbourne Zoo Parkville, www.zoo.org.au. **Collingwood Children's Farm** Abbotsford, www.farm.org.au. **Luna Park** St Kilda, www.lunapark.com.au. **Melbourne Museum** Carlton, www.museumvictoria.com.au.

EVENTS

JANUARY
The Australian Open
www.australianopen.com

MARCH
Moomba Festival
www.moomba.com.au
Formula 1 Grand Prix
www.formula1.com
Melbourne Food
& Wine Festival
www.melbournefood
andwine.com.au

MAY
Australian International
Beer Awards www.beer
awards.com.au
Good Beer Week
www.goodbeerweek.com

JULY-AUGUST
Melbourne International
Film Festival
www.melbournefilm
festival.com.au

SEPTEMBER
AFL Grand Final
www.afl.com.au

SEPTEMBER-OCTOBER
Melbourne Fringe
Festival www.melbourne
fringe.com.au

OCTOBER
Fed Square Microbrew
eries Showcase
www.fedsquare.com.au

OCTOBER-NOVEMER
Melbourne's Spring
Carnival and Melbourne
Cup www.springracing
carnival.com.au

NOVEMBER
Queenscliff Music
Festival www.qmf.net.au

DECEMBER
Boxing Day
Test Match Cricket
www.cricket.com.au

Photography by Rick Besserdin, Chris Canty, Donald Y Tong, Tourism Victoria (select images).

BREWERIES, DISTILLERIES AND BEER COMPANIES

2 Brothers Brewery
4 Joyner St, Moorabbin
(03) 9553 1177
www.2brothers.com.au

3 Ravens Brewery
1 Theobald St, Thornbury
(03) 8480 1046
www.3ravens.com.au

Bakery Hill Distillery
28 Ventnor St,
Balwyn North
(03) 9857 7070
www.bakeryhilldistillery.com.au

Bitch Brewing
www.lifesabitch.com.au

BROO Beer
www.broo.com.au

Boat Rocker Brewing Company
www.boatrocker.com.au

Carlton Brewhouse and CUB Brewery
Cnr Thompson & Nelson Sts, Abbotsford
(03) 9420 6800
www.carltonbrewhouse.com.au

Effen Enterprises
www.effen.com.au

Hawthorn Brewing
www.hawthornbrewing.com.au

James Squire Brewhouse
Portland Hotel,
115-127 Russell St,
Melbourne
(03) 9810 0064
www.portlandhotel.com.au

Kooinda Brewery
www.kooinda.com.au

Moon Dog Craft Brewery
Abbotsford
moondogbrewing.com.au

Mountain Goat Brewery
Cnr North & Clark Sts, Richmond
(03) 9428 1180
www.goatbeer.com.au

Piss Beer Co
www.pi55.com

Sundance Brewing International
www.cricketersarmslager.com

Temple Brewing Company
122 Weston St,
Brunswick East
0418 557 875
www.templebrewing.com.au

Thunder Road Brewing Company
130 Barkly St, Brunswick
www.thunderroadbrewing.com

True South Brewery
298 Beach Rd, Black Rock
1300 878 360
www.truesouth.com.au

Victoria Valley Distillery
www.victoriavalley.com.au

BREWERY TOURS

Take a guided tour of the breweries in Melbourne, the Yarra Valley, Mornington Peninsula or Macedon Ranges with Aussie Brewery Tours; 1300 787 039 or www.aussiebrewerytours.com.au.

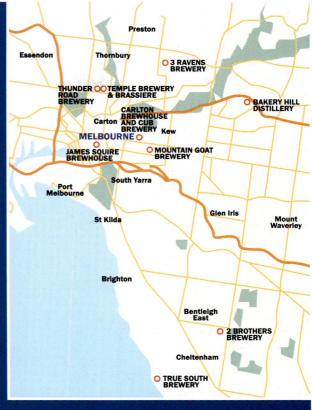

VIC

MORNINGTON PENINSULA AND PHILLIP ISLAND

Bathing boxes line the beach at Mornington Peninsula

When you need to get away from it all, head to the Victorian coast. The locals there have a little something to refresh you, body and soul. **By Julie Holland**

Just an hour's drive south of Melbourne is a land of microbreweries, award-winning restaurants and wineries, buzzing bars and a huge range of activities the whole family will enjoy.

■ MAP IT OUT

Visit The Tasting Station in Rosebud and sample a range of local produce, ciders, Mornington Peninsula cool-climate wines and microbrewery beers. Breakfast at Merricks General Wine Store's buzzing café while you pore over visitor guides (there are 50 cellar doors to visit!), but don't miss stocking the car boot at T'Gallant and Ten Minutes by Tractor (both in Main Ridge), Montalto Vineyard & Olive Grove in Red Hill South, or Stoniers in Merricks.

If you missed The Tasting Station's malty ice-cream made from Red Hill Brewery's Weizenbock seasonal beer, then head across the hills to the brewery itself for David and Karen Golding's handcrafted boutique Ales, from the crisp light-bodied Golden Ale to the malt-driven Scotch Ale and winter Imperial Stout. There's even a Brewer's Choice India Black Ale. This microbrewery, a Victorian Finalist in the 2010 *Beer & Brewer* Awards for Overall Best Beer Venue and Best Brew Bar/Pub, grows all its own hops (organically) on site. The eatery providing beer-matched foods is a must.

Fifth-generation wine maker Andrew Hickinbotham is enjoying producing his 'sideline' HIX Beer range of a German-style Pilsener, Brown Ale, Lager and Irish Stout. Hickinbotham of Dromana has a laidback atmosphere and is perfect for spending a chilled afternoon. There's a range of house-brewed beers, cider and wine to sample, plus hearty meals and live music on weekends. Bliss.

Twenty minutes up the highway, in the backblocks of Mornington, is the rather industrial-looking Mornington Peninsula Brewery. Head brewer Andrew Gow produces what he calls 'drinkable gold' – Pale Ale, Brown Ale, a Belgian-style Witbier and a regularly changing specialty on tap.

Around the corner from Mornington Peninsula Brewery is the One Stop Bar Shop, where you can replenish homebrewing equipment or order a state-of-the-art bar. It's open every day and holds a Home Brew Club meeting every three months.

While you swap homebrewing ideas and enjoy one of the five beers on tap, the family can head for the shops or Mornington Park overlooking Mothers Beach. Meet

The bar and Scotch Ale at Red Hill Brewery

Andrew Hickinbotham and Cameron Turner toast their award winning hobby

them later at The Rocks for a meal overlooking the bay and marina, or head up to Main Street for a pizza at DOC.

■ GET AROUND

Stop by Sorrento's main strip for some retail therapy – a coffee and vanilla slice at Just Fine Foods Deli, MP Chocolates, Main Ridge Dairy for goats' cheese platters and Sunny Ridge Strawberry Farm for every conceivable strawberry indulgence.

Horse-riding along rugged Rye beach will thrill; afterwards, warm up next to the fireplace at McRae Pavilion, near McRae Lighthouse. It's open until late and showcases the best local produce and music, plus local and international wines and beers – six on tap plus a floating tap and a wide range in the fridge.

Alternatively, head up to Arthurs Seat to take in the view, then let loose at The Enchanted Maze Garden. There are children's labyrinths, hedge mazes, more than 20 themed gardens and a 3D indoor maze. Picnic here or at nearby Seawinds Gardens, then head back down the hill to unwind at the Peninsula Hot Springs and Day Spa Centre, Rye.

■ WHERE TO BUY OR TRY

Local microbrewery beers are on tap at bars and hotels in the area. Taste at: The Bay Hotel, Mornington; Flinders Hotel, Flinders; Pavilion, Rye; Hotel Sorrento. Buy from: Red Hill Cellar & Pantry, Red Hill South; Tasting Station, Rosebud; Stringers Stores, Sorrento. Also try: Nepean Highway Cellars, Mornington; Ritchies, Mt Eliza; Thirsty Camel, Mornington; Dan Murphy's Mornington and Frankston.

■ PHILLIP ISLAND

Rusty Water Brewery Restaurant & Bar beckons from across the water at Cowes, Phillip Island. Either drive the 90-minute journey or head to Hastings and jump on an inter-island ferry from Stony Point with your bicycle (a leisurely 20-minute boat trip followed by a 15-minute bike ride). Enjoy Rusty Water's five handcrafted ales on tap – Koala Pale Ale, Dark Malt Burnt Toffee Ale, Raspberry Pale Ale, Caramelised Banana Wheat Beer or the hop driven Mako IPA. Also on offer are limited-release and specialty Ales from the Otways' Prickly Moses and Byron Bay's Stone & Wood breweries and Coldstream Brewery's Draught Cider.

Rusty Water Brewery

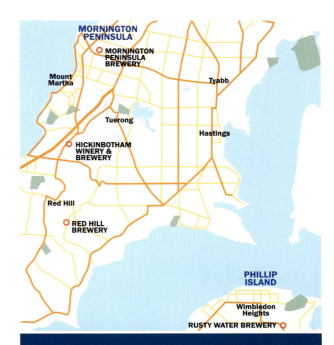

BREWERIES

Hickinbotham Winery & Brewery
194 Nepean Hwy, Dromana
(03) 5981 0355
www.hickinbotham.biz

Mornington Peninsula Brewery
72 Watt Rd, Mornington
(03) 5976 3663
www.mpbrew.com.au

Red Hill Brewery
88 Shoreham Rd, Red Hill South
(03) 5989 2959
www.redhillbrewery.com.au

Rusty Water Brewery
1821 Phillip Island Tourist Rd, Cowes, Phillip Island
(03) 5952 1666
www.rustywaterbrewery.com.au

EVENTS
OCTOBER
OKTOBERFEST

Oktoberfest is a joint event between Hickinbotham of Dromana and Bayside Brewers. On tasting are numerous handcrafted beers of various styles produced by members of local and Melbourne based amateur brew clubs and judged by well-respected beer aficionados. Bryce van Denderen, President of Bayside Brewers says: "Homebrewing on the Mornington Peninsula is thriving with our club attracting many enthusiastic new members in the last year." For more info, go to www.baysidebrewers.org.au

THINGS TO SEE AND DO

Bayside/surf beaches (kayak, dolphin swims, fishing, sailing, surfing). **Montalto Vineyard & Olive Grove** www.montalto.com.au. **Sunny Ridge Strawberry Farm** www.sunnyridge.com.au. **McCrae Pavilion** www.mccraepavilion.com.au. **Enchanted Maze Garden** www.enchantedmaze.com.au. **Peninsula Hot Springs & Day Spa** www.peninsulahotsprings.com.

Photography from Tourism Victoria, Nic Crilly-Hargrave (select images)

VIC

Ned Kelly's legend looms large in Glenrowan.

NORTH EAST

Victoria's north east is famous for Ned Kelly and his last stand. See it for yourself before the bartender shouts "Last orders!" **By Sandy Guy**

Folklore has it that the young smiling woman gracing the labels of Buffalo Brewery beer is Lily Arabella Cherry, thought to be a girlfriend of Kelly Gang member Steve Hart. What's for sure is that Hart enjoyed a cooling Ale at the Boorhaman Hotel, just a gunshot from Wangaratta, in the late 1870s.

■ BREWERIES

Visiting microbreweries in the region, you soon realise that there's beer and there's beer. And a lazy weekend touring Ned Kelly's old stomping ground is a great way to get acquainted with the differences.

The historic town of Beechworth is home to Bridge Road Brewers, where beer aficionado Ben Kraus, who cut his teeth brewing in Innsbruck, Austria, recently produced his 500th brew, creating a black Belgian IPA in 750ml bottles to celebrate five fruitful years of craft brewing.

From humble beginnings in the family's garage, Bridge Road Brewery has grown to become a Victorian microbrewery favourite. Today, the brewery is situated in a rustic coach house behind the historic Tanswell's Hotel in Beechworth's main thoroughfare. Ben brews nine full-bodied beers, including Bridge Road's original brew, Australian Ale, Hefeweizen, hugely hopped Beechworth Pale Ale, Celtic Red Ale, a robust Porter, and Chestnut Lager – all crafted from yeasts cultured from some of the world's best ales.

Boyntons Feathertop Winery

It's all about the beer at Bright Brewery.

Sweetwater Brewing Company

Business is booming, and Ben recently employed two brewers, Steve Matthews and trainee Jay Howlett, to help him brew Bridge Road favourites as well as limited-release beers including The Big Red Rocket – a beer fermented in 50-year old muscat barrels - and Fresh Wet Hop beer – using freshly picked hops from Rostrevor Hop Garden.

Bright Brewery, on the banks of the Ovens River in Bright, has been producing quality Ales since it opened in 2006. Head Brewer/Owner Scott Brandon and new brewer Jon Seltin craft six beers: Bright Lager, English-style Hellfire Amber Ale, Razor Witbier, Staircase Porter, Fainters Dubbel, and American-style Blowhard Pale Ale, as well as a range of seasonal beers. A new seasonal offering, Raspberry Lambic (brewed with raspberries), has proven a hit with beer lovers from the north-east to a bevy of Melbourne's trendy bars, while Bright's new Topaz Harvest Lager is made from Topaz hops grown in nearby Rostrevor Hop Gardens.

Visit Bright Brewery on a Sunday, when you can taste beers and dine on gourmet pizzas while listening to blues music. If you're in town during the week, the brewery hosts tours and tastings every Friday at 3pm ($18 per person), as well as a range of beer-related events throughout the year.

At Sweetwater Brewing Company, based at Annapurna Estate winery at nearby Tawonga South, all beers are brewed on site in a small-batch brewery by owner and brewer Peter Hull. Flavours of malt, hops and yeast enhance soft mountain water in Sweetwater's tasty American-style Pale Ale, malty English Golden Bitter, refreshing and fruity Summer Ale, Weissbier and a Porter.

Sweetwater has a brewery bar in conjunction with Annapurna's cellar door, where Hull's beers are available on tap, and where you can dine at the restaurant from menus stressing fine regional produce. The brewery bar is open Friday to Sunday, 12-4pm.

Beef and beer pies and lamb shanks in Stout are on the menu at Jamieson Brewery, 25 kilometres from Mansfield at Lake Eildon. Head brewer Jeff Whyte uses traditional brewing styles to create preservative-free beers with no added sugars, including Raspberry Ale, Jamieson Beast India Pale Ale, Brown Ale, and popular Mountain Ale, which is brewed with 60 per cent wheat to give it a thick, foamy head and a distinctive chocolate-malt flavour with caramel tones. Open daily from 10am. Free brewery tours held daily at 12.30pm.

The iconic Victorian Bitter Ale was first brewed at the Buffalo Brewery in Wangaratta, two-and-a-half hours' drive north of Melbourne, more than a century ago. Today, the tradition continues at the Buffalo Brewery Boorhaman Hotel.

Boorhaman Hotel co-owner and brewer Greg Fanning grinds his own wheat and barley and uses pure water from a spring on the property to produce Lager, Wheat Beer, Stout, Dark Ale, and a zesty Ginger Beer.

Fanning once turned a century-old grinding wheel by hand, but recently installed a motor to do the job. He still hand fills and caps the bottles at this welcoming pub, said to be Australia's smallest commercially operating brewery, producing 180L per batch, one of a number of small-scale breweries scattered across north-eastern Victoria.

Boyntons Feathertop Winery, at Porepunkah near Mt Buffalo, serve their contract brewed Ales and Pilseners in a setting that will take your breath away. Drop into Feathertop's cellar door to taste Kel Boynton's Ales – he is as passionate about beer as he is about making wine.

Ben Kraus (left) at Bridge Road Brewery

Photography from Tourism Victoria (select images)

■ CIDER

Another local winner in Beechworth, is Beechworth Cider, launched in 2008 by Ben Clifton and his mother Sue Thornton as an addition to the family's Amulet Vineyard. Slightly sweet, lightly-spritzed, and containing no artificial flavours, this boutique cider is made from apples sourced from local orchards. Open weekends, public and school holidays 10am-5pm, other times by arrangement.

Greg Fanning, Buffalo Brewery

Mt Hotham Ski Resort

■ ELLERSLIE HOP ESTATE

Nestled among the picturesque hills and valleys of the King Valley, is Australia's largest family owned independent hop growing company, Ellerslie Hop Estate. With a hop-growing history dating back to the late 1800s, the Myrrhee district of north-east Victoria remains the home of the Australian developed Pride of Ringwood hop as well as the Cluster variety hop and several exciting new varieties. Hops grown in the region support both the domestic and international brewing industry, with the north-east Victorian hops providing an authentic flavour to the major Australian-style beers as well as unique characteristics to many of the fantastic boutique breweries Australia wide.

During the late summer months, the air is filled with the distinct aroma of hops and with first harvest (starting in mid-February), visitors to the area get to take advantage of the long days and warm nights while exploring this unique hop-growing region.

■ ROSTREVOR HOP GARDENS

Hop Products Australia (HPA) has its main estate in Bushy Park, Tasmania, and operates Rostrevor Hop Gardens situated in the Ovens Valley between Myrtleford and Bright beneath Mount Buffalo in north-east Victoria. Rostrevor grows approximately 150 hectares of hop cultivars such as Super Pride, Topaz and Galaxy. HPA supplies international and major Australian brewers, as well as craft brewers. Several Victorian craft brewers specify Victorian grown hops for their brews, so seek them out to taste the flavour of locally grown hops.

■ WHILE IN NORTH EASTERN VICTORIA

Beechworth is one of Australia's best preserved gold rush towns, with more than 30 National Trust-listed buildings. Tree-lined streets have an eclectic mix of shops, cafes and several good restaurants.

Mt Beauty, in the foothills of Mt Bogong, is blanketed with a riot of russet-coloured leaves during autumn, and is a popular pitstop during the winter months for skiers heading to Mt Hotham and Falls Creek.

The historic town of Yackandandah has a National Trust-classified main street and several traditional pubs – a charming way to spend a lazy afternoon. There are some good bushwalking trails if you're feeling active (or need to walk off a meal), or try your luck gold-panning in the Yackandandah Creek.

Milawa, 15 kilometres south-east of Wangaratta, is home to Brown Brothers Winery, which began operating in 1889. Sample wines while dining at the winery's Epicurean Centre. Just north of town is Milawa Cheese Factory, where you can dine on cheese-inspired cuisine at The Factory Restaurant.

Jeff and Jeanette Whyte, Jamieson Brewery

Harvesting hops at Ellerslie Hop Estate

EVENTS

VARIOUS
Bright Brewery "Brewer for a Day"
www.brightbrewery.com.au

MARCH
Yackandandah Folk Festival
www.folkfestival.yackandandah.com

APRIL
Bright Autumn Festival
www.brightautumnfestival.org.au

MAY
Harvest Celebration, Beechworth and beyond
www.harvestcelebration.com.au

JUNE
Rutherglen Winery Walkabout
www.rutherglenvic.com
Weekend Fit for a King
King Valley, www.winesofthekingvalley.com.au

AUGUST
Highland Games
www.amuletwines.com.au
Ned Kelly Weekend
www.beechworth.com

SEPTEMBER
Spring Migration Festival
Yackandandah
www.springmigration.com.au

OCTOBER
Beechworth Oktoberfest
Bridge Road Brewers, Beechworth,
www.bridgeroadbrewers.com.au
Bright Spring Festival
www.brightspringfestival.com.au
Wangaratta Festival of Jazz,
www.wangaratta-jazz.org.au

OCTOBER-NOVEMBER
Mansfield High Country Festival
www.highcountryfestival.com.au

NOVEMBER
La Dolce Vita King Valley
www.winesofthekingvalley.com.au

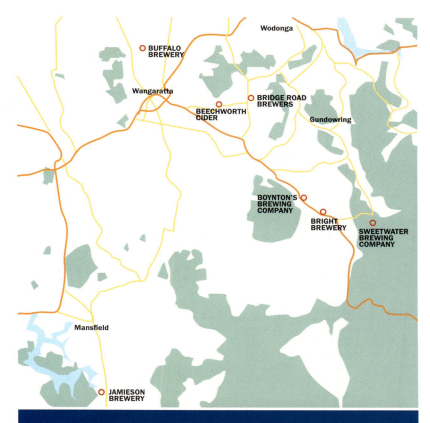

BREWERIES, CIDER AND BEER COMPANY

Beechworth Cider
Amulet Vineyard
1036 Wangaratta Rd, Beechworth
(03) 5727 0420
www.beechworthcider.com.au

Boyntons Feathertop Winery
www.boynton.com.au

Bridge Road Brewers
Old Coach House, Brewers Lane
50 Ford St, Beechworth
(03) 5728 2703
www.bridgeroadbrewers.com.au

Bright Brewery
121 Great Alpine Road, Bright
(03) 5755 1301
www.brightbrewery.com.au

Buffalo Brewery
Boorhaman Hotel
1570 Boorhaman Rd, Boorhaman
(03) 5726 9215

Jamieson Brewery
Eildon Rd, Jamieson
(03) 5777 0515
www.jamiesonbrewery.com.au

Sweetwater Brewing Company
Annapurna Estate Winery
217 Simmonds Creek Rd,
Tawonga South
(03) 5754 1881
www.sweetwaterbrewing.com.au

PLACES TO STAY

Lindenwarrah, Milawa, www.lindenwarrah.com.au. **Blacksprings Bakery**, Beechworth, www.blackspringsbakery.com. **Koendidda**, Barnawartha, www.koendidda.com.au. **Bright's official Visitor Information Centre** www.greatalpinevalleys.com.au 1800 111 885.

Pictures courtesy Mount Hothan Ski Resort

VIC

NORTH WEST

Take a leap back to goldrush times at Sovereign Hill.

There's a lot of history – and craft breweries – in them thar hills, so take an educational trip to Victoria's north west. **By Pammy Kokoras**

Victoria's north west is well known for its fertile farmlands and scenic allure, and offers liberty for adventure, escape or relaxation.

■ MILDURA

Situated on the banks of the Murray River, the bucolic town of Mildura has an outdoor leisure culture that makes water activities and houseboat holidays to the town popular. Hot-air ballooning over the picturesque farms and vineyards is an activity worth getting up early for. Back on terra firma, explore the sand hills, ancient aboriginal sites at nearby Lake Mungo National Park, or glide down the Murray on a paddle steamer.

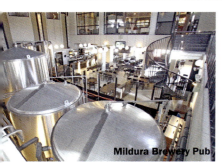

Mildura Brewery Pub

First stop for the beer enthusiast is the Mildura Brewery, located in what was once the Astor Theatre. Four naturally brewed signaure beers (plus monthly specialty brews) were inspired by and named for local stories, produce and attractions. Be sure to check out the ground-floor bar, where there's a three-vessel brewhouse and bottling line.

After a day of explring the town and surrounds, a spot of dinner is just the thing to help you recharge those batteries. If it's gourmet food you're after, head to the Quality Hotel Mildura Grand – chef Stefano de Pieri (author of *Gondola on the Murray*) is one reason for Mildura's reputation for quality food and wine. Sample his house-made cured meats, local Murray cod and yabbies in the award-winning restaurant.

■ SWAN HILL

Nearby, the Murray runs right through the centre of Swan Hill, which is surrounded by farmland and named after the noisy black swans that used to inhabit the region. A weekend can't accommodate all the activities on offer – fishing, scenic discovery trails, water-skiing, golfing and visiting markets – but Swan Hill promises to satisfy, whatever your tastes.

A visit to the three-hectare, open-air Pioneer Settlement Museum is essential. Here, agricultural machinery, historic items, activities and demonstrations show the routine activities of riverland pioneers. From horse rides to displays of blacksmithing, baking and printing the museum gives a hands-on insight into Australian history.

Echuca Brewery

Paul and Tash of Holgate Brewery

Historical discoveries extend to the region's wineries. The region's first winery, St Andrews, was built by the Thomson family in 1930 and is still operating today. Other wineries, cellar doors and vineyards include Andrew Peace, Best's Wines Lake Boga, Buller's Beverford and Oak Dale Winery.

A good meal is always recommended to counter the effects of all that wine. Try Quo Vadis Restaurant & Pizza Parlour, Java Spice for tasty Thai, or Yutaka Sawa if you're in the mood for Japanese.

■ ECHUCA

Echuca, also on the banks of the Murray, offers a variety of water activities, events and day spas for those who fancy a little pampering. It's a great base for tours of the region too.

Beer aficionados should make a beeline for the Echuca Bar and Grill Brewery. Specialising in Australian craft beers, the bar has more than 40 on offer, ranging from Dark Ales to delicate Lagers. Meals are proudly prepared with locally sourced produce – spending a leisurely afternoon or evening on one of the Brewery's comfy couches seems inevitable.

Oscar W's Wharfside Redgum Grill & Deck Bar is another great eatery by the water. Alternatively, try a cruising restaurant with a 360-degree view of the river on the paddle steamer *Emmylou* or *M.V Mary Ann*.

For collectors of all things beer, Echuca is also home to The Great Aussie Beer Shed, the only museum of its kind in Australia. Here, you'll find more than 16,000 beer cans from Australia and around the world (including the world's rarest can, made for the coronation of King George VI in 1937), and other brewery related items including beer tap tops and tap handles, trays, wooden beer barrels, bottles, signs, brewery manufacturing equipment and machinery and more. Guided tours are available. A unique experience for the whole family.

Avonmore Estate

Half an hour from Echuca, Avonmore Estate winery offers a range of biodynamic wines and a Pale Ale that is a rich golden colour, full-bodied and a well-hopped brew. (NB the beer is only available from September to March, as it is brewed under contract off site.)

■ BENDIGO

Gold was discovered in Bendigo in 1851, and the town is still rich with gold-related attractions and activities. Along the tree-lined streets, 19th century buildings house antique shops, bookstores, galleries, restaurants and wineries.

Tour underground mines and see the talking tram at the Central Deborah Mine complex, which runs through a restored gold mine and other Bendigo sights. Visit the Art Gallery or Golden Dragon Museum to take in some history, or visit the southern hemisphere's largest Gothic cathedral, Sacred Heart Cathedral, built in 1896.

For wine connoisseurs, a self-drive wine tasting experience can't be missed. Passing through Balgownie Estate, Sandhurst Ridge and Connor Park, you'll understand why Bendigo's wine region is often referred to as "charming".

If you're not wined out by the end of a day of tasting, Whirrakee Restaurant & Wine Bar's menu offers French-influenced cuisine made from local produce and a selection of more than 200 wines to choose from.

For a Mediterranean or mod-Oz meal, visit The Dispensary Enoteca. To go with the divine fare, there are 70 local and imported bottled beers, 100 single-malt whiskies, 100 French Champagnes, plus lists of gins, tequilas and other spirits that will make a connoisseur weep with joy. A must-visit on your trip.

If you're looking for a real Aussie country pub experience, head to The Rifle Brigade Pub. The team has previously won awards for its home-brand brews, however the Brigade is sadly no longer operating the brewery.

About one hour's drive south of Bendigo, the Holgate Brewhouse offers a wonderful range of full-flavoured beers, all handcrafted by the brewery's small team. Settle down with a beer from the core range, a seasonal beer or try a limited-release or one-off specialty. The Temptress Chocolate Porter is a standout. Open Monday from 2pm; Tuesday to Sunday from noon.

Before leaving town, be sure to stop at The Shamrock Hotel in their Gold Dust Lounge or The Dispensary Enoteca, for the award winning Three Troupers, Pyrenees premium handcrafted beers. Also available at these venues and at the Wine Bank on View is Harcourt Valley Vineyards'

Sightings American Pale Ale. Both beers are contract brewed. Harcourt's have a cellar door 30 kilometres from Bendigo to taste Sightings and their range of wines.

■ BALLARAT

Keep heading south to Ballarat for an Ale or Lager at O'Brien Brewing. O'Brien's makes preservative-free, artificial-colouring free, gluten-free and naturally brewed beer that tastes like real beer. Honest!

For a meal afterwards, head to Phoenix Brewery Restaurant, just 10 minutes down the road opposite the Ballarat University. The menu is filled with dishes made using seasonal local and regional produce, giving vistors an excellent idea of the quality that Ballarat can produce.

For those with more than a passing curiosity, Ballarat University also offers brewing and distilling courses. You can contact the campus to visit its brewery, or view the action through the glass in The Union Building.

■ DAYLESFORD

About 45 minutes' drive north of Ballarat is the charming town of Daylesford. Here, you can find Breakfast & Beer,

O'Brien Brewing

a finalist in the 2010 *Beer & Brewer* Awards for Best Restaurant/Café. A wide range of local and international beers, including Theresianer (Italy) and Emerson's Taieri George (NZ), is offered as an accompaniment with every meal – breakfast, lunch and dinner. Perfect for the night-shift worker or those who like to start early.

Operating out of a garage, Dolphin Brewery is a genuine local brewery. Although you can't tour the brewery itself, the Dolphin product is well worth hunting down. Tastings are available at Daylesford Farmer's Market on the first Saturday of every month, Castlemaine Farmer's Market on the first Sunday of every month and Trentham Farmer's Market on the third Saturday of every month. Also look out for Dolphin brews within Hepburn Shire and Mt Alexander Shire.

Hepburn Springs Day Spa is just five minutes away from Daylesford. It's currently undergoing redevelopment, but reopening is planned for late 2012. Check the Hepburn Springs website for updates when planning your visit.

■ TOOBORAC

Further east, Tooborac (population 277) is home to Tooborac Hotel & Brewery. It offers three specialty beers that are ignored at your peril. Stonemasons is a Pale Ale is made in memory of the local craftsmen while Woodcutters is an Amber brew, named for those who felled the trees of the nearby McHarg ranges. The Stout is called Blacksmiths after the coke furnaces that glowed next to the anvil. The care and craftsmanship evident in the brewery is likewise seen in the accommodation and dining areas.

A tour group marvels at the wonders in the Great Aussie Beer Shed.

The University of Ballarat's training centre also produces Uni Gold and Uni Dark.

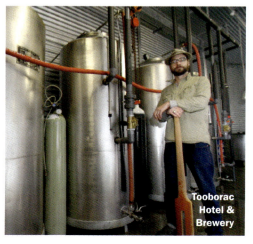
Tooborac Hotel & Brewery

The towns of north west Victoria are a Utopia for those with a thirst for good beer, wine and food, adventure, relaxation and history fanatics. Whether just passing through or spending some time discovering the area, there is no scarcity of remarkable places to visit, taste or experience.

EAT AND DRINK

Breakfast & Beer
(03) 5348 1778
www.breakfastandbeer.com.au

Phoenix Brewery Restaurant
(03) 5333 2686
www.ballarat.com/phoenix

The Rifle Brigade Hotel
(03) 5443 4092
www.riflebrigadehotel.com.au

The Dispensary Enoteca
(03) 5444 5885
www.thedispensaryenoteca.com

The Shamrock Hotel
(03) 5443 0333
www.hotelshamrock.com.au

Wine Bank on View
(03) 5444 4655
www.winebankonview.com

THINGS TO SEE AND DO

BENDIGO Central Deborah Mine complex, Golden Dragon Museum, **Sacred Heart Cathedral**, Wineries.
ECHUCA The Great Aussie Beer Shed, Oscar W's Wharfside Redgum Grill & Deck Bar, **Paddle steamer** *Emmylou* or *M.V Mary Ann*.
MILDURA Lake Mungo National Park, Murray River cruise, **Quality Hotel Mildura Grand**. **SWAN HILL** Pioneer Settlement Museum, Wineries – St Andrews, Andrew Peace, Best's Wines Lake Boga, Buller's Beverford and Oak Dale Winery.

BREWERIES AND BEER COMPANIES

Avonmore Estate Biodynamic Wines
Mayreef/Avonmore Rd,
Avonmore (via Elmore)
(03) 5432 6291
www.avonmoreestatewine.com

Echuca Brewing Company Brewery Bar & Grill
609 High St, Echuca
(03) 5482 4282
www.echucabrewingco.com.au

Harcourt Valley Vineyards
3339 Old Calder Hwy,
Harcourt
(03) 5474 2223
www.harcourtvalley.com.au

Holgate Brewhouse
79 High St, Woodend
Tel: (03) 5427 2510
www.holgatebrewhouse.com

Mildura Brewery
20 Langtree Ave, Mildura
(03) 5022 2988
www.mildurabrewery.com.au

Dolphin Brewery
Daylesford
www.dolphinbrewery.com.au

O'Brien Brewing
110 Creswick Rd,
Ballarat
(03) 4308 0136
www.obrienbrewing.com.au

Tooborac Hotel & Brewery
5115 Northern Highway,
Tooborac
(03) 5433 5201
www.tooborachotel.com.au

Three Troupers Brewery
www.threetroupers.com.au

University of Ballarat
The Union Building,
University Dr,
Mt Helen
1800 811 711
www.ballarat.edu.au

EVENTS

FEBRUARY
Riverboats Jazz, Food & Wine Festival
www.riverboatsjazzfoodandwine.com.au

FEBRUARY-MARCH
Mildura Wentworth Arts Festival www.artsmildura.com.au/mwaf

MARCH
Swan Hill Region Food & Wine Festival
www.swanhillfoodandwine.com.au

MARCH-APRIL
Echuca Moama RSL & Citizens Club Fishing Classic

OCTOBER
Australian Inland Wine Show Swan Hill
www.inlandwine.com
Bendigo Heritage Uncorked
www.bendigowine.org.au

Heathcote Wine & Food Festival
www.heathcotewinegrowers.com.au

NOVEMBER
Australian Alternative Varieties Wine Show
www.aavws.com

NOVEMBER- DECEMBER
RACV Great Victorian Bike Ride www.bv.com.au

VIC

SOUTH EAST

The rolling green hills of West Gippsland, Victoria

Things move slowly down here, but there's a whiff of change in the air. Craft brewers are giving Gippsland's wine industry a shake up. **By Paul Edwards**

Gippsland – that high, wide slab of land stretching from Melbourne's south-eastern suburbs to the NSW border – rarely hits the news unless there's a fire or a flood. For the most part, it's a tranquil expanse of hills and valleys sweeping down through rich farmland and long stretches of beaches.

This is wonderful touring country, with spectacular scenery, historic mining towns, several corny but well-meaning theme parks and a wide range of restaurants, wineries, delis and produce stores. To get a handle on the many faces of Gippsland, you need at least three days, starting and finishing in Melbourne and covering more than 1000 kilometres.

■ DANDENONG

Cosmopolitan Dandenong is the logical start to this journey, and according to brewer Fabian Apps, it's the logical place to start a microbrewery. Fabian, a former metalworker, found his skills came in handy when building his plant, which is modelled on a scaled-up homebrew kit.

Arctic Fox currently produces American and English Pale Ales, a Lager, Chocolate Stout and an apple-pear cider using local fruit. The brewery isn't open to the public, but you can find the product (from 330ml bottles up to 50L kegs) in around 50 restaurants and bottle shops around Melbourne.

Fabian says he's happy to grow slowly, devoting most of his profits to streamlining the plant. "Currently we spend a whole day on bottling, using a bench capper. We need to speed that up and then we'll be ready to increase our output. But there's no hurry – quality is much more important than quantity."

Just 10 minutes away in Dandenong South is the Matilda Bay Brewing Company's Garage Brewery. Here, Head Brewer Scott Vincent and the team brew limited and seasonal releases for beer lovers to enjoy, sustained by coffee from the onsite coffee roaster and treats cooked in the pizza oven. The brewery is not open to the public. Household

Owner and brewer Fabian Apps (right) at Arctic Fox Brewery

Head Brewer Scott Vincent and the team for the Big Helga launch at Matilda Bay Brewing Company's Garage Brewery

Coldwater Creek Tavern & Microbrewery at Chifley Doveton Hotel

Bacchus Distillery

brands in the Matilda Bay stable such as Redback and Beez Neez are brewed at Cascade Brewery due to the higher production capacity required. Matilda Bay is also well known for its craft beers including the highly awarded Alpha Pale Ale, Fat Yak, Big Helga and Dogbolter.

Right next door to Matilda Bay Brewing Company is the Bacchus Distillery. Bacchus is the largest cream liqueur manufacturer in the Asia Pacific region. It's open to the public, so drop in for some butterscotch schnapps or vodka. Tastings are available 9am–5.30pm Monday to Friday and the first Saturday of each month 10am-4pm.

While you're in the Dandenong area, stop by the Chifley Hotel at Doveton, home of the Coldwater Creek Tavern & Microbrewery, where you'll find its Red Raw Amber Ale and Coldwater Creek Pilsner on tap. Also available are 32 local and imported bottled beers and wood-fired pizzas.

From Dandenong, the Princes Highway winds through Gippsland and eventually on to Sydney. To the left is the Great Dividing Range, with side roads luring the tourist to towns such as Walhalla, a one-time ghost town now experiencing a revival based on weekend residents who love the quiet hills and valleys. Quiet, that is, until the tourists turn up to explore the Long Tunnel mine and other reminders of the days when 5000 miners briefly hacked out more gold than at any other field in the world.

Another side trip leads from Drouin towards Mt Baw Baw, where you'll find the wonderful Brandy Creek winery and restaurant – open weekends and public holidays for feasts of paella and churrascos.

Drive on for another 30 minutes and you'll come to the Yarragon Ale House. Currently stocking more than 400 local and imported beers, the shop is also Gippsland's largest homebrew store. Yarragon runs homebrew and beer appreciation classes twice a month. Owner John Greenwood also consults to the microbrewing industry.

■ STRZELECKI RANGES

The next major brewery on the Gippsland trail is one of the nation's most successful, the critically acclaimed Grand Ridge Brewery at Mirboo North. Find it by turning south at Trafalgar and heading into the Strzelecki Ranges.

Just past Thorpdale, the Grand Ridge Road snakes along the peaks of the south Gippsland hills. The grandeur applies to the ridge rather than the road, which is for the most part a winding byway with spectacular views down towards Wilsons Promontory and Bass Strait. And then, joy of joys, Mirboo North and its brewery complex.

The Grand Ridge Brewery has been in existence since 1987, when it opened and went into receivership within a year. Current owner Eric Walters and a consortium of friends bought the failed enterprise and almost immediately began winning awards, creating a demand which required them to build a second brewery.

Since then, a restaurant has flourished, together with accommodation that is in hot demand with visiting connoisseurs of fine beers. The current production line covers nine varieties including a couple of fiendishly strong numbers. They contrast with Moonlight, a mid-strength

Grand Ridge Brewery

Bullant Brewery

Ale that – almost a contradiction in terms – has won awards as Australia's Best Ale in consecutive years.

The Strzelecki Ranges form one side of the Latrobe Valley, which allegedly has enough brown coal to power Victoria for about 1000 years. It also has an intriguing orientation centre at Powerworks, on the Morwell coal field, which runs tours on Tuesdays and Thursdays. Cynics would say this is a major exercise in PR spin; most others find it a fascinating exploration of boilers, turbines, generators and an open-cut mine that is large enough to house a country town.

The highway leads through clusters of cooling towers, often used as visuals to represent pollution spewing into the atmosphere. In fact most of the clouds that billow from the vast structures are composed of little more than steam.

■ SALE

The next major centre on your run around Gippsland is Sale, which is officially classified a port despite being many kilometres from the sea. Confused? It's all thanks to a canal that leads to Australia's first swing bridge and then into the Gippsland Lakes, the nation's largest inland network of waterways.

All very interesting, but the main reason to come to Sale is a cosy restaurant called El Sombrero Mexican, where brewing graduate Martin Treasure makes his staple beer, an aromatic Brown Ale.

Martin describes his enterprise as a nano-brewery, and hopes soon to reach micro status: "I started SavaraIn Brewery in 2008, unsure of the market," says Martin. "Happily, the Brown Ale has been so well received that I've released a seasonal Amber Ale with plans to make it a permanent product. My Brown Ale is a solid session beer which appeals to many tastes so I'm bottling it later this year and may do the same with the Amber."

■ GREAT ALPINE ROAD

Our Gippsland road trip now takes us through Bairnsdale and away from the highway in the general direction of the Victorian snowfields. The next brewhouse is the well established Bullant Brewery at Bruthen, a whistlestop town on the Great Alpine Road. Although the population is only 600, Bruthen punches way above its weight in the culture stakes and community stakes, staging regular art exhibitions, monthly farmers' markets and an annual blues festival.

But pride of this is place is Bullant Brewery, the enterprise operated by longtime brewing enthusiasts Neil and Lois Triggs. After working as an architect for many years, Neil went back to the drawing boards to design the impressive brewery, which houses glowing copper brewhouses imported from Richmond, Virginia, USA, after the Richbrau Brewing Company went broke.

Current brews on tap in the sleek restaurant and bar include Mossiface Pale Ale, Bark Sheds Wheat Beer, Double Bridges IPA, Piano Bridge Stout and Pig & Whistle Brown Ale. Mossiface is on tap at the nearby Albion Hotel, Swifts Creek, and the Bullant bar also stocks guest brews including Mildura Honey Wheat, Mildura Stefano's Pilsner and Mildura Light, and in the past, Hargreaves Hill ESB. Also on tap is Kelly Brothers cider.

Around here, the Great Alpine Road starts to justify its name, with the high plains and ski resorts of Mt Hotham, Dinner Plain and Falls Creek coming nearer with every bend in the road. But before you decide whether to make this into a round trip 'over the top' or return on the faster Princes Highway route, you should definitely make a slight diversion and visit the ghost town Cassilis.

Specifically, you should visit the Mt Markey Winery & Lone Hand BrewHouse on the former wine palace site in the centre of town. It produces wine, mead and cider and since 2006, a Pale Ale as well.

"I dabbled with a small-brew system capable of producing between 20 to 40 cases of ale at a time," says owner Howard Reddish. "Now a 160L stainless-steel boiler/mash tun and a strainer/sparger knocked up from 360 stainless mesh seem an improvement from a plastic dustbin I used in the 1970s!"

John Greenwood, Yarragon Ale House

SavaraIn Brewery

Mt Markey Winery & Lone Hand BrewHouse

BREWERIES, DISTILLERY & WHERE TO BUY

Arctic Fox Brewery
Dandenong
www.arcticfox.com.au

Bacchus Distillery
132-142 Bangholme Rd,
Dandenong South
(03) 9706 6589
www.bacchus
distillery.com.au

Bullant Brewery
46 Main St, Bruthen
(03) 5157 5307
www.bullantbrewery.com

Coldwater Creek Tavern & Microbrewery
Chifley Doveton Hotel
Cnr Doveton Ave and
Princes Hwy, Doveton
(03) 9771 6000
www.chifleyhotels.com.au

Grand Ridge Brewery
Main St, Mirboo North
Tel: (03) 5668 2222
www.grand-ridge.com.au

Matilda Bay Garage Brewery
Dandenong South
www.matildabay.com

Mt Markey Winery & Lone Hand BrewHouse
1346 Cassilis Rd, Omeo
(03) 5159 4328

Savarain Brewery
El Sombrero
Mexican Restaurant
168 Raymond St, Sale
(03) 5143 1855
www.savarainbrewery.com.au

Yarragon Ale House
Lot 2, Rollo St, Yarragon
(03) 5634 2367

EVENTS

FEBRUARY
BeerFest Homebrewing Competition
Grand Ridge Brewery,
www.beerfest.org.au
Melbourne Brewers Home Brew Club's BeerFest is the longest-running competition of its kind in Australia, and attracts more than 200 entries from around the country.

Bruthen Blues and Arts Festival
Bruthen home.vicnet.net.au/~bruthen
Trucks In Action and

Civil Works Expo Lardner Park,
www.lardnerpark.com.au

MARCH
Farm World Lardner Park,
www.lardnerpark.com.au
The Jindi Harvest of Gippsland
Lardner Park, www.lardnerpark.com.au

JUNE/JULY
Great Alpine Roast
www.lardnerpark.com.au

AUGUST
East Gippsland Food Fair
Bairnsdale, www.egipps.vic.gov.au or 0409 549 453

VARIOUS
East Gippsland Farmers' Markets and Craft Markets
www.farmersmarkets.org.au or
www.discovereastgippsland.com.au

QUARTERLY
Pub Plays Australia Bullant Brewery,
www.pubplays.com

THINGS TO SEE AND DO

Long Tunnel mine, Walhalla. **Mt Baw Baw, Brandy Creek winery**, Drouin East. Thorpdale, **Wilsons Promontory and the Bass Strait view along Grand Ridge Road,** Gippsland hills, **Powerworks**, Latrobe Valley, www.powerworks.com.au. www.visitvictoria.com.

Select images from Milk Magazine Gippsland (www.themilkmag.com).

VIC

VIC

SOUTH WEST

The Twelve Apostles, one of the jewels in south-west Victoria's shining crown

Enjoy some of the state's finest brews in the country's most spectacular scenery. **By Laura MacIntosh**

When you hear the words 'weekend away' used in conjunction with 'south-west Victoria', then I wouldn't blame you for thinking of The Twelve Apostles, Bells Beach, and maybe a humpback whale or two if you can stretch your imagination. But if getting in touch with nature isn't really your thing, this corner of the country also offers some of the most sparkling of Ales in the whole of Victoria.

■ GEELONG & SURROUNDS

Believe it or not, there is more to this Bellarine city than AFL and elite private schools – only an hour from Melbourne lies the home of some of Victoria's most iconic watering holes.

In the heart of downtown Geelong lies the Scottish Chief's Tavern Brewery. Established in 1848 as the Scottish Chief's Inn, today it still stands as Australia's oldest *working* brewery. Scottish Chief's has Beacon Bitter and Beacon Pale Ale on tap, both from The Beacon Brewing Co, a Barwon Heads-established homebrew company. Brewer Dan Cunningham hopes to expand to a line of bottled specialty beers. Beacon currently operates out of Scottish Chief's, however this arrangement is soon to end, with the Tavern recently sold.

If you're looking for an attraction away from Geelong's hustle and bustle, head to Waurn Ponds and Pettavel Winery and Restaurant, or Anakie for Del Rios of Mt Anakie Winery (both 20-40 minutes from Geelong's inner-city hub).

■ BELLARINE

About half an hour south of Geelong is Bellarine Estate, which besides being home to great wine, fine food and a breathtaking function area, is the home of Bellarine Brewing Company. The Peninsula's only microbrewery,

Bellarine Estate and Bellarine Brewing Company

Forrest Brewing

Bellarine's signature brews include Queenscliff Ale, a honey-wheat Pale Ale, Lonsdale Lager, beer with a citrus twist, and Mussel Stout, the infamous Dark Ale brewed with Portarlington's Australian blue mussels.

Anytime is a great time to visit Bellarine Estate and Bellarine Brewing Company – both indoor and outdoor seating areas are available year-round for patrons hoping to avoid or make the most of Victoria's four seasons in one day. The cellar door is open for tastings between 11am and 4pm daily. While you're there, pick up some local produce to go with your beverage of choice. There's house-made Drysdale goats' cheese, 'screaming' seeds, olive oils, and much more.

Attached to the tasting room is a relaxed dining area, with views to the expanse of vineyards and the bay, where you can sample some of the region's best produce. It is a family-friendly environment, which sprawls out onto a vast lawn and has a sandpit for the littlies to play in.

If you can't make it down the Peninsula but still want to check out some of the Bellarine brews, a variety of Dan Murphy's, Vintage Cellars, Foodworks and IGA Liquor Stores across Melbourne and down the Surf Coast stock the Estate's brews, including in Ocean Grove, Torquay, St Leonards, Portarlington, Anglesea and Geelong.

■ FORREST

An approximate 1.5 hour drive from Bellarine Estate brings you to the township of Forrest, home to the newly-opened Forrest Brewing Company. Open four days a week (Thursday to Sunday), the Forrest Brewing Company is an independently owned microbrewery, specialising in handcrafted beers fresh from the hinterland of the Otways.

The crew at Forrest brews three types of beer – a Pale Ale, an Amber Ale, and a Kolsch. The signature beer is the Forrest Mountain Ale, and while its brews are presently only available on tap, they are due to be released in stubbies by July. Initially the stubbies will only be available from the Forrest Brewery's cellar door, but the company hopes to make them available through specialty beer sellers by spring or summer this year.

However, if you're looking for more than just a clean, crisp Ale during your visit to Forrest, the Forrest Brewing Company can provide a great day out that caters for the entire family, even the dog! The Forrest Brewhouse boasts a 50-seat restaurant that specialised in breakfast, lunch and dinner, as well as coffee and cake.

The warmer months are the best time to visit Forrest, where you can sit, brew in hand, soaking up the rays in the outdoor beer garden while the kids rummage through the seemingly bottomless toy box. And if you're not planning to stay overnight at one of the region's fantastic, boutique self-contained accommodation options, the Forrest Brewing Company also produces a range of non-alcoholic beverages, so you won't have to worry about getting pulled over by the boys in blue.

■ BARONGAROOK

From Forrest, head to Barongarook via Beech Forest to experience the amazing rainforest drive through Turtons Track. On your way view the many waterfalls and stop by for a forest walk.

Barongarook is ten minutes' drive south of Colac and home to the Otway Estate Winery & Brewery. Otway Estate are known for its range of Prickly Moses standard and specialist beers, including the Organic Lager, made from certified-organic hops, malt and pure Otway rainwater, and the 2008 silver medal-winning Summer Ale, with refreshing flavours of passionfruit, pineapple and citrus.

As well as four-and-a-half star self-contained spa cottages on site and a cafe serving superb meals (open all weekend), Otway Estate is a wannabe brewer's dream. The cellar door operates seven days a week, and Otway Estate provides an exclusive Prickly Moses Brewer's Experience. Participants can join a one- to three-day brewing course, where you can sample the Prickly Moses range accompanied by a four-course degustation menu, tour the brew house, and even make your own Prickly Moses brew. Otway Estate also has a fantastic range of house-made cordials available at the cafe.

Head Brewer Luke Scott, Otway Estate Winery & Brewery

Photography from Tourism Victoria, Visions of Victoria

Red Duck Provedore

Timboon Railway Shed Distillery

■ CAMPERDOWN

About 50 kilometres along the highway from the inland hub of Colac is Camperdown, home to Red Duck Beer. Although Red Duck's classy range of premium Ales have been available for sale through Victorian retailers for some time now, they are now available year round in the Red Duck Provedore. Seven days a week, Camperdown's main drag has the pleasure of offering beer aficionados and gourmands everything they could wish for in one place: the range of latest-release Red Duck Ales, fine wines, gourmet coffee, and sumptuous meals made from local produce.

Red Duck has a simple and classic range of quality beers. As well as its Pale, Amber and Bengal India Ales, the team brews a delicious Porter, as well an exclusive range of Red Duck Limited-Release Ales. And they're not kidding when they say 'limited' – only 500-litre batches of these Ales are ever brewed, and they are gobbled up like candy at Christmas. The best way to ensure you don't miss out on limited-release offerings such as the Burton, Golden Dragon, or The Ox (just to name a few previous ones), make sure you sign up to Red Duck's mailing list online.

■ TIMBOON

A trip down to south-west Victoria would be incomplete without a trip to the Timboon Railway Shed Distillery. Located about 20 minutes inland from the seaside town of Port Campbell, the Timboon Railway Shed Distillery is literally just that – a railway shed from the early 1900s that has been transformed into a distillery. You can taste and buy all of the Railway Shed's house-made spirits, from the Single Malt Whisky to the decadent Coffee Cream aperitif, at The Shed, although if your car is already fully stocked from your gourmet weekend away, you can also order the products online.

But if you have the time to put your single malt down for a second, Timboon is also a great place for a family getaway. The kids will love the locally made Timboon Fine Ice Cream, available all around town including at The Shed, while the adults will enjoy indulging on gourmet local produce at the Distillery's 140-seat restaurant, including local wines, as well as Prickly Moses and Red Duck beers. For the more outdoorsy types, the Distillery is situated at the foot of the famous Timboon Rail Trail walk and ride route. So whether it's basking outdoors in the summer rays or rugging up inside by the log fire, any time of year is a great time to visit the Railway Shed Distillery.

Although there is no on-site accommodation, Whiskey Villas Timboon or Anchors at Port Campbell are great locations for visitors to the Distillery to stay.

■ WARRNAMBOOL

If peacefully sipping a beer out of a dainty tulip glass is what you have in mind when you stop in at Warrnambool, then your expectations will be blown away at The Flying Horse Bar & Brewery. Opening in July 2008 on the site of a former service station and caravan park, the site, which has been affectionately known as the "Flying Horse" for the past 65 years due to the servo's former logo, is no stranger to raucousness.

The Flying Horse beers themselves are not backwards in coming forwards. From the award-winning, smooth Dirty Angel Stout, to the citrusy Whale Ale and tawny Savage Seagull, your experience at the Flying Horse is bound to be a unique one. The brewery's other in-house beers include the Wollaston Wheaty, a distinctive and unique combination of allspice, cloves, bananas, pear drops and bubble gum, the Lady Bar Lager, crafted specifically to drink with hot, spicy food, and the Billy Goat, which is pretty much like the beer drinkers' alternative to red wine.

And with an onsite microbrewery, TAB, sports bar, kids' room, restaurant and lounge bar, you'll want to bunk down for good!

Flying Horse Bar & Brewery

BREWERIES AND BEER COMPANIES

Beacon Brewing Co.
0417 544 542
www.beaconbrewingco.com

Bellarine Estate and Bellarine Brewing Co
2270 Portarlington Rd, Bellarine
(03) 5259 3310
www.bellarineestate.com.au

Forrest Brewing Co
Apollo Bay Rd, Forrest
(03) 5236 6170
www.forrestbrewing.com.au

Independent Distillers
50 Swann Dr, Laverton
(03) 8369 0300
www.independentdistillers.com

Otway Estate Winery & Brewery
10-30 Hoveys Rd, Barongarook
(03) 5233 8400
www.otwayestate.com.au

Port Pier Cafe
6 Pier Street
Portarlington
(03) 5259 1080

Red Duck Provedore
243 Manifold St, Camperdown
(03) 5593 3303
www.redduckbeer.com.au
Brewery located at 11a Michaels Drive, Alfredton (Ballarat). Open Monday to Friday 10am-3pm (other times by arrangement).

Scottish Chief's Tavern Brewery*
99 Corio St, Geelong
(03) 5223 1736
www.scottishchiefs.com.au
*Check if operating prior visit.

Southern Bay Brewing Company
80 Point Henry Rd, Moolap
1300 766 219
www.southernbay.com.au

The Flying Horse Bar & Brewery
Princes Hwy (cnr Mahoneys Rd and Raglan Pde), Warrnambool
(03) 5562 2254
www.theflyinghorse.com.au

Timboon Railway Shed Distillery
The Railway Yard, Bailey St, Timboon
(03) 5598 3555
www.timboondistillery.com

EVENTS

JANUARY
Royal Geelong Show Geelong, **Pier to Pub Swim** Lorne, **Apollo Bay Show** and **Food & Wine Festival** Apollo Bay, **Custom Car & Bike Show** Colac, **Grand Annual Sprintcar Classic** Warrnambool

FEBRUARY
Australian International Airshow Avalon Airport, **Otway Odyssey Mountain Bike Event and Forrest Festival** Apollo Bay, **Great Ocean Sports Festival** Apollo Bay, **Wood, Wine & Roses Festival** Heywood

MARCH
Victorian Surf Life-Saving Championships Apollo Bay **Apollo Bay Music Festival** Apollo Bay, **Port Fairy Folk Festival** Port Fairy, **Lara Food and Wine Festival** Bellarine Peninsula

APRIL
Rip Curl Pro World Surfing Titles Bells Beach, Torquay

MAY
Great Ocean Road Marathon Lorne to Apollo Bay, **Warrnambool Racing Carnival and Grand Annual Steeplechase** Warrnambool

JUNE
National Celtic Festival Portarlington

JULY
Fun4Kids Festival Warrnambool

SEPTEMBER
Angair Wildflower and Art Show Anglesea

OCTOBER
Spring Music Festival Port Fairy **Glenelg River Fishing Competition** Nelson

NOVEMBER
Toast to the Coast Geelong **Portland Bay Festival** Portland

DECEMBER
Rock to Ramp Ocean Swim Anglesea **High Tide Festival** Torquay

THINGS TO SEE AND DO & PLACES TO STAY

Pettavel Winery and Restaurant, Waurn Ponds, **Del Rios of Mt Anakie Winery**, **Rail Trail walk and ride route**, Timboon. **Whiskey Villas** Timboon, **Anchors at Port Campbell**. **Turtons Track**, http://www.gdaypubs.com.au/pubtrails/turtonstrack.html.

VIC

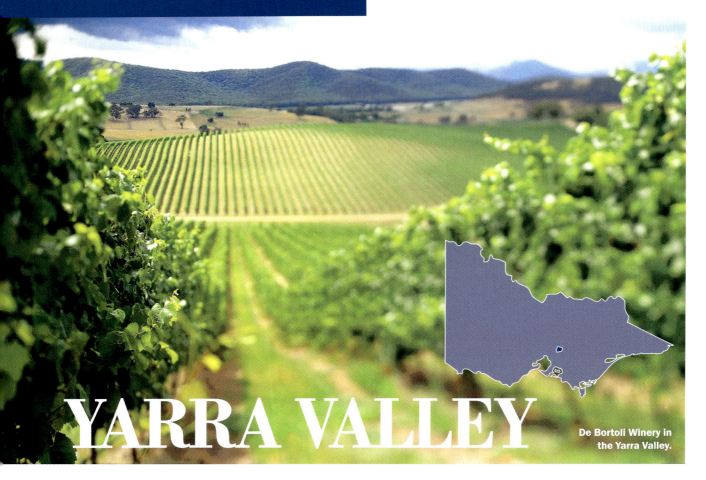

De Bortoli Winery in the Yarra Valley.

YARRA VALLEY

If you thought the Yarra Valley was all about wine, think again. Boutique breweries and innovative cider-makers are leading a changing of the guard in this hotbed of gourmet produce.

By Helen Alexander

It might boast more than 120 wineries, producing some of Australia's award-winning bottles of chardonnay, pinot noir and shiraz, but Victoria's Yarra Valley is also home to a number of excellent breweries that showcase the variety, quality and ingenuity of Australia's boutique beer makers.

■ TAKING ON THE TASTE TRAIL

Three easy-to-navigate highways connect the handful of towns in the region, and the Coldstream Brewery in Coldstream is a good place to kick off a weekend away. The steady flow of punters entering the welcoming red-brick building on the Maroondah Highway means the brewery is almost always bursting at the seams, with bartenders frantically filling shot glasses and sharing tasting notes.

Opened by DIY-enthusiast turned professional brewer Alan Harding and a group of friends in 2007, highlights here include the Naked Ale – an aromatic Golden Ale made with Fuggles and East Kent Goldings hops – as well as rotating seasonal brews, including the six-malt Spring Lager and

Coldstream Brewery's tasting card

Buckley's little bottlers

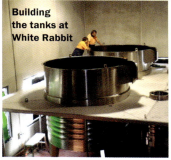
Building the tanks at White Rabbit

White Rabbit Brewery

creamy Autumn Porter. Take a tour of this impressive microbrewery (Wednesday-Saturday 11am-11pm, Sunday 11am-10pm) and stick around for dinner (if you can bag a table amid the merry-making).

Next, head north along the Melba Highway to Yarra Glen and the Hargreaves Hill Brewing Company. Here, confidently executed European-style draught and bottled offerings keep locals and visitors propping up the bar long after they have worked their way though the $8 tasting paddle. Open Monday-Saturday from 11.30am, Sunday from 8.30am.

Housed in a historic bank building and serving a refined restaurant menu, brewer Simon Walkenhorst's six craft beers (produced at the family-run microbrewery in Steels Creek) range from the clove, nutmeg and vanilla flavours of a Hefeweizen to the lively unfiltered Pilsner Kellerbier and the hefty 7.5% ABV kick administered by the Abbey Dubbel.

■ HEALESVILLE HAUNTS

On an industrial estate off Healesville's increasingly chic main drag, Buckley's Beer offers a slightly more no-thrills

Hargreaves Hill Brewing Company

approach to the cellar door experience – although one of the small, friendly team will whip up a pizza on request.

Forget design-led premises and flashy marketing, nothing gets in the way of brewer John O'Callaghan's quest for perfection. Unfazed by what others might see as significant local competition, his focus on quality over quantity has seen the brewery's repertoire of two Lagers and two Ales go from strength to strength, and the warehouse operation leads the way when it to green credentials as the first solar-boosted microbrewery in the region.

Make sure you try a Buckley's Dark Bock while you're there. This flavourful take on Germany's Dunkel (dark lager) is made with a mix of six different grains in the mash. The Golden Pilsner 'Pilz', originally conceived for daughter Lucy's wedding celebrations, is a winner too. Open Saturday and Sunday 11am-5pm.

Feeling inspired? Enthusiastic homebrewers should head to nearby Brewer's Choice for owner Colin Penrose's extensive selection of brewing supplies and bottle shop. Open Monday to Friday, 9am-5.30pm, Saturdays, 9am-1pm.

From small-scale charm to the super-slick operation... A tour of the Yarra Valley's

Brewer's Choice Home Brew Shop

Healesville Sanctuary

The Kelly brothers employ winemaking techniques in their cider production

breweries would not be complete without a lazy Sunday afternoon spent lounging in one of the comfy armchairs at the cavernous White Rabbit brewery, where buzzing bar and experimentation lab sit side by side against a backdrop of giant stainless-steel tanks. The little sister to Fremantle's popular Little Creatures label (also available here), White Rabbit produces two bottlings – the fresh fruity aromas of the Cloudy White Ale offer a tempting prelude to flavourful notes of coriander, bitter orange and juniper berry; the addition of local honey naturally conditions the Ale. While the Dark Ale's contradictory mix of malt-driven richness and refreshingly aromatic hops is a result of the company's self-proclaimed "fermentation with imagination", a comforting reassurance that however big this place becomes it will hopefully continue to innovate and invent. Open Sunday, Monday, Thursday 12-5pm, Friday and Saturday 12-7pm.

Unashamedly appealing to the masses, however, is the Innocent Bystander/Giant Steps building next door. Grab a glass to sip and slurp your way through premium vinous offerings, or linger a while longer to immerse yourself fully in this on-site foodie extravaganza – gourmet pizzas, artisan bakery and cheese room. For the designated driver, they serve a decent cup of coffee, too. If your little ones are getting restless, take a trip to Healesville Sanctuary, where they can make like a wildlife ranger and get up close to koalas, snakes and kangaroos.

■ GRAPES ARE NOT THE ONLY FRUIT

Wild Cattle Creek

Just as Yarra Valley brewers are constantly honing their craft, a handful of the region's wine producers have turned their attention to cider making. With around 150 hectares of orchards on their doorstep Behn Payten, the guy behind Punt Road Wines' Napoleone & Co cider label, believes it was the logical step forward. Today, Behn's handcrafted apple and pear ciders are sold at bars and bottle shops nationwide, while a sparkling cider was recently trialled at the cellar door. The verdict was unanimous. Make more. Open daily 10am-5pm.

But when it comes to zingy Champagne-style ciders, the Kellys of Wonga Park have been leading the way for years. With their first commercial release in 1969 brothers Phil and Gus currently shift up to 400 cases a year, in addition to smaller 330ml bottles of sparkling cider. Applying wine know-how to cider making, they use the same traditional hand-finished Méthode Champenoise that is applied to winery Kellybrook's pinot noir-chardonnay sparkling wine. The result? Lively bubbles and crisp apple flavours that stay true to the source fruit. Cellar door open Monday-Saturday 10am-5pm, Sunday 11am-5pm.

■ GREAT GRUB

In between tours and tastings, check out the region's artisan food scene and visit Yarra Valley Dairy and nibble on some of its much-coveted cheeses, or simply delight in the local produce used in the posh pub grub served at Healesville's charming hotel. While a number of wineries have high-end restaurants on site, mid-range options abound, such as Train Trak winery's Italian eatery Zonzo, housed in a huge conservatory with stunning views over surrounding vineyards.

When it comes to bedding down, the options are endless, from family-run B&Bs to luxury lodgings at five-star Balgownie Estate. For the best of both worlds, Wild Cattle Creek winery's self-contained villas offer a super-plush home from home in Seville, while the friendly hosts at the cellar door make it easy to pass a few hours with a glass in hand. Be sure to include a few of the region's wineries in your itinerary. For a real grape fix, visit in October for the Shedfest Wine Festival.

Behn Payten of Napoleone & Co taste tests his cider

BREWERIES, CIDER & HOMEBREW

Brewer's Choice
1389 Healesville Rd,
Woori Yallock
(03) 5964 6222
www.brewerschoice.net.au

Buckley's Beer
30 Hunter Rd, Healesville
0408 354 909
www.buckleysbeer.com.au

Coldstream Brewery
694 Maroondah Hwy,
Coldstream
(03) 9739 1794
www.coldstreambrewery.com.au

Hargreaves Hill Brewing Company
25 Bell St, Yarra Glen
(03) 9730 1905
www.hargreaveshill.com.au

Kellybrook Winery and Kelly Brothers Cider Co.
Fulford Road, Wonga Park
(03) 9722 1304
www.kellybrookwinery.com.au

Punt Road Wines and Napoleone & Co Cider
10 St Huberts Rd,
Coldstream
(03) 9739 0666
www.puntroadwines.com.au

White Rabbit Brewery
316 Maroondah Hwy,
Healesville; (03) 5962 6516
www.whiterabbitbeer.com.au

BREWERY TOURS

Take a tour of the Yarra Valley, Mornington Peninsula, Melbourne or the Macedon Rangers on a guided brewery tour via Aussie Brewery Tours, 1300 787 039 or www.aussiebrewerytours.com.au.

EVENTS

APRIL/MAY
Kellybrook Cider Festival

SEPTEMBER
Yarra Valley Grape Run

Father's Day at Tokar Estate
www.tokarestate.com.au

OCTOBER
Melba Festival
Shedfest Wine Festival

OCTOBER-MARCH
Summer Jazz at Seville
Seville Hill Winery, Seville
(03) 5964 3284
www.sevillehill.com.au

NOVEMBER
Open Garden Weekend
Warratina Lavender Farm,
105 Quayle Rd, Wandin,
Yallock; (03) 5964 4650
www.warratinalavender.com.au

THINGS TO SEE AND DO

Balgownie Estate Yarra Glen, www.balgownieestate.com.au. **Healesville Sanctuary** Healesville, www.zoo.org.au. **Wild Cattle Creek** Seville, www.wildcattlecreek.com.au. **Yarra Valley Dairy** Yering, www.yvd.com.au. **Zonzo at Train Trak** Yarra Glen, www.zonzo.com.au.

Beer & Brewer promotion   VICTORIA – MELBOURNE

2 BROTHERS BREWERY & BEERHALL

2 Brothers Brewery and Beerhall may be one of Bayside Melbourne's best kept secrets. Complimented by simple beer food, 2 Brothers ales and lagers are served directly from brite beer tanks which form a stunning backdrop to the bar. The Beerhall is a watering-hole cherished by locals and beer lovers alike.

The judges at the Australian International Beer Awards like the beer too - awarding the brewery the title of "Best Victorian Beer" for two years running (2010 – Voodoo Baltic Porter, 2011 – Guvnor Extra Strong Ale). If you're in the neighbourhood, stop by for a beer with the two brothers, Andrew and Dave.

4 Joyner St
Moorabbin
Tel: (03) 9553 1177
www.2brothers.com.au

Opening hours:
Thurs 4.00pm – 10.00pm
Fri-Midday – midnight
Live music both nights

MOUNTAIN GOAT BREWERY

Mountain Goat started out as Dave's backyard home brew project. Cam came back from OS in 1995 inspired by the craft beer movement in Canada and hatched a cunning plan with Dave to get Mountain Goat out of Dave's backyard. Today the boys craft their ales in an old warehouse in the back streets of Richmond (Melbourne) and distribute them in bottle and keg around the country The regular beers are Hightail Ale and Organic Steam Ale plus the specialty Rare Breed releases in 640ml bottles.

80 North St
Richmond
Tel: (03) 9428 1180
www.goatbeer.com.au

The brewery opens to public on Wednesday nights from 5 - 10pm (with a free tour at 6:30pm weekly) and Fridays from 5pm - 11:30pm.

AUSSIE BREWERY TOURS

Australia produces great beer. That's a fact. A lesser known fact is that Australia produces a great VARIETY of beer, some of which is considered the best in the world. Aussie Brewery Tours are passionate about showcasing Australia's finest beer and invite you to join us as we visit Australia's finest breweries.

On tour you will sample styles you know and love, some you've never heard of as well as some weird and wonderful creations that are yet to be named! Throw in some amazing food, a few laughs, an iconic Aussie pub (or two), some unbeerlievable stories from your guides and you have all the ingredients for a great day.

Aussie Brewery Tours are always fun, friendly and relaxed as we believe that's the ONLY way to enjoy a beer.•
Meet & chat with Australia's best brewers

- Visit iconic Australian pubs
- Tasting paddles, beer and lunch included
- Learn how beer is made first hand on the brewery floor
- Create your perfect day out with our different tour configurations, visiting Yarra Valley, Mornington Peninsula, Melbourne or the Macedon Rangers
- Our expert guides are always fun and friendly
- Great for buck's parties, birthdays, club and corporate functions

Tel: 1300 787 039
info@aussiebrewerytours.com.au
www.aussiebrewerytours.com.au
Skype: aussie.brewery.tours

Aussie Brewery Tours is a Brewhopper Group product.

YOUNG & JACKSON HOTEL

Y&J's has a long and proud association with beer since opening its doors in 1861.

It has been the flagship for Australia's most exciting brews and continues to showcase Australia's best craft breweries and their range.

Y&J's provides a rich historical culture in the provision, service and characters of beer.

This is as big as it gets!

The History of Beer and Young & Jackson

1861 – John Thomas Toohey - Original Licensee
Several years later made the move to Surry Hills Sydney to establish The Standard Brewery where the Tooheys brand was born.

1888 – Fosters
The Fosters brothers choose Young and Jackson as the first pub to sell their revolutionary lager.

1875-1914 – Henry Figsby Young - Licensee
Established the Melbourne Co operative Brewing Company in 1904 due to Hotelier's concerns at the rising cost of beer produced by existing breweries. The Co op was sold in 1924 and Henry Figsby joined the board of directors at CUB.

1914 – Stephen Morell - Licensee
Established the Abbotsford Brewery and became Mayor of Melbourne in 1926.

1986 – Bond Corporation
The Brewery Division of the Bond Corporation purchase freehold of Y&Js.

1998 – Fosters
The Fosters Brewing Company purchase freehold of Y&J's.

Current Day

Craft Beer & Cider
Since 1998 Young and Jackson has had a vested interest in craft beer which started with the Matilda Bay brand. Today Y&J's showcases 30 beers and nine ciders on tap with it's focus being Australian Craft.

Showcase Brewery Bar

Each year Y&J's celebrates the re birth of craft brewing, showcasing six of Australia's best independent breweries. Each brewery is represented over a month providing four to eight of their best house and seasonal brews or limited release batches on tap. Y&J's also provides the rare opportunity for customers to share an intimate dinner with each head brewer as they take them on a five course dinner journey of epic proportions, matching the meals with five beers as they tell stories of their humble beginnings, crusade and of course love of beer!

'Meet the brewer' evenings are also held from Chloe's bar where the brewers offer complimentary samples of their range in an open forum.

B.C Fest "Before Cider there was Beer"

The annual Australia Beer & Cider Festival hosts up to ten different craft breweries and cider producers from around Oz! $15 a ticket gives you 20 samples and opens the door to a world that includes a portfolio of over 50 of Australia's finest craft beer and ciders to choose from. Live entertainment with great cider and beer food are provided as the festival continues into the early hours.

Cider Bar

'Australia's first and only Cider Bar'
Nine Australian craft & international ciders on tap; more than 25 bottled varieties to choose from - traditional scrumpy blended on site and served from a french oak barrel and choice of four hot mulled ciders including our own house brew- 'Warm Apple Pie'. In an outdoor garden bar, it is the ideal place to relax and unwind.

Other Crafty Ambitions

Rotational Taps - Limited and Seasonal Release and New Brews
Seasonal Beer Lists
Beer Food Menus
Signature Food & Beer Dishes

1 Swanston St
Melbourne
Tel: (03) 9650 3884
www.youngandjackson.com.au

Opening hours:
Mon-Thurs 10.00am – midnight
Fri 10.00am – 3.00am
Sat 9.00am – 3.00am
Sun 9.00am – midnight

Beer & Brewer promotion   VICTORIA – MELBOURNE

BREW CELLAR DISTRIBUTION

BREW Cellar Distribution is an Australian owned national distributor to the home brewing specialty stores.

Representing such iconic brands as Morgan's, Coopers, Samuel Willard's, Ellerslie Hop and their own BREW Cellar branded products. BREW Cellar have the right products and advice for absolute beginners and experienced brewers alike.

If you have never tried brewing your own before you can't go past the popular BREW Cellar 23 litre micro brewery starter kit with everything you need to brew a great tasting beer right in the box – and you get to tell your friends you own a brewery!

Visit their website and use the store locator to find the BREW Cellar stockist closest to you and start brewing today!

Tel: 1300 882 143
www.brewcellar.com.au

GRAIN AND GRAPE

Australia's leading supplier of all grain brewing equipment and ingredients to homebrewers.

Winner of the inaugural 2010 Beer & Brewer Peoples Choice Award as Best Home Brew Shop in Australia.

Grain, hops, pure yeast available from Australia and all over the world. Supplier of Wyeast liquid yeast cultures to breweries and homebrewers.

Importer and Distributor of the Braumeister automated Brewing System. Available in 20 and 50L sizes for homebrewers and 200L for small breweries, bars and cafes.

Stockist of a great range of local & imported beers.

Free twice monthly All Grain Brewing demonstrations. They also make their own line of fresh wort kits at Mountain Goat Brewery.

5/280 Whitehall St
Yarraville
Tel: (03) 9687 0061
www.grainandgrape.com.au

Opening hours:
Mon-Fri 10.00am – 5.30pm
Sat 9.00am - 1.00pm

JAMES SQUIRE BREWHOUSE

The James Squire Brewhouse showcases the experience, life and times of James Squire. The Brewhouse offers the entire Squire range and is Melbourne CBD's only working micro-brewery producing handcrafted ales brewed on site as well as those brewed by the Malt Shovel Brewery.

The Brewhouse is a place for beer lovers. It has everything from crisp easy drinking lagers to big hoppy craft ales with great traditional pub food to match. The easy going traditional pub environment and friendly knowledgeable staff make for the perfect beer drinking experience whether you are just in for a quiet pint or wish to learn more about the inner workings of an operational microbrewery.

Visitors can enjoy one of the Brewhouse's famous six beer tasting paddles with accompanying tasting notes and join one of their guides into the brewery itself to learn all about how beer is crafted from the grain mill to the tap.

Brewhouse award winning original brews include; the Portland Pale Australian style Pale Ale; The Highwayman thrice hopped Red Ale; The Craic traditional Irish Stout and the Speculator robust hop heavy American Pale Ale.

The Brewhouse is open from 11am every day except Christmas so those in search for good full flavoured craft beer will always have this little piece of beer drinking heaven to come to.

Portland Hotel incorporating the James Squire Brewhouse

127 Russell St
Melbourne
Tel: (03) 9810 0064
www.portlandhotel.com.au

Opening hours:
11.00am every day except Christmas

Beer & Brewer promotion   VICTORIA – MELBOURNE

THE FOX HOTEL

A facelift never looked so good as in the case of The Fox Hotel. A grimy pub turned modern eatery; this Collingwood haunt now boasts a first-rate selection of food, beer and wine as well as a rooftop beer garden, that is arguably one of Melbourne's best, for the perfect weekend (or weeknight) drinks.

Unique and cosy, The Fox is designed to instantly make people feel at ease and the welcoming vibe is highlighted by a cast of versatile and colourful clientele. The kitchen is open every night of the week and group bookings and functions are welcome.

Beer is revered at The Fox and this is reflected in a beer list that is designed to give customers a real experience and sample a wide range of styles. Beginning with the best of Australian microbreweries, the list presents outstanding examples of Lagers, Ales and Stouts from around the world. The wine list has also been carefully selected to showcase the best of local varietals and also incorporates award winners from around the globe.

The kitchen at The Fox offers an extensive menu of pub treats and daily specials whilst also incorporating vegan, vegetarian and children's options. Sourcing the best of fresh local produce, The Fox is committed to presenting interesting, delicious meals with a distinctly Australian twist.

A great talking point in the pub is The Fox's collection of 5000 plus beer cans and bottles. Some are the same, some are one offs, some prototypes that never made the shelves, there are cans from all over the world. The most valuable item is a numbered Guinness bottle limited edition for the Queen in 1953 - 54 commemorating a royal visit, the bottle is etched with the crown of St James Gate. Other collectables include a Tenant's Lager Penny set 1976-81, which is the most commented on, TAA Airbus collection, Japanese beer cans, a Duff can that people always want, South Africa Lion set that seems to be in demand, and the premiership AFL cans are very popular.

Alongside an eclectic line up of DJ's, The Fox also has a weekly, rotating roster of live music with a commitment to showcasing the best of local up and coming talent.

351 Wellington St
Collingwood
Tel: (03) 9416 4957
www.thefoxhotel.com.au
thefoxhotel@gmail.com

Opening hours:
Mon-Thurs 3.00pm – late
Fri-Sun 12.00pm – 1.00am
Kitchen: Mon-Thurs 5.00pm – 10.00pm
Fri-Sun 12.00pm – 10.00pm

Beer & Brewer promotion   VICTORIA

BRIDGE ROAD BREWERS

Experience unique hand crafted beers whilst they are being brewed under your nose. The brewery, the bar, and its pizza restaurant are all located in a 150 year old coach house and stables. Picturesque Beechworth is located in Victorian high country at the foothills of the alps. The brewery is a great spot to enjoy lunch, with a large beer garden and children's play area.

Brewer/Founder, Ben Kraus, lives and breathes beer, he is constantly tweaking his huge range of ales, currently 12, or creating new ones to make sure they're up there with the best on offer. There's even a great list of local wines, and great locally roasted coffee.

The Old Coach House
Ford St, Beechworth
Tel: (03) 5728 2703
www.bridgeroadbrewers.com.au

Opening hours:
NOW OPEN - 7 DAYS
Mon & Tue 11.00am – 4.00pm
Wed & Thurs 11.00am – 5.00pm
Fri & Sat 11.00am – 6.00pm
Sun 11.00am – 8.00pm
Lunch Wed-Sun 12.00 – 3.00pm
Dinner Sun nights only

BRIGHT BREWERY

Bright Brewery uses fresh mountain water from the Ovens River, flowing right past the brewery, local ingredients and craft brewing techniques to create their award-winning range of Mountain Crafted beers.

The beer is poured straight from the impressive tanks lined up behind the bar, and you can join a weekly Tour-and-Tasting or even get hands-on as Brewer For A Day.

At this picturesque river-side brewery in the heart of Bright, you can relax with a tasting board of the six regular beers and the ever-changing Brewer's Choice range of seasonal beers. Or you can choose a local wine, light meal or a coffee.

Sunday afternoon live music and free WiFi complete the must-visit experience.

121 Great Alpine Road
Bright
Tel: (03) 5755 1301
www.brightbrewery.com.au

Opening hours:
Open daily, 12 noon till evening

HICKINBOTHAM WINERY & BREWERY

The Hickinbotham family is now making headlines with its new range of beers brewed at the Dromana winery and brewery. Brewing started in 2006 with 30 litre experimental batches, with the brew size growing to 600 litres in 2010.

Entry into the Australian International Beer Awards in May 2011 awarded Hix Pale Ale the top gold medal in the American Pale ale section, and a Bronze medal for the Brown Ale.

All Hix beers use all natural ingredients to reflect their true styles. The range includes Pilsner, Pale Ale, Brown Ale (also available in bottle) and Irish Stout with seasonal beers available on tap which change regularly.

194 Nepean Highway
Dromana
Tel: (03) 5981 0355
www.hickinbotham.biz

Trading Hours
Cellar Door 11.00am – 5.00pm Daily
Events and Functions up to 100 guests
Beer tastings and appreciation by appointment

SWEETWATER BREWING COMPANY

Based in the beautiful town of Mount Beauty where the Kiewa River emerges from steep mountain valleys. Kiewa means 'sweetwater' in the language of the original indigenous visitors to the region and the Brewery has adopted this name in recognition of the history of the area and the important part the pure clear mountain water plays in the beer brewed. The brewer aims to produce beers where the flavours of the malt, hops and yeast are allowed to shine through and enhance the mountain water.

The Brewery Bar provides beer lover's the opportunity to enjoy beer fresh from the brewery in one of Victoria's most beautiful locations.

Simmonds Creek Rd
Tawonga South
Tel/Fax: (03) 5754 1881
www.sweetwaterbrewing.com.au

Opening hours:
Fri-Sun noon – 5:00pm
Check website for seasonal changes

Beer & Brewer promotion   VICTORIA – SOUTH EAST

GRAND RIDGE BREWERY

Set in the picturesque Strzelecki Ranges you'll find one of Gippsland's best kept secrets. Driving through the quiet town of Mirboo North you can't miss the Grand Ridge Brewery, at the end of the main street you're welcomed by an oversized pot of beer and get the feeling you've reached the end of a rainbow.

Set in an original 1920's butter factory, this modern yet beautifully rustic building houses the Brewery, Restaurant, Bar and function space for up to 120 people. You can even pull up a stool and watch the boys hard at work from the glass panelled viewing area.

The freshly renovated bar has been crafted from stunning local timbers and Jarrah with copper taps suspended from the roof and pouring all the favourite Grand Ridge beers. Sit down at the bar with a Gippsland Gold and get lost in the explosion of hops and malt, the perfect winter warmer.

In the restaurant the friendly staff make you feel like part of the Grand Ridge family. 'Man Sized' plates of beautiful food are served, the steak from their own beef farm is sensational and desserts are to die for. It's no surprise their menu has been awarded as one of Victoria's best.

The accommodation is a renovated Edwardian cottage just a few short steps / stumbles across the road. Room features include a fridge stacked with eggs, bacon, tomato and beverages, plus a crackling open fire. The Hatlifter Stout and Moonshine will keep you warm all night.

The brewery has won over 150 international medals, as well as the Australian title in every category of beer at the National Festival of Beers. This trip is a must do adventure for those with the finest of palates for beer, wine, cuisine and all things tasty.

P.S. Don't forget the specialty cheeses; they are as stunning as the beers!

1 Baromi Rd, Mirboo North
Restaurant & Accommodation enquiries: (03) 5668 2222
Wholesale Beer Orders: 0419 303 488
www.grandridgebeer.com.au

Opening hours:
Bar 11.00am – late 7 days
Restaurant Wed-Sun Lunch 12.00pm – 3.00pm &
Dinner 6.00pm – 9.00pm
Open 7 days during holiday periods & on public holidays

Beer & Brewer promotion   VICTORIA – SOUTH EAST

COLDWATER CREEK MICROBREWERY

Beer is good for the soul. Local beer is even better for the soul. Beer brewed meters from where you consume it is virtually instant access to heaven.

The Coldwater Creek Microbrewery has just served it's 10th brew, Red Raw. Preceded by seven Pilsners and two American Pale Ale's the microbrewery has come a long way from its thirsty wait for the very first brew in early 2010.

Located in Doveton the microbrewery boasts 32 bottled beers, 8 tap beers, wood fire pizza's and an extensive menu to please every palate. With live music on Friday's and happy hour from 4pm-7pm you don't have to venture far for the freshest beer in the South East.

Chifley Doveton
Corner Doveton Avenue & Princes Highway, Doveton
Tel: (03) 9771 6000
reservations.doveton@chifleyhotels.com
www.chifleyhotels.com.au/dandenong/chifley-doveton-hotel

Opening hours:
Daily from 5.00pm – 11.00pm

SAVARA IN BREWERY

Possibly Victoria's smallest brewery, Savara In operates out of El Sombrero Mexican Restaurant in Sale, East Gippsland.

A family business stemming from a passion for quality ingredients, producing a single, hand crafted Brown Ale on draught. Savara In's Brown Ale is the first beer to be released for this brewery, it has a rich aromatic smell with earthy undertones and its flavour is rich and smooth, with the right amount of bitterness.

There are big plans for this "nano-brewery" with the bottling machine coming on-line in 2011 and a planned expansion into the greater Melbourne area later in the year.

168 Raymond St
Sale
Tel: (03) 5143 1855
www.savarainbrewery.com.au

Opening hours:
Thurs-Sat 6.00pm – 9.00pm

BULLANT BREWERY

Bullant Brewery Bruthen was opened in 2011 and is located on the Great Alpine Road in Bruthen only 15 minutes from Bairnsdale in East Gippsland.

The Brewery provides the opportunity for visitors and locals to experience locally made beers and excellent restaurant quality food sourced from local producers. Whether a snack or a meal, the beautiful setting allows visitors to dine indoors or outside on the expansive deck overlooking the Tambo Valley and Rail Trail right on its doorstep.

Bullant beers are designed to match their menu just like wine, but they are equally enjoyable as a solely refreshing beverage.

There are eight beers on tap including the Mossiface Pale Ale, Bark Sheds Wheat Beer, Piano Bridge Stout, Pig & Whistle Brown Ale as well as seasonal beers, guest beers and apple cider. Take home your favourite drop in their 640ml bottles or 5 litre party kegs.

The centrepiece is the brewhouse itself, sourced from Richmond Virginia USA, which has a copper clad mash tun and kettle with 4 jacketed uni-tanks used for fermentation and two bright beer tanks. The brewhouse can be viewed through large, wide windows, so, sit, sip and ponder the wonders of beer making.

Feel welcome to visit and experience the Bullant Brewery Bruthen – the home of '**beer with bite**'.

46 Main Street
Bruthen
Tel: (03) 5157 5307
www.bullantbrewery.com

Opening hours:
Wed 11.00am – 5.00pm
Thurs-Sun & Public Holidays
11.00am – 10.00pm

Beer & Brewer promotion   VICTORIA – YARRA VALLEY

BREWER'S CHOICE

Brewers Choice has been open for 6 years. Predominantly servicing the home brewers of Australia. They are very proud of their customer service that they believe to be second to none.

The owner, Colin Penrose has been involved in home brewing for nearly 30 years. He is a regular contributer to Beer & Brewer magazine and started the National Home Brewers Competition in 1995.

Apart from "Make Your Own" beer, wine, spirits, sausages, jerky, chocolates and yoghurt they also stock a range of imported beers from UK, Germany and Belgium.

1389 Healesville Rd
Woori Yallock
Tel: (03) 5964 6222
www.brewerschoice.net.au

Order online

Opening hours:
5 days 9.00am – 5.00pm
Sat 9.00am – 1.00pm

HARGREAVES HILL BREWING COMPANY

Hargreaves Hill commenced brewing in 2004, as owners Simon Walkenhorst and Beth Williams decided Victoria's Yarra Valley was the perfect place to produce an eclectic range of beers. A brewery was set up on Beth's family property, and the journey began.

In 2007, Hargreaves Hill opened a cellar door, bar and restaurant in the historic Colonial State Bank in Yarra Glen, and the award winning ales and lagers can be savoured with perfectly matched food – perhaps a hearty rib eye steak with an ESB, or Spring Bay Mussels with an Abbey Dubbel. The courtyard is great for a tasting paddle on a summer's afternoon, and the open fires roar in the cooler months. Stout anyone?

25 Bell Street
Yarra Glen
Tel: (03) 9730 1905
info@hargreaveshill.com.au

Opening hours:
Mon-Sat 11.30am – late
Sun 8.30am – 4.30pm

NAPOLEONE & CO CIDER

The Napoleone Family have been orchardists in the Yarra Valley since 1948. They planted their first vineyards in 1983 and have since become highly regarded for their Yarra Valley wines under the Punt Road label.

In 2008, Punt Road applied its winemaking skills in a new direction, producing a range of Napoleone & Co. ciders made with fruit from the Napoleone's own local orchards.

Their cider production is much closer to that of sparkling wine than traditional cider making. Using only 100% Yarra Valley fruit and no concentrates, all ciders are fermented using Champagne yeast and are produced in regular, fresh, small batches. The current range includes an apple & pear cider, along with a small-batch Methode Traditionelle pear sparkling.

When visiting the Punt Road and Napoleone & Co Cellar Door, you'll be greeted by their friendly staff offering a complete and relaxing tasting experience. With plenty of room for the kids to run around, you and your friends can also enjoy a fun game of Pétanque, a casual barbecue and indulge in a wide variety of local produce.

The team bring together a wealth of experience and a passion that is reflected in every one of their products.

10 St Huberts Road
Coldstream
Tel: (03) 9739 0666
wine@puntroadwines.com.au
www.napoleonecider.com.au

Opening hours:
Cellar door 10.00am – 5.00pm daily
Open 7 days a week

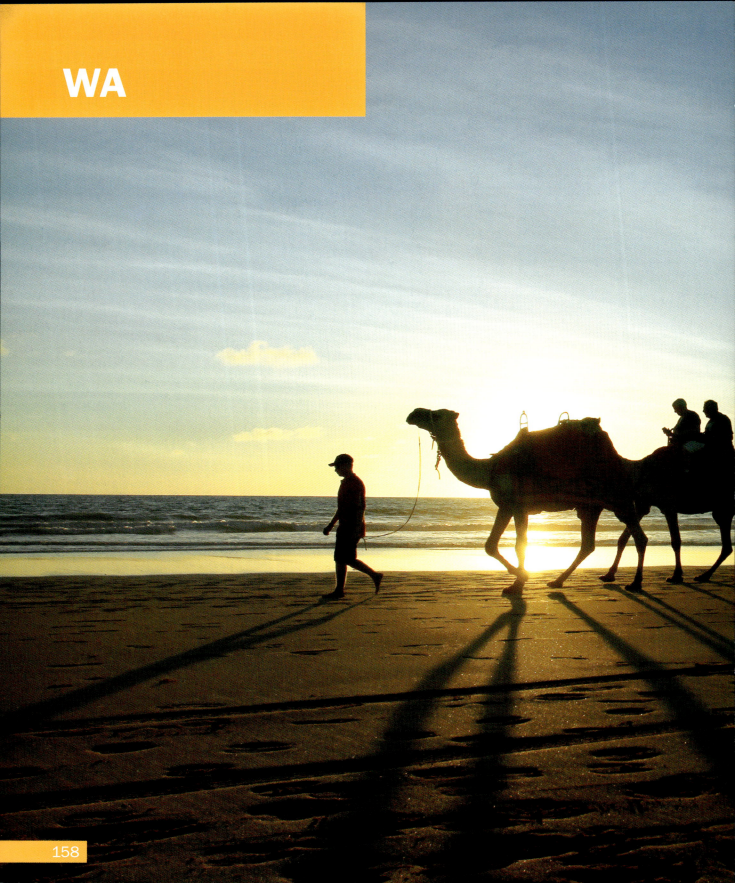
WA

WESTERN AUSTRALIA

Australia's largest state is recognised with the birth of craft beer in Fremantle, at the Sail & Anchor. With 33 breweries and one beer company, WA produces world-class beers in a varied landscape that even offers camel trekking.

Photo: Sunset camel trek on Cable Beach, Broome, courtesy Tourism WA.

WA

WA

A river runs through it: Eagle Vale, near the town of Margaret River.

MARGARET RIVER

The Margaret River region is renowned for stunning scenery and award-winning wines. Watch out grapes – here come the grains. **By Jeremy Sambrooks**

When it opened in 1994, Bootleg Brewery – "an oasis of beer in a desert of wine" – was the only full-mash brewery among the 80 or so cellar doors in the famed Margaret River wine region. Fast-forward 17 years and, while Margaret River is still known primarily for its wine, it is also one of the major players in the craft-brewing revolution.

Located about 290 kilometres south of Perth, the Margaret River region stretches from Cape Naturaliste in the north to Cape Leeuwin in the south, with most towns located within 20 kilometres of the coast.

Heading south on the Bussell Highway, first port of call is the seaside town of Busselton, home to Occy's Brewery. Opened by two surfing mates who refer to themselves as the "beer brothers", Occy's is a place where thongs and board shorts rule, with most punters electing to drink outside in the expansive beer garden. The brewery produces a large range of easy drinking beers, including a Radler, Mexican Lager, Honey Wheat beer and a silky Irish Dry Stout. Also available are beer- and wine-based cocktails.

■ DUNSBOROUGH & SURROUNDS

If you're passing through Dunsborough, stop for a bevy at Malt Market Bar & Kitchen, voted WA's Best Small Beer Bar in the 2010 *Beer & Brewer* Awards. More than 70 beers are on offer (20 on tap), including quality international brews, local craft beers and the latest single-batch release from Little Creatures.

Head west towards Cape Naturaliste and arrive at the region's newest brewery – Eagle Bay Brewing Company. Here is an attractive, modern, open-plan venue where – at least for the moment – a restaurant license dictates that you must stay for a meal if you want to drink beer. Thankfully, the kitchen provides a range of well-priced, quality bistro-style meals and woodfired pizzas,

Beer analysis by Michael Brookes at Bootleg Brewery

Malt Market Bar & Kitchen

Eagle Bay Brewery

making it an ideal lunchtime stop on your brewery trail. Brewer and co-owner Nick D'Espeissis crafts six beers: Kolsch, Vienna Lager, American Pale Ale, English Mild mid-strength, Extra Special Bitter and the current seasonal, a Steam beer brewed with lager yeast at ale temperatures.

Venture south and the next stop is Bush Shack Brewery, a small family run operation previously known as Wicked Ale Brewery. Run by Danial and Coralie Wind, Bush Shack specialises in unusually flavoured beers and wines. The range currently includes a Chilli Beer, Strawberry Pale Ale, Lemon Lager and Chocolate Beer – a staff favourite. Some more conventional beers are also available, including a Dark Wheat Ale and a Stout.

■ MARGARET RIVER

Continue south on the Bussell Highway and you'll arrive in the town of Margaret River. Until the 1960s, it was much like other small towns of the area – a support centre for dairy farms and the timber industry. Since then, through a combination of wine, surf and a laidback lifestyle, Margaret River has become a hit with tourists and sea-changers. The local population has swelled to 5600 and the Shire Council claims there are approximately 1.5 million tourists visiting every year. On any sunny weekend the main street can be found bustling with people shopping at the many boutique stores and eating award winning ice-creams from Simmo's ice-creamery. While a few chain stores have popped up recently, for the most part, the surfie town charm remains.

Venture outside the town centre and there is plenty to do and see, including for those not of drinking age. Rewarding culinary experiences can be had at the region's several topnotch restaurants, cheese factories and a venison farm as well as coffee from Yahava Koffee Works and sweet treats from the Margaret River Chocolate Company and the Fudge Factory in the town centre. Most places offers free samples so you can try (and try and try) before you buy.

Head west of town and you will encounter several kilometres of glorious coastline and some of Australia's best surf beaches. Take the scenic drive down Caves Road and feel dwarfed by the majestic pale barked Karri trees which grow to more than 60 metres high. While you're here, be sure to visit the spectacular show caves. Take a guided or self-guided tour, or just explore for yourself.

Depending on your interests and the time of year, you may wish to time your visit to Margaret River based around one of the many events that take place in the region. Early April is the best time to visit for waxheads, when Surfers Point in Prevelly hosts the Drug Aware Pro Margaret River – a premier international surfing tournament featuring surfers from across the globe. The tournament always attracts large crowds from all over, given the beautiful location and the world-class Margaret River surf.

In spring, the region's spectacular forests burst into life with an array of colour. The Margaret River area is home to some 2500 species of wildflower and more than 150 species of orchid, many of which can be seen on dedicated wildflower tours that run from September to November.

If your interests lie more in fauna than flora, why not head to the capes for a spot of whale watching? Southern Right and Humpback whales make their annual splash in the waters off Cape Leeuwin, Augusta between June and September, with the season continuing in Geographe Bay as the warmer months approach.

■ THE ORIGINAL OASIS

Back on the brewery trail, next up is Margaret River's original beer oasis – Bootleg Brewery. Running the show here is general manager and head brewer, Michael Brookes, whose range includes two Wheat Beers, Tom's Amber Ale, Wils Pils, a decidedly hoppy Pale Ale and Raging Bull Strong Ale. All are impressive, but the standout is the Raging Bull – a smooth, dark and malty

Danial Wind of Bush Shack Brewery

Surfs up at Margaret River

Bootleg Brewery

Grove brewer Nik Hughes hopping an Imperial Red Ale

Jeremy Good, Cowaramup Brewing Company

Ale tasting of caramel, sweet coffee and milk chocolate. In recent times, Bootleg has experimented with a number of seasonal and limited-release beers, including The Grandfather, a Barley Wine that has been fermented in Shiraz oak barrels that weighs in at a powerful 9.2% ABV.

Less than five minutes' drive away from Bootleg is Saracen Estates, home to the newest branch of Duckstein Brewery. The original Swan Valley microbrewery was one of the country's smallest breweries, but the Margaret River venue – which is now responsible for all production – is on a far grander scale. Here, four traditional German styles are on offer: Pilsener, Hefeweizen, Dunkel and Altbier. All are enjoyable, but the seasonal beer – an unfiltered, dry-hopped American Pale Ale is most impressive.

While in this area, consider popping into The Grove Vineyard, home to the Margaret River Liqueur Factory. Tours of the spirit and liqueur range are run daily, so you can gain an insight into the art of distilling and sample the large range of spirits and liqueurs. Also on site is a new nano-brewery; its Pale Ale and Whisky Ale are available on tap.

■ AWARD-WINNING BREWS

Heading south-east, the next stop is Cowaramup Brewing Company, a family-owned brewery just outside the township of Cowaramup, or 'Cowtown' as it is affectionately known by locals. (Those same sharp locals also refer to the designated driver as the Skipper.) Situated on a hillside with rammed-earth walls and a large native garden, Cowaramup Brewing Company could be the most aesthetically pleasing brewery in the region. Brewer Jeremy Good offers a range of five beers: Pilsener, Hefeweizen, Special Pale Ale, IPA and the current seasonal brew, a Porter. An expat Pom, Jeremy is particularly passionate about English-style Ales, and both the Special Pale Ale and IPA have the toasty malt and spicy, earthy hop characteristics associated with the best English brews. The Cowaramup Pilsener, which delights with its pungent hoppy aroma, firm bitterness and elegant, dry finish, was awarded Champion Lager at the 2011 Australian International Beer Awards.

Further south but still just 15 minutes' drive from the town of Margaret River, is the Colonial Brewing Company. Colonial has a strong history of awards and accolades, having won the title of Champion Small Brewery at the 2006 and 2007 Australian International Beer Awards and more recently, the Premier's Trophy for Best WA Beer at the 2009 Perth Royal Beer Show. Head brewer Mal Seccourable brews five beers: Kolsch, Witbier, Pale Ale, English style IPA and Porter. All Colonial's excellent beers are available to take away in two-litre growlers (glass bottles), which can also be refilled at The Royal in East Perth.

Back in the Margaret River town centre, the best place to enjoy a beer is at Settlers Tavern, where you can find Bootleg on tap, as well as a goos variety of local and imported beers. Early in 2011, Settlers played host to a Mad Brewer's beer dinner with special guest Dr Chuck Hahn.

This already-great region is only getting better for those with a fondness for Bacchanalian pursuits. The recently founded Margaret River Ale Company's beers are soon to be tapped at Settlers Tavern, the Cheeky Monkey Brewery & Cidery is due to open in September 2011 and a new branch of Clancy's Fish Pub – long-time supporters of craft beer – is expected to open in Dunsborough by Christmas.

Duckstein Brewery

Colonial Brewing Company

BREWERIES & DISTILLERIES

Bootleg Brewery
Puzey Rd, Willyabrup
(08) 9755 6300
www.bootlegbrewery.com.au

Bush Shack Brewery
Lot 3, Hemsley Rd
Yallingup
(08) 9755 2848
www.bushshackbrewery.com.au

Cheeky Monkey Brewery & Cidery
Lot 100, Caves Rd
Margaret River
(08) 9227 0055
www.cheekymonkeybrewery.com.au

Colonial Brewing Company
Osmington Rd
Margaret River
(08) 9758 8177
www.colonialbrewingco.com.au

Cowaramup Brewing Company
North Treeton Rd,
Cowaramup
(08) 9755 5822
www.cowaramupbrewing.com.au

Duckstein Brewery
Saracen Estates
3517 Caves Rd,
Willyabrup
(08) 9755 6500
www.duckstein.com.au

Eagle Bay Brewing Co
236 Eagle Bay Rd,
Eagle Bay
(08) 9755 3554
www.eaglebaybrewing.com.au

Occy's Brewery
737 Bussell Hwy
Busselton
(08) 9755 8300

The Grove Vineyard
(Liqueur Factory,
Distillery, Nano Brewery
and Cafe)
Cnr Metricup and Carter
Rds, Willyabrup
(08) 9755 7458
www.thegrovevineyard.com.au

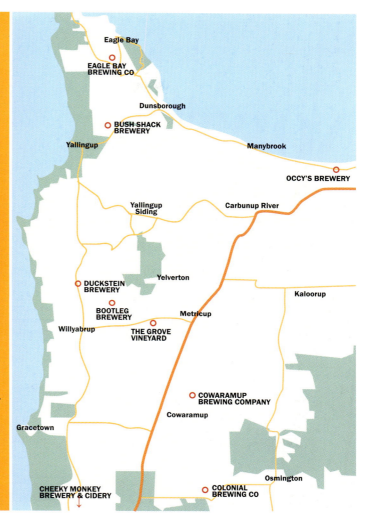

EVENTS

JANUARY
Southbound 2012 Music and Arts Festival www.southboundfestival.com.au

FEBRUARY
Leeuwin Estate Concerts www.leeuwinestate.com.au

MARCH
Margaret River Regional Festival www.margaretriverfestival.com

APRIL
Telstra Drug Aware Pro Margaret River syd1-0003dsb.server-web.com

OCTOBER
Flourish Margaret River www.flourishmargaretriver.com
Cape to Cape MTB capetocapemtb.com

NOVEMBER
Anaconda Adventure Race www.rapidascent.com.au/anacondaadventurerace/wa
Busselton Show www.busseltonshow.com.au

DECEMBER
SunSmart Iron Man WA Triathlon ironmanwesternaustralia.com

THINGS TO SEE & DO
For more info on the attractions of the Margaret River region, go to www.margaretriver.com

BEER BARS

Clancy's Fish Pub
www.clancysfishpub.com.au

Maltmarket Bar & Kitchen
26 Dunn Bay Rd,
Dunsborough
(08) 9759 1720
www.maltmarket.com.au

Settlers Tavern
114 Bussell Hwy,
Margaret River
(08) 9757 2398
www.settlerstavern.com

WA

NORTH

Western Australia's remote far north is known for its wide open spaces, spectacular landscapes and long, dusty 4WD tracks. It's hot and dry country for most of the year, which is probably why you'll find plenty of places to stop and enjoy a well-earned – and well-brewed – beer. **By Vanessa Hayden**

The Roey

It's not surprising that you'll find a boutique brewery in Broome. What is a revelation is that what is probably Australia's most remote microbrewery produces a staggering nine different handcrafted products, including a Dark Lager, Lager Draughts, a Spiced Wheat Beer, Chilli Beer and the locals' favourite, a ginger beer.

Part of the Kimberley region about 2500 kilometres north of Perth, the scenery in and around Broome is breathtaking and has some very fine watering holes.

Situated on a peninsula, the town is literally surrounded by water and has that distinct laidback feel of a beachside destination. Broome is ideal for families, yet equally good as a romantic getaway. There are opportunities to feel at one with nature, as well as great bars for party goers.

Many people travel to Broome just to relax at the beach. However, attractions such as the Willie Creek Pearl Farm and the Malcolm Douglas Wilderness Park, plus events like the Staircase to the Moon and Broome Race Round make it hard for visitors to spend much time on their sunloungers.

Broome was built on pearl fishing and today the Willie Creek Pearl Farm (38 kilometres from town) shows around 50,000 visitors a year what the fuss is all about. Pearls are everywhere in Broome – big names in the biz Paspaley, Kailis and Linney's can be found in the town centre.

Moonlight Bay Suites

Matso's Broome Brewery

There are three or four different beach experiences. The stunning Cable Beach is where you can walk (or drive) for miles and miles. Riddell Beach and Entrance Point harbours dinosaur footprints, rock pools and striking pindan rock formations. Town Beach, in 'Old Broome' is a family favourite; it has a cafe, a great little playground and a new water park that is popular with the little ones.

For wildlife warriors, the new Malcolm Douglas Wilderness Park (16 kilometres from town) is not to be confused with the Malcolm Douglas Crocodile Park at Cable Beach. While the wildlife park does feature two huge billabongs where 200 crocodiles stage a twice-weekly feeding frenzy, it has a much broader representation of Kimberley wildlife. The new night walk, with infra-red lighting, highlights many of Australia's least-known species.

Back on the beer trail, the town's jewel is Matso's Broome Brewery, which has grown from a 300L malt-extract brewery established in the late 1990s to a brewpub/micro brewery capable of producing 1200L per batch.

Head brewer Marcus Muller arrived in Broome 2009 and brings 20 years of brewing experience from around the world to the business. Marcus aims to combine the finest natural ingredients, traditional time-honoured brewing techniques and modern technology to produce a range of beer styles that, above all else, aim to deliver flavour.

Matso's beers are handcrafted, without the use of chemical additives and adjuncts, which makes it harder to brew a more delicate product. But Marcus says this is a more rewarding process as Matso's can obtain immediate feedback at the watering hole.

And he must be doing something right. Matso's draught beers (Mango and Ginger) can be found in an increasing number of bottle shops in Western Australia. Popular pubs and restaurants such as Clancy's Fish Pub in Canning Bridge, The Chapel Farm Restaurant at Middle Swan, The Pickled Fig Café in North Coogee and The Pink Duck in Rockingham are also serving some on tap. The brewery has recently broken into the east-coast market, its products beginning to appear in bottleshops in Melbourne, Canberra and Newcastle, on NSW's central coast.

If you can feel your tastebuds tingling, there is more good news. There are several good quality resorts within walking distance from Matso's. First choice would be Moonlight Bay Suites, which offers one- and two-bedroom apartments, many with a view over magnificent Roebuck Bay. If you're on a budget, check out Bayside Apartments – it's just metres from the brewery's front door! Others within easy walking distance to consider are Captains By The Bay, The Mangrove Hotel and The Oaks.

Once you've tried everything from Matso's menu, there are two more hotspots for you to pull up a barstool at.

Over at Cable Beach, head straight for Zeebar. It's only a few years old, but this is *the* place to be seen. Open until midnight most nights, it offers all the beers you'd expect: an extensive range of Little Creatures brews, including Pipsqueak Cider, plus other boutique beers including Beez Neez, Fat Yak, Big Helga, Bohemian Pilsner and Redback Original. The two tap beers are the very popular Becks and Hahn Super Dry.

The Roebuck Bay Hotel – The Roey – is as much a part of the local landscape as the bay itself, has three bars to choose from (or work your way through) and has more than 100 beers, wines and cocktails on offer. The Oasis Bar is said to be the biggest outdoor beer garden in the west. The Pearler's Bar has just been upgraded again and it's a great place to start your Broome holiday.

■ WHERE TO STAY

Moonlight Bay Suites; www.moonlightbaysuites.com.au. Bayside Holiday Apartments; www.baysideholiday apartments.com.au. Captains By The Bay; www.captainsbroome.com.au. The Mangrove Resort Hotel; www.mangrovehotel.com.au. The Oaks; www.oaks hotelsresorts.com.

BREWERY
Matso's Broome Brewery
Hammersley St, Broome
(08) 9192 7751
www.matsos.com.au

BARS
Zeebar
4 Sanctuary Rd, Cable Beach
(08) 9193 6511
www.zeebar.com.au

The Roebuck Bay Hotel
Carnarvon St, Broome
(08) 9192 1221
www.roey.com.au

EVENTS

MAY
North West Expo www.northwestexpo.com.au
Ord Valley Muster and Kimberley Moon Experience www.ordvalleymuster.com.au

JUNE-AUGUST
Broome Race Round www.broometurfclub.com.au

APRIL-OCTOBER
Staircase to the Moon www.broomevisitorcentre.com.au

AUGUST
Opera Under the Stars www.operaunderthestars.com.au

SEPTEMBER
Shinju Matsuri – Festival of the Pearl www.shinjumatsuri.com.au

THINGS TO SEE AND DO
Willie Creek Pearl Farm www.williecreekpearls.com.au. **Malcolm Douglas Wilderness Park** www.malcolmdouglas.com.au.

WA

Perth, capital of the Craft Beer state.

PERTH & FREMANTLE

Perth might be the world's most isolated capital, but from isolation comes a pioneering spirit. Make a pilgrimage to the breweries that started a nationwide craft-beer revolution, then check out the operations that are blazing a new trail to the top. **By Anthony Williams**

Beer lovers in the west are particularly proud of the (occasionally disputed) fact that Fremantle is the birthplace of Australian craft brewing. Brewers tell stories about formative beer experiences at the Sail & Anchor pub-brewery, where the Matilda Bay Brewing Company – and the once-pioneering Redback Wheat Beer – was born in the mid 1980s. Another generation of craft-beer devotees was born when Little Creatures Brewing opened its doors in late 2000, and yet another group of passionate beer aficionados have brought a new world of craft-brewed flavour to Freo (aka Fremantle) in recent years.

■ FISHING BOATS, CHIPS AND FRESH HOPS

For beer-loving first-time visitors to Perth's port city, all roads lead to the expansive, multi-faceted beer destination that is Little Creatures Brewery. The venue's original brewery, bar and restaurant is perfectly positioned on the

Clancy's Fish Pub, Fremantle

Little Creatures Brewery

edge of Fishing Boat Harbour, and its bohemian, candlelit-shed vibe has been a magnet for tourists and locals alike in the past decade or so. Of course, the massive, market-redefining success of Little Creatures Pale Ale has led to a more-than-a-little expansion since Y2K – with a loft bar, burger bar and whole new brewery built around that original 'shed'. Plans are afoot for a boutique hotel nearby too.

The brewery's flagship American-style Pale Ale has been joined by a core range of widely available bottled beers, but there's something very Freo about drinking a fresh Little Creatures at the source. Whether it's the Pale Ale, Bright Ale, Rogers' or Pilsner, a pint, pizza or seafood lunch, and the Fremantle Doctor (the afternoon sea breeze) is a winning trifecta on a Sunday afternoon during summer. Proximity to the harbour has also been a win for the Creatures beers, with the brewery able to quarantine its imports of whole US hop flowers – essential for the Pale's trademark citrus and grapefruit characters – straight off the boat.

Fresh-caught seafood is another not-to-be-missed experience while visiting Fishing Boat Harbour. Whether your preference is for fine-dining with a selection of Indian Ocean delicacies, or simply for fish 'n' chips wrapped in paper, you'll find a number of waterside restaurants and eateries just a short stroll from Little Creatures.

■ CAFFEINE HITS AND CRAFT-BEER SHIPS

The bustling, cosmopolitan vibe of the South Terrace 'Cappucino Strip' on a Sunday afternoon is classic Freo, with a melting pot of cultures contributing to the area's many cafes and restaurants. The historic Fremantle Markets, part of the Freo way-of-life since 1897, are here too, located right next door to a WA beer icon. Of course, a rummage through more than 150+ market stalls is one way to work up a thirst for good beer.

That's what that iconic neighbour – the Sail & Anchor – has been offering since 1984. With venue manager Matt Marinich at the helm, the Sail has taken its role as an ambassador for good beer to new heights.

The hotel's 43 (and counting) taps serve up a regularly changing line-up of quality, often-local brews, including a number of locally-favoured house beers that are now contract-brewed by the team at Feral Brewing Company. Well-organised, well-run promotions such as 'Novembeer', 'Febreary' and 'Beer Royale' have showcased Australian, international and local craft beers respectively, with Perth's beer geeks quickly realising that they've never had it so good.

Marinich's efforts were recognised in the 2010 *Beer & Brewer* People's Choice Awards, with the Sail & Anchor voted WA's Best Beer Venue. His success also seemed to inspire the team at The Monk Brewery & Kitchen, just across the road, where April 2011's inaugural 'USA Craft Beer Week' delivered more than 50 fresh, first-class American craft beers – many of which hadn't been available in Australia before – to grateful Perth enthusiasts.

That said, The Monk's own craft beers have been warmly welcomed by punters and judges alike. The venue's list of

Matt Marinich at the Sail & Anchor, where it's all about the beer.

The Monk Brewery & Kitchen

house brews includes a Kolsch, (Belgian-style) Wheat Beer, Pale Ale, Porter and a Mild (mid-strength lager) that picked up a Champion Trophy at the 2011 Australian International Beer Awards. A switched-on kitchen provides perfect food matches for those beers, and an expansive outdoor terrace takes full advantage of WA's mostly agreeable weather. Word is that another massive week of American craft-beer bliss is on the cards too.

The Norfolk Hotel adds six regularly changing taps to the range of South Terrace beer options, while The Freo Doctor bottleshop (on Arundel Street) stocks an extensive range of bottled Australian and international specialty brews.

■ OTHER WAYS TO GO FREO

Elsewhere in Fremantle, the original Clancy's Fish Pub is arguably Australia's first craft beer bar, pioneering the promotion and education of WA craft beer to its clientele since 2001. Fish 'n' chips and an array of fresh seafood are also a specialty at this relaxed, welcoming and very Freo venue, while the Governor's Bar at Moondyne Joe's – just to the south of central Fremantle – has a number of local craft brews on its taps. Heading south along South Terrace will

also lead you to a number of quality restaurants and cafes: Missy Moo's Burger Bar, Ruocco's, La Vespa and Ootong & Lincoln have joined Little Creatures, Great Mellie and the Gypsy Tapas House as current Freo favourites.

A stroll around central Fremantle's grand, heritage-listed streets is an ideal way to appreciate the history of Perth's port city. Visits to Fremantle Prison – after dark for an eerie Torchlight Tour if you're game – and the Roundhouse (WA's first convict jail) are definitely worthwhile, with the state's seafaring past on display at the impressive Fremantle Maritime Museum and the WA Museum's Shipwreck Galleries.

Over on the beach in North Fremantle, you'll find the Blacksalt Brewery, a self-described 'nano-brewery' that's a labour of love for brothers Geoff and Dan Goddard. The pair has taken inspiration from German brewing traditions, producing a Kolsch, Altbier, Dunkelweizen and a Hefeweizen that attracted gold and silver plaudits from judges at the Australian International Beer Awards and Perth Royal Beer Show in 2010.

■ A TOAST TO THE WEST COAST

Just beyond Fremantle's city limits, the Billabong and Gage Roads breweries produce bottled and kegged craft beer that you might well find in some of the other licensed premises mentioned here. The latter is purely a commercial brewery (and doesn't cater for visitors), while Billabong also operates as a Brew-It-Yourself business and sells its packaged beers on-site, including an award-winning Porter and a range of gluten-free brews. Gage's range includes the Gage Pils 3.5 (mid-strength), Gage Premium Lager, Wahoo

Taste the options on offer at The Monk.

Alan Proctor, Billabong Brewing

Last Drop Canning Vale

Premium Ale, Atomic Pale Ale and Sleeping Giant India Pale Ale, with a move into contract brewing – for Woolworths – contributing to an annual production capacity of an impressive 1.2 million cases.

At the smaller end of the craft-brewing scale, the Swan Valley-based Mash Brewing Company has recently established the Mash Brasserie in Rockingham, about 30 kilometres to the south of Freo. The brewery's intent is to produce wort – the tea-like blend of water, sugars and proteins created by the mashing process – in the valley, then transfer it to tanks at the Rockingham venue, where the fermentation and conditioning stages of the brewing process will occur. A beer-matched menu adds to the appeal of Mash's second coastal outpost (after Mash Bunbury), which isn't far from the well-stocked Big Brews bottleshop, and The Last Drop Tavern in beachside Warnbro.

Rockingham's other attraction is undoubtedly its oceanside location, with an array of watersports and activities on offer. Marine wildlife is also a major drawcard for the region, with dolphins, seals and fairy penguins calling the sheltered bays and islands of Cockburn Sound home.

If you prefer 'wild things' to wildlife, the Perth Motorplex is just up the road at Kwinana Beach, home to the city's drag racing, speedway and demolition derby action, as well as the annual Motorvation weekend for all things high-octane.

If that's not your bag, a leisurely drive up the coast from Fremantle will lead you to the stylish surrounds of Cottesloe Beach. It's one of Perth's premier strips of white sand and crystal blue water, as well as a place to socialise at the hotels, bars and restaurants that overlook the Indian Ocean on Marine Parade. The Cottesloe Beach Hotel (aka 'The Cott') – with its recently opened Craft Beer Bar – and Ocean Beach Hotel are Sunday session landmarks during the summer months, while Indiana (now serving beers from The Old Brewery), The Blue Duck Café and Il Lido are local dining favourites.

Seafood and craft beer has become a favoured combination up the road at City Beach, where the Clancy's Fish Pub team recently opening its third venue (after Clancy's Freo and Canning Bridge). Scarborough, Trigg, Mullaloo and the Hillarys Boat Harbour are also popular beach destinations, but it's the northern end of the city's coastal strip that holds particular appeal for craft-beer seekers.

Here, at the Mindarie Marina, you'll find the Indian Ocean Brewing Company and its summer-oriented four-beer core range. Brewer Mark Cocks keeps the Indi White (Belgian-style Witbier), Indi Green (Low-Carb Lager), the English-style Indi Pale Ale and Indi Pilsner flowing through the venue's taps, and then flexes his brewing muscles with a range of inventive seasonals. The Indi's Vanilla Milk Stout is definitely one to look out for during the winter months, while the traditional, seasonal flavours of the Best Bitter and India Pale Ale serve to slake the thirsts of Mindarie's local UK expats.

■ ELSEWHERE IN PERTH...

With Czech-born master brewer Jan Bruckner at the helm, the Last Drop Brewery has been supplying first-class Lagers, Wheat Beers and seasonal Ales to a number of Perth venues since 1992. The Elizabethan Village Pub, next door to the brewery in semi-rural Bedfordale (about 40 minutes southeast of the Perth CBD), is one place to sample those brews with lunch or dinner; Canning Vale's Last Drop Brewery Restaurant is another. The aforementioned Last Drop in

Indian Ocean Brewing Company

Warnbro and The Best Drop Tavern in Kalamunda also serve Bruckner's German-flavoured creations – the Last Drop Hefeweizen is a gold-medal-winning highlight in a consistently impressive range.

For consistently impressive craft beer closer to central Perth, The Old Brewery is a destination that also offers million dollar views in an iconic WA location. The Old Brewery – also one of the city's finest steakhouses – is situated in the historic Old Swan Brewery building, on the banks of the Swan River, and home to the original Swan Brewery between 1879 and 1966. A meticulous rebuild and restoration saw brewing return to the site in 2001, with current owners the Fraser's Restaurant Group taking over from Swan/Lion Nathan in 2007.

Brewer Mark Reilly produces a core range of five beers – Narrows Lager (Mid-Strength), Riverside Lager (Helles), Heritage Wheat Beer, Mounts Bay Brown Ale and Angus Pale Ale. A seasonal brew completes a line-up that has attracted gold and silver recognition at the Perth Royal Beer Show and Australian International Beer Awards in recent years; The Old Brewery was also a Best New Exhibitor finalist at the awards in 2009. Reilly's handcrafted beers can be enjoyed with or without lunch or dinner, although carnivorous beer lovers may well find the venue's grill menu – which includes grain-fed Black Angus and Wagyu beef, and WA Dorper lamb – an irresistible opportunity to drink *and* dine in style.

Edith Cowan University (ECU) has a 6HL brewery and Australia's only pilot malting plant at its Joondalup Campus. It hosts a range of malting and brewing science courses, including a one-year postgraduate Diploma of Brewing and a one-week short course in brewing. Beers are produced and sold under the Degrees Brewery brand.

Also calling the ECU Brewery home is John Stallwood from Nail Brewing. Here, John uses the equipment to brew his ales, including an Australian-style Pale Ale, multi-award-winning Oatmeal Stout and Imperial Stout. Nail beers are available at many Perth venues including the Sail & Anchor and Clancy's. John says his new home will be changing in late 2011, having been a gypsy brewer for the last 10 years of Nail's 11-year history.

For drinking and dining options in the Perth CBD, the west end of Murray Street boasts two beer-focused destinations in the Belgian Beer Café Westende and The Generous Squire. Both venues have contemporaries in other states and will be recognisable to visitors from the east. The latter – an often-bustling James Squire pub – has its brewery installed and ready to go, however has been trying to get its producer's license approved since 2009, so far without success.

The Brass Monkey Hotel is an iconic Perth pub over in the city's hotel, restaurant and nightclub precinct of Northbridge. William Street has become the area's hip and

Mark Reilly at The Old Brewery

Belgian Beer Cafe Westende

The pilot malting facility at ECU.

happening shopping and small bar strip in recent years, while the Perth Cultural Centre – which includes the WA Museum, Art Gallery of WA, Perth Institute of Contemporary Arts and the recently opened State Theatre Centre – is a hub of arts and heritage experiences. Where the CBD meets the Swan River, meanwhile, you'll find the Bell Tower and Barrack Street Jetty, where you can catch a ferry across to South Perth and Perth Zoo, or jump on a cruise to Fremantle, the Swan Valley or escape 'overseas' to Rottnest Island.

Just outside the city centre, you'll find an abundance of beer options at The Paddo – otherwise known as The Paddington Ale House – in Mt Hawthorn. Live entertainment and extensive sports coverage seven nights a week suggests a pretty traditional Aussie pub, but it's The Paddo's Beer Hall of Fame – 141 ales and lagers from around the world – that makes the venue a genuine beer destination.

Over in West Leederville, meanwhile, Irish beer and hospitality has well and truly made its mark at J.B. O'Reilly's. This self-described "eatin' and drinkin' emporium" served more Guinness than any other licensed venue in the country in 2008 and '09, and also boasts an extensive range of British and Belgian beers, as well as rare Scotch and Irish whiskies. Mount Lawley's Five Bar is also building an impressive bottled beer range, with some interesting, Swan Valley-flavoured brews set to join the James Squire range on tap.

John Stallwood from Nail Brewing at ECU

If you want to pick up a beverage to savour in the comfort of your own home (or someone else's), you'll find a mind-boggling range of bottled beer at the International Beer Shop (Australia's Best Bottleshop with more than 300 beers, according to voters in the 2010 *Beer & Brewer* People's Choice Awards) – just five minutes from central Perth in West Leederville. With more than 1000 beers on its shelves and in its fridges, this pioneering beer specialist is a must-visit destination for anyone reading this book.

Other quality bottle shops to visit in Perth include Cellarbrations Carlisle, Liquor Barons Mt Lawley, Greenmount Liquor, Mane Liquor, Belmont, Big Brews Liquor, Warnbro and The Beer Store, Morley.

The Generous Squire

International Beer Shop

BEER BARS AND PUBS

Belgian Beer Cafe Westende
Cnr Murray and King Sts, Perth
(08) 9321 4094
www.belgianbeer.com.au

Clancy's Fish Pub Canning Bridge
903 Canning Hwy, Applecross
(08) 9364 7322
www.clancysfishpub.com.au

Clancy's Fishbar City Beach
195 Challenger Drv, City Beach
(08) 9385 7555
www.clancysfishpub.com.au

Clancy's Fish Pub Fremantle
51 Cantonment St, Fremantle
(08) 9335 1351
www.clancysfishpub.com.au

Cottesloe Beach Hotel
104 Marine Pde, Cottesloe
(08) 9383 1100
www.cottesloebeachhotel.com.au

Elizabethan Village Pub
Lot 22, Canns Rd, Bedfordale
(08) 9399 4531
www.elizabethanpub.com.au

Five Bar
560 Beaufort St, Mount Lawley
0407 851 911

J.B. O'Reilly's
99 Cambridge St, West Leederville
(08) 9382 4555
www.jboreillys.com.au

Mash Brasserie Rockingham
1 Council Ave, Rockingham
(08) 9592 9208
www.mashbrewing.com.au

Moondyne Joe's
Cnr Wray Ave and Hampton Rd, Fremantle
(08) 9430 5513
www.moondynejoes.com.au

Ocean Beach Hotel
Cnr Marine Pde and Eric St, Cottesloe
(08) 9384 2555

The Freo Doctor Liquor Store

www.obh.com.au

Queens Tavern
520 Beaufort St, Highgate
(08) 9328 7267
www.thequeens.com.au

Sail & Anchor Hotel
64 South Tce, Fremantle
(08) 9431 1666
www.sailandanchor.com.au

The Best Drop Tavern
18 Haynes Street, Kalamunda
(08) 9293 2993

The Brass Monkey Hotel
Cnr James and William Sts, Northbridge
(08) 9227 9596
www.thebrassmonkey.com.au

The Generous Squire
397 Murray St, Perth
(08) 6311 7071
www.thegeneroussquire.com.au

The Last Drop Tavern Warnbro
Cnr Currie and Hokin Sts, Warnbro
(08) 9593 1597

The Norfolk Hotel
47 South Tce, Fremantle
(08) 9335 5405
www.norfolkhotel.com.au

The Paddo
141 Scarborough Beach Rd, Mt Hawthorn
(08) 9242 3077
www.paddo.com.au

BOTTLE SHOPS

Big Brews Liquor
2 Hokin St, Warnbro; (08) 9593 0904

Cellarbrations Carlisle
Cnr Wright St and Orrong Rd, Kewdale
(08) 9361 1434
www.cellarbrationscarlisle.com.au

Dan Murphy's
1300 72 33 88
www.danmurphys.com.au

Greenmount Liquor
47 Old York Rd, Greenmount
(08) 9294 1451

International Beer Shop
69 McCourt St, West Leederville
(08) 9381 1202
www.internationalbeershop.com.au

Liquor Barons Mt Lawley
654 Beaufort St, Mt Lawley
(08) 9271 0886
www.liquorbarons.com.au

Mane Liquor
237 Great Eastern Hwy, Belmont
(08) 9478 3676
www.maneliquor.com.au

The Beer Store
Cnr Wellington Rd and Noranda Ave, Morley
(08) 9276 1911

The Freo Doctor Liquor Store
27 Arundel St, Fremantle
(08) 9335 2801

BREWERIES & BEER COMPANY

Billabong Brewing
72a McCoy St, Myaree
(08) 9317 2940
www.billabongbrewing.com.au

Blacksalt Brewery
(@ Salt On The Beach)
Cnr Port Beach and
Tydeman Rds,
North Fremantle
(08) 9430 6866
onthebeach.net.au

Edith Cowan University
270 Joondalup Drv,
Joondalup
134 328
www.reachyourpotential.com.au

Gage Roads Brewing Co
Palmyra
www.gageroads.com.au

Indian Ocean Brewing Company
Ocean Falls Blvd,
Mindarie
(08) 9400 1111
www.indibrew.com

Last Drop Brewery & Restaurant
Lot 51 Nicholson Rd,
Canning Vale
(08) 9456 4228
www.lastdropbrewery.com.au

Little Creatures Brewery
40 Mews Rd, Fremantle
(08) 9430 5555
www.littlecreatures.com.au

Nail Brewing
www.nailbrewing.com.au

Swan Brewery
25 Baille Road, Canning Vale
(08) 9350 0222
www.lion-nathan.com.au

The Monk Brewery & Kitchen
33 South Tce, Fremantle
(08) 9336 7666
themonk.com.au

The Old Brewery
173 Mounts Bay Rd,
Perth
(08) 9211 8999
www.theoldbrewery.com.au

EVENTS

JANUARY
Perth Cup (horse racing)
www.perthcup.com.au
Hyundai Hopman Cup (tennis)
www.hopmancup.com
City of Perth Australia Day Skyworks
www.perth.wa.gov.au/skyworks

FEB/MAR
Perth International Arts Festival
www.perthfestival.com.au

MARCH
Eat Drink Perth
eatdrinkperth.showmeperth.com.au

APRIL
Fremantle Street Arts Festival www.fremantle.wa.gov.au

JUNE
WA Beer Week and Perth Royal Beer Show
www.wabeerweek.com.au

JUN/JUL/AUG
Winter Arts Season
www.perthwinterarts.com.au

SEPTEMBER
Kings Park Festival
www.bgpa.wa.gov.au/events/kings-park-festival

OCTOBER
Perth Royal Show www.perthroyalshow.com.au

NOV/DEC
Fremantle Festival
www.fremantle.wa.gov.au

WA
SOUTH WEST

Brew42 brewery

For most Australians, just making the trek to our largest state is a journey and a half. Beer lovers will find it's well worth the effort. **By Jeremy Sambrooks**

The drive from Perth to Albany is 409 kilometres by the most direct route, the Albany Highway. But beer lovers would do much better to take the westerly route, where for a mere 144 kilometres extra, they will be within reach of seven of the state's finest craft breweries.

Just over an hour out of Perth on the Old Coast Road is Brew42 Brewery at Lake Clifton Tavern & Motel. The brew pub is situated alongside the World Heritage-listed Lake Clifton, home to a population of thrombolites – 'living rocks' that represent the earliest record of life on earth. Six all-natural, unfiltered beers are on offer, including two Irish-style beers – a Red Ale and a Cream Stout, both decidedly more flavoursome than their vastly more famous Irish forebears.

William Bay, Denmark. A jewel in southern WA's crown.

Old Coast Rd Brewery

Gnomesville, in the Ferguson Valley

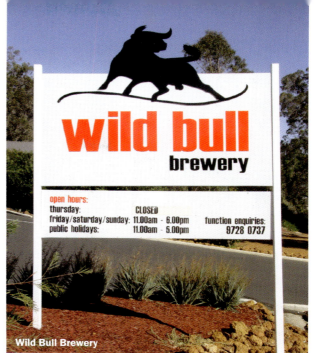
Wild Bull Brewery

Continuing south, the next stop is Old Coast Rd Brewery. Here, brewer Andrew Harris crafts a range of four beers: Pilsener, Acres of Wheat, Harris Bitter Ale and PBH Strong Porter Ale. All are easy drinkers, the Porter impressing most, with its full body and rich palate of chocolate and coffee. All the beers are available in takeaway six packs with each bottle featuring a different label, making for interesting collector's items.

■ BUNBURY AND THE VALLEY OF COWS

A further 30 minutes south is the coastal city of Bunbury, centre of the Geographe region and home to Mash Brewing's third operation. Boasting a waterfront location and a fantastic ocean view, Mash Bunbury has the brewery's core range of beers on tap, plus a few specials produced by its small in-house brewery. Those with less beery interests will find plenty to do in Bunbury's CBD: shopping, relaxing with coffee and cake on Victoria Street or perhaps making a short trip to the Dolphin Discovery Centre.

Next, head inland to the Ferguson Valley. This area is famous to many for Gnomesville, a collection of more than 3000 garden gnomes who reside near the roundabout that joins Wellington Mill Road and Ferguson Road.

The rolling hills in this area evoke thoughts of English countryside and are also home to several small dairy farms. Amusingly, the cow has become something of a mascot for the area, which is displayed no more clearly than in the naming of the region's two breweries.

Mash Brewing's Bunbury operation.

First up is Wild Bull brewery, whose hillside location overlooking vineyards and farmland provides a spectacular view. Ask the friendly staff for a $15 sampler tray, which consists of the brewery's full range of beers: Amber Ale, Irish Ale, Special Irish Ale (nitrogenised),

Moody Cow Brewery

Mark Hollett, brewer at The Cidery – Blackwood Valley Brewing

Bitter and Stout, as well as a sweet cider from the Capel cidery, Cider Works.

A short drive away is the other bovine-themed brewery, the Moody Cow Brewery. Established in May 2010, Moody Cow has a distinctly warm and friendly feel, with its red-cedar construction, log fire and large lawn with young families playing cricket and footy. Grant McClintock is the brewer, his range consisting of two Lagers and four Ales. Grunta's Original Ale is a firm favourite, a full-bodied malty Amber Ale with assertive bitterness from spicy Saaz hops.

■ CIDER COUNTRY

Back on the road, next stop is in the picturesque valley town of Bridgetown. This place claims to be home to Australia's foremost boutique-drinks producer, The Cidery. Once inside it becomes clear there is substance behind the claim – The Cidery produces a range of all-natural ciders made from Pink Lady apples and Champagne yeast, four wines available in 330ml bottles and six beers brewed under the name of Blackwood Valley Brewing. All are good, but most impressive is the multi-award-winning Stout Porter, a sweet, rich and complex Stout which pairs exceptionally well with a sticky date pudding.

For cider fans, another worthwhile port of call is Mountford Wines in Pemberton, where you can drink three varieties of Tangletoe organic cider. A couple of hours' drive south through majestic Karri forest and we find ourselves in the town of Denmark, home to Denmark Brew & Ales, a relatively new brewery operating out of the Southern End Restaurant. A range of Ales to suit most palates is available, from a crisp, light Bitter to a rich, malty Stout.

■ TO THE GREAT SOUTHERN

A further 60 kilometres east and we arrive at the port city of Albany, the hub of the Great Southern region. Here is a place deserving of at least a weekend's visit, as there is plenty to do and see in and around the city. The area is rich in natural beauty – spots worth checking out include the blowholes, the gap and natural bridge, and the tree-top walk in Walpole (130 kilometres west of Albany, but totally worth the drive). For a spot of history, go to Whale World and take an interactive journey through the site of Australia's last operating whaling station, or alternatively, go on a whale watching tour and see the real thing (whales that is, not whaling!).

While in Albany, be sure to try the beers at White Star Hotel, home of the Tanglehead Brewery. Try its cleverly named Wheat Beer, Southern White Ale, or take home bottles of the annual Christmas Ale and Old White Hart barley wine. In the mood for something a little stronger? Go to the Great Southern Distilling Company's cellar door to sample some Limeburners – WA's first single-malt whiskey.

As you can see, there is plenty for the beer lover to enjoy in WA's south-west, if you are willing to put in the miles.

Great Southern Distilling Company

Tanglehead Brewery (White Star Hotel)

BREWERIES & DISTILLERIES

Blackwood Valley Brewing – The Cidery
43 Gifford Rd, Bridgetown
08) 9761 2204
www.thecidery.com.au

Brew42 Brewery
19 Old Coast Rd,
Lake Clifton
(08) 9739 1010
www.brew42.com

Denmark Brew & Ales
Southern End Restaurant
427 Mount Shadforth Rd,
Denmark
(08) 9848 2600
www.southernend.com.au

Great Southern Distilling Company
252 Frenchman Bay Rd,
Robinson
(08) 9842 5363
www.distillery.com.au

Mash Bunbury
11 Bonnefoi Blvd, Bunbury
(08) 9721 6111
www.mashbrewing.com.au

Moody Cow Brewery
791 Ferguson Rd,
Dardanup
(08) 9728 3553
www.moodycow.com.au

Mountford Wines (Tangletoe Cider)
Bamess Rd, Pemberton
(08) 9776 1345
www.mountfordwines.com.au

Old Coast Rd Brewery
West Break Rd, Myalup
1300 792 106
www.ocrb.com.au

Tanglehead Brewing Company
White Star Hotel
72 Stirling Tce, Albany
(08) 9841 1733
www.tanglehead.com.au

Wild Bull Brewery
Lot 11, Pile Rd, Ferguson
(08) 9728 0737
www.wildbullbrewery.com.au

EVENTS

FEBRUARY
Taste Great Southern www.greatsoutherntastewa.com

MAY
Pemberton Autumn Festival festival.pemberton.org.au

JUNE
Manjimup 15000
www.williethomson.com/manjimup

AUGUST
Balingup Medieval Carnivale www.balingupmedievalcarnivale.com.au

OCTOBER
Dardanup Bull & Barrel Festival
www.bullandbarrel.net.au
The Funtabulous Bunbury Kidsfest
www.bunburykidsfest.com.au

NOVEMBER
Geographe Crush Food & Wine Festival richard@cmevents.com.au
Blues at Bridgetown www.bluesatbridgetown.com

DECEMBER
Manjimup Cherry Harmony Festival
www.cherryfestival.com.au

FOR MORE INFORMATION on places mentioned in this article, see www.visitbunbury.com.au, www.fergusonvalley.net.au and www.albanytourist.com.au

Take a load off in the Swan Valley

WA
SWAN VALLEY

A drive into the Swan Valley is always accompanied by a wonderful sense of escape. You're less than half an hour from the ever-increasing hustle and bustle of the Perth CBD, but the landscape of vineyards, market gardens and semi-rural calm seems a million miles from the city's rush.

By Anthony Williams

Craft breweries have become an important part of the Swan Valley landscape in the past 12 years, adding to the huge range of gourmet flavours that Perth's 'Valley of Taste' now offers to foodies, wine lovers and, of course, beer connoisseurs.

■ BASKERVILLE (NORTHEAST)

First stop should be the Feral Brewing Company, a bastion of craft-beer excellence that has called the northeast corner of the valley home since 2003. The multi-award-winning brewery scooped the pool at the 2009 Australian International Beer Awards and claimed the Champion Exhibitor and Champion Small Brewery trophies. Brewers Brendan Varis and Will Irving also collected the Champion Hybrid Beer (for Feral White), Champion Ale (for Hop Hog IPA) and Champion Scotch & Barley Wines (for Razorback) trophies that year, a result that seemed to inspire the pair to embark on bigger, and bolder, brewing adventures.

Feral's bar now boasts 16 taps (up from six in 2009!), offering a range of craft beer options that's unsurpassed in WA, if not Australia. Those aforementioned champions have been joined by such treats as Boris (a Russian Imperial Stout, naturally), the Fantapants Red Ale and Golden Ace (a Belgian-style Golden Ale that recently became the brewery's third bottled beer). Also contributing to the tap range is

Fabulous food and award-winning beer at Feral

Varis and Irving's ambitious barrel-fermentation program, which uses old oak barrels and wild yeast strains to create the distinctively sour characters of the remarkable Funky Junkie and Dark Funk ales.

Add a quality-focused modern Australian menu to the attractions on offer, and it's hardly surprising that the brewery-restaurant is often a full house for Sunday lunch. You can pick up the White, Hop Hog and Golden Ace at well-stocked bottleshops around Perth (and a couple of the house beers at The Sail & Anchor – see Perth & Fremantle – are actually brewed at Feral these days), but a pre-booked visit to Feral certainly offers flavoursome reward for effort. Its wide verandahs and spray-mist, air-cooling system create an ideal retreat during the summer months, while nearby attractions include the Lamont's and Upper Reach wineries, and Brookleigh estate – with Upper Reach and Brookleigh boasting award-winning restaurants in Broad's and Stewart's respectively.

■ HENLEY BROOK & WEST SWAN (CENTRAL)

To the west of Feral and its neighbours, over in the heart of the valley, you'll find a hive of brewing, wining, dining and distilling activity along a four-kilometre stretch of West Swan Road. The Duckstein Brewery was the first microbrewery in the area, introducing authentic German beer, food and hospitality to the valley in 1999. Its first brews were created using the tiny 100-litre plant that still stands in the middle of the brewery's restaurant, but demand eventually outstripped what original owner-brewer Erich Massberg could possibly supply on site. As a result, the venue's beers were produced elsewhere for a number of years, a situation resolved somewhat with the opening of the Duckstein Brewery at Saracen Estates, in the Margaret River region, in 2008.

Duckstein's craft beers are now produced at the much bigger Margaret River brewery, with kegs of the Pils, Hefeweiss, Dunkel, Altbier and seasonal beers delivered up to the Swan Valley as required. Each adheres to the strict traditions of the German Purity Law, or *Reinheitsgebot*, and each has a perfect match or two among the brewery restaurant's range of traditional German meals, including the Brewer's Pan – a hearty serve of pan-fried potatoes, smoked pork cutlets and bratwurst sausages. Add an 'oompah' band – albeit an automated, plaster cast three-piece – to proceedings and it won't be long before you're contemplating a beer-change to the Bavarian motherland.

Elmar's In The Valley is the area's second German-style beer-and-food destination. Purpose-built in 2005, this brewery-restaurant seriously amplifies the scale of Duckstein's cosy operation (located just 500 metres to the north), catering for up to 1000 visitors and featuring a huge indoor bar and dining area, a two-acre beer garden and the largest micro-glass-brewery in the Southern Hemisphere.

Elmar's brewer Brad Harris imports the finest German ingredients for his brews – Ein Stein Pilsner, Over Draft Altbier, Kick Back Hefeweizen and a range of seasonals – and also sticks to the Purity Law. Bock, Marzen, Rauch and Schwarz beers are among the seasonal treats that have accompanied the wursts, schnitzels and pork shanks served in the restaurant, while

Duckstein Brewery's 'Oompah Band'

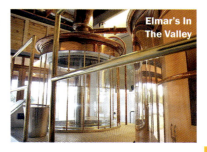

Elmar's In The Valley

You're spoilt for choice at Elmar's

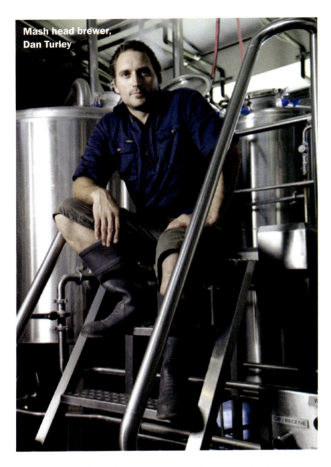

Mash head brewer, Dan Turley

Mash Brewing Company's Mash Eisbock

owner Elmar Dieren's range of traditional, smoked smallgoods offer plenty of take-home options for visitors to the valley.

The third destination in the Henley Brook craft-brewing precinct is Mash Brewing Company, situated about a kilometre north of Duckstein and also on West Swan Road. With the polished concrete, cut-stone and stainless steel of its brewery-brasserie, Mash cleverly places a city-style eatery within the functional, industrial realms of a craft-brewing operation, matching its accessible range of handcrafted beers with a largely local mod-Oz menu. As a result, the venue has been one of the Swan Valley's Sunday-lunch favourites since it opened its doors in April 2006.

Mash's core range of brews includes the Freo Doctor Pale Lager, West Coast Wheat, 'Pale' Pale Ale, Sgt. Pepper Golden Ale and two ciders (Crush Apple and Press Pear). Perhaps surprisingly, though, it's the brewery's seasonals that have really attracted the attention of beer judges in recent years, with the Mash Baltic Porter collecting the Best Stout Draught trophy at the Perth Royal Beer Show in 2009, and again in 2010. The Mash Eisbock, Scotch Ale and Flying Monk (a Belgian-style Tripel) have also been limited-release medal winners, and should definitely be sampled when available – especially if you've taken steps to exclude driving from the list of post-tipple activities.

Indeed, with the Swan Valley Oasis Resort – an accommodation, restaurant and function centre complex – situated right behind the Mash brewery, that's always a possibility. The family-friendly nine- or 18-hole stroll of Supa Golf is also right next door, as is the laser-combat action of Laser Corps. The Wild Swan Distilling Company, Merrich Estate Olive Farm, Oggie's Ice Cream Cafe and the WA Reptile Park are all just a short stroll away.

Wild Swan Distilling Company's world-class pure and flavoured vodkas have won medals at the San Francisco World Spirits Competition in recent years, and the distillery's range also includes whisky, brandy and a medal-winning gin that's flavoured with a selection of organic botanicals including native lemon myrtle. Good spirits can also be found at the Great Northern Distillery over on Great Northern Highway, home to The Kimberley Rum Company and its award-winning Canefire Rum. The delicious home cooking of Taylor's Art & Coffee House is close by, as are the traditional Italian flavours of Mondo Nougat and the delightful wining, dining and valley views of Sittella winery and restaurant.

You'll find plenty more Swan Valley flavours back on West Swan Road, with Chesters Restaurant and Heafod Glen Winery, and the Black Swan Winery & Restaurant, offering everything a gourmand could want. Snacking and sampling are more the norm at Lancaster Wines, home to some of the oldest vines in the valley, while the Margaret River Chocolate Company and Yahava Koffeeworks bring the irresistible attractions of chocolate and coffee to the region's gourmet mix. Then it's back to the craft beer at the Ironbark Brewery, located at the Valencia Complex in Caversham, just north of Guildford.

CAVERSHAM & GUILDFORD (SOUTHERN GATEWAY)

Ironbark Brewery is a family-run venture that's testament to the perseverance and passion of director Graeme White. The farmer-turned-brewer actually built Ironbark's full-mash decoction plant from scratch and since 2001 has developed a beer range that includes

Why not take a brewery tour?

the award-winning, lambic-style Cherry Ale (featuring 40 per cent pureed cherries), Ironbock Lager and Aussie Pils. Hannan's Lager is based on a beer that was once popular in WA's Goldfields, and a native fruit lends its name and flavour to the Desert Lime.

Graeme's passion for all things Australian is reflected in Ironbark's decor and menu. The solid jarrah tables in the brewery's leafy beer garden are just the place to enjoy a Big Mallee Bull steak sandwich, a Roustabout platter for two, or a Boundary Rider (kangaroo) burger.

The Vineyard Restaurant – which has been serving home-cooked meals since 1992 – is right next door to Ironbark, as is the cellar door for Lilac Hill Estate Wines, and the must-see heritage town of Guildford is just a short drive away.

Often described as the 'Gateway to the Swan Valley', Guildford has a history that dates back to the beginnings of the Swan River Colony in 1829. The settlement was established as a market town and inland port that same year, and developed an English-village character that – having been preserved by the National Trust – lives on through its original buildings, the strip of antique shops on James Street, and the Devonshire teas served by local cafes. The beautifully restored Rose & Crown Hotel, built in 1841, is well worth a visit, and the Swan Valley Visitor Centre – located in the Old Guildford Courthouse (circa 1866) – is the place to go for the latest info and assistance.

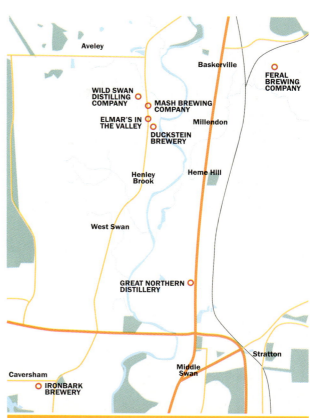

The magnificent beer garden at Ironbark Brewery

EVENTS

MARCH
Guildford Heritage Festival
Stirling Square,
www.swanvalley.com.au

JULY
Seafood & Shiraz Weekend
www.swanvalley.com.au

OCTOBER
Spring In The Valley
www.swanvalley.com.au
Oktoberfest
Elmar's in the Valley,
Henley Brook
www.elmars.com.au

BREWERIES & DISTILLERIES

Duckstein Brewery
9720 West Swan Rd,
Henley Brook
(08) 9296 0620
www.duckstein.com.au

Elmar's In The Valley
8731 West Swan Rd,
Henley Brook
(08) 9296 6354
www.elmars.com.au

Feral Brewing Company
152 Haddrill Rd,
Baskerville
(08) 9296 4657
www.feralbrewing.com.au

Mash Brewing Company
10250 West Swan Road,
Henley Brook
(08) 9296 5588
www.mashbrewing.com.au

Great Northern Distillery (The Kimberley Rum Company)
496 Great Northern Hwy
(08) 9250 5422
www.canefire.net

Ironbark Brewery
(in the Valencia Complex)
55 Benara Road,
Caversham
(08) 9377 4400
www.ironbarkbrewery.com.au

Wild Swan Distilling Co
10581 West Swan Road,
Henley Brook
(08) 9296 6656
www.wildswandistillery.com.au

Brewery Tours
0423 976 116
tours@thebrewersdray.com.au

Beer & Brewer promotion   WESTERN AUSTRALIA – MARGARET RIVER

COWARAMUP BREWING COMPANY

Located in a picturesque rural setting 4km east of the Bussell Highway, offering award winning quality hand crafted ales and lagers, a range of local wines with an excellent menu focusing on local produce. The brewery has also become a popular function venue.

The brewery/restaurant building is made from rammed earth, a popular locally sourced building material. A large decking and grassed area, with an adjacent kids playing area, allow patrons to relax and enjoy the rural surroundings.

Five beers are available on tap, a Pilsener, awarded Champion Lager at the Australian International Beer Awards 2011, Hefeweizen, Special Pale Ale, India Pale Ale and a Robust Porter.

North Treeton Rd
Cowaramup
Tel: (08) 9755 5822
www.cowaramupbrewing.com.au

Opening hours:
10.00am – 6.00pm daily

THE GROVE VINEYARD LIQUEUR FACTORY, DISTILLERY AND NANO BREWERY & CAFE

Located in the heart of the Margaret River Wine Region. Tastings of the liqueur and spirit ranges are available daily. Food is available everyday, starting with breakfast, through to lunch and afternoon tapas to accompany the brews and cocktails available in the bar. Visit The Grove for a unique experience in the region.

Cnr Carter & Metricup Rd
Willyabrup
Margaret River Wine Region
Tel: (08) 97557458
www.thegrovevineyard.com.au

Opening hours
Open 9.00am – 5.00pm daily

MALTMARKET BAR & KITCHEN

Maltmarket Bar & Kitchen is a small two level bar devoted to all things beer! Located in Dunsborough just metres from the Bay in the Margaret River Region.

Ground Level: Maltmarket Bar & Kitchen is an original eclectic bar featuring great beer and bistro style food to match. The bar features over 100 beers and ciders available by the bottle as well as 16 taps pouring local, West Australian and international brews. Consistently featuring locally produced and specialty beer with 4 rotating taps, Maltmarket is the southwest home of craft beer.

Upstairs: The Lawn is a summer terrace bar serving more great beers, gourmet burgers and featuring live music and DJ's on weekends. The bar has craft beer designed for summer with White Rabbit White Ale, Weinstephaner Weiss Bier and Little Creatures Pale Ale all featuring as well as some interesting local and eastern state craft beers on tap. The Lawn is a perfect summer hangout!

26 Dunn Bay Road
Dunsborough
Tel: (08) 9759 1720
maltmarket@westnet.com.au
www.maltmarket.com.au

Opening hours:
7 days from 4pm 'til late
Upstairs - The Lawn open
Wed-Fri from 4.00pm
Sat-Sun 12.00pm 'til late

Beer & Brewer promotion　　　　WESTERN AUSTRALIA – MARGARET RIVER

BOOTLEG BREWERY

An Oasis of Beer in a Desert of Wine

Open since 1994, Bootleg Brewery, situated in the heart of the Margaret River Wine Region, is a favourite to both visitors and locals alike. Set against a backdrop of pine trees and on the edge of a picturesque lake, Bootleg Brewery is a casual yet scenic location to enjoy.

Their beers speak for themselves, having created a range of award-winning boutique beers to suit every palate. Bootleg Brewery also has a terrific reputation for creating some of the most distinctive seasonal beers. All of the regular beers are bottled for purchase to take home.

The restaurant is also well known for serving moderately-priced meals in a casual atmosphere, using only fresh locally grown produces. To enhance the vibe, they have live bands perform most weekends and a great playground for the kids to explore. With viewing windows into the brewery and brewing museum, Bootleg Brewery truly is an oasis of beer in a desert of wine.

Puzey Road, Cnr of Johnson Rd
Wilyabrup
Tel: (08) 9755 6300
brewery@bootlegbrewery.com.au

Opening hours:
Daily from 11.00am – 6.00pm
Lunch from 12.00pm

EAGLE BAY BREWING CO

Eagle Bay Brewing Co opened its doors in December 2010. It was founded by the d'Espeissis siblings, who share a passion for local produce, wine and most importantly handcrafted brews. The venue houses a 1,000L micro-brewery, relaxed restaurant and farm shop overlooking a rolling rural landscape and the Indian Ocean.

Eagle Bay Brewing Co is located in the north of the Margaret River Wine Region, just five minutes from Dunsborough, and one minute from the pristine beaches of Eagle Bay.

Eagle Bay Brewing Co beers are brewed on site by Executive Brewer and co-owner Nick d'Espeissis. Nick adheres to the German Purity Law, and uses only rainwater, malted barley, hops and yeast. Regular brews include; Kolsch, Vienna, English Mild, Pale Ale and Extra Special Bitter.

Eagle Bay Brewing Co's restaurant is located in a rural setting, with a relaxed, family-friendly, vibrant atmosphere, ample lawns and a playground. Head Chef, Rupert Brown creates seasonal menus full of good honest fare, using local produce and ingredients freshly plucked from the kitchen garden. Open daily for lunch, all day grazing and special events by arrangement.

236 Eagle Bay Rd
Eagle Bay
Tel: (08) 9755 3554
www.eaglebaybrewing.com.au

Opening hours:
Open daily for lunch and all day grazing

Beer & Brewer promotion WESTERN AUSTRALIA

BUSH SHACK BREWERY

Located between Yallingup and Dunsborough this is a micro-brewery with a difference. From the classic Australian Bitter with a chilli bite, to the deep roasted coffee flavour of the Dark Wheat beer, the Bush Shack is the full pint.

Even the non-beer aficionado won't miss out. Try their range of flavoured wine-spirit based drinks for a taste of something completely different.

Built from recycled bricks, timber and tin, the rustic tasting bar sits well in the Australian bush. Relax in the beer garden, complete with a nearby children's playground. Choose from the Snack Attack menu served from 11am - 4pm daily, or bring your own picnic, or use the free onsite BBQ facilities.

Hemsley Rd
Yallingup
Tel: (08) 9755 2848
info@bushshackbrewery.com.au
www.bushshackbrewery.com.au

Opening hours:
Sun-Thu 10.00am – 5.00pm
Fri-Sat 10.00am – 6.00pm

THE FREO DOCTOR LIQUOR STORE

With over 500 beers in stock, and the best customer service in town, this is a beer lovers paradise.

The Freo Doctor is named after the afternoon sea breeze. Located right in the heart of Fremantle, which many consider as the spiritual home of Australian microbrewing. Built in the 1920's the beautiful heritage listed building embraces both the strong history and heritage of the area and was a working winery up till the early 90's, with an amazing underground limestone and Jarrah cellar.

Regular Beer Club functions and Beer tastings. Wholesale pricing is available. 10% off any mixed 6. Delivery anywhere in Australia.

27 Arundel Street
Fremantle
Tel: (08) 9335 2801
info@thefreodoctor.com

Opening hours:
Mon-Sat 10.00am – 8.00pm
Sun 11.00am – 7.00pm

MOODY COW BREWERY

This family run brewery was opened in May 2010. Set on five acres in the picturesque Ferguson Valley 8kms from Dardanup on Ferguson Rd.

The limestone and western red cedar building utilises eight different timbers in it's construction. The use of Marri, Jarrah, Tuart, Wandoo and American Oak timbers create a warm and inviting environment.

Watch the brewing process from close quarters, sit round the log fire or enjoy a meal on the large decked area or grassed terraces.

The children are well catered for, with a large grassed area that runs from the terraces to a winter creek. You can kick a footy, have a game of cricket or bocce or merely take in the ambiance that is the Ferguson Valley.

791 Ferguson Rd
Ferguson Valley
Tel: (08) 9728 3553
moodycowbrewery@bigpond.com
www.moodycow.com.au

Opening hours:
Thurs/Fri/Sat/Sun and public holidays from 11.00am. Available for Corporate and Private Functions by arrangement.

THE MONK BREWERY

The Monk Brewery & Kitchen, offers an ever growing range of award winning, handcrafted ales, brewed on site in their custom small batch brew house. The resident head brewer mixes and mashes water, malt, hops and yeast to deliver fresh, crisp beer, free of additives and preservatives. The Monk's kitchen is open till late and has created a menu to match the range of featured beers. Using only locally sourced, real and honest produce to create a quality driven and diverse menu selection. The Monk loves its beer and look forward to seeing you soon for one!

33 South Terrace
Fremantle
Tel: (08) 9336 7666
beer@themonk.com.au
www.themonk.com.au

Opening hours:
Open every day from 11.30am 'til late

SAIL & ANCHOR HOTEL

In fermentation, there is truth. Beer was never meant to be bland, tasteless & apathetic

Being the spiritual home of craft brewing in Western Australia, it was decided from the start that The Sail would stay true to craft beer. It would become a showcase venue for hand-sculpted beer in Australia. Anyone can provide package beer but to specialise in tap beer is the cutting edge. The consistent maintenance & thorough beer hunting required to showcase 250+ beers every year is a huge undertaking. The mission has been accepted, executed and is prevailing with flying colours! Currently pouring 27 different beers through 43 taps and another 16 being installed, the Sail is pushing the upper limits of the tap beer atmosphere.

Calender of events…

Febreway International Craft Beer Showcase
Collect your Beer Passport complete with score sheets & beer notes, and then get stamped as you travel the beer world in 28 days.

June - Annual "Beer Royale" Wa Craft Beer Showcase
In conjunction with the Royal Agricultural Society of WA they showcase WA's finest brews. Brewers & beers from across the state come together over the 2 day event to engage the public face to face. There's nothing like a 2-day Beer Circus to cap off WA Beer Week! Vote for your favourite beer over the 2 days to go in the running to win your very own keg fridge!

Novembeer
The Australian wide monster showcase. Hand-sculpted beers from passionate brewers are transported to the Sail for this month of beer glory.

Novembeer Hall of Fame

"Keg that drained the quickest" – McLaren Vale Ale 32mins.
"Most talked about beer" – Feral Funkie Junkie.
"Most anticipated tapping" - 2 Brothers James Brown Belgian Dubbel.
"Under the Radar" - 3 Ravens Rauchbier.
"First Choice Pale Ale" – Moo Brew Pale Ale.
"Attack of the Hops" – Old Brewery Tomahawk 2IPA.

Night Of The Barrels
The pinnacle of the Novembeer celebrations is Night of the Barrels. 9 Specialty beers & limited small batch release tapped from kegs and firkins on the bar top!

Seven Seas Homebrew Brewing Competition
A gold medal Seven Seas Recipe from 1999 is available to any one game enough to clone brew one of the beers from the original stable, when the brewery opened in 1984. The brewer of the winning entry will have the honour of brewing a 40 keg batch to go on tap at the Sail & Anchor! Thanks to the Sponsors: Cryer Malt, Hopco and Beer Men TV. For more information contact Matt Marinich.

Beer Head…

Join the BEER HEAD database to receive updates on beer showcases, events, and beer launches. You can follow the Sail on twitter @Sail_Anchor. And Facebook.

64 South Tce
Fremantle
Tel: (08) 9431 1666
www.sailandanchor.com.au

Opening hours:
Sun 10.00am – 10.00pm
Mon-Tues 11.00am – 11pm
Wed-Thurs 11.00am – 12.00am
Fri-Sat 11.00am – 1.00am

Beer & Brewer promotion   WESTERN AUSTRALIA – NORTH

MATSO'S BROOME BREWERY

You simply must visit the only full mash hand crafted brewery in Australia's North West. Sit back, relax on the verandah and enjoy spectacular views over Roebuck Bay whilst sipping on an award winning beer. Matso's boasts their own Indian chef with his authentic North Indian curries or choose from an extensive a la carte menu.

Matso's is the Kimberley's award wining microbrewery. The owners of Matso's Broome Brewery (Martin and Kim Peirson-Jones) are committed to the Kimberley region and the Western Australian tourism industry with an investment in accommodation throughout the region.

At the helm of Matso's Broome Brewery is Marcus Mueller, a German Master Brewer who has over 16 years brewing experience around the world. Marcus combines the finest natural ingredients, traditional time honoured brewing techniques and modern technology, to produce a range of beer styles that, above all else, aim to deliver flavour.

The Kimberley lifestyle, climate and natural environment is unique and unfettered, and Matso's have an objective to create beers of individuality that will reflect the region. With the knowledge and wisdom of 'Old World' brewing to draw from, and the imagination and innovation of 'New World' brewers as their inspiration, Matso's hope to contribute to the future of Australian beer.

Matso's Broome Brewery is an ideal function venue. They cater for stand up cocktails, a Kimberley BBQ or a lavish sit down meal.

When looking for a place to stay in Broome, Matso's has conveniently located accommodation on Roebuck Bay with its sister property Moonlight Bay Suites.

60 Hamersley St
Broome
Tel: (08) 9193 5811
drink@matsosbroomebrewery.com.au
www.matsos.com.au
www.moonlightbaysuites.com.au

Opening hours:
Open 7 days 7am-late
Events and Functions up to 100 guests Beer tastings and appreciation Brewery tours by appointment

Beer & Brewer promotion   **WESTERN AUSTRALIA – PERTH & FREMANTLE**

EDITH COWAN UNIVERSITY (ECU)

The Malting and Brewing Research and Education Facility located at the Joondalup Campus of Perth's Edith Cowan University (ECU), hosts a range of malting and brewing science courses.

The facility houses a six hundred litre brewery and associated equipment for filtration, bottling and kegging of both student and commercial beers. In addition, smaller brewing equipment is available for individual student and project work. The facility also boasts the only pilot malting facility in Australia, with the recent addition of the 100kg National Pilot Malting unit installed in partnership with the Department of Agriculture and Food, Western Australia (DAFWA).

ECU teaches a one year postgraduate Diploma of Brewing through it's School of Natural Sciences. This allows students to learn the science and practice of brewing in depth. The course is available to those with an undergraduate degree or with relevant industry experience. Previous science education is not a prerequisite. Students are given a solid foundation in the chemical, biochemical and microbiological science involved in brewing as well as the engineering, plant design and packaging concepts required for working in a modern large or small brewery.

Graduates from the course are in demand with some working as far afield as England and Holland as well as in large and small breweries across Australia.

For those wishing to gain a greater understanding of the brewing process but who are unable to commit to extended study, the University also teaches a one week short course in brewing each year in June. This course will prepare students to sit the industry recognised General Certificate in Brewing exams through the Institute of Brewing and Distilling (IBD) if they so wish. There are no entry requirements and the course has proved popular with brewery operators, new brewers to the industry and professional home brewers.

ECU has established a number of relationships with industry and consumer groups which have led to practicum opportunities for students in breweries in Western Australia and interstate as well as awards and prizes for students for academic achievement. The University's brewing staff and students are encouraged to actively engage with industry and support industry initiatives such as judging and stewarding at the Perth Royal Beer Show each year.

Teaching in these courses includes industry experienced guest lecturers and IBD accredited trainers as well as the School's full-time brewing lecturer Hugh Dunn, himself an IBD accredited trainer with over 25 years experience in the industry.

270 Joondalup Drive
Joondalup
Tel: 134 ECU (134 328)
futurestudy@ecu.edu.au
www.reachyourpotential.com.au

Beer & Brewer promotion   WESTERN AUSTRALIA – PERTH & FREMANTLE

CELLARBRATIONS CARLISLE

Cellarbrations Carlisle has been a family owned business for over 25 years. Over that period of time they have dedicated themselves to deliver only the finest service and produce.

Their extensive beer range is but one of the sections that they are proud to provide for their clientele. With over 750 different beers and ciders in their range, their knowledgeable staff are keen to assist in procuring rare and premium beers for ultimate consuming satisfaction.

The creation of their new beer club, 'Grain Cru' has enabled them to take the extra step over the beer horizon with amazing tastings, dinners and events.

2 Wright St
Kewdale, Perth
Tel: (08) 9361 1434
carlisle.wine.bin@bigpond.com

www.cellarbrationscarlisle.com.au
Under construction

Opening hours:
Mon-Thurs 8.30am – 8.30pm
Fri-Sat 8.30am – 9.00pm
Sun & Public Holidays
10.00am – 7.00pm

LIQUOR BARONS MT LAWLEY

Liquor Barons Mt Lawley's premium wine cellar has been an attraction for many years, but the growth of its specialty beer range in the past 12 months has added another string to its already impressive bow.

The family-owned store is committed to offering a decidedly different bottleshop experience, and more than 300 of the world's finest beers – think Nogne-O, Mikkeller, Rogue, De Molen, Hitachino Nest and BrewDog – are now an integral part of that quality-focussed approach.

Add Australia's best craft-brews, an extensive wine and spirit range, and friendly, knowledgeable staff to the equation, and Liquor Barons Mt Lawley offers a real alternative to the impersonal world of 'liquor supermarkets'.

654 Beaufort St
Mount Lawley
Tel: (08) 9271 0886
mtlawley@liquorbarons.com.au

Opening hours:
Mon-Thurs 9.00am – 8.45pm
Fri-Sat 9.00am – 9.30pm
Sun 11.00am – 7.00pm

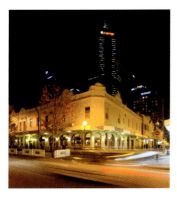

BELGIAN BEER CAFÉ WESTENDE

Constructed with authentic 1930s Belgian architecture in mind, providing unique surroundings & atmosphere.

At the Belgian Beer Cafe beer service is of a particularly high standard, observing the 7 step Belgian Beer Pouring Ritual. Bar staff are armed with the knowledge to assist you in all of your beer needs. They are all about the beer and pride themselves on an organic evolution of the beer offering, dependant on season & often of very limited availability, making Westende a true beer aficionado venue in Perth.

The Beer menu is extensive; over 100 beers are seasonally available! Belgian Blondes, Brunes, Tripels, Wit & Saisons feature prominently. Also featured is a large range of naturally fermented lambic beers, known for their added fruit flavors, from Sour cherry to Candy Sugar and more. The Reserve List is comprised of one-off imports & more extreme styles for the true beer adventurer. Food matches are listed with each beer.

Cuisine is classic European with a modern twist. The menu is varied enough to suit all palates & tasting & tapas style servings are available to better complement dinning with beer. Mussels feature prominently with a choice of sauces & several dishes feature beer based sauces.

347 Murray Street
(Cnr King St)
Perth
Tel: (08) 9321 4094
www.belgianbeer.com.au

Opening hours:
Mon-Tue 11.00am – late
Wed-Sat 11.00am – midnight
Sun 11.00am – 10.00pm

Beer & Brewer promotion   WESTERN AUSTRALIA – PERTH & FREMANTLE

MANE LIQUOR BEER SPECIALISTS

Good People Drink Good Beer.

Take your beer seriously? Searching for beer with real flavour, character and intensity? Find everything you've been looking for at Mane Liquor in Ascot.

Mane Liquor is a beer and spirit specialty store with over 650 beers and ciders from around the world, including all the essential brewers and limited edition beers. Their experienced staff are always on hand to offer expert advice or source that beer you can't find anywhere else.

There is a dedicated research station for you to review and comment on everything regarding craft beers. In addition Mane Liquor hosts a monthly beer club for the beer enthusiast which ranges from tastings to beer and food degustation.

Join the Mane Liquor database through their website for updates on upcoming events and new arrivals, or follow them on Facebook.

In 2010 Mane was named top 5 beer store in Western Australia in the 2010 Beer & Brewer Awards.

237 Great Eastern Hwy
Ascot
Tel: (08) 9478 3676
www.maneliquor.com

Opening hours:
10.00am 'til late
7 days/week

Beer & Brewer promotion WESTERN AUSTRALIA

BILLABONG BREWING

Billabong was the first Brew On Premise to be set up in Australia in 1993. Facilities are provided for people to brew over 120 styles of beers, similar to local and international beers. Brewers enjoy the experience of brewing their own quality beer with fun and savings part of the mix.

They now also have a commercial licence and production includes award winning Gluten Free and main stream boutique styles. Check out the web site.

72a McCoy St
Myaree
Tel: (08) 93176099
(Commercial)
Tel: (08) 9317 2940
(Brew on Premise)
billbrew@westnet.com.au
www.billabongbrewing.com.au

Opening hours:
Brew On Premise
Mon-Fri 1.00pm – 7.30pm
Sat 8.00am – 1.00pm
Commercial enquiries
Mon-Fri 8.00am – 5.00pm
Sat 8.00am – 1.00pm

ELMAR'S IN THE VALLEY

Elmar's in the Valley is a multi-award winning German style microbrewery, restaurant, function and event venue.

Located in the heart of the Swan Valley tourist region, just 25 minutes from the Perth city centre, the venue is renowned for the quality of its food and beverage, with the versatility of the venue lending itself to being a great restaurant for every day dining, or the perfect venue for larger functions, including corporate events and outdoor concerts.

Elmar's in the Valley is family friendly, offering friendly service in a relaxed casual environment, with the 'backyard style' fully licensed Beer Garden a very unique offering.

8731 West Swan Rd
Henley Brook
Tel: (08) 9296 6354
www.elmars.com.au

Opening hours:
Wed-Thurs 11.00am – 5.00pm
Fri-Sun 11.00am – 10.00pm

THE BREWERS DRAY

Perth's premier beer & brewery tour operator.

Let us guide you through some of the wonderful award winning breweries of Western Australia on a day to tantalise your senses, stimulate your grey matter and invigorate your spirits!

We provide a relaxed and informal experience and pride ourselves on delivering a fantastic value tour focusing on the three F's, Fun; Food & Froth.

It doesn't stop there! We also produce delicious hand crafted Beer Chutney's and Relishes and even have our own range of unique, all natural Beer Soaps.

Tel: 0423 976 116
tours@thebrewersdray.com.au
www.thebrewersdray.com.au

Tour times:
Full Day Tours run Wed-Sun.

Corporate midweek tours available.

MASH BREWING COMPANY

Opening in 2006, Mash Brewing has rapidly expanded since, and now counts three brewery / restaurant venues in the budding empire. The original brewery is in the Swan Valley, Perth, but has now been joined by Mash Bunbury and Mash Rockingham, each serving beers from the Mash range, as well as specialty beers brewed in-house.

The Mash "Homegrown Range" reflects all beer and cider being naturally brewed in WA using premium raw materials. These include Freo Doctor Pale Lager, West Coast Wheat Beer, Pale, Crush Apple cider and Press Pear cider. Available on tap at all Mash Venues, as well as from local Bottle Shops.

Mash Swan Valley
10250 West Swan Rd
Henley Brook WA 6055
Tel: (08) 9296 5588

Opening hours:
Mon-Thu 11.00am – 5.00pm
Fri-Sun 11.00am-late

Mash Bunbury
2/11 Bonnefoi Blvd
Bunbury WA 6230
Tel: (08) 9721 6111

Opening hours:
7 days from 11.00am

Mash Rockingham
Shop T208 Council Rd
Rockingham Shopping Centre
Rockingham WA 6168
Tel: (08) 9592 9208

Opening hours:
7 days from 11.00am

www.mashbrewing.com.au

Beer & Brewer promotion   WESTERN AUSTRALIA – SWAN VALLEY

FERAL BREWING COMPANY

Feral Brewing Company is a micro brewery situated in the beautiful Swan Valley. Around half an hours drive from the Perth CBD you'll find a unique selection of hand crafted award winning beers and premium wines made with grapes from their own vines.

To complement their outstanding beers and wines, the restaurant serves an exciting menu of modern Australian cuisine. Diners can choose from a full a-la-carte menu at very reasonable prices. Their food philosophy is to use the freshest available local produce. The menu changes regularly to reflect this.

FERAL BEERS

Feral White is produced in the true Belgian style with 50 percent barley and 50 percent wheat and an imported Belgium yeast strain. It is cloudy and unfiltered with coriander and orange peel added during the boil to contribute a spicy citrus flavour. This is a fantastic beer for all occasions and pairs particularly well with seafood and Japanese cuisine.

The India Pale Ale style originated in the eighteenth century when beer was to be shipped from England to India. The brewer's only weapons against spoilage were alcohol and hops. Higher rates of both of these saved the bitter brew on its long sea voyage. A common American variant on the IPA style used more citric hops. Hop Hog is an American style IPA with strong pine needle and citrus aroma followed by an aggressive bitterness and dry finish.

FERAL FUNCTIONS

Are you planning a birthday, engagement or corporate sundowner? Well, why not have it at Feral Brewing Company.

Their venue offers four great function spaces and a range of packages to suit any event.

For all the information you need, email or call Jo functions @feralbrewing.com.au or (08) 9296 4657.

FERAL WEDDINGS

Imagine the birds chirping and the leaves blowing in the wind. Now imagine what it would be like to share your special day in a uniquely special venue like Feral Brewing.

Imagine no more. Feral Brewing is now available for weddings. From the ceremony, to pre wedding drinks and the reception, Feral Brewing has a wedding package to suit everyone.

Let the team organise it for you. Email or call Jo functions@feralbrewing.com.au or (08) 9296 4657.

152 Haddrili Road
Baskerville, Swan Valley
Tel/Fax: (08) 9296 4657
www.feralbrewing.com.au

Opening hours:
7 Days for lunch, Fri and Sat for dinner

NEW ZEALAND BREWING DIRECTORY

LEGEND

- 🟢 NATIONAL/REGIONAL BREWERY
- 🔵 BREW PUB
- 🟡 MICROBREWERY
- 🔴 BREW ON PREMISE
- (BC) BREWING COMPANY

NEW ZEALAND NORTH ISLAND

1.1	Lion-Nathan, Auckland
1.2	DB, Waitemata, Auckland
1.3	Steam Brewing, Auckland
1.4	Independent, Auckland
1.5	Hallertau, Auckland
1.6	Galbraith's Alehouse, Auckland
3	Roosters Brew House, Hastings
4.1	Croucher, Rotorua
4.2	Waipa, Rotorua
5	Waiheke Island Microbrewery
6	Sawmill, Leigh
7	Brewhaus Frings, Whangerei
8	Sunshine Brewery, Gisborne
9	The Filter Room, Hawkes Bay, Napier
10	Kiwi, Morrinsville
11	Peak, Masterton
12	Shamrock, Palmerston North
13	DB, Tui, Mangatainoka
14	Tuatara, Waikanae
15	Mike's Organic Brewery, Urenui
16	Aoteoroa, Kawerau
17	Brewers Bar, Mt Maunganui
18	Waituna, Rewa
19	Coromandel Brewing Company
20	Rogue Brewery, Taupo
21	Kaimai Brewing Company, Mount Manganui, Tauranga (BC)
22	Scott's Brewing
23	Cassels & Sons, Christchurch
24	St Katherines Brewing, Auckland (BC)
25	Epic Brewing Company, Auckland (BC)
26	Island Bay Brewing, Wellington (BC)
27	BREW, Rotorua (BC)
28	Shunters Yard Brewing, Matangi (BC)
29	Kea Brewing, Hartiner, Hawkes Bay (BC)
30	Zeetandt Brewing Co, Kumeu (BC)
(BC)	Liberty Brewing Company, Karaka, New Plymouth
(BC)	Anchor Brewing
(BC)	Yeastie Boys
(BC)	666 Brewing, Auckland
(BC)	Bennett's Beer
(BC)	Ben Middlemiss Brewing Co, Auckland
(BC)	Valkyrie Brewing Co, Auckland

NEW ZEALAND SOUTH ISLAND

1.1	Lion-Nathan, Canterbury
1.2	Dux de Lux, Christchurch
1.3	The Twisted Hop, Christchurch
1.4	Wigram, Christchurch
1.5	Matson's, Christchurch
1.6	Harrington's, Christchurch
1.7	Three Boys, Christchurch
2.1	Lion-Nathan, Speights
2.2	Emerson, Dunedin
2.3	Green Man, Dunedin
2.4	McDuff's, Dunedin
2.5	Meenans, Dunedin
3.1	Founders, Nelson
3.2	Nelson Bays Brewery
3.3	Lighthouse, Nelson
4.1	Moa, Blenheim
4.2	Renaissance, Blenheim
4.3	Pink Elephant, Blenheim
5	Kaiapoi Brewing Co.
6	Brew Moon, Amberley
7	DB, Mainland
8	Invercargill Brewery
9	Dux de Lux, Queenstown
10	Wanaka Beerworks
11	DB, Monteith's, Greymouth
12	West Coast, Westport
13	Mussel Inn, Onekaka
14	Arrow Brewing Company, Arrowtown
15	Townshend Brewery, Upper Moutere
16	Golden Bear Brewing
17	Monkey Wizard Brewery
18	Totara Brewing Co.
19	Sprig & Fern Brewery, Richmond
20	McCashin's Brewery
21	Green Fern Brewery
22	Boundary Road Brewery, Red Hill
23	8 Wired, Blenheim (BC)
24	Dead Good Beers (BC)
(BC)	Golden Ticket Brewing, Christchurch
(BC)	AdLib Brewing, Christchurch

PROUDLY SUPPORTED BY

NZ HOPS
Providing the brewer with the dual benefits of both outstanding aroma and quality bittering. www.nzhops.co.nz

Zymus
We add value by discovering and delivering innovative solutions that vitalise our customer's business. www.zymus.net

NZ

NEW ZEALAND

Kia ora Aotearoa (welcome to NZ in Māori), an island country, with the most breweries per capita in Australasia. The North Island has 35 breweries and five beer companies and South Island has 38 breweries and two beer companies.

Haast River in the remote Wahipounamu World Heritage area, photo courtesy Tourism New Zealand

NZ

NZ

Beautiful Lake Taupo is one of the big drawcards of New Zealand's central North Island.

CENTRAL NORTH ISLAND

Craft beer in New Zealand is a challenge of the trainspotter type. Great little breweries and bars are hidden in all sorts of out-of-the-way places, and trying to get around them all will test the patience of the designated driver. **By Neil Miller**

Auckland is the economic engine and Wellington is the political capital, but the people who live in the plains, hills and mountains of the central North Island of New Zealand pride themselves on their sunny weather and relaxed approach to life. In keeping with this laidback spirit, a large number of smaller breweries are dotted around the region, with most of them more than happy to show thirsty visitors round the tanks, sample the brews and maybe sell a bottle or two for later.

■ PROUDLY ORGANIC

One of the oldest breweries in the region is Mike's Organic Brewery, though for much of its first 21 years it was called White Cliffs Brewery. It was the second brewery in New Zealand to be certified organic (after Founder's in Blenheim) and remains one of only four breweries in the country to hold that accreditation. Mike's is fiercely proud of its fully organic status and low environmental impact brewery operations.

Mike's held the mantle of being the country's smallest commercial brewery for many years, but it has steadily expanded since the Trigg family took over in 2007. As well as a larger and more modern brewery, a tasting room, store and beer garden have recently been constructed in the spacious grounds. Bookings are recommended but it is always worth dropping in as it is a great place to drink beer. The enormous "beer" sign is hard to miss though it does annoy some local bureaucrats.

Mike's has traditionally been known for moderate, balanced beers but the range now includes a hoppy Pilsner, an organic Strawberry Lager and several huge seasonal releases, such as a barrel-aged Whisky Porter and a Double IPA.

The team at Mike's Organic Brewery.

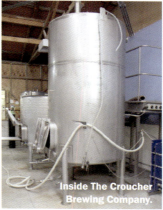

Inside The Croucher Brewing Company.

Andrew Larson of Kaimai Brewing Co samples a new batch.

■ GROWING IN NEW ZEALAND, GROWING OVERSEAS

The Croucher Brewing Co is based in Rotorua. Established by a former university lecturer in 2004, Croucher has developed impressively and in 2010 scooped the prestigious award for Champion International Lager at the New Zealand Beer Awards. Its range also includes a Pale Ale, Hefeweizen and a changing range of limited-edition beers including Christmas Ales and Belgian Strong Ales. While Paul Croucher and Nigel Gregory are champion hosts, it pays to give them advance notice of visits or tours.

Kaimai Brewing Co is based in the same building as Croucher and actually owns the brewing plant. Brewer Andrew Larson does things very differently from most Kiwi and Aussie brewers. His beers are made using a high proportion of rye mixed with the more usual barley. Brewing with rye is generally considered difficult, but Andrew says it brings an added dimension to his beers. Kaimai also started selling its products overseas before selling them in New Zealand, reversing the usual model of starting small and eventually building up to exporting. The range is anchored by a Golden Ale and a Porter.

■ OLD-SCHOOL BREWERIES

Roosters Brew House has been operating just outside of Hastings for many years. The brewery is attached to a casual café which offers tastings of the beers as well as drinks and food. Roosters has always been a brewery very comfortable in its own skin, never looking to bottle its beers or send them too far. It rarely enters competitions either, preferring instead to concentrate on making fresh natural beers for locals and visitors.

Roosters' range is uncomplicated. From time to time, it produces specialty beers that are always eagerly sought out. Roosters is an old-style brewery that epitomises the pace of the region.

It is a similar story at the Brewer's Bar in Mount Manganui. The brewery sits directly behind a largely blue-collar bar and makes 500-litre batches of its seven beers. The range includes such staples as a pilsner, draught and stout, and is sold on tap on the premises or in hand-labelled bottles or kegs to take away. Brewer's Bar is a popular stop for tour groups.

On the east coast, Sunshine Brewery has a modern feel, although it was founded way back in 1989 by Geoff Logan. Tired of American surfers making fun of New Zealand beer, Geoff created Gisborne Gold, a brew that quickly became the country's first iconic craft beer of the modern era. It is available nationally in bottles, but a number of Sunshine's specialty beers, such as Black Magic, are limited to kegs and riggers (large plastic bottles). The brewery in Gisborne takes its brewing seriously but there is still a subtle surfer vibe and the hospitality is rightly renowned.

■ TAKING A MODERN APPROACH

Hawkes Bay Independent Brewery is a growing brewery in Napier that produces its own brand of beers and the mainstream Mates beer range, plus ginger beer, ciders and some pre-mixed spirits. Established in 1995, the company moved to its high-tech, custom-built brewery in 2007, and opened the adjourning tasting room and restaurant – The Filter Room – soon after. The Filter Room serves the brewery's full range of drinks and occasionally pilot brews as well.

The Liberty Brewing Company has opened in New Plymouth as the venture of top homebrewer Joseph Wood. He also commercially supplies hops, yeast and malt. Liberty's products span the beery spectrum from hoppy ales to rich Stouts.

The Aotearoa Breweries in Kawerau in Eastern Bay of Plenty is a family-run brewery that makes the Mata range of "beers from the edge." For a number of years, Aotearoa Breweries concentrated on making a Pale Ale, a Manuka-flavoured Lager and a seasonal Feijoa beer. In 2010, the company added a Stout (Black-Bru) and an Amber Ale (Brown Boy) to its repertoire. Specialty beers are frequent additions to the menu and the brewers have freely experimented with ingredients such as kumara (native sweet potato) and horopito (a peppery native herb). Aotearoa Breweries puts a strong emphasis on beer and food matching and it has done well in a number of competitions, winning a number

Wassail Brauhaus

BREW

Bungy jumping at Taupo Bungy, Lake Taupo.

of medals at the BrewNZ Beer Awards. As usual, it is best to organise a visit or brewery tour in advance.

Unfortunately, not all breweries are welcoming. The Kiwi Brewery in Morrinsville and the Rogue Brewery in Taupo do not allow tours and their products can be hard to find, even locally. The tiny Waipai Brewery, which evolved out of a homebrewing operation, closed after a business deal turned sour. It will not be reopening as a brewery.

■ BLUES, BREWS AND BBQS

Many of the breweries in the central region of the North Island have a strong presence at the annual Blues, Brews and BBQs festival in Mount Manganui. This is a huge event that celebrates all things music, beer, wine, food and fun. The focus is unashamedly on promoting craft beer, particularly local craft beer, and for many it is the highlight of the beer year. It is held annually in January and tickets should be booked early.

■ PLACES TO DRINK AND STAY

Pubs serving good beer can be hard to find outside the main centres, as the big breweries look to lock in often struggling establishments to limited beer selections. Notable exceptions include the craft-beer pub BREW in Rotorua, which is operated by The Croucher Brewing Co. BREW showcases its own beers as well as the best offerings of other craft producers.

Also in Rotorua, the Great Kiwi Ale House on Hinemoa Street is also a must-visit beer destination.

Easily one of the country's most unique beer destinations is the Wassail Brauhaus, the first and still only Bed, Breakfast and Beer. Basically, it is a lovely modern cottage located at the base of Mount Egmont with a small brewery which opens directly into the lounge. The Wassail hosts are first rate and the food outstanding.

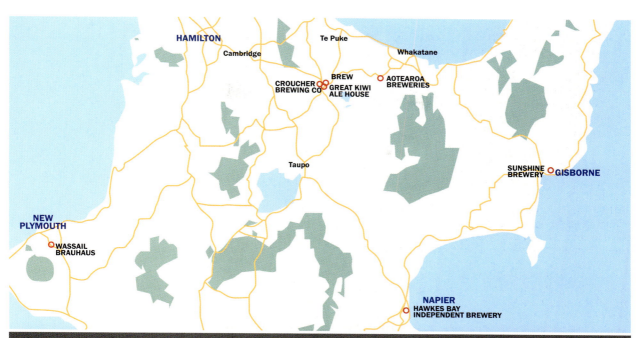

BREWERIES & BEER BARS

Aotearoa Breweries
Kawerau, www.mata.net.nz

BREW
Rotorua, www.brewpub.co.nz

Brewers Bar
Mt Maunganui, (07) 575 2739

Croucher Brewing Co
Rotorua,
www.croucherbrewing.co.nz

Great Kiwi Ale House
Rotorua, www.greatkiwialehouse.co.nz

Hawkes Bay Independent Brewery
Napier, www.thefilterroom.co.nz

Kaimai Brewing Company
Tauranga, www.kaimaibrewing.com

Kiwi Breweries
Morringsville, (07) 887 7742

Liberty Brewing Company
www.libertybrewing.co.nz

Mike's
Taranaki, www.organicbeer.co.nz

Roosters Brew House
Hastings, (06) 879 4127

Sunshine Brewery
Gisborne, www.gisbornegold.co.nz

Waipa Brewery
Rotorua, (07) 343 9576

Wassail Brauhaus
Egmont Village, www.brauhaus.co.nz

■ TOURISM ATTRACTIONS APLENTY

Rotorua is renowned for its geo-thermal activity and Maori cultural displays; beautiful Lake Taupo is a top spot for boating and fishing. The world-famous Waitomo Caves remain hugely popular and newer eco-tourism activities are flourishing. In Taranaki, enjoy the Forgotten Highway, the White Cliffs walkway and Egmont National Park.

The central North Island showcases a vast range of scenery and settlements. The pace is gentler and while the breweries are generally smaller than their city counterparts, several are growing strongly – Mike's, Croucher and Hawkes Bay Independent are all now established national brands.

After a long day out in the sun, nothing beats relaxing with a tasty local beer.

THINGS TO SEE AND DO

Forgotten Highway – www.taranaki.info/visit/theme.php/page/forgotten-world-highway

JANUARY
Blues, Brews and BBQs
www.bluesbrews.co.nz

MARCH
Surf Lifesaving Championships
www.surflifesaving.org.nz

SEPTEMBER
Rally Gisborne
www.rallynz.org.nz
Deco Wine and Surprise Tour
www.artdeconapier.com
Hastings Blossom Festival www.visithastings.co.nz/eventlisting/hastings-blossom-festival
The Running of the Lambs www.facebook.com/event.php?eid=209929002371196

OCTOBER
Poverty Bay A&P Show
www.gisborneshow.co.nz

NOVEMBER
Lake Taupo Cycle Challenge
www.cyclechallenge.com

Oriental Bay, Wellington

NZ

LOWER NORTH ISLAND

The lower half of the North Island may only have a relative smattering of breweries, but it offers a great deal to the beer aficionado or casual drinker who enjoys a good pint.

By Neil Miller

The main craft brewery in the region is Tuatara Brewing Company which is based near Waikanae on the Kapiti Coast. Founded in 2001, Tuatara was the inaugural champion brewery of New Zealand in 2008/2009. The rapidly growing brewery is located on a working farm but tours can be arranged on request. The growth of Tuatara was so impressive that it has been named as one of the 50 fastest growing Kiwi companies in 2009 and 2010.

Head brewer Carl Vasta, a young veteran of craft brewing, produces a range of European-style beers made with local ingredients. His range includes a Hefe, Pilsner, Porter, Pale Ale and a strong Belgian Ale called Ardennes. These were joined in 2011 by Tuatara APA which is made with generous additions of imported American hops. It is proving a real hit with drinkers with the brewery constantly struggling to keep up with demand.

Wellington is the capital of New Zealand and, in the view of many, the craft-beer capital as well. One report estimates that nearly half the craft beer consumed in this country is drunk in Wellington. The city has a dedicated customer base that is willing to pay decent prices for quality products. That makes it even more surprising that there is not really a brewery in the city (though Tuatara is within the Greater Wellington region).

Mac's Brewery on the Wellington waterfront closed in 2010 and shipped south to become part of the larger Lion Brewery in Christchurch, which was extensively damaged by the 2011 Canterbury earthquake. Estadio Bar (formerly The Temperance) has a small brewing kit in its massive bar that can produce batches of around 500 litres. The brewer is the talented Dion Paige, but the bar's Latin theme means the emphasis is generally on lighter lagers.

Further north, Peak Brewery in Masterton is going from strength to strength. Production of its traditional-style

Tuatara, the region's most famous beer

Tui Brewery

ales is growing, and Peak is one of only four certified organic breweries in the country. Each of the brewery's beers is named after a prominent geographical feature. For example, Mendip Bitter is named after the Mendip Hills near Glastonbury in the UK. The Peak Brewery is appropriately located on a lifestyle block and, while visitors are welcome, appointments are required.

By far the biggest brewery in the region is the giant DB Tui brewing complex at Mangatainoka. More than 40,000 visitors pass through the doors each year, with professional tours and tastings available (bookings essential). This huge commercial brewery makes Tui and a range of other mainstream DB brands but may be of interest to beer lovers because it uses the rare continuous fermentation process for some of the brews. Virtually all breweries today use batch brewing instead.

■ VIRTUAL BREWERIES & BEER FESTIVALS

Stu McKinlay, one of the creative geniuses behind Yeastie Boys, is based in Wellington and many of the company's test batches are brewed there. However, commercial production of Yeastie Boys beers takes place at Invercargill Brewery, an arrangement the Boys describe as "post-modern brewing".

One of Yeastie Boys' most famous offerings is Rex Attitude, a Golden Ale made with 100 per cent peat-smoked malt usually destined for whisky distilling. It was billed as a world first, and there certainly aren't many clear golden beers that have an aroma of smoked kippers and medicine.

The Waituna Brewing Company is based in Rewa, but its flagship TaaKawa beer, made with the native herb Kawakawa, is contract brewed in Auckland by Steam Brewing. Similarly, the Island Bay Brewing Company, brainchild of beer-loving artist Maurice Bennett, has its beers contract brewed by Harrington's. The Shamrock Brewing Company in Palmerston North has closed.

Beervana, New Zealand's largest and most prestigious beer festival, is held in Wellington each August in conjunction with the New Zealand Beer Awards. In June, the Society of Beer Advocates organises a beer festival to celebrate Matariki (Maori New Year).

■ SOME OF THE BEST BARS IN THE COUNTRY

Given the relative paucity of local breweries – tiny Nelson alone has more than the entire lower North Island – the real strength of the region lies in its bars, restaurants and stores, particularly in Wellington. In the 2010 *Beer*

Casual drinkers and connoisseurs alike flock to the annual Beervana festival.

The many delights of Regional Wines & Spirits

Malthouse offers the largest range of beers in NZ

The Hop Garden

■ BEER AT THE FINE-DINING TABLE

Wellington diners are spoilt for choice with a huge number of eateries offering cuisines from Kiwi classic to Creole. Many places still have a token beer selection but a gratifying number are beginning to take beer seriously, accepting it as an integral part of the dining experience. This shift is being led by a number of fine-dining establishments, which have lifted the quality of both their beer lists and service.

One of the pioneers was noted chef Martin Bosley, who regularly champions beer and food matching at the Beervana festival. At his award-winning Yacht Club Restaurant, patrons can even order his famous degustation menu with beer matches instead of the traditional wine.

The winner of the 2010 *Beer & Brewer* Award for Best Restaurant was Ortega Fish Shack. Ortega combines fine dining with an extensive, well-balanced beer list. The proprietors take their beer as seriously as their seafood, which is very seriously indeed. The menu is compiled daily based on the best ingredients available, and the beer list regularly includes seasonal and limited-edition brews.

Top restaurants Logan Brown (modern-New Zealand cuisine) and Ambeli (cutting-edge Mediterranean) pride themselves on their beer matches and the advocacy of their staff. Quality beer has a place on the finest tables in Wellington and other restaurants and cafés are taking notice of the growing popularity and respectability of beer.

You're spoilt for choice at Hashigo Zake

& Brewer Annual Awards, the top two New Zealand Beer Venues were both in Wellington.

Malthouse on Courtenay Place serves the largest range of beers in New Zealand, including an ever-changing selection of Kiwi craft beers and exotic imports. The friendly staff, led by the affable Colin Mallon, pour beer from 30 taps, six fridges, two English hand pumps, an innovative hopinator and a large cellar selection.

Named after Japanese slang for a pub crawl, Hashigo Zake is a central city basement bar with a strong selection of craft beers and unusual imported beers, particularly from Japan and the US. Owner Dominic Kelly spent years in Japan, an experience that has influenced the beer selection, food and décor. The tiny kitchen whips up some of the best gourmet pies in the land, and one of the most popular bar snacks is octopus dumplings.

Out in Newtown, Bar Edward is an established haven for quality beers and hearty pub food. It was also the venue for a charity event that raised more than $8000 for earthquake relief in a single night. Proprietor James Henderson has recently expanded his bar portfolio, opening The Hop Garden on the slopes of Mount Victoria. This spacious bar and restaurant has a strong tap selection, a growing bottled-beer list and delicious beer-friendly food.

The Brühaus opened quietly at the end of 2010. It has taken over from a long-closed café and its Willeston Street premises are spacious and smart. The beer selection has passed 100 offerings with a mix of beers primarily from New Zealand, the UK and Belgium. Food and service have significantly lifted since opening, and has become a popular choice for business lunches and lazy weekend brunches.

■ EVER-IMPROVING SELECTION ON THE SHELVES

In New Zealand, beer can be sold in supermarkets and grocery stores as well as bottle shops. Dairies (small convenience stores) can also sell beer, but could lose that right under new legislation expected to pass in early 2012. The quality of the selection varies wildly from store to store but in general the situation is steadily improving. A number of supermarkets – particularly New World supermarkets – have extensive selections.

The best beer store in New Zealand is Wellington's Regional Wines & Spirits, which has a tremendous selection and quality education programs. Moore Wilson's on Tory

Chef Martin Bosley champions beer and food matching at his award-winning eatery, Martin Bosley's Yacht Club Restaurant.

Moore Wilson's

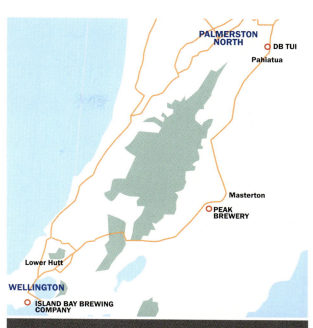

Street is the best small bottle store while New World Island Bay and New World Thorndon have probably the largest selections in the nation.

■ LOTS TO DO AND SEE AND DRINK

For a long time, visitors bypassed Wellington, which was derided as a city of bureaucrats. Extensive redevelopment of the waterfront and CBD has transformed the city; now, Wellington is renowned for its coffee, culture and history. Parliament is sited there but the biggest visitor attraction is the modern and interactive Museum of New Zealand – Te Papa (Our Place). It is a world-class museum and art gallery.

The historic cable car offers panoramic views to those on their way to the expansive botanical gardens. Nature lovers should also head to Zealandia wildlife sanctuary, where native birds and lizards can be viewed at close quarters. Zealandia is a hit with adults and children alike.

Another form of animal behaviour is on display at the annual Wellington Rugby Sevens tournament. Every February, the city is awash with colour as 35,000 people enjoy two days of action at the Wellington Stadium and party throughout the city. It is the biggest hospitality time of the year – beating out even Saint Patrick's Day.

The lower North Island might not have the most breweries, but it has great local products backed up by the venues and stores to help people enjoy the best of beer.

FEBRUARY
Wellington Sevens
www.nzisevens.co.nz

JUNE
SOBA Matariki Beer Festival www.soba.org.nz
Baby Pops www.wellingtonorchestra.co.nz

AUGUST
Beervana
www.beervana.co.nz

Visa Wellington on a Plate
www.wellingtononaplate.com
World of WearableArt
www.worldofwearableart.com

NOVEMBER
Toast Martinborough
www.toastmartinborough.co.nz

EVERY SUNDAY
City Market
www.citymarket.co.nz

THINGS TO SEE AND DO

Beervana www.beervana.co.nz **Cable Car** www.wellingtoncablecar.co.nz **Estadio** www.estadio.co.nz **Logan Brown** www.loganbrown.co.nz **Martin Bosley's Yacht Club Restaurant** www.martin-bosley.com **Ortega Fish Shack** www.ortega.co.nz **SOBA** www.soba.org.nz **Te Papa** www.tepapa.govt.nz **Wellington Sevens** www.nzisevens.co.nz **Zealandia** www.visitzealandia.com

BREWERIES AND BEER BARS

Bar Edward
167 Riddiford St, Newtown
(04) 389 9933
www.baredward.co.nz

The Brühaus
24 Willeston St, Wellington
(04) 472 2120

DB Tui
(06) 376 0815
www.tui.co.nz

Hashigo Zake
25 Taranaki St, Te Aro
(04) 384 7300
www.hashigozake.com

The Hop Garden
13 Pirie St, Mt Victoria
(04) 801 8807
www.hopgarden.co.nz

Island Bay Brewing
35 Milne Tce, Island Bay
(04) 383 8190
www.bennettsbeer.co.nz

Malthouse
48 Courtenay Pl, Wellington
(04) 802 5484
www.themalthouse.co.nz

Moore Wilson's
93 Tory St, Te Aro
(04) 384 9906
www.moorewilson.co.nz

New World
Island Bay and Thorndon
ww.newworld.co.nz

Peak Brewery
160 East Taratahi Rd, RD 7
Masterton
(0211) 496 996
www.peak-brewery.co.nz

Regional Wines & Spirits
15 Ellice St, Mt Victoria
(04) 385 6952
www.regionalwines.co.nz

Tuatara Brewing Co
Akatarawa Rd, Waikanae
(04) 293 3351
www.tuatarabrewing.co.nz

Waituna Brewing
Rangitikei Valley Rd, Rewa
(06) 328 6707
www.waitunabrewing.com

Yeastie Boys
www.yeastieboys.co.nz

Photography from The Hop Garden (Hop Garden) Richard Catto

NZ

TOP OF THE NORTH ISLAND

Auckland

Cosmopolitan Auckland is a regular stop on the NZ tourist trail – with good reason. As a beer destination, however, the city and surrounds are not so popular. Look a little deeper and you'll find craft breweries aplenty. Let's take it from the top. **By Greig McGill**

The upper part of the North Island is often overlooked on beer destinations due to its paucity of craft breweries. If you know where to look, however, the liquid rewards await.

■ NORTHLAND

This popular tourist destination is flush with great food and wine, friendly people and colonial history. For lovers of flavourful beer though, it's as devoid of joy as parliament debating alcohol reform. Happily, there are a few shining beacons for the thirsty cerevisaphile.

The Pear Tree in Kerikeri is well known for its excellent cuisine and has recently added the tasty Mata range of beer to go with it. Experiments with food matches are underway, though are yet to make it to the menu.

The historic Duke of Marlborough in Russell would be worth visiting even if it didn't have the rather wonderful and equally iconic Emerson's beers in the fridge.

For an educational offset to these epicurean opportunities, head to the Waitangi Treaty Grounds. New Zealand's founding document, the treaty of Waitangi, was signed there in February 1840. Today, the grounds house cultural displays, an historic home, and *Ngatokimatawhaorua* – one of the world's largest Maori ceremonial war canoes.

The Brauhaus Frings in Whangarei is something of an institution. Run by a Braumeister from Bremen, you might expect frothing Maß of Helles borne to you by striking examples of Teutonic womanhood, while you heroically set about your dish consisting of most of a pig. Brauhaus Frings breaks that stereotype with a laidback take on the Kiwi pub. It offers a simple but tasty traditional pub menu (the

Waitangi Treaty Grounds

Hallertau

burgers are highly recommended). The beers are unassuming, but the locals rave about them.

Five minutes' drive from Whangarei is Kiwi North. It offers plenty of entertainment for the family, including a nocturnal kiwi viewing experience, heritage park and local museum.

It's a beautiful drive out to Leigh, and to make it even better, there's a brew-bar/café at the end of it. The Leigh Sawmill Café is known for live music as well as for its well-appointed brewery (tours available). The café offers a sample tray of the beers – not including the rather strong Doctor, so you'll have to take your medicine separately! There are many vineyards to explore in the area too, so oenophiles should be fairly happy here.

Tahi Bar in Warkworth is one of the most individual bars in New Zealand. Set up by Ian and Silke Marriott in 2008, it combines many different elements into a charming whole. Tahi offers a veritable beer tour through New Zealand craft brewing, and Ian personally chooses beers which he thinks are drinking at their best. The tap line-up is small but well-chosen, usually featuring the excellent beers from Hallertau, and the contents of the well-stocked fridges will keep even the most avid beer geek happy for quite some time. Tahi is in a slightly quirky back-alley location but has a great vibe. Ian loves talking beer, so bend his ear if he's around.

■ AUCKLAND

While it might be controversial to include the town of Riverhead as part of Auckland, there's nothing debatable about the quality of the ales brewed at nearby Hallertau Brewbar and Restaurant. Originally a winery, under the passionate and energetic guidance of owner and brewer Stephen Plowman, this up-market yet rustic brewbar has become one of the places for Auckland's cool kids to be seen. Don't let that put you off though – Plowman and his staff have worked very hard to make this a place where everyone feels welcome, and the diversity of the crowd is matched by the variety of the beers. The balanced house beers and beer-matched menu work in perfect harmony, and the kitchen more than lives up to the high standard set by the brewer. Tours are not generally offered, but ask at the bar in case Steve is around and feels like showing off the tools of his trade.

Known for its range of American-influenced hop-driven Ales, Epic Beer is based out of the Steam Brewing facility in Otahuhu. Tours of the brewery are not regularly available, but Epic beers can be sampled at many locations around Auckland such as Andrew Andrew, the new craft-beer haven down by the waterfront. Epic produces several of the most awarded beers in New Zealand. Owner and head brewer Luke Nicholas recently hired the ex-Thornbridge (UK) "brewing rockstar" Kelly Ryan, so you can expect Epic beers to push even more boundaries in the future.

Steam Brewing Company primarily brews for its own English-styled Cock & Bull pubs. Pop into any one of them – there are several around Auckland – to try fresh Epic Pale Ale on tap or the excellent range of Ales including the tasty Fuggles Best Bitter on handpump. Monk's Habit (more an American-style Imperial Red Ale than a Belgian beer) is a favourite of many of New Zealand's beer geeks.

Speaking of beer geeks, if they have a temple in Auckland, it might well be Galbraith's Alehouse. Built inside a former library, Galbraith's is a homage to the better sort of English pub. The brewery workings are on show, viewed through panes of perspex, and the massive carved-kauri bar and ornate fittings add to the atmosphere. The house beers are mainly in the English style and showcase Keith

Galbraith's Alehouse

Shunters Yard

Epic's Luke Nicholas

Waiheke Island Brewery

The boys from homebrew Mecca, Brewers Coop

Galbraith and brewer Ian Ramsay's perfect sense of balance. Bob Hudson's Bitter is highly recommended, but you really can't go wrong. A recent feature is the addition of several rotating guest taps to complement the house brews and the plentiful and cosmopolitan fridge selection.

A short ferry trip takes you to Waiheke Island, which will be a hit with the family due to the wealth of impressive scenery, vineyards and boutiques. Since you're there anyway, it would be silly not to take a tour of the Waiheke Island Brewery. Brewer Alan Knight is a stalwart of the New Zealand brewing scene, and a tour of the brewery is well worth taking. The brewery's gift shop is an attraction in its own right too, with all sorts of local goodies to go with the freshly filled flagons of beer.

For the keen homebrewer, a visit to *Beer & Brewer*'s 2010 Best Homebrew Shop, Brewers Coop, is a must. It's a haven for homebrewers of beer, wine or spirits, and proprietor Mike Ellwood is one of the friendliest people around.

The City of Sails is also home to the big boys of brewing – Lion Nathan and DB Breweries. Unfortunately, neither offer tours of their impressive facilities, but you can sample their many and varied wares at bars throughout Auckland, such as the Bluestone Room on Durham Lane and the stylish Brew on Quay bar down by the waterfront.

There is plenty to do in Auckland other than bar hopping. Kelly Tarlton's Underwater World offers an amazing look at life under the sea and is highly recommended for the whole family. For the more adventurous, there's also Snowplanet, New Zealand's only indoor snowdome.

■ HAMILTON AND COROMANDEL

Hamilton is fast becoming a beer destination, with some great craft-beer bars opening up in recent times. It's not all beer though, as there's plenty to do in this river city. Take a romantic stroll through the tranquil Hamilton Gardens, head to the Hamilton Zoo for a family day out, or take a scenic drive out to the Coromandel Peninsula.

The rugged and beautiful Coromandel Peninsula is home to one of New Zealand's newest breweries, The Coromandel Brewing Company. It's run by Englishman Neil Vowles, who is passionate about bringing New Zealand hop flavours to his growing range of easy drinking beers. Tours are by arrangement only at this stage, and distribution is fiercely local, so you'll need to hunt!

Back in Hamilton itself, Gothenburg is a Euro-styled bar with friendly service and Hamilton's largest selection of beers. There are often up to 80 beers in the bar fridges, mostly Belgian flavour bombs, personally selected by owners Carl and Susanna, as well as something local on tap to complement the excellent food.

The most overtly craft-beer friendly bar in Hamilton has to be House on Hood. With the tagline "the home of great beer" and up to 12 taps pouring a changing selection of some of New Zealand's most interesting and flavourful beers, the team at House go all out to show that Hamilton is a real beer city. All the staff know their beer, and will happily recommend a match for their pub-food-with-a-twist menu items. House also runs regular beer events, such as Beer versus Wine dinners, and has a weekly Beer Club which showcases new or rare releases.

Hamilton also has the Shunters Yard brewery. Originally a hobby for brewers Dave Smith and Peter McKenzie, this little venture is rapidly expanding based on consistently good product and consumer demand. The brewery can be toured by arrangement – just ask at the café. The duo produces a Stout and a Pilsner year round, but is looking to expand its range soon. Of course, by the time it does, there will most likely be at least one new brewery and bar open in Hamilton… but that's another story!

Gothenburg, Hamilton

BREWERIES, BEER COMPANIES

666 Brewing Co
www.666brewing.com

Boundary Road Brewery
Red Hill, www.boundaryroadbrewery.co.nz

Brauhaus Frings
Whangarei, www.frings.co.nz

DB – Waitemata Brewery
Auckland, www.dbbreweries.co.nz

Epic Beer/Steam Brewing Company
Otahuhu, www.epicbeer.com
www.steambrewing.co.nz

Galbraith's Alehouse
Auckland, www.alehouse.co.nz

Hallertau Brewbar and Restaurant
Riverhead, www.hallertau.co.nz

Independent Liquor
Papakura, www.independentliquor.co.nz

Lion Breweries
Newmarket, (09) 377 8840

Saratoga Estate
Weiheke Island, www.saratogaestate.com

Shunters Yard Brewery
Matangi, (07) 829 5826

The Coromandel Brewing Company
Matarangi, (07) 866 2927

The Leigh Sawmill Café
Leigh, www.sawmillcafe.co.nz

Waiheke Island Brewery
Waiheke Island, www.waihekebrewery.co.nz

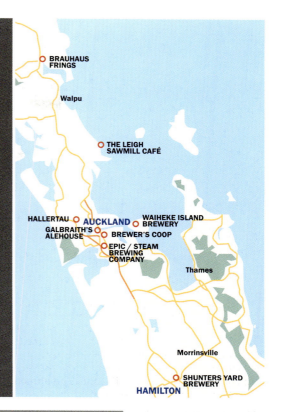

BEER BARS

Andrew Andrew
201 Quay St, Auckland
(09) 377 0040

Brew on Quay
102 Quay St, Auckland
www.brewonquay.co.nz

Cock & Bull
Botany: (09) 271 2001
Ellerslie: (09) 579 5592
Lynfield: (09) 626 0640
Hamilton: (07) 850 5254
Newmarket: (09) 529 2485
www.cockandbull.co.nz

Fort Street Union
Level 1, 16 Fort St,
Auckland
(09) 309 0315

Golden Dawn
134 Ponsonby Rd,
Ponsonby, Auckland
(09) 376 9929

Gothenburg
15 Hood St,
Hamilton
www.gothenburg.co.nz

House on Hood
27 Hood St, Hamilton
www.houseonhood.co.nz

O'Carrolls
10 Vulcan Lane, Auckland
(09) 300 7117

Tahi Bar
1 Neville St, Warkworth
www.tahibar.com

The Bluestone Room
9-11 Durham Lane,
Auckland
www.thebluestoneroom.co.nz

The Duke of Marlborough Hotel
35 The Strand, Russell,
Bay of Islands
www.theduke.co.nz

The Occidental
Belgian Beer Cafe
6-8 Vulcan Lane, Auckland
www.occidentalbar.co.nz

The Pear Tree
215 Kerikeri Rd,
Kerikeri, Bay of Islands
www.thepeartre.co.nz

HOMEBREW SHOP

Brewers Coop
3 Prescott St, Penrose
(09) 525 2448
www.brewerscoop.co.nz

EVENTS

FEBRUARY
Devonport Food Wine & Music Festival
www.devonportwinefestival.co.nz

Kumeu Beer Food & Wine Festival
Kumea Showgrounds

SUMMER
The New Zealand Beer Festival
www.beerfestival.co.nz

NZ

Lake Wakatipu, Queenstown

BOTTOM OF THE SOUTH ISLAND

There's a strong brewing culture in the south, and the region's beer- and winemakers are working together to get their industries back on track after recent natural disasters. **By Liz Lewis**

Speight's Brewery Heritage tour participants

Otago might be best known for it's award-winning wines, but beer connoisseurs will tell you it's also home to some pretty fine brews.

■ DUNEDIN'S PRIDE OF THE SOUTH

Taking pride of place is Dunedin's Speight's Brewery. Since 1876, the Speight's Brewery has been supplying the city's residents, and the world, with some mighty fine beers. The hour-and-a-half tour of the working brewery and museum is a popular tourist attraction. And those with a sweet tooth or children in tow should also consider visiting Cadbury World, a working chocolate factory on Cumberland Street.

Being a university town, there is no shortage of beer in Dunedin. Local microbreweries such as Emerson's, McDuff,

Richard Emerson (centre right) with the brewing team at Emerson's, Dunedin

Beer & Brewer 2010 People's Choice Award runner-up, Tonic bar, in Dunedin

Some of the organic Green Man range

and the certified-organic Green Man don't offer brewery tours, but their beers can be purchased onsite or tasted at the many pubs around town.

Emerson's Brewery makes a variety of award-winning craft beers, including the 1812 India Pale Ale once rated by renowned English beer critic Michael Jackson as one of the best 500 beers in the world.

The Green Man Brewery is as green as it gets, producing natural, organic beers in more than a dozen varieties, ranging from a traditional Stout (one of only 13 New Zealand beers listed in the book *1001 Beers You Must Taste Before You Die*) and German-style Lager to the unique Tequila Beer and Whiskey Bock.

Dunedin also boasts a host of craft-beer bars, including Tonic (a runner-up in the 2010 *Beer & Brewer* People's Choice Awards for best beer venues in New Zealand), Albar and Metro Cafe and Bar. All of which are within walking distance of each other in the Octagon, Dunedin's bustling city centre.

■ DAY TRIPS FROM DUNEDIN

To the east is the Otago Peninsula, considered by many to be the wildlife capital of New Zealand. Yellow-eyed penguins, hooker sea lions and royal albatrosses make their home in the hidden coves and beaches here. And atop the hill, overlooking it all, is the fascinating Larnach Castle.

To the west is the Otago Rail Trail, with its numerous historic gold-mining towns, many with their original pubs still standing. You could pedal your way around in three to four days, staying in some of the numerous historic hotels along the way. But an easier option for those short of time would be driving along Route 85 to St Bathans for a drink at the infamous Vulcan Hotel and the Royal Hotel at nearby Naseby, where you can also have a go at curling, too.

To the south is moonshine country, easily reached by driving along what has been dubbed the Presidential Highway between the towns of Clinton and Gore. The region's colourful history of illicit stills and moonshine runners can be discovered at Gore's Hokonui Moonshine Museum. Better still, visit in February for the Hokonui Moonshiners' Festival.

From Gore, it's only a short drive via State Highway One to New Zealand's southernmost brewery. The award-winning Invercargill Brewery produces a diverse selection of handcrafted beers and ciders, including Farmhouse Ale SA!son and limited-edition Strong Scotch Ale Men'nskurts

■ ACTION-PACKED QUEENSTOWN

On Church Street, a charming old stone cottage houses the popular Dux de Lux. A combination of bar and brewhouse, The Dux produces a variety of beers, ranging from the slightly nutty Alpine Ale to the sweet Sou'Wester Stout.

For a more intimate beer experience, try out the compact Atlas Beer Bar on Steamers Wharf, featuring beers from Dunedin and Invercargill. Or, if you want to compare local to international beers, head over to the equally small Minibar in Eureka Arcade. Space might be limited, but its selection of international beers is anything but.

A weekend spent in Queenstown shouldn't just be about beer, however. Those just wanting to mellow out should take

Pomeroy's

Harrington's Bar

Dux de Lux, Queenstown

some time to cruise Lake Wakatipu on the HMS *Earnslaw* or check out the Queenstown skyline with a trip up the gondola. The views are truly spectacular.

Skiers, on the other hand, will want to spend their days up at Coronet Peak or the Remarkables, taking advantage of the region's impressive ski fields and maybe even having a try at heli-skiing.

■ DAY TRIPS FROM QUEENSTOWN

For something different, catch the double-decker bus to Arrowtown and check out the Arrow Brewing Company. Or, take a scenic drive north to Wanaka, stopping off along the way at the historic Cordrona Hotel that was featured in a Speight's television advertisement.

The Wanaka Beerworks, located next to the New Zealand Fighter Pilots Museum, offers a daily brewery tour and sampling from Monday to Saturday at 2pm.

Sample a few brews and then head to The Puzzling World of Stuart Landsborough, a unique attraction featuring illusion rooms, crooked buildings, and possibly New Zealand's most unusual public toilets.

And once you've built up an appetite, you can't go wrong with the Speight's Ale House, where you can not only get huge meals but learn the Southern Man song and watch rugby on large-screen TVs while trying out a variety of Speight's beers.

■ CHRISTCHURCH'S BREWING FUTURE

Christchurch has been a leader in craft breweries for the past couple of decades. But with the city having been hit hard by heavy seismic activity recently, the breweries' futures remain up in the air.

Three Boys Brewery suffered a lot of damage in the earthquakes, causing them to shut down temporarily. But plans are afoot to reopen and start brewing again as soon as possible – something that will please devotees of The Three Boys Indian Pale Ale.

Close by, new start-up Cassels & Sons Brewery, in the old Woolston Tannery, took a heavy hit. A long-awaited brew-pub is due to open in 2011, serving brews including the elderberry-infused Elder Ale and the roast dark Lager Dunkel.

Two brew-bars in central Christchurch, The Twisted Hop (winner of the 2010 *Beer & Brewer* People's Choice Award for best brew-bar/pub) and Dux de Lux, remain closed until further notice.

Sadly, the Christchurch Dux de Lux, located in the The Arts Centre, has since had its tenancy cancelled, leaving its future in Christchurch uncertain.

The Twisted Hop has been doing a little brewing out at Three Boys Brewery. But its brew-pub, located in the inaccessible red zone, will be out of action for some time.

The good news is that The Twisted Hop management is looking at alternative locations – either with a pub in the suburbs or a new brewery and pub in a rural setting just outside of Christchurch city limits.

Meanwhile, Pomeroy's Old Brewery Inn, located just outside the red zone, is open for business. Owners Steve and Victoria Pomeroy have created a really community-oriented pub on the site of what was Wards Brewery, offering a great range of New Zealand craft beers and wines.

The suburban breweries faired much better, with Matson's Brewery, a large-scale independent brewery located behind the Parkhouse Tavern in Sockburn, continuing to produce its naturally crafted premium beers.

Harringtons' Breweries on Ferry Road is still producing a variety of beers to suit every taste, from the Belgium Tempest Golden Lager to the Kentucky bourbon-infused Big John Special Reserve. Wigram Brewing Company, too, suffered minimal to no damage.

The Brew Moon Cafe and Brewery, just 30 minutes north of Christchurch on State Highway One, is a popular stop-off point for locals and travellers alike. The $10 tasting platter is the perfect way to sample its brews. Add a gourmet pizza or ploughman's platter and you'll not want to leave in a hurry.

And for those looking to escape Christchurch for a while, it's an easy half-day drive over either Arthur's Pass or the Lewis Pass to the west coast town of Westport and its West Coast Brewing Company, makers of the certified-organic Green Fern Lager.

Quake damage at The Twisted Hop

Wanaka Beerworks

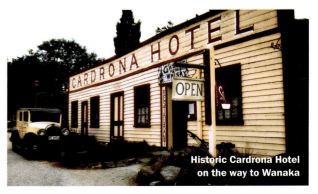

Historic Cardrona Hotel on the way to Wanaka

BEER BARS

Albar
135 Stuart St, Dunedin
(03) 479 2468

Atlas Beer Cafe
Steamer Wharf, Queenstown
(03) 442 5995

Cardrona Hotel
Crown Range Rd, RD1 Wanaka
(03) 443 8153
www.cardronahotel.co.nz

Metro Cafe and Bar
153 Stuart St, Dunedin
(03) 477 7084

Minibar
Eureka Arcade, The Mall, Queenstown
PH: 03 441 3212

Pomeroy's Old Brewery Inn
292 Kilmore St, Christchurch
(03) 374 3532

Tonic
138 Princes St, Dunedin
(03) 471 9194
www.tonicbar.co.nz

EVENTS

FEBRUARY
4 **Rippon Music Festival**
www.ripponfestival.co.nz

MARCH
Gibbston Harvest Festival
www.gibbstonharvestfestival.co.nz

Dunedin Fringe Festival
www.dunedinfringe.org.nz

APRIL
Warbirds over Wanaka
www.warbirdsoverwanaka.com

Festival of Colour
www.festivalofcolour.co.nz

SEPTEMBER
The Remarkables Spring Carnival
www.nzski.com

BREWERIES

Arrow Brewing Co
Arrowtown
(03) 409 8849
www.arrowbrewing.co.nz

Brew Moon Brewery
North Canterbury
(03) 389 1852

Cassels & Sons Brewery, Christchurch
(03) 389 1852

DB Mainland Brewery
Washdyke, Timaru
www.dbbreweries.co.nz

Dux de Lux
Christchurch and Queenstown
www.thedux.co.nz

The Emerson Brewing Company, Dunedin
(03) 477 1812
www.emersons.co.nz

Green Man Brewery
Dunedin; (03) 477 7755; www.greenmanbrewery.co.nz

Harrington's Breweries
Christchurch
(03) 366 6323
www.harringtonsbreweries.co.nz

Invercargill Brewery
(03) 214 5070; www.invercargillbrewery.co.nz

Lion Nathan
Christchurch
www.maltexo.co.nz

Matson's Brewery
Christchurch
(03) 341 3229; www.matsonsbrewery.co.nz

McDuff's Brewery
Dunedin, (03) 477 7276

Speight's Brewery
Dunedin (03) 477 7697
www.speights.co.nz

The Twisted Hop
Christchurch
(03) 962 3688
www.thetwistedhop.co.nz

Three Boys Brewery
Christchurch, www.threeboysbrewery.co.nz

Wanaka Beerworks
Wanaka; www.wanakabeerworks.co.nz

Wigram Brewing Co
Christchurch; www.wigrambrewing.co.nz

THINGS TO SEE AND DO

Cadbury World 280 Cumberland St, Dunedin. 0800 223 2879 or www.cadburyworld.co.nz. **Gore's Hokonui Moonshine Museum** 16 Hokonui Drive, Gore. (03) 208 9907 or www.hokonuiwhiskey.com. **Larnach Castle** 145 Camp Rd, Otago Peninsula, Dunedin. (03) 476 1616 or www.larnachcastle.co.nz/index. **The Puzzling World** 188 Wanaka Luggate Hwy 84, Wanaka. (03) 443 7489 or www.puzzlingworld.co.nz.

NZ

The beach at Kaiteriteri

TOP OF THE SOUTH ISLAND

There's more than sun, sea and sand to keep punters smiling at the top of New Zealand's South Island.

By Monica Mead

Wine is king at the 'Top of the South,' but there's more than grapes and temperate climes to satisfy visitors. Craft brewers, from Marlborough to Golden Bay, are a hot regional commodity.

■ BLENHEIM, MARLBOROUGH WINE COUNTRY

Blenheim is the heart of Marlborough wine country, so tastings are de rigueur, and Marlborough Wine Tours offers outings through the labyrinth of vines and vintners.

February brings the annual Marlborough Wine Festival, a chance for local wineries and fans to champion the region's most famed tipple. But you'd be foolish for thinking the terroir is dedicated solely to Sauvignon Blanc, as this vine town is home to some of the best Kiwi brewers.

Minutes from Blenheim's CBD is Renaissance Brewing, helmed by expat American brothers-in-law Andy Deuchars (a former winemaker) and Brian Thiel. Assistant Brewer Soren Eriksen, an expat Dane and erstwhile sea urchin researcher, makes his name here, too, as 8 Wired Brewing.

No formal brewery tour exists, but if you give the boys some notice, they'll likely let you have a peek. The adjacent The Malthouse on Dodson offers both brewers' wares on tap and moreish pizzas plus windows at one side of the tavern for watching the men at work.

Deeper into the vines, Moa Brewing has brought notoriety to the winemaking Scott family. Moa beers are available at the bar and on taps and in bottles around town.

The Scotch Wine Bar, despite its name, is keen on craft brew, counting Moa co-owner Josh Scott as one of its principals.

Dick Tout of the Lighthouse Brewery in Stoke

In addition to gin and whisky tastings, Josh's working partners, Tim and Hamish Thomas, regularly showcase regional brews.

The Secret Garden Ale House & Wine Bar, just up the road, boasts an equally impressive real ale roster. With a sunny courtyard out back, this urban respite offering bottles of the legendary Mammoth, a Strong Ale (at a hefty 7% ABV) from Roger Pink of Blenheim's pioneering Pink Elephant Brewing.

Townshend Brewery in Upper Moutere

Dean and Emma McCashin

Stoke tastings

The Old Bank Tavern might not warrant second glances from the street, but all of its six taps host regional brews, with one hand-pull dedicated to Nelson's Townshend Brewery. Owner Mike Pink's ardour for real Ale comes from his British roots and time spent running a 16th-century pub in Devonshire. That he's a card-carrying member of both CAMRA and New Zealand's Society of Beer Advocates (SOBA) doesn't hurt his credibility one iota.

■ NELSON

West through the Rai Valley is Nelson, New Zealand's geographical centre and holder of the country's title for most sunshine hours.

New Zealand's sole commercial hop-growing region thrives here, and it's the biggest commercial fishing port in Australasia. Nelson lacks port-side culture a la Sydney or Seattle, but redemption comes in spades with no less than 10 regional breweries, though Wellingtonians rankle at the notion of this being the country's craft-brew capital.

Navigable by foot, the CBD harbours local brews worthy of real ale disciples, while regional world-class wineries are easily reached by car and either Bay Tours or Nelson Tours & Travel, both of which are more than happy to show off local breweries.

Festivals are perennially popular here, too. January brings the esteemed Nelson Jazz and Blues Festival and March sees hair-raising downhill speed in the form of Richardson's Trolley Derby, with racers barrelling down the length of Collingwood Street in impressive homemade, gravity-driven kits. But you're here for beer, and Nelson is steeped in artisan brew.

Firebrand Terry McCashin's Mac's Brewery was defiantly born here in 1981, standing against the Kiwi brewing duopoly until it was gobbled up and production spirited away. Others, including Nelson Bays Brewery, Dick Tout's Lighthouse Brewery (reportedly New Zealand's smallest), and newbie Totara Brewing, have since been established. Dean McCashin, Terry's son, now distills and brews on

John Duncan, Founders Brewery

Founders Brewery

the site of his father's historic venture as Stoke by the McCashin Family.

■ WORLD CUP RUGBY 2011

World Cup rugby is on the horizon and, fittingly, Nelson hosted New Zealand's first ever rugby match (circa 1870) on the green of the Botanical Reserve.

It's a short walk up Botanical Hill before the city and neighbouring Maitai Valley unfold in a 360-degree panorama around a commemorative spire marking the centre of New Zealand.

Take a quick, easy tramp through nearby Sir Stanley Whitehead Reserve and you're rewarded with a pint from Australasia's first organic craft brewer at trail's end, tucked inside Nelson's thematic homage to early settlers.

It's here in Founders Park that fifth-generation brewer John Duncan and wife Carol established Founders Organic Brewery & Cafe, with light meals and house-made brews on tap, including Generation Ale, a velvety Nut Brown Ale with subtle hops and tender, balanced biscuit notes and malt.

Around the bend is the first in the five-strong Sprig & Fern Brewery family of regional taverns. Each runs upwards of 18 taps, and all beers are brewed locally under the watchful eyes of owners Tracy Banner and Dave Barrett. Banner, formerly of Lion Nathan and Mac's, is noted as New Zealand's first female commercial brewer.

Restaurants boasting local brew are few, but at the area's most renowned independent, The Free House, bringing in local takeaways is heartily encouraged (though no corporate fast food, please).

Set in a converted Dutch Reform church with a spacious new adjoining beer garden, owners Mic Dover and Eelco

Mic Dover and Eelco Boswijk welcome you to The Free House

The Sprig & Fern Tavern in Milton Street, Nelson

New Zealand Hops, Nelson

Golden Bear's Jim Matranga and wife, Anne, with dog, Dudley

Boswijk are advocates of good regional and national brews, so names like Townshend Brewery from nearby Upper Moutere appear alongside Invercargill Brewery from the bottom of the South. The Free House's own label, Dead Good Beer, is featured regularly, too.

Hit town in March and you'll be treated to MarchFest, the premier craft-beer event of the year. A hip, seasonal homage to hops, it's the biggest of numerous beer fetes Mic and Eelco hold year-round, where beer lovers can hear local brewers talk real beer and mingle with like-minded craft brew fanatics in a refreshingly family-friendly environment.

■ ON THE BANDWAGON

Pick up the plank-straight stretch called the Appleby Highway from State Highway 6 west, and you'll find no fewer than two spots on the craft-brew bandwagon.

The Abbey Ale House is an enticing spread with a reputation for its meandering indoor-outdoor tree and vines. While a stone's throw away the Traveller's Rest serves up local brew and cafe fare with authentic Thai.

At the centre of the hop-growing region is New Zealand Hops, a co-operative in place since 2005, following its previous incarnation as the New Zealand Hop Marketing Board. It may be small potatoes on the international hop-growing scene (accounting for only one percent of the global market), but this region's antipodean nature makes it well-poised to fill the gap when northern hemisphere growers are dormant.

Aromatic cones like the Riwaka and Sauvin or the high-alpha Pacific Jade and Green Bullet are particularly fruitful in the temperate climes here, with roughly 17 grower-owners harvesting a respectable 700,000kg of

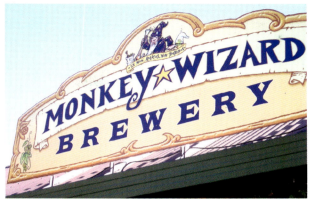

hops each year. Even outside of harvest time (late February through March), tours of the plant are a difficult prospect, though the helpful staff are always eager to answer questions and direct the curious to local hop farms.

Up the coast is Mapua, home to Golden Bear Brewing, Jim Matranga's popular wharf-side brewery and pub. An expat Californian and self-proclaimed big IPA guy, Matranga's hop-driven ales lead an ephemeral roster.

Golden Bear is also one of the country's 'crème de la crème' small breweries. With a 1200L brew length with 10,000L conditioning capacity, it's a drool-worthy glimmering stainless steel construct designed and built by local engineering whiz Chris Little of CLE Brewsystems.

A scant drive west on the pastoral Moutere Highway sits Redwood Cellars and the home of Old Mout Cider. The tasting room is completely revamped and you'll find cider-maker Merophy Hyslop's artful apple blends on taps and in bottles nation-wide.

New Zealand's oldest standing pub, The Moutere Inn, is just up the road, and while two of its 16 taps are still dedicated to hard-boiled locals with a penchant for standard-issue lager, the others, including one hand-pull, are true blue Kiwi craft. Owners Andrew Cole and Dave Watson have also unveiled Moutere Brewing Co, a new house label staying true to the pub's German-settler roots with an inaugural crisp, quenching Munich Helles-style brew dubbed Sarau Lager.

Andrew's even developed a free, uber-cool, brew-centric website, The Beer Tourist, to aid enthusiasts traversing New Zealand by way of real beer. Just click on a region and maps spring to life, highlighting the area's artisan brewers, free houses and homebrew suppliers.

■ RIWAKA

North of Motueka, in hop-drenched Riwaka, is one of the most eclectic small regional breweries, Monkey Wizard. If you're lucky enough to have had Mat Elmhirst's alchemical ales locally (at The Free House or The Moutere Inn), then you'll recognise this expat Brit's nous for well-crafted creations – whatever the style. Fruit beers can be hit-or-miss, but his seasonal Boysenberry Stout is balanced, with fruit rightly in a supporting role, and it's not treacly or heavy-handed in the least. So stop in Friday through Sunday for a taste and a chat.

■ GOLDEN BAY

Nelson may routinely get kudos for an eclectic, artsy vibe, but Golden Bay, just one hour north over Takaka Hill, is the real deal. Gateway to the stark wonder of Farewell Spit and the pristine pools of Te Waikoropupu Springs, it's also a beloved coastal hippie enclave, and you very nearly catch patchouli on the air as you

The rustic charm of The Mussel Inn

peruse the bedecked rainbow of shops and cafes on its main drag.

In the township of Takaka you'll find Roots Bar, a funky little place with 12 craft beer taps and regular live music.

From here, it's not far to cherished tavern and brewery The Mussel Inn. Captain Cooker, the inn's take on James Cook's renowned curative Manuka hop brew, put this craft-beer Mecca on the lips of self-respecting devotees.

You'll find this celebrated elixir around the country and world-wide, but nothing beats a fresh pint from the tap, a bowl of 'sossys' and a relax on the deck under the cover of verdant native trees.

Just take care to stow that mobile phone before sipping into the cool native vibe or, as the inn's website chides (and the on-deck pole with cell phones crudely nailed to its sides demonstrates): 'If necessary, we can fix them.'

The Mussel Inn telephone pole

BEER BARS

Roots Bar
1 Commercial St, Takaka,
(03) 5259592

Scotch Wine Bar
26 Maxwell Rd, Blenheim
(03) 579 1176

Sprig & Fern Tavern
134 Milton St, Nelson
(03) 545 7117
280 Hardy St, Nelson
(03) 548 1154
108 Queen St, Richmond
(03) 544 4900
54 Ellis St, Brightwater
(03) 542 2323
Wallace St, Motueka
(03) 528 4684
www.sprigandfern.co.nz

The Abbey Ale House
Highway 60, Appleby
(03) 544 1908

The Free House
95 Collingwood St, Nelson
(03) 548 9391
www.thefreehouse.co.nz

The Malthouse on Dodson
1 Dodson St, Blenheim
(03) 577 8348

The Moutere Inn
1406 Moutere Hwy, Upper Moutere
(03) 543 2759
www.moutereinn.co.nz

The Old Bank Café & Bar
81 Cleghorn St, Blenheim
(03) 579 1230
www.theoldbank.co.nz

The Secret Garde Ale House & Wine Bar
30 Maxwell Rd, Blenheim
(03) 579 5025
www.secretgardencafe.co.nz

Traveller's Rest
Highway 60, Appleby
(03) 544 8450

EVENTS

www.itson.co.nz

MARKETS
Nelson and Marlborough Farmers' Markets
Every weekend.
Fashion Island, Nelson.
www.marketground.co.nz/fmnznelson

Nelson Saturday Market
Every Saturday (except religious holidays).
Montgomery Square.
www.nelsonmarket.co.nz

McCashin's Market
Every Saturday from October to March. Stoke, Nelson.
www.mccashinsmarket.co.nz

JANUARY
Port Nelson Street Races
www.portnelsonstreetracing.co.nz

Nelson Jazz & Blues Festival
www.nelsonjazzfest.co.nz

Nelson Kite Festival
www.rainbowflight.co.nz

Luminate Festival
www.luminatefestival.co.nz

FEBRUARY
Marlborough Wine Festival
www.marlboroughwinefestival.co.nz

Blues, Brews & BBQs Blenheim
www.bluesbrews.co.nz.

Brightwater Wine and Food Festival
www.bwff.co.nz

MARCH
Havelock Mussel Festival
www.havelockmusselfestival.co.nz

MarchFest
www.marchfest.com

Robertson's Trolley Derby
www.derby.co.nz

Sprig & Fern Summer Fare
www.sprigandfern.co.nz

Taste Nelson
www.tastenelson.co.nz

JUNE
Rollo's Nelson Adventure Race
www.adventurenelson.co.nz

JUNE/JULY
Monteith's Beer & Wild Food Challenge
www.monteiths.co.nz

JULY
Nelson Winter Music Festival
www.nelsonwinterfestival.co.nz

SEPTEMBER
Rugby World Cup
www.rugbyworldcup.com

RugBeer HopFest
www.hopfest.co.nz

OCTOBER
Nelson Arts Festival
www.nelsonfestivals.co.nz

NOVEMBER
Hunter's Garden Marlborough
www.gardenmarlborough.com

DECEMBER
Nelson Summer Beer Fete
www.deadgoodbeerevents.com

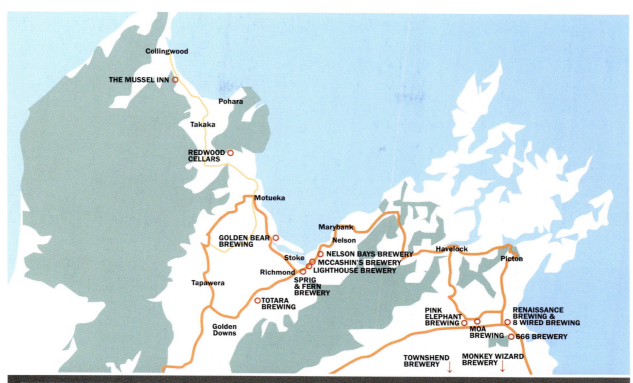

BREWERIES, BEER COMPANIES & CIDER

8 Wired Brewing
www.8wired.co.nz

Dead Good Beers
www.deadgoodbeerevents.com

Founders Brewery
Athawhai Dr, Nelson
(03) 548 4638
www.foundersbrewery.co.nz

Golden Bear Brewing
Mapua Wharf, Mapua
(03) 540 3210
www.goldenbearbrewing.com

Lighthouse Brewery
21 Echodale Pl, Stoke
(03) 547 0983

McCashin's Brewery Bar
660 Main Rd, Stoke
(03) 547 5357
www.mccashins.co.nz

Moa Brewing
Jackson's Rd, Blenheim
(03) 572 5146
www.moabeer.co.nz

Monkey Wizard Brewery
483 Main Rd, Riwaka
027 333 4617
www.monkeywizard.co.nz

Monteith's Brewing Co.
Cnr Turumaha & Herbert Streets, Greymouth
(03) 768 4149
www.monteiths.co.nz

Nelson Bays Brewery
89 Pascoe St, Nelson
(03) 547 8097
www.baysbrewery.co.nz

Pink Elephant Brewing
RD3, Blenheim
(03) 572 9467

Redwood Cellars
523 Moutere Hwy, RD 1, Richmond, Nelson
(03) 544 2706
www.redwoodcellars.co.nz

Renaissance Brewing
1 Dodson St, Blenheim
(03) 579 3400
www.renaissancebrewing.co.nz

Sprig & Fern Brewery
53 Beach Rd, Richmond
Nelson; (03) 544 8675
www.sprigandfern.co.nz

The Mussel Inn
Onekaka, Golden Bay
(03) 525 9241
www.musselinn.co.nz

Totara Brewing
249 State Highway 6, RD1, Nelson; 021 624 322
www.totarabrewing.co.nz

Townshend Brewery
Upper Moutere
(03) 543 2170
www.townshendbrewery.co.nz

West Coast Brewing
10 Lyndhurst Street, Westport; (03) 789 6253
www.westcoastbrewing.com

THINGS TO SEE AND DO Bay Tours 03 548 6486 www.baytoursnelson.co.nz **Nelson Tours & Travel** 027 237 5007 or 0800 222 373 www.nelsontoursandtravel.co.nz **NZ Hops** Blackbyre Road, Appleby, Richmond 03 544 8989 www.nzhops.co.nz **Marlborough Wine Tours** 03 578 9515 www.marlboroughwinetours.co.nz **Society of Beer Advocates (SOBA)** www.soba.org.nz **The Beer Tourist** www.beertourist.co.nz

Beer & Brewer promotion   NEW ZEALAND – NORTH ISLAND

BREWERS COOP

Brewers Coop has recently moved to larger premises. Now operating out of a renovated warehouse, Mike, Bryan and Roger between them provide excellent advice and service on all forms of home brewing from making beer, wines and spirits to making cheese and sausages.

Still NZ's leading home brew shop, Brewers Coop has the largest selection of malted barley and extracts for New Zealand homebrewers.

Coupled with its range of stills and essences, wine ingredients and the mad millie cheese range, brewers coop is well worth a visit.

Unit 2, 3 Prescott Street,
Penrose, Auckland
Tel: (09) 5252448
www.brewerscoop.co.nz

Opening hours:
Mon-Fri 10.00am – 5.00pm
Thurs (late night)
10.00am – 6:30pm
Sat 9.00am – 3.00pm

MALTHOUSE

Pouring the largest range of beers in the country, Malthouse was the inaugural winner of the 2010 Beer & Brewer Magazine Awards for Best Kiwi Small Pub and the overall accolade of Best New Zealand Beer Venue.

With over 160 craft beers consistently available, this Courtenay Place institution has 29 individual taps, two hand pumps, six fridges at different temperatures and a cellar selection of Vintage Ales. The state-of-the-art Hopinator allows staff to add bold late flavours to any beer.

Malthouse is the home of Tuatara – Champion Brewery 2009 – and the home of Beervana – New Zealand's biggest and best beer festival. It is a must-visit beer destination.

48 Courtenay Place,
Wellington
Tel: (04) 802 5484
www.themalthouse.co.nz

Opening hours:
Sun-Wed 3.00pm – Late
Thurs-Sat 12 noon – 3.00am

ST KATHERINE'S BREWING CO.

St Katherine's Brewing Co., based in Herne Bay Auckland, brew Tawny Ale as their flagship beer. This is a vintage beer only released annually in October, which brewer Andrew Larsen has named after his daughter, Katherine.

Tawny Ale is a copper-coloured beauty, matured in port barrels, which provide complex flavours and subtle vinous aromas.

This beer is brewed in small batches making it hard to find. So hard, it could be on a 'Rarest Top 100' beers of the world list!

While you travel on beer adventures across the USA, New Zealand and Australia, where Tawny Ale is available off-premise and in leading restaurants, put on your 'Beer Hunter' hat and find a bottle of Tawny Ale and experience what makes this beer so special.

Herne Bay
Auckland
Tel Aus: +61 427 007 800
Tel NZ: +64 274 874 283
Tel USA: +1 413 336 8877
info@stkatherinesbeer.com

Beer & Brewer promotion   NEW ZEALAND – NORTH ISLAND CENTRAL

KAIMAI BREWING COMPANY

It's no secret that rye makes for a great tasting beer – in fact its use in brewing can be traced back to medieval times. However it is only recently that Rye Beer has been produced in any great quantity. That's because the brew actually disappeared for 500 years.

Originating in the Bavarian region of southern Germany during the Middle Ages, rye beer became a staple beverage. But in 1516 a law was passed, following a period of bad harvests, which ruled that rye could only be used to bake bread. Rye beer didn't reappear again until 1988, after a repeal of the law by the European Court of Justice.

Crafting rye beer involves combining rye malt with the traditional brewing base of barley malt. Its inclusion presents a challenge to the brewer as extracting sugars from the huskless grain is technically difficult, however brewer Andrew Larsen has achieved this by creating a distinctive crisp flavour with a unique smooth silky sensation on the palate.

Kaimai Brewing Company is New Zealand's only brewer that specialises in an innovative range of Rye Ales.

Kaimai beers are available in all good beer retailers and restaurants across North America, Asia and here at home in New Zealand and Australia.

PO Box 101210
Mount Manganui
Tauranga 3152
Tel: 0508 RYE BEER (874 783)
info@kaimaibrewing.com
www.kaimaibrewing.com

Not open to the public.

Beer & Brewer promotion NEW ZEALAND

MCCASHIN'S BREWERY

McCashin's Brewery was started in 1981 by Terry McCashin, the same year as the infamous underarm bowling incident. The only beer available in New Zealand at the time was sweet and bland and brewed by Lion or DB. This period was termed the "beer drinking dark ages". Terry has been credited as starting the craft beer revolution in New Zealand when he opened the Brewery and introduced New Zealander's to Real Ale. Lion Nathan purchased the Macs brand from the family in 1999 and leased the Brewery in Stoke until 2009 when McCashin's Brewery was re-opened in 2009 by Terry's eldest son Dean. The Brewery is housed in the historic Rochdale Cider Factory and Rochdale Cider is still brewed on site.

660 Main Road,
Stoke Nelson
Tel (03) 547-0329
www.mccashins.co.nz

Opening hours
7 Days
Sun-Wed 8.00am – 6.00pm
Thurs-Sat 8.00am – 9.00pm
Tours: Mon-Sat 11.00am and 2.00pm

THE MUSSEL INN CAFÉ BAR AND BREWERY

Home of the famous 'Captain Cooker Manuka Beer'

Situated in the heart of Golden Bay, a two hours drive north west of Nelson city. The picturesque drive over the 'marble mountain' will whet your appetite for a nice bowl of fresh steamed mussels and a tasty beer or three from the extensive range created in our adjacent brewery.

Established in 1992, the Mussel Inn is a focal point of the local community and an iconic land mark for both beer lovers and appreciators of original live music.

Onekaka, RD 2
Takaka, Golden Bay
Tel: +64 35259241
(after 11.00am)
www.musselinn.co.nz

Opening hours:
1.00am to late, every day from mid September to mid July. Brewery tours by arrangement only.

REGIONAL WINES & SPIRITS

Regional (as the locals call it) doesn't have beer in the name, but don't be fooled. These guys are obsessed – with over 300 different bottled beers from around the globe, and 11 taps dispensing the finest craft beers from around New Zealand.

Sitting right on Wellington's Basin Reserve, Regional carries nearly any beer you can think of - from Affligem to Zyiwiec - and everything in between.

They specialise in New Zealand craft beer and are at the forefront of the national uprising against crap beer.

Regional is more than just a bottle store - it's a cathedral of beer - with 300 whiskies and 3000 wines rounding out the congregation.

15 Ellice St, Mt Victoria
Wellington
Tel: +64 4 385 6952
www.regionalbeers.co.nz

Opening hours:
Mon-Sat 9.00am – 10.00pm
Sunday & Public Holidays
11.00am – 7.30pm

RENAISSANCE BREWING COMPANY

In the heart of the gourmet province of New Zealand, their modern 2000 litre brewery is located on Blenheim's Dodson Street, alongside - Marlborough's oldest commercial building, originally built in 1858 for local brewer Henry Dodson.

Adjacent to the brewery and below ground level - is The Malthouse on Dodson Street featuring the entire Renaissance range on tap, offering a comprehensive menu which includes a selection of beerfriendly home-made pizzas making it a destination where you can enjoy craft beer and great food.

At the 2011 Australian International Beer Awards – Renaissance was the highest ranking New Zealand brewery with a best-in-class trophy and a gold medal for their Craftsman Oatmeal Chocolate Stout.

1 Dodson Street
(next to Lansdowne Park)
Blenheim
Tel: (03) 577 8348
www.olde-malthouse.co.nz

Opening hours:
Tue-Sun 4.00pm daily (winter)
Tue-Sun Mid-day (summer)
Brewery tours available by arrangement

Beer & Brewer promotion   NEW ZEALAND – SOUTH ISLAND

SPRIG & FERN BREWERY

World Famous in Nelson

The Sprig & Fern Brewery is located in the heart of Richmond, Nelson. Originally established in 1996, the brewery changed its name to Sprig & Fern in 2009 - a name first used for its taverns of which there are now five throughout the Nelson region.

Highly respected co-owner and head brewer Tracy Banner together with brewers Gary Giblin and Ric Valentine have nearly six decades of combined brewing experience which is reflected in the extensive and multi-award winning range of ales and lagers they produce.

There are 18 all natural craft products on offer running from Ginger Lager, Pilsner & Blonde to Porter, IPA, Scotch Ale & Doppelbock. A 'must try' while visiting the brewery is the unique and sensational Berry Cider.

All Sprig & Fern Taverns pour the full range of S&F products and provide a genuine kiwi tavern experience – welcoming and unpretentious. There are deliberately no pokies, pool tables or TV's, just great conversation, awesome beer and a fine selection of Nelson wine. And just like the brewery, all the taverns have off-licenses, allowing you to take away your favourite drop after having a pint - or two! (Yes, they serve true pints).

Drop in to the brewery or one of the taverns and find out why Sprig & Fern is 'World famous in Nelson'.

53 Beach Rd
Richmond, Nelson
Tel: (03) 544 8675
david@sprigandfern.co.nz

Opening hours:
Tues-Sat 12 Noon – 6.00pm
Free tastings with purchase. Tours by arrangement.

THE FREE HOUSE

Nelson is at the heart of New Zealand's hop growing region at the top of the South Island. The Free House is a craft beer and real ales Mecca - untied to any brewery and changing its beer menu on a daily basis - 44 different breweries and 240+ different tap beers featured since 2009.

Plus local ciders, juices, wines, spirits, hot food, real piano, live music, wood fire and beer garden. No pokies or TV screens. Currently the only pub in New Zealand where you can taste the Dead Good Beer range on tap including their IPA, Pilsner and seasonal specials such as Porter and Weizen.

How good is The Free House? Don't take our word for it, here's what Lonely Planet 2011 says about us: "OUR PICK: Come rejoice at this church of ales. Tastefully converted from its original, more reverent purpose; it's now home to an excellent, oft-changing selection of NZ craft beers. You can imbibe inside or out and even bring takeaway food in from elsewhere. Hallelujah!"

95-97 Collingwood St
Nelson
Tel: +64 3 548 9391
www.thefreehouse.co.nz

Opening hours:
Mon-Thurs 4.00pm – 10-ish
Fri 4.00pm – 11-ish
Sat Noon – 11-ish
Sun: Noon – 10-ish

DIRECTORY

Cold

DIRECTORY OF BEER & CIDER

MIX & MATCH ANY 10, GET 10% OFF.

Beer

A comprehensive listing of 1800+ local and imported beers and ciders available in Australia &/or New Zealand. Listings are sorted by country, then alphabetically by brewery or brand, including name, style, ABV and unit size.

Beer & Cider Styles

STYLE	OG	FG	ABV%	IBU	COLOR SRM
1. LIGHT LAGER					
A. Lite American Lager	1.028-40	0.998-1.008	2.8-4.2	8-12	2-3
B. Standard American Lager	1.040-50	1.004-10	4.2-5.3	8-15	2-4
C. Premium American Lager	1.046-56	1.008-12	4.6-6.0	15-25	2-6
D. Munich Helles	1.045-51	1.008-12	4.7-5.4	16-22	3-5
E. Dortmunder Export	1.048-56	1.010-15	4.8-6.0	23-30	4-6
2. PILSNER					
A. German Pilsner (Pils)	1.044-50	1.008-13	4.4-5.2	25-45	2-5
B. Bohemian Pilsener	1.044-56	1.013-17	4.2-5.4	35-45	3.5-6
C. Classic American Pilsner	1.044-60	1.010-15	4.5-6.0	25-40	3-6
3. EUROPEAN AMBER LAGER					
A. Vienna Lager	1.046-52	1.010-14	4.5-5.5	18-30	10-16
B. Oktoberfest/Märzen	1.050-57	1.012-16	4.8-5.7	20-28	7-14
4. DARK LAGER					
A. Dark American Lager	1.044-56	1.008-12	4.2-6.0	8-20	14-22
B. Munich Dunkel	1.048-56	1.010-16	4.5-5.6	18-28	14-28
C. Schwarzbier	1.046-52	1.010-16	4.4-5.4	22-32	17-30
5. BOCK					
A. Maibock/Helles Bock	1.064-72	1.011-18	6.3-7.4	23-35	6-11
B. Traditional Bock	1.064-72	1.013-19	6.3-7.2	20-27	14-22
C. Doppelbock	1.072-112	1.016-24	7.0-10.0	16-26	6-25
D. Eisbock	1.078-120	1.020-35	9.0-14.0	25-35	18-30
6. LIGHT HYBRID BEER					
A. Cream Ale	1.042-55	1.006-12	4.2-5.6	15-20	2.5-5
B. Blonde Ale	1.038-54	1.008-13	3.8-5.5	15-28	3-6
C. Kölsch	1.044-50	1.007-11	4.4-5.2	20-30	3.5-5
D. American Wheat or Rye Beer	1.040-55	1.008-15	4.0-5.5	15-30	3-6
7. AMBER HYBRID BEER					
A. North German Altbier	1.046-54	1.010-15	4.5-5.2	25-40	13-19
B. California Common Beer	1.048-54	1.011-14	4.5-5.5	30-45	10-14
C. Düsseldorf Altbier	1.046-54	1.010-15	4.5-5.2	35-50	11-17
8. ENGLISH PALE ALE					
A. Standard/Ordinary Bitter	1.032-40	1.007-11	3.2-3.8	25-35	4-14
B. Special/Best/Premium Bitter	1.040-48	1.008-12	3.8-4.6	25-40	5-16
C. Extra Special/Strong Bitter (English Pale Ale)	1.048-60	1.010-16	4.6-6.2	30-50	6-18
9. SCOTTISH AND IRISH ALE					
A. Scottish Light 60/-	1.030-35	1.010-13	2.5-3.2	10-20	9-17
B. Scottish Heavy 70/-	1.035-40	1.010-15	3.2-3.9	10-25	9-17
C. Scottish Export 80/-	1.040-54	1.010-16	3.9-5.0	15-30	9-17
D. Irish Red Ale	1.044-60	1.010-14	4.0-6.0	17-28	9-18
E. Strong Scotch Ale	1.070-130	1.018-56	6.5-10.0	17-35	14-25
10. AMERICAN ALE					
A. American Pale Ale	1.045-60	1.010-15	4.5-6.0	30-45	5-14
B. American Amber Ale	1.045-60	1.010-15	4.5-6.0	25-40	10-17
C. American Brown Ale	1.045-60	1.010-16	4.3-6.2	20-40	18-35
11. ENGLISH BROWN ALE					
A. Mild	1.030-38	1.008-13	2.8-4.5	10-25	12-25
B. Southern English Brown Ale	1.033-42	1.011-14	2.8-4.1	12-20	19-35
C. Northern English Brown Ale	1.040-52	1.008-13	4.2-5.4	20-30	12-22
12. PORTER					
A. Brown Porter	1.040-52	1.008-14	4.0-5.4	18-35	20-30
B. Robust Porter	1.048-65	1.012-16	4.8-6.5	25-50	22-35
C. Baltic Porter	1.060-90	1.016-24	5.5-9.5	20-40	17-30
13. STOUT					
A. Dry Stout	1.036-50	1.007-11	4.0-5.0	30-45	25-40
B. Sweet Stout	1.044-60	1.012-24	4.0-6.0	20-40	30-40
C. Oatmeal Stout	1.048-65	1.010-18	4.2-5.9	25-40	22-40
D. Foreign Extra Stout	1.056-75	1.010-18	5.5-8.0	30-70	30-40
E. American Stout	1.050-75	1.010-22	5.0-7.0	35-75	30-40
F. Imperial Stout	1.075-115	1.018-30	8.0-12.0	50-90	30-40
14. INDIA PALE ALE (IPA)					
A. English IPA	1.050-75	1.010-18	5.0-7.5	40-60	8-14
B. American IPA	1.056-75	1.010-18	5.5-7.5	40-70	6-15
C. Imperial IPA	1.075-90	1.010-20	7.5-10.0	60-120	8-15
15. GERMAN WHEAT AND RYE BEER					
A. Weizen/Weissbier	1.044-52	1.010-14	4.3-5.6	8-15	2-8
B. Dunkelweizen	1.044-56	1.010-14	4.3-5.6	10-18	14-23
C. Weizenbock	1.064-90	1.015-22	6.5-8.0	15-30	12-25
D. Roggenbier (German Rye Beer)	1.046-56	1.010-14	4.5-6.0	10-20	14-19
16. BELGIAN AND FRENCH ALE					
A. Witbier	1.044-52	1.008-12	4.5-5.5	10-20	2-4
B. Belgian Pale Ale	1.048-54	1.010-14	4.8-5.5	20-30	8-14
C. Saison	1.048-65	1.002-12	5.0-7.0	20-35	5-14
D. Bière de Garde	1.060-80	1.008-16	6.0-8.5	18-28	6-19
E. Belgian Specialty Ale	Variable	Variable	Variable	Variable	Variable
17. SOUR ALE					
A. Berliner Weisse	1.028-32	1.003-06	2.8-3.8	3-8	2-3
B. Flanders Red Ale	1.048-57	1.002-12	4.6-6.5	10-25	10-16
C. Flanders Brown Ale/Oud Bruin	1.040-74	1.008-12	4.0-8.0	20-25	15-22
D. Straight (Unblended) Lambic	1.040-54	1.001-10	5.0-6.5	0-10	3-7
E. Gueuze	1.040-60	1.000-06	5.0-8.0	0-10	3-7
F. Fruit Lambic	1.040-60	1.000-10	5.0-7.0	0-10	3-7
18. BELGIAN STRONG ALE					
A. Belgian Blond Ale	1.062-75	1.008-18	6.0-7.5	15-30	4-7
B. Belgian Dubbel	1.062-75	1.008-18	6.0-7.6	15-25	10-17
C. Belgian Tripel	1.075-85	1.008-14	7.5-9.5	20-40	4.5-7
D. Belgian Golden Strong Ale	1.070-95	1.005-16	7.5-10.5	22-35	3-6
E. Belgian Dark Strong Ale	1.075-110	1.010-24	8.0-11.0	20-35	12-22
19. STRONG ALE					
A. Old Ale	1.060-90	1.015-22	6.0-9.0	30-60	10-22
B. English Barleywine	1.080-120	1.018-30	8.0-12.0	35-70	8-22
C. American Barleywine	1.080-120	1.016-30	8.0-12.0	50-120	10-19
20. FRUIT BEER	Varies	with	base	beer	style
21. SPICE/HERB/VEGETABLE BEER					
A. Spice, Herb, or Vegetable Beer	Varies with base beer style				
B. Christmas/Winter Specialty Spiced Beer	Varies with base beer style				
22. SMOKE-FLAVORED & WOOD-AGED BEER					
A. Classic Rauchbier	1.050-57	1.012-16	4.8-6.0	20-30	12-22
B. Other Smoked Beer	Varies with base beer style				
C. Wood-Aged Beer	Varies with base beer style				
23. SPECIALTY BEER	Varies	with	base	beer	style
24. TRADITIONAL MEAD					
A. Dry Mead	Varies	0.990-1.010	Varies	N/A	N/A
B. Semi-Sweet Mead	Varies	1.010-25	Varies	N/A	N/A
C. Sweet Mead	Varies	1.025-50	Varies	N/A	N/A
25. MELOMEL (FRUIT MEAD)					
A. Cyser (Apple Melomel)	Variable	See	Guidelines	N/A	N/A
B. Pyment (Grape Melomel)	Variable	See	Guidelines	N/A	N/A
C. Other Fruit Melomel	Variable	See	Guidelines	N/A	N/A
26. OTHER MEAD					
A. Metheglin	Variable	See	Guidelines	N/A	N/A
B. Braggot	Variable	See	Guidelines	N/A	N/A
C. Open Category Mead	Variable	See	Guidelines	N/A	N/A
27. STANDARD CIDER AND PERRY					
A. Common Cider	1.045-65	1.000-20	5-8%	N/A	N/A
B. English Cider	1.050-75	0.995-1.010	6-9%	N/A	N/A
C. French Cider	1.050-65	1.010-20	3-6%	N/A	N/A
D. Common Perry	1.050-60	1.000-20	5-7%	N/A	N/A
E. Traditional Perry	1.050-70	1.000-20	5-9%	N/A	N/A
28. SPECIALTY CIDER AND PERRY					
A. New England Cider	1.060-100	0.995-1.010	7-13%	N/A	N/A
B. Fruit Cider	1.045-70	0.995-1.010	5-9%	N/A	N/A
C. Apple Wine	1.070-100	0.995-1.010	9-12%	N/A	N/A
D. Other Specialty Cider or Perry	1.045-100	0.995-1.020	5-12%	N/A	N/A

Source: Copyright © 2008, Beer Judge Certification Program (BJCP), Inc. Used with permission. www.bjcp.org.

Note this list of styles doesn't include Australia or New Zealand styles, eg Australian Lager, Australian Pale Ale, New Zealand Lager

Directory

BEER: AUSTRALIA

ACT

Brand/Distributor/Name	Style	ABV	Unit
Stricklands Beer Group	www.1842beer.com.au		
1842	German Pilsner	4.6%	50L Kegs
Wig & Pen	www.wigandpen.com.au		
Ballyragget	Irish Red	4.6 - 4.9%	Keg 50L
Big Brown Beaver	Double American Brown Ale	6.0%	Keg 50L
Blonde	Wit Beer	4.3 - 4.6%	Keg 50L
Bob's Armpit	Unstyled	7.0%	Keg 50L
Brewers' IPA	English IPA	5.6 - 6%	Cask
Kembery	Kolsch	4.5 - 4.8%	Keg/Bottle
Kiandra Gold	Czech Pilsner	4.9 - 5.2%	Keg 50L
London Porter	Brown Porter	5.6 - 5.9%	Cask
Lunch with the Monks	Tripel	9.0%	Keg 50L
Marv Man's Mild	Unstyled	3 - 3.3%	Cask
Rumpole	Unstyled	5.1 - 5.4%	Keg 50L
The Judges are Old Codgers	Russian Imperial Stout	10.5 - 11%	Keg 50L
Velvet Cream	Dry Stout	5.4 - 5.7%	Keg 50L
Venom	Double IPA	7.0%	Keg 50L
Wig & Pen Pale Ale	Unstyled	5.0 - 5.8%	Cask
Zierholz Premium Brewery	Local Liquor, ALM, www.localliquor.com.au		
Zierholz Amber Ale	Altbier	4.9%	5L minikeg
Zierholz German Ale	Kolsch	4.3%	5L minikeg
Zierholz Hopmeister	Pale Ale	5.0%	5L minikeg
Zierholz Pils	German Pilsner	5.0%	5L minikeg
Zierholz Porter	Porter	5.0%	5L minikeg
ZIERHOLZ Schankbier	Lager	2.7%	5L minikeg
Zierholz Weizen	Hefeweizen	4.4%	5L minikeg

NSW

Brand/Distributor/Name	Style	ABV	Unit
4 Pines Brewing Co.	NSW - ALM, ILG, VIC - Paramount, ALM, WA - Liquid Mix, TAS - Polkadot		
4 Pines Hefeweizen	Weizen/Weissbier	5.2%	6pack 330mL
4 Pines Kolsch	Premium Light Lager	4.6%	6pack 330mL
4 Pines Pale Ale	American Pale Ale	5.1%	6pack 330mL
4 Pines Stout	Dry Stout	5.1%	6pack 330mL
Akuna Brewery			
Akuna Brewery			
Badlands Brewery	www.badlandsbrewery.com.au		
Badlands Dark	Brown Porter	4.8%	
Badlands Pale Ale	English Pale Ale	4.6%	330ml 6 pack
Man Singh IPA	English Indian Pale Ale	5.4%	750ml swingtop
Balmain Brewing Company	www.balmainbrewing.com.au		
Balmain Original Bock	Dark Lager	5.5%	Keg
Balmain Original Lager	Bohemian Pilsner	4.5%	Keg
Balmain Original Pale Ale	English Pale Ale	4.9%	Keg
Barons Brewing	www.baronsbrewing.com		
Barons Brewing			
Black Duck Brewery	www.blackduckbrewery.com.au		
Dark Ale	Dark Ale	4.0%	50L keg, 18L keg
Golden Goose	American Ale	5.0%	50L keg
Proper Bitter	English Pale Ale	4.0%	50L, 18L keg, 500mL bottle
Bluetongue Brewery	Coca-Cola Amatil, 13 COKE (13 2653)		
Bluetongue Alcoholic Ginger Beer	Ginger	4.0%	49.5L keg, 330ml btl
Bluetongue Premium Lager	Lager	4.9%	49.5L keg, 330ml btl
Bluetongue Premium Light	Lager	2.7%	49.5L keg, 330ml btl
Bluetongue Traditional Pilsener	Pilsener	4.5%	49.5L keg, 330ml btl
Bruers Bright	Lager	4.2%	49.5L keg
Grolsch Premium Lager	European Lager	5.0%	330ml, 49.5L keg
Miller Chill	Flavour-infused Low Carb Lager	4.2%	330ml bottle
Miller Genuine Draft	Draught Lager	4.7%	330ml btl, 49.5L keg
Peroni	Lager	5.1%	330ml btl, 49.5L keg
Peroni Leggera	Lager	3.5%	330ml bottle
Bowral Brewing Company	www.pigsfly.com.au		
Pigs Fly			
Brewtopia Pty Ltd	www.brewtopia.com.au		
Brewtopia Custom Branded Ale	Pale Ale	4.5%	330ml / case 24
Brewtopia Custom Branded Lager	European Style Lager	4.5%	330ml / case 24
Brothers Ink	ALM, ILG, HLW, SALD, Capital		
Gold Digger	Golden Ale	4.5%	50L kegs, 24x330ml
Skinny Blonde	Lager	5.0%	24x330ml, 50L kegs
Byron Bay Brewery	www.byronbaybrewing.com.au		
Byron Bay Brewery			
Central Ranges Brewing Co	www.beekeepersinn.com		
Central Ranges Brewing Co			
Dalgety Brewing Co	www.snowyvineyard.com		
Dalgety Brewing Co			
Doctor's Orders Brewing	www.doctorsordersbrewing.com		
Doctor's Orders			
Ekim Brewing	www.ekimbrewing.com.au		
Ekim Brewing			
Endeavour Beverages	1300 BUY BEER. www.endeavourbeer.com		
End. True Vintage Reserve Amber Ale	Australian Amber Ale	5.2%	4x330ml, 24x330ml
End. True Vintage Reserve Pale Ale	Australian Pale Ale	4.5%	4x330ml, 24x330ml
Federal Hotel	www.federalhotel.com.au		
Bellingen Darkwood Ale	Ale		
Five Islands Brewing Company	Illawarra Brewing Company, brew@fibc.com.au		
Autumn E.S.B.	E.S.B.	5.1%	50L Keg
Bulli Black	Porter	5.1%	50L Keg
"Colombian Black" Coffee Porter	Coffee Porter	5.1%	50L Keg
Draught Ale	American Wheat	4.9%	50L Keg
Kolsch	Kolsch	5.0%	50L Keg
Rust	American Amber Ale	5.1%	50L Keg
Wit	Belgian Wit	5.2%	50L Keg
Fusion Brewing	www.fusionbrewing.com.au		
Fusion Brewing			
Happy Goblin Brewing Company	www.happygoblin.com		
Happy Goblin Brewing Company			
HopDog BeerWorks	HopDog BeerWorks, 0428 293 132		
Black Sunshine	Oatmeal Stout	4.8%	330ml 4-pack
Horns Up Rye IPA	American IPA	5.8%	330ml 4-pack
Midgee - South Coast Mild Ale	English Ordinary Bitter	2.8%	330ml 4-pack
The Pale	American Pale Ale	5.0% abv	330ml 4-pack
Hunter Beer Co.	www.hunterbeer.com.au		
Chocolate Porter (Annual Seasonal)	Brown Porter	5.0%	Keg 750ml Champagne
Christmas Beer (Annual Seasonal)	Dark Spiced Beer	7-8.5%	Keg 750ml Champagne
Crankypants (Annual Seasonal)	American India Pale Ale	6-8.5%	Keg 750ml Champagne
Hunter Bock	Traditional Bock	5.5%	Keg 750ml Champagne
Hunter Ginger Beer	Spiced Beer	4.5%	Keg 750ml Champagne
Hunter Kolsch	Kolsch	4.5%	Keg 750ml Champagne
Hunter Lager	Bohemian Pilsner	4.8%	Keg 750ml Champagne
Hunter Pale Ale	American Pale Ale	5.2%	Keg 750ml Champagne
Oktoberfest Lager (Annual Seasonal)	Oktoberfest Lager	5.8%	Keg 750ml Champagne
Oyster Stout (Annual Seasonal)	Oyster Stout	4.5-6.5%	Keg 750ml Champagne
Witbier	Non-traditional Belgian Witbier	4.5%	Keg 750ml Champagne
Infusion Restaurant Bar Brewery	www.rydges.com/campbelltown		
Infusion Restaurant Bar Brewery			
Iron Bark Brewery	SSS BBQ		
SSS beer			
John Boston Premium Beverages	www.johnboston.com.au		
Boston's Mill Pale Ale	Pale Ale	4.9%	330ml bottle, 6 pack, carton
John Boston Premium Lager	Lager	4.9%	330ml bottle, 6 pack, carton
King St Brewhouse	www.kingstbrewhouse.com.au		
King St Brewhouse			
Koala Beer t/as Burragum Billi	www.burragumbilli.com.au		
Burragum billi	Certified Organic beer	4.0%	6 pack, 24 case
Wilde	Certified Organic beer	4.0%	6 pack, 24 case
Kosciuszko Brewing Company	www.malt-shovel.com.au		
Kosciuszko Pale Ale	Australian Pale Ale	4.5%	345 ml bottle, 6 pack
Lion Nathan Australia	www.lion-nathan.com.au		
Bare Cove Radler	Radler	4.2%	
Long Board Brewing Company	www.longboardbeer.com.au		
Long Board Brewing Company			
Lord Nelson Brewery	www.samsmith.com		
Lord Nelson Old Admiral	Dark Ale	6.1%	24x330ml bottle
Lord Nelson Three Sheets Pale Ale	Australian Pale Ale	4.9%	24x330ml bottle
Lovells Lager	www.lovellslager.com		
Lovells Lager	Lager		
Malt Shovel Brewery	www.lion-nathan.com.au		
James Squire Amber Ale	English Brown Ale	5.0%	345 ml bottle, 6 pack
James Squire Golden Ale	English Summer Ale	4.5%	345 ml bottle, 6 pack
James Squire IPA	India Pale Ale	5.6%	345 ml bottle, 6 pack
James Squire Pilsener	Bohemian Pilsner	5.0%	345 ml bottle, 6 pack
James Squire Porter	Porter	5.0%	345 ml bottle, 6 pack
James Squire Sundown Lager	Australian All-Malt Craft Lager	4.4%	345 ml bottle, 6 pack
New Norcia Abbey Ale	Belgian Strong Golden Ale	7.0%	345 ml bottle, 6 pack
Mountain Ridge Brewery	www.mountainridgebrewery.com		
Mountain Ridge Brewery			
Mudgee Brewing Co	www.mudgeebrewing.com.au		
Mudgee Nectar	Strong Belgium Ale	6.5%	750mL bottle
Mudgee Pale Ale	Pale Ale	4.4%	330mL bottle
Mudgee Porter	Porter	4.3%	330mL bottle
Mudgee Spring	American Pale Ale	5.0%	330mL bottle
Mudgee Wheat Beer	Wheat Beer	4.7%	330mL bottle

Brand/Distributor/Name	Style	ABV	Unit
Murray's Craft Brewing Co.	www.murraysbrewingco.com.au		
Anniversary Ale 5			
Murray's Angry Man			
Murray's Anniversary Ale 4			
Murray's Aphrodite			
Murray's Best Extra Porter			
Murray's Big Wednesday IPA			
Murray's Dark Knight			
Murray's Easter Ale			
Murray's Endless Summer			
Murray's Grand Cru	Belgian Trippel/Golden Strong Ale	8.8%	
Murray's Heart of Darkness	Belgian Inspired Imperial Stout	9.6%	
Murray's Icon 2IPA	Double India Pale Ale	7.5%	
Murray's Imperious			
Murray's Nirvana Pale Ale	American Pale Ale	5.0%	
Murray's Pilsner			
Murray's Pumpkin Ale			
Murray's Punch & Judy's	New World Bitter	3.9%	
Murray's Punk Monk			
Murray's Retro Rocket Ale			
Murray's Sassy Belgian Blond			
Murray's Sassy Blonder			
Murray's Shawn's Fault			
Murray's Spartacus Imperial IPA			
Murray's Whale Ale			
Murray's 'Wild Thing' Imperial Stout	Russian Imperial Stout	10.0%	
Old Goulburn Brewery	Old Goulburn Brewery		
Old Goulburn Brewery			
Outback Brewery	Outback Brewery		
Outback Brewery			
Paddy's Brewery (The Markets Hotel)	www.paddysbrewery.com		
Paddy's Brewery (The Markets Hotel)			
Pinchgut Brewing Co.	Pinchgut Brewing Co.		
Pinchgut BLK PLZ	Dark Lager	4.8%	50 litre kegs draught only
Pinchgut PLZ	Czech Pilz	4.8%	50 litre kegs draught only
Redoak	www.redoak.com.au		
2006 Vintage (Seasonal)	Scottish Strong Scotch Ale	30.0%	
2007 Vintage (Seasonal)	Scottish Strong Scotch Ale	20.0%	
2008 Vintage (Seasonal)	Scottish Strong Scotch Ale	15.0%	
2009 Vintage (Seasonal)	Scottish Strong Scotch Ale	12.0%	
Belgian Wit (Seasonal)	Belgian Witbier	5.0%	gls
Redoak Aussie Ale	Australian Ale with Aussie spices	5.4%	gls
Redoak Belgian Chocolate Stout (Seasonal)	Specialty	5.0%	250ml bottle
Redoak Belgian Pale Ale (Seasonal)	Belgian Pale Ale	4.5%	gls
Redoak Berlinerweiss (Seasonal)	Sour Ale Berlinerweisse	2.9%	250ml bottle
Redoak Bitter	English Pale Ale Ordinary Bitter	3.5%	6 pack (330ml)
Redoak Blackberry Wheat Beer	Fruit Wheat Beer	5.0%	250ml bottle
Redoak Bock (Seasonal)	Bock	6.7%	gls
Redoak Christmas Cheer	Spiced Christmas Beer	6.2%	250ml bottle
Redoak Dunkel Weiss (Seasonal)	Dark Lager Munich Dunkel	5.7%	gls
Redoak Eis Bock (Seasonal)	Eisbock	14.0%	250ml bottle
Redoak Framboise Froment (Seasonal)	Fruit Beer	5.0%	250ml bottle
Redoak Framboise Reserve (Seasonal)	Specialty	11.0%	250ml bottle
Redoak Hefeweizen (Seasonal)	German Wheat Beer	5.0%	gls
Redoak Honey Ale	Australian Pale Ale with honey	4.9%	6 pack (330ml)
Redoak India Pale Ale	India Pale Ale English	6.5%	gls
Redoak Irish Red Ale	Irish Red Ale		
Redoak Oatmeal Stout	Stout Dry	4.8%	gls
Redoak Oktoberfest Lager (Seasonal)	European Amber Lager Oktoberfest	5.8%	gls
Redoak Old English Ale	Strong Ale Old Ale	5.4%	gls
Redoak Organic Pale Ale	English Pale Ale	4.6%	6 pack (330ml)
Redoak Paddy's Big Stout (Seasonal)	Stout Dry	6.0%	gls
Redoak Porter	Brown Porter		gls
Redoak Rauch Bier (Seasonal)	Smoked Classic Rauch Bier	5.5%	gls
Redoak Special Reserve (Seasonal)	English Barley Wine	12.0%	250ml bottle
Redoak Special Strong Bitter	English Pale Ale	5.6%	gls
Redoak Summer Lager	Australian Lager	4.5%	gls
Redoak Vienna Lager (Seasonal)	European Amber Lager Vienna	5.2%	gls
Redoak wee Heavy Ale vintages (Seasonal)	Scotch Ale	8.0%	250ml bottle
Redoak Weizen Dopplebock (Seasonal)	Weizenbock	8.4%	250ml bottle
Rocks Brewing Co.	Rocks Brewing Co - Nick Becker (0421 059 969)		
The Boxer	Irish Red Ale	4.1%	50 Litre Kegs
The Butcher	Porter	4.7%	50 Litre Kegs
The Governor	Golden Ale	4.5%	50 Litre Kegs
The Hangman	American Pale Ale	4.9%	50 Litre Kegs
The Pickpocket	Common Cider	5.0%	50 Litre Kegs
Scharers Little Brewery	www.scharers.com.au		
Scharers Little Brewery			

Brand/Distributor/Name	Style	ABV	Unit
Schwartz Brewery Hotel	www.schwartzbrewery.com		
Dr Schwartz Bavarian Red	Vienna Lager	5.0%	
Dr Schwartz Belgian	Belgian Double	7.5%	
DR Schwartz Pale Ale	American Pale Ale	5.0%	
Dr Schwartz Pils	Pilsner	5.0%	
Dr Schwartz Porter	Porter	5.5%	
Dr Schwartz Schwarzbier	Dark lager	4.9%	
Sydney Summertime	Blonde	4.6%	
Snowy Mountains Brewery	Paramount, SIL, ALM, ILG, HLW		
Bullocks Pilsner	Czech Pilsner	4.5%	Bottle 6-pack
Charlotte's Hefeweizen	German Wheat	4.7%	Keg 50L, Bottle 6-pack
Crackenback Pale Ale	American Pale Ale	4.9%	Keg 50L, Bottle 6-pack
Razorback Red Ale	Irish Red	4.8%	6-pack
St Arnou Brewing	www.st-arnou.com.au		
St Arnou Brewing			
St Peters Brewery	St Peters Brewery		
Blonde Ale	Wheat		
Green Star Lager	Lager		
Killagh Stout	Stout		
Cinnamon Girl	Spiced Beer		
Steel River Brewery	www.steelriverbrewery.com.au		
Steel River Brewery			
Stone and Wood Brewing Co	www.stoneandwood.com.au		
Pacific Ale			
Stone Beer			
The Australian Brewery	www.australianhotelandbrewery.com.au		
AB 3.3	Reduced Alcohol	3.3%	Draught
AB Champion Pale Ale	Australian Pale Ale	4.8%	Draught
AB Dark Lager	Bock	5.2%	Draught
AB Mexican Lager	Light Lager	4.5%	Draught
The Little Brewing Company	Clive Edmonds Wine Merchants, ALM, ILG, High Spirits Wholesale, HLW, Polkadot Liquor, Boutique Beverage Distributors		
Mad Abbot Dubbel 'Cellar Release'	Belgian Trappist/Abbey Ale	6.9%	330ml 4-pack, 50L keg
Mad Abbot Tripel 'Cellar Release'	Belgian Trappist/Abbey Ale	9.5%	330ml 4-pack, 50L keg
Wicked Elf Pale Ale	American Pale Ale	5.4%	330ml 4-pack, 50L keg
Wicked Elf Witbier	Belgian White Ale	5.0%	330ml 4-pack, 50L keg
Thirsty Crow	info@thirstycrow.com.au		
American Pale Ale	APA	5.0%	Keg
ESB	ESB	5.2%	Keg
Hefeweizen	Hefeweizen	4.9%	Keg
Jiminy Cricket	Milk Stout	5.2%	Keg
Kolsch	Kolsch	4.5%	Keg
Liquid Bacon	Rauch	5.0%	Keg
Red Light	Light Beer	2.9%	Keg
Robust Porter	Robust Porter	5.5%	Keg
Tooheys Brewery	www.lion-nathan.com.au		
Becks	Lager	5.0%	330mL, 50L
Blue Bitter	Light Lager	2.3%	
Gold Bitter	Mid Strength	3.0%	
Hahn Premium	Premium Lager	5.0%	
Hahn Premium Light	Light Lager	2.6%	
Hahn Super Dry	European Lager	4.6%	
Hahn Super Dry 3.5	Mid Strength Lager	3.5%	
Hahn White	Belgian Witbier	4.2%	330mL
Heineken	Lager		330mL, 50L
Ice Beer	Ice Brewed	4.0%	
Kirin	Lager		330mL
Red Bitter	Lager	3.4%	
Tooheys Extra Dry	Dry Lager	5.0%	
Tooheys Extra Dry Platinum	Lager	6.5%	
Tooheys New	Lager	4.6%	
Tooheys New White Stag	Lager	4.4%	
Tooheys Old	Dark, top fermented ale	4.4%	
Tooheys Pils	European Pilsener	4.5%	
Underground Brewing	www.underbrew.com		
Underground Brewing			
William Bull Brewery	www.williambull.com.au		
Red Angus Pilsener	Pilsener	4.8%	330mL
William's Organic Pale Ale	Australian Pale Ale	4.5%	330mL
Woolworths Liquor Brands	www.woolworths.com.au		
Platinum Blonde	Low Carb Lager	4.6%	4X6X330ML
Sail & Anchor BOLT	Low Carb Lager	4.6%	4 X 6 X 330ML
Sail & Anchor CLIPPER LIGHT	Lager	2.7%	4 X 6 X 330ML
Sail & Anchor DRY DOCK	Lager	5.0%	4 X 6 X 330ML

■ QLD

Brand/Distributor/Name	Style	ABV	Unit
Blue Sky Brewery	www.blueskybrewery.com.au		
Blue Sky Pilsner	Czech Style Pilsener	4.5%	330Ml 4 x 6 packs/ctn
Blue Sky Wheat Beer	Hefeweizen	5.0%	49.5L keg
Cairns Gold	Midstrenth Lager	3.3%	330Ml 4 x 6 packs/ctn

Brand/Distributor/Name	Style	ABV	Unit
FNQ Lager	Australian Style Lager	4.4%	330Ml 4x6 packs/ctn
IPA	American Pale Ale	5.2%	49.5L KEG
Reef Blonde	Lower Carb Lager	4.7%	330Ml 4x6 packs/ctn
True Blue Stout	Dark Porter	4.4%	49.5L keg
Brewhouse Brisbane	www.brewhouse.com.au		
Brewhouse Brisbane			
Burleigh Brewing	www.burleighbrewing.com		
28 Pale Ale	70's Style Pale Ale	4.8%	330ml x 6pk, 50L Kegs
Bighead	No Carb Lager	4.2%	330ml x 6pk, 50L Kegs
Black Giraffe	Black Coffee Lager	5.0%	650ml dinner bottle; 50L kegs
Duke Helles	German Helles	3.5%	330ml x 6pk, 50L Kegs
Duke Premium Lager	German Pilsner	4.8%	330ml x 6pk, 50L Kegs
Fanny Gertrude's Bickie Beer	Creamy Ale	5.0%	650ml dinner bottle; 50L kegs
HEF	German Hefeweizen	5.0%	330ml x 6pk, 50L Kegs
My Wife's Bitter	English Bitter	4.8%	650ml dinner bottle; 50L kegs
Carlton & United Breweries - Yatala	www.cub.com.au		
Great Northern Brewing Co	Lager		
KB Lager	Lager		
Power's Gold Bitter	Lager		
Castlemaine Perkins Brewery	www.lion-nathan.com.au		
XXXX Bitter	Lager	4.6%	
XXXX Gold	Mid Strength Lager	3.5%	
XXXX Light Bitter	Light Lager	2.3%	
XXXX Summer Bright Lager	Lager	4.2%	
MT Brewery	www.mtbeer.com		
0909 Cuvee Blonde	Belgian Pale Ale	5.3%	
Black Cockatoo	Schwarzbier	4.8%	
Czech Mate	Pilsener	5.0%	
Moderation Golden Ale	American Pale Ale	2.8%	
Rainforest Lager	German Lager	4.3%	
Sonntag	Kolsch	5.0%	
St Bridget	Dubel	7.2%	
Yippy IPA	I.P.A	6.5%	
Spring Hill Craft Brewery	www.internationalhotel.com.au		
Spring Hill Craft Brewery			
The Sunshine Coast Brewery	www.sunshinecoastbrewery.com		
Best Bitter	English Pale Ale-Best Bitter	4.6%	4x330mL
Chilli Beer	Spice Beer	4.6%	4x330mL
Czech Mate	American Pilsner	4.6%	Draught beer
Ginger Kegs	Spice Beer	3.0%	4x330mL
Hefeweizen	Weiss Bier	4.6%	4x330mL
Hot Chilli Beer	Spice Beer	4.6%	4x330mL
Porter	Brown Porter	4.6%	Draught beer
Rauch Bier	Smoked beer	6.1%	4x330mL
Rye ESB	English Pale Ale-Extra Special Bitter	5.8%	4x330mL
Summer Ale	English Pale Ale	4.6%	4x330mL
Townsville Brewing Co	www.townsvillebrewery.com.au		
Bandito Loco	Mexican Lager	5.0%	
Belgian Blonde	Witbier	4.9%	
Diggers Golden Ale	Aussie Ale	4.8%	
Flanagans Dry Irish Stout	Dry Irish Stout	4.4%	
Neds Red Ale	Irish Red Ale	4.4%	
Townsville Bitter Premium	Premium Lager	5.0%	
Townsville Bitter Premium Light	Premium Light Lager	3.0%	

■ SA

Brand/Distributor/Name	Style	ABV	Unit
Barossa Brewing Company	www.barossabrewingcompany.com		
Barossa Brewing Company			
Barossa Valley Brewing	www.bvbeer.com.au		
Barossa Valley Brewing			
Beard and Brau	SA/NT - www.empireliquor.com.au, VIC - Boutique Beverage Distributors		
Black Snout	English Milk Stout	5.0%	750ml bottle, 50L Keg
Bon Chiens	French Farmhouse Ale	7.9%	4x330ml, 24x330ml, 50L Keg
Cheeky Hound	Dortmunder	5.0%	50L Keg
Golden Paw	American Steam Ale	4.7%	4x330ml, 24x330ml, 50L Keg
Red Tail	UK Amber Ale	5.1%	4x330ml, 24x330ml, 50L Keg
Boar's Rock Beer	www.boarsrock.com.au		
Boar's Rock Beer			
Brewboys	www.brewboys.com.au		
Brew Boys			
Coopers Brewery Ltd	www.coopers.com.au, www.premiumbeverages.com.au		
Coopers 62 Pilsner	Pilsner	5.0%	355ml bottle
Coopers Best Extra Stout	Stout	6.3%	50 litre keg, 375ml, 750ml
Coopers Birell	Ultra Light Lager	<0.5%	375ml bottle
Coopers Clear	Low Carb Lager	4.5%	50 litre keg, 355ml bottle & can
Coopers Dark Ale	Dark Ale	4.5%	50L keg 375ml bottle
Coopers Mild Ale	Mid-strength Ale	3.5%	50L keg, 355ml bottle & can
Coopers Original Pale Ale	Pale Ale	4.5%	50L keg 375ml, 750ml
Coopers Premium Lager	Lager	4.8%	50L keg, 355ml bottle & can
Coopers Premium Light	Light Beer	2.9%	50L keg, 355ml bottle & can
Coopers Sparkling Ale	Ale	5.8%	50L keg, 375ml, 750ml
Coopers Vintage	Vintage Ale	7.5%	50L keg 375ml bottle
Goodieson Brewery	www.goodiesonbrewery.com.au		
Pale Ale	Australian Style Pale Ale	4.5%	330ml bottle - 6 pack
Pilsner	European Pilsner	5.0%	330ml bottle - 6 pack
Stout	Imperial Stout	6.5%	330ml bottle - 6 pack
Wheat Beer	German Hefeweizen	5.2%	330ml bottle - 6 pack
Grumpy's Brewhaus	www.grumpys.com.au		
Grumpy's Brewhaus			
Gulf Brewery	www.gulfbrewery.com.au		
Fish Tale Pilsner	Bohemian Pilsner	4.2%	24
Harvest Moon	Specialty - Organic Lager	4.6%	24
Humpback Pale Ale	Special/Best/Premium Bitter	4.2%	24
Kitten 9 Tails	Oktoberfest	4.3%	24
Madam Rouge	Specialty - Strawberry infused lager	4.6%	24
Pilot's Light	Lite Lager	2.7%	24
Sou'Wester Stout	Dry Stout - Choc stout	4.6%	24
Trade Winds IPA	English IPA	6.0%	24
Holdfast Bay Brewing Company	www.holdfasthotel.com.au		
Holdfast Bay Brewing Company			
Knappstein Enterprise Winery & Brewery	www.lion-nathan.com.au		
Knappstein Reserve Lager	Bavarian Style Lager	5.6%	4 pack x 330ml
Lobethal Bierhaus	www.bierhaus.com.au		
Lobethal Bierhaus			
Lovely Valley Beverage Factory / Myponga Brewery	www.lovelyvalley.websyte.com.au		
Lovely Valley Beverage Factory / Myponga Brewery			
McLaren Vale Beer Company	1300 MVBEER, www.valeale.com		
Vale Ale	Australian Pale Ale	4.5%	4x330ml, 24x330ml, Keg 50L
Vale Dark	American Dark Lager	4.5%	4x330ml, 24x330ml, Keg 50L
Vale Dry	Australian Dry Lager	4.5%	4x330ml, 24x330ml, Keg 50L
Vale IPA	India Pale Ale	5.0%	50L Keg
Pepperjack of Barossa	www.saltramestate.com.au		
Pepperjack of Barossa			
Pikes Wines	Fine Wine Partners		
Pike's Oakbank Beer	Pilsener	4.5%	24 X 330ml
Port Dock Brewery	www.portdockbreweryhotel.com.au		
Port Dock Brewery			
Regency Tafe Brewery	www.tafesa.edu.au		
Regency Tafe Brewery			
South Australian Brewing Company	www.lion-nathan.com.au		
Southwark Bitter	Bitter Lager	4.5%	
Southwark Old Stout	Stout	7.4%	
West End Draught	Australian Lager	4.5%	
Swanky	swankybeer.com.au		
Swanky			
Swell Brewing Co.	www.swellbeer.com.au		
SWELL GOLDEN ALE	Light Hybrid Ale	4.7%	49.5lt Keg, 4x500ml
SWELL PALE ALE	American Ale	4.9%	49.5lt Keg, 4x500ml
The Steam Exchange Brewery	www.steamexchange.com.au		
Family Reserve	Belgian Dubbel	8.7%	50L Keg
Oak Aged Pale Ale	English Ale aged on oak	5.8%	50L Keg
Pale Ale	English Ale	5.8%	6-pack 330ml bottle 24-carton
Santa's Wobbler	Porter	5.3%	50L Keg
Southerly Buster	Northern English Brown Ale	5.5%	6-pack 330ml bottle 24-carton
Steam Ale	California Common	4.9%	6-pack 330ml bottle 24-carton
Stout	Sweet Stout	5.2%	6-pack 330ml bottle 24-carton
Truffles	Bourbon Fortified Dessert Beer	6.5%	6-pack 330ml bottle 24-carton
Woolshed Brewery	A-List Fine Wines		
Amazon Ale	Australian Pale Ale	4.5% - 4.7%	330ml, 19 & 50L kegs.
Yorke Brewing	www.yorkebrewing.com.au		
White Sands Wheat	Weizen	4.5%	50L Keg

■ TAS

Brand/Distributor/Name	Style	ABV	Unit
Cascade Brewery	www.cascadebreweryco.com.au		
Cascade Bitter	Australian Lager		
Cascade Blonde			
Cascade Draught	Australian Lager		
Cascade First Harvest			
Cascade Pale Ale	Australian Pale Ale		
Cascade Premium	Australian Lager		
Cascade Premium Light	Australian Lager		
Cascade Pure	Australian Lager		
Cascade Stout	Stout		
Iron House Brewery	www.ironhouse.com.au		
Iron House Brewery			
James Boag & Son Brewing	www.lion-nathan.com.au		
Boag's Draught	Australian Lager	4.6%	
Boag's Draught Light	Light Lager	2.7%	
Boag's St George	Tropical Dry Lager	4.8%	
Boag's Wizards Smith's Ale	English Pale Ale	5.0%	

Brand/Distributor/Name	Style	ABV	Unit
Boag's XXX Ale	Australian Lager	4.8%	
James Baog's Pure	Lager	4.5%	
James Boag's Classic Blonde	Low Carb Lager	4.5%	
James Boag's Premium	Australian Premium Lager	5.0%	
James Boag's Premium Light	Light Lager	2.9%	
Moo Brew Brewery www.moobrew.com.au, SA - Jon Tolley Wine Merchants, QLD - Lock Stock & Barrel			
Moo Brew Dark Ale	Dark Ale	5.0%	50L Keg, 24 x 330ml
Moo Brew Hefeweizen	Hefeweizen	5.1%	50L Keg, 24 x 330ml
Moo Brew Imperial Stout	Imperial Stout	8.5%	330ml Bottle
Moo Brew Pale Ale	American Pale Ale	4.9%	50L Keg, 24 x 330ml
Moo Brew Pilsner	Pilsner	5.0%	50L Keg, 24 x 330ml
Seven Sheds	www.sevensheds.com		
Seven Sheds			
Taverner's	www.ozhoney.com.au		
Honey Pale Ale	Pale Ale	5.5%	330ml
Honey Porter	Double Honey Porter	6.0%	330ml
Strong Honey Ale	Medieval style Strong Ale	8.0%	330ml
The Tasmanian Chilli Beer Co	www.tasmanianchillibeercompany.com.au		
The Tasmanian Chilli Beer Co			
The Two Metre Tall Company	Boutique Beverage Distributors (VIC), Fine Drop (TAS)		
'One-Off' Seasonal Real Ale	Real Ale	Variable	750ml bottle
Derwent Real Ale	Aromatic Wheat based Real Ale	5.2%	330ml, 500ml bottle
Forester Real Ale	Bitter Real Ale	5.3%	330ml, 500ml bottle
Huon Dark Apple Ale	Unique Dark, Fruit based Real Ale	5.5%	330ml, 500ml bottle
Two Metre Tall Cleansing Ale	Aromatic Amber Real Ale	4.9%	330ml bottle
Van Dieman Brewing	www.vandiemanbrewing.com.au		
Jacobs Ladder	British Style Amber Ale	4.2%	330ml Bottle/50L keg
Van Dieman Brewing	www.vandiemanbrewing.com.au		
Ragged Jack	British Style Pale Ale	4.2%	330ml Bottle/50L keg
Stacks Bluff	Oatmeal Stout	5.0%	330ml Bottle/50L keg
White Hills	Belgian Witbier	4.6%	330ml Bottle/50L keg
Wineglass Bay Brewing Co.	Freycinet Vineyards		
Hazards Ale	Bottle conditioned ale	5.2%	330 ml Bottle, 50L keg (Tas only)

■ VIC

Brand/Distributor/Name	Style	ABV	Unit
2 Brothers Brewery	www.2brothers.com.au		
Chief (seasonal)	Marzen	6.0%	330ml
Grizz	American Amber Ale	5.7%	330mL
Growler	American Brown Ale	4.7%	330ml
Guvnor (seasonal)	Extra Strong Ale	10.3%	330ml
James Brown (Seasonal)	Belgian Brown	8.8%	330mL
Taxi	Pilsner	4.7%	330ml
Voodoo (Seasonal)	Baltic Porter	7.0%	330ml
Arctic Fox Brewery	David Hardcastle 0400 332 006		
American Pale Ale	American Pale Ale	4.7%	Bottle 330ml 6-Pack
Chocolate Stout	Stout	5.9%	Bottle 500mL Single
English Pale Ale	English Pale Ale	4.7%	Bottle 330ml 6-Pack
Ice Cap Lager			Bottle 330ml 6-Pack
Avonmore Estate Biodynamic Wines	www.avonmoreestatewine.com		
Avonmore			
Beacon Brewing Company	www.beaconbrewing.com.au		
Beacon Brewing			
Bellarine Brewing Company	www.bellarinestate.com.au		
Bellarine Brewing Company			
Bitch Brewing Pty Ltd	www.lifesabitch.com.au		
Bitch Brewing Pty Ltd			
Boat Rocker	www.boatrocker.com.au		
Boat Rocker			
Boynton's Brewing Company	www.boynton.com.au		
Boynton's Brewing Company			
Bridge Road Brewers	info@bridgeroadbrewers.com.au		
Australian Ale	English Pale Ale	4.4%	Bottle 330ml 6-Pack
Beechworth Pale Ale	American Pale	4.8%	Bottle 330ml 6-Pack
Bling India Pale Ale	India Pale Ale	5.8%	Bottle 330ml 6-Pack
Celtic Red Ale	Scottish and Irish Ale	5.3%	Bottle 330ml 6-Pack
Chestnut Pilsner	Pilsner	5.0%	Bottle 330ml 6-Pack
Chevalier BiereDe Garde	Belgian Strong Ale	7.5%	750ml Bottle and Case of 6
Chevalier Hefe Weizen Dunkel	German Wheat	5.2%	750ml Bottle and Case of 6
Chevalier Saison	Belgian and French Ale	6.0%	750ml Bottle and Case of 6
Hefe Weizen	German Wheat	5.0%	Bottle 330ml 6-Pack
Robust Porter	Porter	5.2%	Bottle 330ml 6-Pack
Bright Brewery	www.brightbrewery.com.au		
Blowhard Pale	American Pale Ale	5.0%	Keg, 330ml btl, 5 litre MiniKegs
Bright Lager	Lager	4.7%	Keg, 330ml btl, 5 litre MiniKegs
Fainters Dubbel	Dubbel	8.5%	Keg, 330ml btl, 5 litre MiniKegs
Hellfire Amber	English Bitter	5.0%	Keg, 330ml btl, 5 litre MiniKegs
Pinky Framboise (Seasonal)	Raspberry Lambic-Style	5.4%	750ml bottles, 5 litre MiniKegs
Razor Witbier	Witbier	5.0%	Keg, 330ml btl, 5 litre MiniKegs
Russian Imperial Stout (Seasonal)	Russian Imperial Stout	10.0%	750ml bottles, 5 litre MiniKegs
Staircase Porter	Porter	5.7%	Keg, 330ml btl, 5 litre MiniKegs
Topaz Lager (Seasonal)	Harvest Lager	5.7%	750ml bottles, 5 litre Minikegs
BROO Pty Ltd	www.broo.com.au		
BROO Pty Ltd			
Buckley's Beers	www.buckleysbeer.com.au		
Buckley's Beers			
Buffalo Brewery	www.buffalobrewery.com.au		
Buffalo Brewery			
Bullant Brewery	www.bullantbrewery.com		
Bark Sheds Wheat Beer	German Wheat	5.1%	50 litre, 5 litre, 640mL
Double Bridges IPA	English IPA	5.8%	50 litre, 5 litre, 640mL
Mossiface Pale Ale	American Pale Ale	4.8%	50 litre, 5 litre, 640mL
Piano Bridge Stout	Stout	6.7%	50 litre, 5 litre
Pig & Whistle Brown Ale	English Brown Ale	4.7%	50 litre, 5 litre, 640mL
Carlton & United Breweries	www.cub.com.au		
Abbotsford Invalid Stout	Stout		
Carlsberg	Lager	5.0%	330mL, 50L
Carlton Draught	Australian Lager	4.6%	
Crown Lager	Australian Lager		
Fosters Lager	Lager		
Kronenbourg	Lager		330mL, 50L
Melbourne Bitter	Australian Lager		
NT Draught	Lager		
Pure Blonde	Lager		
Resche Real			
Sheaf Stout	Stout		
Stella Artois	Lager		330mL, 50L
VB	Australian Lager	4.6%	
Coldstream Brewery	www.coldstreambrewery.com.au		
Coldstream Naked Ale	English Bitter	4.9%	6 x 330ml Stubby
Coldstream Pilsner	Pilsner	4.5%	6 x 330ml Stubby
Coldstream Porter	Porter	4.8%	6 x 330ml Stubby
Coldwater Creek Microbrewery	www.chifleydoveton.com.au		
Coldwater Creek American Pale Ale	Americal Pale Ale	5.1%	Draught on-site
Coldwater Creek Pilsner	Pilsner	4.8%	Draught on-site
Red Raw	Amber Ale	4.8%	Draught on-site
DOLPHIN BREWERY	www.dolphinbrewery.com.au		
Amber Ale	Traditional Country-style Amber Ale	4.0%	6X330ml
Best Bitter Ale	English Best Bitter Ale	5.0%	6X330ml
Pale Ale	English Pale Ale	4.5%	6X330ml
Penguin Porter Ale	Chocolate Porter Ale	4.5%	6X330ml
Shag	Spiced Honey Ale With Ginger	4.0%	6X330ml
Echuca Brewing Co	www.echucabrewingco.com.au		
Echuca Brewing Co			
Effen Enterprises Pty Ltd	ALM, SIL, Monacellars, Paramount Liquor		
effen Lager	European Lager	4.6%	330ml bottle
Flying Horse	www.theflyinghorse.com.au		
Billy Goat	Bock	6.9%	6 x 330ml, Keg 50lts
Dirty Angel	Porter	5.8%	6 x 330ml, Keg 50lts
Lady Bay Lager	Lager	4.6%	6 x 330ml, Keg 50lts
Savage Seagull	Dark Ale	4.8%	6 x 330ml, Keg 50lts
Whale Ale	British Style Pale Ale	4.6%	6 x 330ml, Keg 50lts
Wollaston Wheat	Wheat Beer	4.6%	6 x 330ml, Keg 50lts
Forrest Brewing Company	www.forrestbrewing.com.au		
Amber Ale	Amber Hybrid Beer	4.2%	Keg
Blackwood Stout	Stout	4.5%	Keg
Golden Ale	American Ale	4.8%	Keg
Mountain Ale	American Ale	4.6%	Keg
Silvertop Ale	Light Hybrid Beer	4.1%	Keg
Grand Ridge Brewery	Alm, Sil, Capital Liquor, Paramount		
Almighty Light	Lager	2.7%	330ml, 50l
Black & Tan (Seasonal)	Porter	4.9%	330ml, 50l
Brewers Pilsener	Pilsener	4.9%	330ml, 50l
Gippsland Gold	Pale Ale	4.9%	330ml, 50l
Grand Ridge Draught	Lager	4.9%	330ml, 50l
Hatlifter Stout	Stout	4.9%	330ml, 50l
Mirboo Madness (Limitedl)	American Red Ale	6.0%	330ml, 50l
Mirboo Midnight (Limitedl)	Dark Oaked Ale	6.5%	330ml, 50l
Moonlight (Seasonal)	Nut Brown Ale	3.3%	330ml, 50l
Moonshine	Dark Scotch Ale	8.5%	330ml, 50l
Natural Blonde	Belgian Wheat	4.5%	330ml, 50l
Supershine	Barley Wine	11.0%	330ml
Whoa (Limitedl)	Wet Hopped Oatmeal Ale	4.5%	330ml, 50l
Yarra Valley Gold	Real Ale	4.9%	330ml, 50l
Harcourt Valley Brewing Co	www.harcourtvalley.com.au		
Harcourt Valley Brewing Co			
Hargreaves Hill Brewing Co	www.hargreaveshill.com.au		
AD	Abbey Dubbel	7.5%	750ml, keg
Extra Special Bitter	New World ESB	5.2%	4x330ml, keg
Hefeweizen	Hefeweizen	4.9%	6x330ml, keg
Pale Ale	English Pale Ale	4.9%	6x330ml, keg
R.I.S.	Russian Imperial Stout	13.5%	750ml, keg

Brand/Distributor/Name	Style	ABV	Unit
Stout	Foreign Extra Stout	6.2%	4x330ml, keg
The Phoenix	Imperial Red Ale	9.8%	750ml, keg
Yarra Valley Pilsner	New World Pilsner	4.9%	keg
Hawthorn Brewing	BID (Vic/Tas): (03) 9310 3130. 1300 HBC Beer (422233)		
Hawthorn Amber Ale	English Pale Ale	4.7%	6x330ml
Hawthorn Pale Ale	American / English Pale Ale hybrid	4.7%	6x330ml
Hawthorn Pale Ale	American / English Pale Ale hybrid	4.7%	50lt Keg
Hawthorn Pilsner	German Pilsner	4.6%	6x330ml
Hickinbotham Winery & Brewery	www.hickinbotham.biz		
HIX PILSENER	German Pilsner	5.7%	500ml, draught on-site
HIX PALE ALE	Pale Ale	5.2%	500ml, draught on-site
HIX BROWN ALE	Brown Ale	4.3%	500ml, draught on-site
HIX IRISH STOUT	Stout	4.3%	draught on-site
Holgate Brewhouse	Julian Nelson 0419 460 259		
Beelzebub's Jewels (Seasonal)	Belgian Quadrupel	12.0%	750mL
Double Trouble (Seasonal)	Belgian Abbey-Ale	8.0%	330mL
Empress (Seasonal)	Imperial Mocha Porter	10.0%	750mL, 50L
ESB	English Extra Special Bitter	5.0%	330mL, 50L
Hopinator	American Double IPA	7.0%	330mL
Mt Macedon Ale	American Pale Ale	4.5%	330mL, 50L
Pilsner	German-Style Pilsner	5.1%	330mL, 50L
Road Trip	American IPA	5.5%	Keg 50L
Temptress	Chocolate Porter	6.0%	330mL, 50L
White Ale (Seasonal)	Belgian Witbier	5.0%	330mL, 50L
Independent Distillers	www.independentdistillers.com		
3 Kings			
James Squire Brewhouse	www.portlandhotel.com.au		
House beers and James Squire range			
Jamieson Brewery	www.jamiesonbrewery.com.au		
Jamieson Brewery			
Kooinda Boutique Brewery	www.kooinda.com.au		
Kooinda Belgian Wit	Belgian Wit	5.5%	Keg Only
Kooinda Pale Ale	American Pale Ale	4.7%	330ml and Draught
Lone Hand Brewery	lonehand@aussiebroadband.com.au		
Lone Hand Brewery			
Matilda Bay Brewing Company	www.cub.com.au		
Alpha Pale Ale	American Pale Ale	5.2%	6 Pack, Carton, Keg
Beez Neez	Honey Wheat	4.7%	6 Pack, Carton, Keg
Big Helga	Munich Helles Lager	4.7%	6 Pack, Carton, Keg
Bohemian Pilsner	Bohemian Pilsner	4.7%	6 Pack, Carton, Keg
Dogbolter	Munich Dunkel Dark Lager	5.2%	4 Pack, Carton, Keg
Fat Yak	American Pale Ale	4.7%	6 Pack, Carton, Keg
Redback	German Wheat - Weizen	4.7%	6 Pack, Carton, Keg
Mildura Brewery	www.mildurabrewery.com.au		
Mildura Brewery			
Moon Dog Craft Brewery	www.moondogbrewing.com.au		
Moon Dog Craft Brewery			
Mornington Peninsula Brewery	www.mpbrew.com.au		
Hightail Ale	Amber Ale	4.5%	330ml
Mornington Brown	English Brown Ale	5.0%	50Lt
Mornington Imperial IPA	Indian Pale Ale	8.3%	50Lt
Mornington IPA	Indian Pale Ale	6.1%	50Lt
Mornington Pale	American Ale	4.7%	50Lt
Mornington Pale	American Ale	4.7%	6x330ml
Mornington Porter	Porter	6.0%	50Lt
Mornington Saison	Belgian and French Ale	6.0%	50Lt
Mornington Sorachi Koslch	Light Hybrid Beer	5.2%	50Lt
Mornington Witbier	Belgian and French Ale	4.7%	50Lt
Mornington Witbier	Belgian and French Ale	4.7%	6x330ml
Mountain Goat	www.goatbeer.com.au		
Double Hightail	Strong Ale	6.8%	640ml
India Pale Ale	IPA	6.2%	640ml
Steam Ale	Pale Ale	4.5%	330ml
Surefoot Stout	Sweet Stout	4.9%	640ml
Otway Estate	NSW & QLD www.australiantradepartners.com.au		
Otway Brewing Organic Lager	German Pilsner	4.5%	6x330ml, 50L
Prickly Moses Farmhouse Ale	Belgian Farmhouse Ale	6.3%	6X750ml
Prickly Moses Otway Ale	Original Pale Ale	4.9%	6x330ml, 50L
Prickly Moses Otway Light	Light Ale	2.9%	6x330ml, 50L
Prickly Moses Otway Pilsner	Bohemian Pilsner	4.8%	6x330ml, 50L
Prickly Moses Otway Stout	Dry Stout	5.0%	6x330ml, 50L
Prickly Moses Red Ale	Irish Red Ale	5.0%	6x330ml, 50L
Prickly Moses Reserve De Otway	Biere De Garde	6.8%	6X750ml
Prickly Moses Saison 2011	Saison	7.2%	6X750ml
Prickly Moses Summer Ale	Kolsch	4.5%	6x330ml, 50L
Prickly Moses Wheat Beer	Witbier	4.3%	6x330ml, 50L
Piss Beer Co	www.pi55.com		
Piss Beer Co			
Port Pier Café	(03) 5259 1080		
Port Pier Café			
Ranga Brewing Co	Paramount Liquor		
RANGA Premium Red Ale	Red Ale	4.5%	16x330ml, 50L
Rebellion Brewery	www.therat.com.au		
The Rat Bitter Ale	Australian Pale Ale	4.5%	50L, 6x330ml
Red Duck	www.redduckbeer.com.au		
Red Duck Amber Ale	Amber Ale	4.9%	6pack/30l keg
Red Duck Bengal IPA	English IPA	7.0%	6pack/30l keg
Red Duck Burton	English Pale Ale	5.4%	6pack/30l keg
Red Duck Canute the Gruit	Dark Medieval	4.4%	6 pack
Red Duck Loch Ness	Barrel-aged Scotch Ale	6.7%	6pack
Red Duck Overland	Kolsch	4.2%	6pack/30l keg
Red Duck Pale Ale	Australian Pale Ale	4.5%	6pack/30l keg
Red Duck Pale Rider	APA	5.6%	6pack/30l keg
Red Duck Porter	Porter	6.4%	6pack/30l keg
Red Duck Queen Bee	Honey Porter	6.6%	6pack/30l keg
Red Duck Red Admiral	Celtic Red Ale	6.2%	6pack/30l keg
Red Duck The Ox	Imperial Stout	9.4%	6pack/30l keg
Red Duck Vanilla Porter	Belgian Porter	6.5%	6pack/30l keg
Red Duck White Garden	Hybrid Fruit Beer	4.1%	6pack/30l keg
Red Hill Brewery	www.redhillbrewery.com.au		
Belgian Blonde (Seasonal Release)	Belgian Pale Ale	6.0%	Keg & 330ml bottle
Bohemian Pilsner (Seasonal Release)	Bohemian Pilsner	6.0%	Keg & 330ml bottle
Christmas Ale (Seasonal Release)	Belgian Abbey Ale	8.3%	Keg & 330ml bottle
Golden Ale	Kolsch	5.0%	Keg & 330ml bottle
Hop Harvest Ale (Seasonal Release)	ESB	6.0%	Keg & 330ml bottle
Imperial Stout (Seasonal Release)	Imperial Stout	8.1%	Keg & 330ml bottle
Scotch Ale	Scotch Ale	5.8%	Keg & 330ml bottle
Temptation (Seasonal Release)	Strong Golden Ale	8.0%	Keg & 330ml bottle
Weizenbock (Seasonal Release)	Weizenbock	8.1%	Keg & 330ml bottle
Wheat Beer	Hefeweizen	5.0%	Keg & 330ml bottle
Rusty Water Brewery	www.rustywaterbrewery.com.au		
Rusty Water Brewery	Rusty Water Brewery		
Savaraln	www.savarainbrewery.com.au, El Sombrero Mexican Restaurant		
Savaraln Brown Ale	Brown Ale	4.6%	19L Keg
Scottish Chiefs Tavern Brewery	www.scottishchiefs.com.au		
Scottish Chiefs Tavern Brewery			
Southern Bay Brewing Co.	www.southernbay.com.au		
Bearings Lager	Lager	4.6%	24x330ml, 50L Keg
Sundance Brewing	www.calager.com		
Cricketers Arms Lager	Lager		
Sweetwater Brewing Company	www.sweetwaterbrewing.com.au		
Sweetwater Golden Bitter	English Special Bitter	5.2%	330ml
Sweetwater IPA	India Pale Ale	5.0%	330ml
Sweetwater Pale Ale	American Pale Ale	5.0%	330ml
Sweetwater Porter	Robust Porter	4.8%	330ml
Sweetwater Summer Ale	Australian Pale Ale	4.5%	330ml
Sweetwater Wiessbier	Hefeweizen	5.0%	330ml
Temple Brewing	www.templebrewing.com.au		
Temple Brewing			
The Three Ravens Brewing Company	www.3ravens.com.au		
55	American Ale	5.5%	330ml
Ale Noir	Specialty Beer	5.5%	750mL
Alt Beer	Alt Beer	5.0%	330mL
Black	Oatmeal Stout	5.5%	330mL
Dark	Smoke Beer	5.2%	330mL
Double Ale Noir	Specialty Beer	6.5%	750mL
English Ale	English Ale	4.6%	330mL
Hell	Munich Helles	5.0%	500mL
Oktoberfest Beer	Amber Lager	6.0%	500mL
Rye	Rye Beer	5.6%	500mL
The Ravenator	Bock	5.8%	500mL
Uber Special Bitter (USB)	Strong Ale	6.0%	500mL
White	Belgian Wit	5.2%	330ml
Three Troupers	www.threetroupers.com.au		
Three Troupers			
Thunder Road Brewing Company	www.thunderroadbrewing.com		
Thunder Road Brewing Company	Pale Lager		
Toborac Hotel & Brewery	www.tooborachotel.com.au		
Tooborac Hotel & Brewery			
True South Brewery	www.truesouth.com.au		
True South Brewery			
University of Ballarat	www.ballarat.edu.au		
Ballarat University Brewery			
White Rabbit	www.littlecreatures.com.au		
White Rabbit Dark Ale	Dark Ale	4.9%	330ml, 50L Kegs
White Rabbit White Ale	Belgian White Ale	4.5%	330ml, 50L Kegs

WA

Brand/Distributor/Name	Style	ABV	Unit
Billabong Brewing	www.billabongbrewing.com.au		
Bavarian Wheat	German Style Kristall	5.0%	330x24 and 50LKegs
Mango Beer	Fruity Lager	4.9%	50 Liter kegs only
Nelson Sauvin Ale	American Pale Ale	515.0%	330x24 and 50LKegs
Porter	Robust Porter	4.9%	330x24 and 50LKegs
Blacksalt Brewery	www.onthebeach.net.au		
Blacksalt Brewery			
Blackwood Valley Brewing Company	www.blackwoodvalley.com.au		
Blackwood Valley Bitter	Best Bitter	5.5%	(10lt/50lt)
Blackwood Valley Irish Red	Robust Irish Red Ale	5.3%	(10lt/50lt)
Blackwood Valley Lager	Bohemian Lager	5.2%	(10lt/50lt)
Blackwood Valley Nut Brown	Nut Brown Ale	5.2%	(10lt/50lt)
Blackwood Valley Stout	Sweet Stout	5.0%	(10lt/50lt)
Blackwood Valley Summer Ale	Reduced Alc Pale Ale	3.5%	(10lt/50lt)
Bootleg Brewery	www.bootlegbrewery.com.au		
Black Market	Black Ipa	5.6%	50L / 330ml / 6-pack
Hefe	Hefeweizen	4.7%	50L / 330ml / 6-pack
Oatmeal Stout	Oatmeal Stout	5.5%	50L / 330ml / 6-pack
Raging Bull	Porter	7.1%	50L / 330ml / 6-pack
Settler's Pale Ale	American Style Pale Ale	4.8%	50L / 330ml / 6-pack
Sou West Wheat	Wheat Beer	4.7%	50L / 330ml / 6-pack
Tom's Amber Ale	Amber Ale	4.0%	50L / 330ml / 6-pack
Wils Pils	European Style Pilsner	4.9%	50L / 330ml / 6-pack
Brew 42 at Lake Clifton	www.brew42.com		
Brew 42			
Bush Shack Brewery	www.bushshackbrewery.com.au		
Chilli	Pilsner	5.0%	335ml 6 Pack
Chocolate	Milk Stout	5.5%	335ml 6 Pack
Dark Roast Wheat	Dunkle	4.5%	335ml 6 Pack
Dirty Dans Dark Delight	Imerial Stout	7.5%	335ml 6 Pack
Ginger Beer	Ginger Beer	4.5%	335ml 6 Pack
Kick'n Kole'	RTD	4.5%	335ml 6 Pack
Mango Madness	RTD	4.5%	335ml 6 Pack
Old Pa's Sar's	RTD	4.5%	335ml 6 Pack
Passionfruit Beer	RTD	4.5%	335ml 6 Pack
Scream'n Cream'n	RTD	4.5%	335ml 6 Pack
Spelt Wheat	Raw Wheat	4.5%	335ml 6 Pack
Strawberry Blonde	Lager	6.4%	335ml 6 Pack
Twisted Lemon	Pale Ale	5.5%	335ml 6 Pack
Yallingup Old	Scotich Ale	5.5%	335ml 6 Pack
Cheeky Monkey Brewery & Cidery	www.cheekymonkeybrewery.com.au		
Cheeky Monkey			
Colonial Brewing Company	www.colonialbrewingco.com.au		
Colonial			
Cowaramup Brewing Company	www.cowaramupbrewing.com.au		
Cowaramup Hefeweizen	Weizen/Weissbier	5.1%	50litre
Cowaramup India Pale Ale	English India Pale Ale	5.8%	50litre
Cowaramup Pilsener	German Pilsener	5.1%	50litre
Cowaramup Porter	Robust Porter	6.0%	50litre
Cowaramup Special Pale Ale	English Extra Special Bitter	5.4%	50litre
Denmark Brews & Ales	www.southernend.com.au		
Denmark Brews & Ales			
Duckstein Brewery	www.duckstein.com.au		
Duckstein Brewery			
Eagle Bay Brewing Company	www.eaglebaybrewing.com.au		
Eagle Bay Brewing Company			
Edith Cowan University (ECU)	www.ecu.edu.au		
Edith Cowan University (ECU)			
Elmar's in the Valley	www.elmars.com.au		
ChristBock (Seasonal)	German Style Bock	5.8-6%	Keg Draught
Cloudy Pilsener (Seasonal)	German Style unfiltered Pilsener	4.8%	Keg Draught
Dunkle (Seasonal)	German Style dunkle beer	5.0%	Keg Draught
Einstein Pilsener	German Style Pilsener	4.8%	Keg, 5L Party Keg
Kickback Weizen	German Style HefeWeizen	4.8%	Keg Draught
Maibock (Seasonal)	German Style Maibock	5.8 - 6%	Keg Draught
Marzen (Seasonal)	German Oktoberfest Beer	5.0%	Keg Draught
Overdraft Alt	German Style Alt Ale	4.8%	Keg Draught
Schwarz Dark	German Style Schwarz Beer	5.0%	Keg Draught
Feral Brewing Company	www.feralbrewing.com.au		
Feral White	Wheat Beer	4.6%	24 x 330ml
Golden Ace	Belgian Ale	5.5%	16 x 330ml
Hop Hog	American IPA	5.8%	16 x 330ml
Gage Roads Brewing Co	www.gageroads.com.au		
Atomic Pale Ale	Pale Ale	4.7%	Bottle 330ml
Gage Pils 3.5	Pilsner	3.5%	Bottle 330ml, Keg 50L
Gage Premium Lager	Lager	4.7%	Bottle 330ml
Sleeping Giant IPA	IPA	5.4%	Bottle 330ml
Wahoo Premium Ale	Kolsch style Ale	4.6%	Bottle 330ml, Keg 50L
Indian Ocean Brewing Co	www.indibrew.com		
Indi Best Bitter	Handpump Best Bitter	5.2%	50Ltr Keg
Indi Green	Low Carb Lager	4.7%	50Ltr Keg
Indi Pale Ale	English Pale Ale	5.2%	50Ltr Keg
Indi Pils	Pilsner	4.9%	50Ltr Keg
Indi Vanilla Milk Stout	Sweet Stout	6.2%	50Ltr Keg
Indi White	Witbier	4.5%	50Ltr Keg
Ironbark Brewing	www.ironbarkbrewery.com.au		
Ironbark Brewing			
Last Drop Brewery	www.lastdropbrewery.com.au		
Last Drop Brewery			
Little Creatures Brewing	www.littlecreatures.com.au		
Little Creatures Bright Ale	Pale Ale	4.5%	330ml, 568ml, 50L
Little Creatures Pale Ale	American Pale Ale	5.2%	330ml, 568ml, 50L
Little Creatures Pilsner	European Pilsner	4.6%	330ml bottles, 50L
Little Creatures Rogers	Amber Ale	3.8%	330ml bottles, 50L
Mash Brewing	www.mashbrewing.com.au		
Bunbury Blonde	American Blonde	4.8%	Draught - Mash Bunbury
Haze	Hefeweizen	4.8%	On Draught
Killer Ale	Changing Range		On Draught
Pale	American Pale Ale	5.0%	On Draught
Sgt. Pepper	Golden Ale	4.8%	On Draught
Summer Lager	Low-Carb Lager	4.6%	Bottles
Chilli-Out-Beer	Spiced Beer	4.5%	50L Keg
Matso's Broome Brewery	www.matsosbroomebrewery.com.au sales@davemullenwines.com.au		
Divers Porter	Porter	5.2%	50L Keg
Ginger Beer	Wine Cooler	3.5%	bottle, 50L Keg
Hit The Toad Lager	Lager	4.6%	50L Keg
Mango Beer	Fruit Beer	4.5%	bottle, 50L Keg
Monsoonal Blonde	Belgium Wheat	4.7%	bottle, 50L Keg
Pearlers Pale	(West) Australian Pale Ale	4.5%	50L Keg
Smokey Bishop	German Style Dark Lager	4.9%	bottle, 50L Keg
Moody Cow Brewery	www.moodycow.com.au		
Black Dog Pils	Pilsner		
Fergus Dark Ale	Dark Ale		
Grunta's Original Ale	Original Ale		
Pale Ale	Pale Ale		
Simply Red Irish Ale	Irish Red Ale		
Nail Brewing Australia	www.nailbrewing.com		
Clout Stout (Annual Release)	Imperial Stout	10%+	Bottle only
Nail Ale	Australian Pale Ale	4.7%	Keg, bottle
Nail Stout	Oatmeal Stout	6.0%	Keg Bottle
Occy's Brewery	Occy's (08) 9755 8300		
Occy's Brewery			
Old Coast Rd Brewery	www.ocrb.com.au		
Acres of Wheat	Hefe Weizen	5.3%	500ml singles
Harris Bitter	English Pale Ale	4.0%	330ml 6 pack
OCRB Pilsener	Bohemian Pilsener	5.5%	330ml 6 pack
PBH Strong Porter	Porter	5.7%	330ml 6 pack
Old Swan Brewery	www.oldswanbrewery.com.au		
Old Swan Brewery			
The Grove Vineyard	www.thegrovevineyard.com.au		
The Grove			
The Monk	www.themonk.com.au		
Chief	American India Pale Ale	6.3%	
Kolsch	German Kölsch	4.9%	Keg
Mild	European Low-Alcohol Lager	3.5%	Keg
Pale	Australian Pale Ale	5.0%	
Porter	Brown Porter	4.6%	
Rauch	Bamberg Marzen Rauchbier	5.3%	
Seasonal	Currently - Foreign Extra Stout with Whiskey Infused		
The Wheat	Belgian Witbier	6.0%	Keg
The Swan Brewery Company	www.lion-nathan.com.au		
Emu Bitter	Lager	4.6%	
Emu Draught	Mid Strength Lager	3.0%	
Emu Export	Lager	4.5%	
Swan Draught	Lager	4.5%	
Wild Bull Brewery	www.wildbullbrewery.com.au		
Amber Ale	Ale	4.8%	glass, 2lt bottle, 5lt keg
English Bitter	Ale	3.5%	glass, 2lt bottle, 5lt keg
Irish Red Ale	Ale	5.0%	glass, 2lt bottle, 5lt keg
Irish Special Ale	Ale	5.0%	glass, 2lt bottle, 5lt keg
Stout	Stout	5.8%	glass, 2lt bottle, 5lt keg
Tanglehead Brewery	www.tanglehead.com.au		
Tanglehead Christmas Ale 2011 Release	Belgian-Style Spiced Beer	8.1%	750ml

CIDER & PERRY: AUSTRALIA

ACT

Brand/Distributor/Name	Style	ABV	Unit
Wig & Pen	www.wigandpen.com.au		
Nockers	Perry	4.5 - 4.8%	Keg 50L
Thirsty Worm	Apple Cider	5.7 - 6%	Keg 50L

NSW

Brand/Distributor/Name	Style	ABV	Unit
Redoak	www.redoak.com.au		
Redoak Dry Cider	Cider	4.5%	gls
Redoak Original Cider	Cider	4.5%	gls
Redoak Perry	Perry	4.5%	gls
Schwartz Brewery Hotel	www.schwartzbrewery.com		
Sydney Cider	Cider	4.5%	
Tooheys Brewery	www.lion-nathan.com.au		
Tooheys 5 Seeds	Cider	5.0%	
Woolworths Liquor Brands	www.woolworths.com.au		
CASTAWAY	Cider		4X6X330ML

QLD

Brand/Distributor/Name	Style	ABV	Unit
Blue Sky Brewery	www.blueskybrewery.com.au		
Wicked Cider	Apple Cider	5.0%	330ml 4X6 Packs/ctn

SA

Brand/Distributor/Name	Style	ABV	Unit
Thorogoods Cider	www.thorogoods.com.au		
Thorogoods Cider	Cider		
VOK Beverages	VOK Beverages		
Three Oaks Cider	Original	5.0%	330mL Bottle
Three Oaks Cider	Sweet	5.0%	330mL Bottle
Three Oaks Cider	Dry	5.0%	330mL Bottle

TAS

Brand/Distributor/Name	Style	ABV	Unit
The Two Metre Tall Company	Boutique Beverage Distributors (VIC), Fine Drop (TAS)		
Huon Farmhouse Dry Cider	Real Cider	7.5%	500ml, 750ml bottle
Poiré	Real Perry	7.0%	500ml, 750ml bottle

VIC

Brand/Distributor/Name	Style	ABV	Unit
2 Brothers Brewery	www.2brothers.com.au		
Gypsy	Pear Cider	4.9%	330mL
Beechworth Cider	www.beechworthcider.com.au		
Beechworth Cider			
Carlton & United Breweries	www.cub.com.au		
Bullmers	Cider		
Mercury	Cider		
Strongbow	Apple Cider		
Coldstream Brewery	www.coldstreambrewery.com.au		
Coldstream Crushed Apple Cider	Apple Cider	5.0%	6x330ml Stubby
Coldstream Original Cider	Apple Cider	7.0%	6x330ml Stubby
Independent Distillers	Independent Distillers		
3 Kings			
Kelly Brothers Cider Co.	Beer Importers and Distributors		
Kelly Brothers Pear Cider	Cider	5.0%	330ml, 30L Keg
Kelly Brothers Sparkling Apple Cider	Cider	7.0%	330ml, 50L Keg
Matilda Bay Brewing Company	www.matildabay.com		
Dirty Granny	Common Cider	5.5%	bottle, 49.5L Keg
Otway Estate	NSW & QLD www.australiantradepartners.com.au		
Otway Estate Organic Cider	French Dry Cider	6.8%	15x330ml
Punt Road Wines	www.negociantsaustralia.com		
Napoleone & Co	Apple	5.5%	330ml, 50L Keg
Napoleone & Co	Pear	5.4%	330ml, 50L keg

WA

Brand/Distributor/Name	Style	ABV	Unit
Bootleg Brewery	www.bootlegbrewery.com.au		
ILLICIT CIDER	Cider	5.0%	50L/330ml/6-pack
Cheeky Monkey Brewery & Cidery	www.cheekymonkeybrewery.com.au		
Cheeky Monkey			
Ciderworks	www.ciderworks.com.au		
Cider	Dry	6.0%	glass, 2lt bottle, 5lt keg
Cider	Sweet	6.0%	glass, 2lt bottle, 5lt keg
Gage Roads Brewing	www.gageroads.com.au		
Blue Angel Cider	Cider	7.0%	Bottle 330ml
Little Creatures Brewing	www.littlecreatures.com.au		
Pipsqueak Cider	Apple Cider	5.2%	330ml, 50L Kegs

Brand/Distributor/Name	Style	ABV	Unit
Mash Brewing	www.mashbrewing.com.au		
CRUSH	Cider	4.9%	On Draught
Mountford Wines	www.mountfordwines.com.au		
Tangletoe Cider			
The Cidery	www.thecidery.com.au		
Apple Kiss	Still/Non-Alc/Sweet	0.0%	330ml
Bitter Sweet	Bitter Sweet	6.5%	500ml, (10lt/50lt)
Scudamores Scrumpy	Still/Dry/Aged	8.0%	bottle, keg
Soft Cider	Non-Alc/Sweet	0.0%	330ml
Spider Cider	Dry	5.5%	330ml, (10lt/50lt)
Sweet Rosie	Sweet	4.5%	330ml, (10lt/50lt)
Vintage Gold	Stll/Dry/Cloudy	6.5%	500ml, (10lt/50lt)
Cargans Perry	Dry	6.5%	500ml, (10lt/50lt)

GLUTEN FREE BEER: AUSTRALIA

NSW

Brand/Distributor/Name	Style	ABV	Unit
Koala Beer t/as Burragum Billi	www.burragumbilli.com.au		
Wilde	Gluten Free	4.5%	6 pack, 24 case

VIC

Brand/Distributor/Name	Style	ABV	Unit
O'Brien Brewing Pty Ltd	www.gfbeer.com.au		
O'Brien Brown Ale	English Brown Ale	4.5%	24x330ml bottle
O'Brien Natural Light	Low Alcohol European Lager	2.7%	24x330ml bottle
O'Brien Pale Ale	American Pale Ale	4.5%	24x330ml bottle
O'Brien Premium Lager	German Pilsner	4.5%	24 x 330ml bottle

WA

Brand/Distributor/Name	Style	ABV	Unit
Billabong	www.billabongbrewing.com.au		
Australia's Pale Ale	American Pale Ale	5.1%	330x24
Blonde	Fruity Lager	4.5%	330x24
Ginger Beer	More Ginger than beer	4.5%	330x24

JUST TASTED A GREAT BEER OR CIDER?

Share your own tasting note on the Beer & Brewer forums at www.beerandbrewer.com

BEER

NEW ZEALAND - NORTH ISLAND

Brand/Distributor/Name	Style	ABV	Unit
666 Brewing			
666 Brewing			
Anchor Brewing			
Anchor Brewing			
Aotearoa Breweries			
MATA Artesian	Kolsch	5.0%	
MATA Black-Bru	Irish Stout	5.0%	
MATA Blondie	Belgian Wit Beer	5.0%	
MATA Brown-Boy	Amber Ale	5.0%	
MATA Feijoa	Fruit Wheat Beer	4.5%	
MATA Manuka	Honey Ale	5.0%	
Ben Middlemiss Brewing		beernz	
Nota Bene	Belgian Ale	8.7%	
Boundary Road Brewery			
Boundary Road Brewery			
Brauhaus Frings			
Brewhaus Frings			
Brewers Bar			
Brewers Bar			
Coromandel Brewing Company			
Coromandel Brewing Company			
Croucher Brewing Co	www.northdown.com.au		
NZ Pilsner	Pilsner	5.0%	500ml
Pale Ale	Pale Ale	5.0%	500ml
Patriot Black Ale	Black IPA	5.5%	500ml
DB Breweries			
Tui Brewery			
Waitemata Brewery			
Epic Brewing Company	www.epicbeer.com, Aus - www.betterbeerimports.com		
Epic Armageddon	Imperial IPA	6.7%	500ml
Epic Lager	Munich Helles	5.0%	330ml/500mL
Epic Mayhem	American Pale Ale	6.2%	500ml
Epic Pale Ale	American Pale Ale	5.4%	330ml/500mL
Epic Portamarillo	Smoked Beer	7.0%	500ml
Epic Thornbridge Stout	American Stout	6.8%	500ml

Brand/Distributor/Name	Style	ABV	Unit
Galbraith's Alehouse			
Galbraith's Alehouse			
Hallertau Brewery			
#1 Luxe	Kölsch	4.5%	
#2 Statesman	Pale Ale	5.3%	
#3 Copper Tart	Red Ale	4.2%	
#4 Deception	Schwarzbier	5.1%	
Barley Wine	Barley Wine	9.4%	
Hallertau Brewery			
Maximus Humulus Lupulus	IPA	6.8%	50, 30L keg, 750 ml
Porter Noir	Wood aged Sour beer	6.8%	50, 30L keg, 750 ml
Hallertau Brewery			
Stuntman	Imperial IPA	9.0%	50, 30L keg, 750 ml
Hawkes Bay Independent Brewery	Qld: www.q-vino.com, NSW: www.grandeurbrew.com.au		
Amber Ale	NZ amber	4.0%	12 x 330mL, 12 x 500mL
Black Duck Porter	Brown Porter	4.0%	
Pilsner	NZ pils	5.0%	12 x 330mL, 12 x 500mL
Pure Lager	NZ lager	4.0%	12 x 500mL
Special Reserve	NZ summer ale	5.0%	12 x 330mL, 12 x 500mL
Independent Liquor			
Independent Liquor			
Island Bay Brewing			
Island Bay Brewing			
Kaimai Brewing Co			
Kaimai Brewing Co			
Kea Brewing Company			
Kea Brewing Company			
Kiwi Breweries			
Kiwi Breweries			
Liberty Brewing Co	NZ - www.beernz.co.nz		
West Coast Blonde	Blonde Ale	5.5%	Keg
American Landlord	Blonde Ale	5.1%	Keg
Darkest Days	American Stout	6.0%	Keg
Welcome Back	English IPA	3.7%	Keg
High Carb Ale	STRONG ALE	7.3%	750ml Bottle
MMMMoMMftCHv3	SPECIALTY BEER	10.5%	750ml Bottle
Never Go Back	Imperial Stout	10.6%	750ml Bottle
Debilitated Defender	American Barleywine	11.0%	750ml Bottle
C!tra	Imperial IPA	9.5%	750ml Bottle
Liberty Brewing Co / mike's	NZ - www.beernz.co.nz		
Taranaki Pale Ale	American IPA	7.0%	Keg
Yakima Warrior	American IPA	7.0%	Keg
Lion New Zealand			
Black Ice			
Black Mac			
Canterbury Draught			
Castlepoint			
Greenstone Lager			
Light Ice			
Lion Brown			
Lion Ice			
Lion Red			
Mac's Gold			
Mac's Great White			
Mac's Hop Rocker			
Mac's Light			
Mac's Sassy Red			
Mac's Spring Tide			
Speights Distinction Ale			
Speights Gold Medal Ale			
Speights Old Dark			
Speights Pale Ale			
Speights Pilsener			
Speights Porter			
Speights Summit Lager			
Speights Traverse			
Steinlager Classic			
Steinlager Edge			
Steinlager Premium Light			
Steinlager Pure			
Waikato Draught			
Mike's Organic Brewery			
Mike's Organic Brewery			
Peak Brewery	Pure Wairarapa, +64-6-377-7064		
Alb Weiss	Weizen	5.0%	500mL
Cornhll Porter	Robust Porter	5.0%	500mL
Drachenfels Lager	Kölsch	5.0%	500mL
Great End ESB	Extra Special/Strong Bitter	6.5%	500mL
Mendip Bitter	Special/Best/Premium Bitter	4.0%	500mL
Monkey Point IPA	British IPA	6.5%	500mL

Brand/Distributor/Name	Style	ABV	Unit
Sollinger Bock	Maibock/Helles Bock	6.5%	500mL
Mile Gully Ginger Beer	Ginger Beer	5.0%	500mL
Rogue Brewery			
Rogue Brewery			
Roosters Brew House			
Roosters Brew House			
Saratoga Estate			
Saratoga Estate			
Shakespeare Brewery & Hotel			
Shakespeare Tavern & Brewery			
Shamrock Brewing Company			
Shamrock Brewing Company			
Shunters Yard Brewery			
Shunters Yard Brewery			
Steam Brewing Company			
Cock & Bull Blue Goose			
Australian Lager		4.6%	Keg - 50L
Cock & Bull Brewer's Choice	Various - Seasonals	5.0%	Keg - 50L
Cock & Bull Buxom Blonde	American Wheat Ale no Yeast	4.7%	Keg - 50L
Cock & Bull Classic Draught	American Amber Ale	4.0%	Keg - 50L
Cock & Bull Dark Star	Robust Porter	5.0%	Keg - 50L
Cock & Bull Fuggles	English Pale Ale	4.8%	Keg - 50L
Cock & Bull Monk's Habit	American IPA	7.0%	Keg - 50L
Sunshine Brewery			
Black Magic	Stout	5.0%	50L & 30L Keg, 0.5 - 2L PET
Gisborne Gold	Lager	4.0%	50L & 30L Keg, 0.5 - 2L PET
Gisborne Green	Pilsner	5.0%	50L & 30L Keg, 0.5 - 2L PET
Reserve Ale	Red Ale	4.0%	50L & 30L Keg, 0.5 - 2L PET
The Brewhaus Frings			
The Brewhaus Frings			
The Cock & Bull Traditional English Pub and Brewery			
The Cock & Bull Traditional English Pub and Brewery			
The Coromandel Brewing Company			
Cloud 9	Witbier	5.0%	500ml Bottle
Easy Rider	English Pale Ale	5.0%	500ml Bottle
Good as Gold	Bohemian Pilsner	5.0%	500ml Bottle
The Leigh Sawmill Café			
The Leigh Sawmill Café			
Trident Tavern			
Trident Tavern			
Tuatara Brewery	Aus - www.betterbeerimports.com		
Tuatara APA	American IPA	5.6%	500ml
Tuatara Ardennes	Belgian Dubbel	6.5%	6x330ml
Tuatara Hefe	Weizen/Weissbier	5.0%	6x330ml
Tuatara Helles	Munich Helles	5.0%	6x330ml
Tuatara IPA	English IPA	5.0%	6x330ml
Tuatara Pilsner	Bohemian Pilsner	5.0%	6x330ml
Tuatara Porter	Brown Porter	5.0%	6x330ml
Tuatara Brewing Co			
Tuatara Brewing Co			
Waiheke Island Brewery			
Baroona Original Pale Ale	Pale Ale	4.4%	Any
Hauraki Ginger Beer	Ginger	0.0%	Any
Matiatia Malt	Malt	7.2%	Any
Onetangi Dark Ale	Porter	4.3%	Any
Wharf Rd Wheat	Wheat	4.5%	Any
Waipa			
Waipa			
Waituna Brewing Company			
Waituna			
Wassail Brauhaus			
Wassail Brauhaus			
Yeastie Boys	NZ - www.beernz.co.nz, Aus - www.innspire.com.au		
Her Majesty	Vintage release, style varies	varies	750ml bottle (single)
His Majesty	Vintage release, style varies	varies	750ml bottle (single)
Hud-a-wa' Strong	Imperial ESB	6.8%	330ml bottle (single)
PKB Remix	Vintage release, style varies	varies	750ml bottle (single)
Pot Kettle Black	Hoppy Porter	6.0%	330ml bottle (single)
Rex Attitude	Islay Strong Golden Ale	7.0%	330ml bottle (single)
Zeelandt Brewing Company			
Zeelandt Brewing Company			

■ NEW ZEALAND - SOUTH ISLAND

Brand/Distributor/Name	Style	ABV	Unit
8 Wired Brewing	NZ - www.beernz.co.nz, Aus - www.betterbeerimports.com, www.innspire.com.au		
Hopwired	IPA	7.3%	500ml bottle
iStout	Imperial Stout	10.5%	500ml Bottle
Rewired	Brown Ale	5.7%	500ml Bottle
Tall Poppy	Amber Ale	7.0%	500ml Bottle
The Big Smoke	Porter	6.2%	500ml bottle

Brand/Distributor/Name	Style	ABV	Unit
Arrow Brewing			
Arrow Brewing			
Bennett's			
Bennett's 4 seasons ale	Fruit beer		6x330ml bottles
Bennett's belgium strong	belgian strong ale	7.2%	6X330ml bottles
Bennett's classic black	Dark Lager	5.0%	6X330ml bottles
Bennett's Wellington lager	lager	5.0%	6X330ml bottles
Brew Moon			
Brew Moon			
Cassels & Sons			
Cassels & Sons			
DB Breweries - Mainland Brewery			
DB Breweries - Mainland Brewery			
DB Breweries - Monteith's Brewing Company			
DB Breweries - Monteith's Brewing Company			
Dead Good Beers	www.deadgoodbeerevents.com		
Dead Good Pilsner	Pilsner	4.4%	50l keg or 1.25l PET
Dead Good IPA	IPA	5.2%	50l keg or 1.25l PET
Dead Good Weizen	Wheat	5.2%	50l keg or 1.25l PET
Dead Good Porter	Porter	4.7%	50l keg or 1.25l PET
Dux Brew Co.	www.hancocks.co.nz		
Dux Lager	Pilsner style lager	5.0%	500ml
Ginger Tom	alcoholic ginger beer	5.0%	500ml
Hereford Bitter	Munich style, dark lager	5.0%	500ml
NorWester Strong Pale Ale	Pale Ale	6.5%	500ml
SouWester Strong Dark Stout	Dark ale	6.5%	500ml
Founders Organic Brewery			
Founders Organic Brewery			
Golden Bear Brewing			
Golden Bear Brewing			
Green Fern Brewery			
Green Fern Brewery			
Green Man Brewery Ltd			
Best Bitter	Special/Best/Premium Bitter	4.2%	500ml Bottle, 30 & 50L Kegs
Black Lager	Schwarzbier	4.5%	500ml Bottle, 30 & 50L Kegs
Celt	Wood-Aged Beer	6.5%	500ml Bottle, 30 & 50L Kegs
Chocolate Krystal Weiss	Dunkelweizen	5.0%	500ml Bottle, 30 & 50L Kegs
Cyclist	Fruit/Spice Beer	2.4%	500ml Bottle, 30 & 50L Kegs
Enrico's Cure	English Barley Wine	14.5%	330ml Bottle
Ginger Beer	Fruit/Spice Beer	4.5%	500ml Bottle, 30 & 50L Kegs
IPA	English IPA	5.0%	500ml Bottle, 30 & 50L Kegs
Keller		4.8%	500ml Bottle, 30 & 50L Kegs
Krystal Weiss	Weizen/Weissbier	5.0%	500ml Bottle, 30 & 50L Kegs
Lager	Dortmunder Export	4.8%	500ml Bottle, 30 & 50L Kegs
Premiun Pils	German Pilsner (Pils)	5.0%	500ml Bottle, 30 & 50L Kegs
Stout	Imperial Stout	7.0%	500ml Bottle, 30 & 50L Kegs
Strong	Wood-Aged Beer	6.5%	500ml Bottle, 30 & 50L Kegs
Tequila Beer	Fruit/Spice Beer	5.6%	500ml Bottle, 30 & 50L Kegs
Whisky Bock	Wood-Aged Beer	9.2%	330ml Bottle
Harrington's Breweries	Aus - www.grandeurbrew.com.au		
Belgium Tempest	Strong Golden Ale	8.0%	330ml, 500ml
Clydesdale - Stout	Stout	5.0%	4x6 packs 330ml
Doppelbock - Strong Amber Brew	Bock	8.0%	330ml, 500ml
East Indies - Indian Lager	Indian Style Lager	5.0%	330ml, 500ml
Kiwi Draught - Classic Draught	New Zealand commercial style draught	4.0%	330ml, 500ml
Ngahere Gold - Strong Lager	Strong New Zealand lager	7.2%	330ml
Pig and Whistle - Dark	New Zealand classic dark beer	4.0%	500ml
Razor Back - Bitter	New Zealand classic bitter beer	5.2%	330ml, 500ml
Strong Man - Strong Lager	Hoppy New Zealand lager	6.5%	330ml, 500ml
Rogue Hop organic Pilsner	Bohemian Pilsener	5.0%	4x6 packs
Wobbly Boot - Porter Ale	Porter	5.0%	4x6 packs
Invercargill Brewery			
B.Man	NZ Pilsner	5.2%	Bottle
Boysenbeery	Fruit Beer	6.5%	Bottle
Pitch Black	Stout	4.5%	Bottle
Sa!son	Belgium Farmhouse	6.5%	Bottle
Smokin Bishop	Smoked Beer	7.0%	Bottle
Stanley Green	Pale Ale	4.7%	Bottle
Wasp	NZ Pilsner	5.2%	Bottle
Kaiapoi Brewing Co			
Kaiapoi Brewing Co			
Lighthouse Brewery			
Lighthouse Brewery			
Lion Breweries - Christchurch Brewery			
Speights			
Matson's Brewery NZ Ltd			
Matson's 100% Premium Lager	Lager	4.8%	330ml Bottle x 4 Pack
Matson's Black	Black	4.0%	330ml Bottle x 4 Pack
Matson's Classic Draught	Draught	4.0%	330ml Bottle x 4 Pack
Matson's FRENZ ALE	Ale	4.0%	330ml Bottle x 4 Pack
Matson's Irish Mild	Black	4.0%	330ml Bottle x 4 Pack
Matson's Lager	Lager	4.5%	330ml Bottle x 4 Pack
Matson's Pilsner	Pilsner	4.8%	330ml Bottle x 4 Pack
Matson's XL Draught	Draught	4.0%	330ml Bottle x 4 Pack
McCashin's Brewery			
Stoke Amber	Ale	4.5%	30L, 50L, 6, 12 Pack (330ml)
Stoke Dark	Regular/Brown Porter	4.5%	30L, 50L, 6, 12 Pack (330ml)
Stoke Gold	Golden Ale	4.5%	30L, 50L, 6, 12 Pack (330ml)
McDuff's Brewery			
McDuff's Brewery			
Meenans Wines & Spirits			
Meenans Wines & Spirits			
Monkey Wizard Brewery			
Abel Ale	IPA	5.0%	Riggers 2lt or 1.25lt
Black Mass Stout	Stout	6.0%	Riggers 2lt or 1.25lt
Brass Monkey Lager	Lager	4.0%	Riggers 2lt or 1.25lt
George Best	Strong Ale	6.5%	Riggers 2lt or 1.25lt
Savvy Blonde	Blonde	4.0%	Riggers 2lt or 1.25lt
Steam Punk Ale	Strong Ale	7.5%	Riggers 2lt or 1.25lt
Nelson Bays Brewery			
Nelson Bays Brewery			
Pink Elephant Brewery	NZ - www.beernz.co.nz		
Mammoth	Strong Ale	7.0%	330 mls bottles. 12 pack
Golden Tusk	Special Bitter	7.0%	330 mls bottles. 12 pack
Renaissance Brewing Ltd.	Aus - www.innspire.com.au, NZ - info@hopandvine.co.nz		
Craftsman	Chocolate Oatmeal Stout	4.9%	506 ml Bottle
Discovery APA	American Pale Ale	4.5%	501 ml Bottle
Elemental	Robust Porter	6.0%	503 ml Bottle
MPA	Imperial IPA	8.5%	505 ml Bottle
Paradox	Blonde Ale	4.0%	500 ml Bottle
Perfection	Pale ale	5.0%	502 ml Bottle
Stonecutter	Strong Scotch Ale	7.0%	504 ml Bottle
Sprig & Fern Brewery	www.sprigandfern.co.nz		
Best Bitter	Ale	5.0%	1,3,2L rig 25-50L keg
Blonde	Ale	5.0%	1,3,2L rig 25-50L keg
Doppelbock	Dark Lager	8%	1,3,2L rig 25-50L keg
Fern Dark	Ale	4%	1,3,2L rig 25-50L keg
Fern Draught	Ale	4%	1,3,2L rig 25-50L keg
Fern Lager	Lager	4%	1,3,2L rig 25-50L keg
Ginger Lager	Lager	5.0%	1,3,2L rig 25-50L keg
I.P.A.	Ale	5.0%	1,3,2L rig 25-50L keg
Pale Ale	Ale	5.0%	1,3,2L rig 25-50L keg
Pilsner	Lager	5.0%	1,3,2L rig 25-50L keg
Porter	Ale	5.0%	1,3,2L rig 25-50L keg
Scotch Ale	Ale	6.50%	1,3,2L rig 25-50L keg
Tasman Lager	Lager	6.50%	1,3,2L rig 25-50L keg
Harvest Pilsner (Limited Release)	Lager	5.0%	1,3,2L rig 25-50L keg
Belgian Pale Ale (Limited Release)	Ale	5.50%	1,3,2L rig 25-50L keg
Stout (Limited Release)	Ale	5.0%	1,3,2L rig 25-50L keg
Summer Ale (Limited Release)	Ale	5.0%	1,3,2L rig 25-50L keg
Bush Honey Ale (Limited Release)	Ale	9%	1,3,2L rig 25-50L keg
The Emerson Brewing Company Ltd	Various - see www.emersons.co.nz		
1812	Pale ale	4.9%	50L kegs, 500 ml bottles
Bookbinder	Ordinary bitter	3.7%	50L kegs, 500 ml bottles
Dunkel	Bavarian hefe-weizenbier	6.3%	500 ml bottles
JP	Belgian	Varies	500 ml bottles
London Porter	Porter	4.9%	50L kegs, 500 ml bottles
Pilsner	Pilsner	4.9%	50L kegs, 500 ml bottles
Southern Clam Stout	Stout	6.0%	500 ml bottles
Taieri George	Spiced ale	6.8%	500 ml bottles
Weissbier	Bavarian Hefe-weizenbier	5.0%	500 ml bottles
Weizenbock	Bavarian Hefe-weizenbier	8.0%	500 ml bottles
The Moa Brewing Company			
Moa			
The Mussel Inn			
Bitter Ass Extra Bitter Beer	Double IPA	8.5%	500ml
Captain Cooker Manuka Beer	Spice / herb	5.0%	330ml
Dark Horse Black Beer	Dark Lager	5.0%	330ml
Golden Goose Lager	Lager	5.0%	330ml
Hear Rash Chilli Beer	Spice / herb		330ml
Lambagreeny	Geueze	4.5%	330ml
Monkey Puzzel Extra Strong Ale	Belgian strong ale	10.0%	330ml
Pale Whale Ale	IPA	6.0%	500ml
Strong Ox Stron Dark Ale	Dark ale	6.0%	500ml
Weka	Sour Porter	5.0%	330ml
White Heron	Wheat Beer	4.0%	1.25L
The Twisted Hop	NZ - www.beernz.co.nz		
Challenger	ESB	5.0%	Real Ale only
Enigma	Barley Wine	10.0%	330ml bottle
Golding Bitter	English Pale Ale	3.7%	Real Ale only
Honey Dew	Braggot	4.0%	Keg
India Pale Ale	American IPA	6.4%	Real Ale/Keg/500ml bottle

Brand/Distributor/Name	Style	ABV	Unit
Nokabollokov	Imperial Stout	8.6%	330ml bottle
Sauvn Pilsner	Lager	5.0%	Keg/500ml bottle
Twsited Ankle	Robust Porter	5.9%	Real Ale only
The West Coast Brewery			
West Coast Black	German-Style Schwarzbier	4.0%	Keg, Bottle
West Coast Lager	NZ Lager	4.0%	Keg, Bottle
West Coast Draught	NZ Draught	4.0%	Keg, Bottle
Green Fern	Nz Premuim Lager	5.0%	Keg, Bottle
West Coast Pale Ale	International Pale Ale	5.0%	Keg, Bottle
West Coast Session	Ordinary Bitter	3.6%	Keg
West Coast Marzen	German-Style Marzen	6.5%	Keg
West Coast Wheat	Hefeweizen	5.0%	Keg
West Coast Stout	Oatmaeal Stout	6.0%	Keg
Three Boys			
Three Boys			
Totara Brewery			
Totara Brewery			
Townshend Brewery			
Townshend Brewery			
Wanaka Beerworks			
Wanaka Beerworks			
Wigram Brewing Company	NZ - www.beernz.co.nz		
Bavarian Pils	Pilsner	5.0%	330ml 500ml
Briston Best Bitter	Best Bitter	4.5%	500ml bottle
Captain Cook Spruce	Specialty Ale	5.0%	500ml bottle
Dakota Dark	Porter	5.0%	500ml bottle
Ginger Jerry	Ginger Wit Bier	4.0%	330ml
Harvard Honey Ale	Honey Ale	6.0%	500ml bottle
Hefe Weizen	Wheat Beer	5.0%	500ml bottle
Kortegast	Irish Red Ale	5.0%	500ml bottle
Morning Glory	Breakfast Beer	5.0%	330ml 500ml
Munchner Dunkel	German Dark Lager	5.2%	500ml bottle
Mustang Pale Ale	APA	5.0%	500ml bottle
Phoenix Golden Ale	Golden Ale	5.0%	330ml
Propeller Lager	Lager	5.0%	500ml bottle
The Tzar	Russian Imperial Stout	8.5%	500ml bottle
Vienna Lager	Amber Lager	5.0%	500ml bottle

CIDER & PERRY
■ NEW ZEALAND

Brand/Distributor/Name	Style	ABV	Unit
Harrington's Breweries	Aus - www.grandeurbrew.com.au		
Fat Ass Scrumpy	Scrumpy	9.0%	1L bottle
Hawkes Bay Independent Brewery	Qld: www.q-vino.com		
Kingston Apple Cider	Cider	5.0%	1L, 500ml, 330ml
Kingston Perry	Perry	5.0%	1L, 500ml, 330ml
Kingston Fusion	English Cider	2.5%	12 x 1 Litre
Kingston Scrumpy	English Cider	9.0%	12 x 500mL, 12 x 1 Litre
Invercargill Brewery			
Nallys Cider	Cider	5.0%	Bottle
Lion New Zealand			
Mac's Isaac's Cider			
McCashin's Brewery	NZ - www.hancocks.co.nz		
Frute Berry	Cider	5.0%	4, 24 pack (275ml bottle)
Frute Mango Lime	Cider	5.0%	4, 24 pack (275ml bottle)
Frute Vanilla Orange	Cider	5.0%	4, 24 pack (275ml bottle)
Rochdale Ginger Lime	Cider	5.0%	30L, 50L, 4, 24 pack (330ml bottle)
Rochdale Pear	Cider	5.0%	30L, 50L, 4, 24 pack (330ml bottle)
Rochdale Traditional	Cider	5.0%	30L, 50L, 4, 24 pack (330ml bottle)
Monkey Wizard Brewery			
Pomona Cider	Dry Cider	6.0%	Riggers 2lt or 1.25lt
Peak Brewery	Pure Wairarapa, +64-6-377-7064		
Wills Neck Cider	English Cider	5.0%	500mL
Redwood Cellars	Aus - www.baw.com.au		
Old Mout Scrumpy	Cider	8.0%	330ml Glass bottles (4 pack)
Old Mout Classic Apple	Cider	4.5%	330ml Glass bottles (4 pack)
Old Mout Feijoa and Cider	Fruit Cider	8.0%	330ml Glass bottles (4 pack)
Old Mout Boysencider	Fruit Cider	8.0%	330ml Glass bottles (4 pack)
Old Mout Scrumpy	Cider	8.0%	330ml Glass bottle (single)
Old Mout Classic Apple	Cider	4.5%	330ml Glass bottle (single)
Old Mout Feijoa and Cider	Fruit Cider	8.0%	330ml Glass bottle (single)
Old Mout Boysencider	Fruit Cider	8.0%	330ml Glass bottle (single)
Old Mout Scrumpy	Cider	8.0%	750ml Glass Bottle
Old Mout Classic Apple	Cider	4.5%	750ml Glass Bottle
Old Mout Feijoa and Cider	Fruit Cider	8.0%	750ml Glass Bottle
Old Mout Boysencider	Fruit Cider	8.0%	750ml Glass Bottle
Old Mout Classic Apple	Cider	8.0%	Keg 50 LTR
Old Mout Classic Apple	Cider	4.5%	Keg 30 LTR
Old Mout Scrumpy	Cider	8.0%	Pint Glass (on premise)
Old Mout Scrumpy	Cider	8.0%	Pot Glass (on premise)
Old Mout Classic Apple	Cider	4.5%	Pint Glass (on premise)
Old Mout Classic Apple	Cider	4.5%	Pint Glass (on premise)
Sprig & Fern Brewery	www.sprigandfern.co.nz		
Apple Cider	Cider	5.7%	1.3, 2Lrig 25-50L keg
Berry Cider	Cider	4.5%	1.3, 2Lrig 25-50L keg
The Mussel Inn			
Apple Roughy	Country	5.0%	50L
Freckled Frog	Fruit	5.0%	330ml
The Twisted Hop			
Incid'er	English Cider	6.5%	330ml bottle

GLUTEN FREE BEER
■ NEW ZEALAND

Brand/Distributor/Name	Style	ABV	Unit
Scotts Brewing Co.			
Gluten Free Beer	Gluten Free: Amber Ale	4.5%	6 Pack 6 x 330ml bottles
Gluten Free Beer	Gluten Free: Pale Ale	4.5%	6 Pack 6 x 330ml bottles

BEER: INTERNATIONAL
ARGENTINA

Brand/Distributor/Name	Style	ABV	Unit
Malteria Quilmes Vic - www.redislandmarketing.com.au, Qld - www.australiantradepartners.com.au			
Quilmes	Pale Lager	4.9%	24x330

AUSTRIA

Brand/Distributor/Name	Style	ABV	Unit
Eggenberg	Enoteca Sileno		
Hopfenkonig Pilsner			
German Pilsner (Pils)	5.1%		330ml
Samichlaus Bier	English Barley Wine	14.0%	330ml
Urbock 23 Degrees	Doppelbock	9.6%	330ml
Gosser	www.baw.com.au		
Gosser Dark	Dark Lager	4.6%	330ml
Gosser Pale	Lager	5.1%	330ml, 500m can
Kaiser	www.baw.com.au		
Kaiser Lager	Lager	4.9%	330ml, 500m can
Kaltenhausen	www.australiantradepartners.com.au		
Snowfresh	Pale Lager	4.8%	24x330
Stieglbrauerei	German Beverage Imports		
Stiegl Goldbräu	Munich Helles	4.9%	6 Pack
Zipf	www.australiantradepartners.com.au		
Zipfer	Pale Lager	5.4%	24x330

BELGIUM

Brand/Distributor/Name	Style	ABV	Unit
Achel Brewery	Beer Importers and Distributors		
Achel Blonde	Belgian Blond Ale	8.0%	330ml x 24
Achel Brune	Belgian Dubbel	8.0%	330ml x 24
Alken Maes	www.beerandcider.com.au		
Judas	Belgium Strong Ale	8.5	12 x 330ml btl
Judas	Belgium Strong Ale	9.5	24 x 500ml can, 4 pack
Mort Subite Original Kriek	Fruit Lambic	4.5	12 x 250ml btl
Mort Subite Xtreme Framboise	Fruit Lambic	4.3	12 x 250ml btl
Mort Subite Xtreme Kriek	Fruit Lambic	5.3	12 x 250ml btl
Anheuser-Busch InBev	www.cub.com.au		
Hoegaarden	Belgian Witbier	4.9%	50L Keg
Leffe Blond	Belgian Dubbel	6.6%	50L Keg
Leffe Brune	Belgian Dubbel	6.5%	50L Keg
Leffe Radieuse	Strong Ale	8.5%	330mL
Anheuser-Busch InBev	Beer Importers and Distributors		
Leffe Brune	Belgian Dubbel	6.5%	330ml x 24
Leffe Vieille Cuvee	Belgian Dark Strong Ale	8.2%	330ml x 24
Bavik	www.australiantradepartners.com.au		
Petrus Aged Pale	Aged Pale Ale	7.3%	24x330
Petrus Blond	Pale Ale	6.5%	24x330
Petrus Double Brown	Brown Ale	6.5%	24x330
Petrus Gold Triple	Tripel	7.5%	24x330
Petrus Oude Bruin	Old Ale	5.5%	24x330
Petrus Speciale	Ale	5.5%	24x330
Wittekerke	Witbier	5.2%	24x330
Wittekerke Rose	Fruit Beer	4.3%	24x250
Bosteels Brewery	Beer Importers and Distributors		
Deus "Brut des Flandres"	Belgian Specialty Ale	11.5%	750ml x 6
Karmeliet Tripel	Belgian Tripel	8.0%	330ml x 24
KWAK	Belgian Specialty Ale	8.0%	330ml

Brand/Distributor/Name	Style	ABV	Unit
Brasserie du Bocq	www.phoenixbeers.com.au		
Blanche de Namur	Belgian Wit	4.5%	24x330ml, 12x750ml, Keg
Gauloise Ambree	Belgian Dubbel	5.5%	24x330ml, Keg
Gauloise Blonde	Belgian Blonde	6.4%	24x330ml, Keg
Gauloise Brune	Belgian Dubbel	8.1%	24x330ml, Keg
Triple Moine	Belgian Tripel	7.0%	12x750ml
Brasserie Dupont	www.phoenixbeers.com.au		
Biere de Beloiel	Biere de Garde	8.5%	12x750ml
Biere De Miel Biologique	Saison (Honey)	8.0%	12x750ml
Bons Voeux	Sasion	9.5%	750ml, 12x375ml, Keg
Cervesia	Traditional Ale	8.0%	12x750ml
Moinette Bio	Saison	7.5%	12x750ml, Keg
Moinette Blonde	Belgian Blonde	8.5%	24x330ml, Keg
Moinette Brune	Belgian Dubbel	8.5%	24x330ml, Keg
Monks Stout	Stout	5.2%	24x330
Redor Pils	Pilsner	5.3%	24x330
Saison Dupont	Saison	6.5%	750ml, 24x330ml, Keg
Saison Dupont Biologique	Saison	5.5%	12x750ml, Keg
Saison Dupont Dry Hopped	Saison	6.9%	4x1.5ltr
Brasserie Lefebvre	www.phoenixbeers.com.au		
Barbar	Honey Ale	8.0%	24x330ml
Barbar Bok	Honey Ale	8.0%	24x330ml
Hopus	Belgian Strong Ale	8.5%	20x330ml
Mannekin Pilsner	Pilsner	5.2%	24x330ml
Brasserie St Bernard	www.phoenixbeers.com.au		
Grottenbier	Belgian Dubbel	6.5%	24x330ml, 12x750ml
St Bernardus ABT 12	Belgian Quad / Strong Ale	10.5%	24x330ml, 12x750ml
St Bernardus Christmas	Belgian Quad / Strong Ale	10.5%	12x750ml
St Bernardus Pater 6	Belgian Dubbel	6.7%	24x330ml
St Bernardus Prior 8	Belgian Dubbel	8.0%	24x330ml, 12x750ml
St Bernardus Tripel	Belgian Tripel	8.0%	24x330ml, 12x750ml
St Bernardus Wit	Belgian Wit	5.5%	24x330ml
Brewery Dubuisson	Beer Importers and Distributors		
Bush Beer Amber	Belgian Dark Strong Ale	12.0%	250ml x 24
Bush Beer Blonde Belgian Golden	Strong Ale	10.5%	250ml x 24
Cantillon Brewery	www.phoenixbeers.com.au		
Cantillon Fou Fonne	Fruit Lambic	5.0%	6x750ml
Cantillon Grand Cru Bruoscella	Lambic	5.0%	6x750ml
Cantillon Gueuze	Lambic	5.0%	12x375ml, 6x750ml
Cantillon Iris	Lambic	5.0%	6x750ml
Cantillon Kriek	Fruit Lambic	5.0%	12x375ml, 6x750ml
Cantillon Lou Pepe Framboise	Fruit Lambic	5.0%	6x750ml
Cantillon Lou Pepe Gueuze	Lambic	5.0%	6x750ml
Cantillon Lou Pepe Kriek	Fruit Lambic	5.0%	6x750ml
Cantillon Mamouche	Fruit Lambic	5.0%	6x750ml
Cantillon Rosé de Gambrims	Fruit Lambic	5.0%	12x375ml, 6x750ml
Cantillon St Lamvinus	Fruit Lambic	5.0%	6x750ml
Cantillon Vigneronne	Fruit Lambic	5.0%	6x750ml
Caulier	www.australiantradepartners.com.au		
Bon Secour Ambre	Strong Ale	8.0%	12x330
Bon Secour Blond	Strong Ale	8.0%	12x330
Bon Secour Blueberry	Fruit Beer	7.0%	12x330
Bon Secour Brown	Dubbel	8.0%	12x330
Bon Secour Rasberry	Fruit Beer	7.0%	12x330
Chimay Brewery	Beer Importers and Distributors		
Chimay Blanche	Belgian Tripel	8.0%	330ml, 20L, 30L
Chimay Bleue	Belgian Dark Strong Ale	9.0%	330ml x 12
Chimay Cinq Cents	Belgian Tripel	8.0%	750ml x 12
Chimay Grand Reserve	Belgian Dark Strong Ale	9.0%	750ml, 1500ml, 3000ml
Chimay Premiere	Belgian Dubbel	7.0%	750ml x 12
Chimay Rouge	Belgian Dubbel	7.0%	330ml x 12
CUVEE DES TROLLS	www.baw.com.au		
CUVEE DES TROLLS	Strong Ale	7.0%	250ml
De Block	www.fmliquor.com.au		
Abbaye Dendermonde Ale	Ale	8.0%	330ml bottle
Kastaar Ale	Ale	6.0%	330ml bottle
Satan Gold	Ale	8.0%	330ml, 750ml
Satan Red	Ale	8.0%	330ml, 750ml
Special 6 Ale	Ale	6.0%	330ml bottle
De Halve Maan	www.australiantradepartners.com.au		
Brugse Zot Blond	Ale	6.0%	24x330
Brugse Zot Double	Abbey Dubbel	7.5%	24x330
Straffe Hendrik	Abbey Tripel	9.0%	24x330
De Koninck	www.australiantradepartners.com.au		
De Koninck	Ale	5.0%	24x250
De Koninck Blond	Ale	6.2%	24x330
De Koninck Triple	Abbey Tripel	8.3%	24x330
De Landtsheer	www.australiantradepartners.com.au		
Malheur 10	Strong Ale	10.0%	24x330
Malheur 12	Strong Ale	12.0%	24x330
Malheur 6	Ale	6.0%	24x330
Malheur Brut	Strong Ale	11.0%	6x750
De Troch	www.australiantradepartners.com.au		
De Troch Framboise	Lambic	3.5%	24x250
De Troch Kriek	Lambic	3.5%	24x250
Delirium Tremens	www.baw.com.au		
Delirium Tremens	Belgian Golden Strong Ale	9.0%	330ml
Duvel Moortgaat Brewery	Beer Importers and Distributors		
Duvel	Belgian Golden Strong Ale	8.5%	330ml, 750ml
Duvel Jeroboam	Belgian Golden Strong Ale	8.5%	3000ml x 1
Duvel Magnum	Belgian Golden Strong Ale	8.5%	1500ml x 3
Maredsous Blonde	Belgian Blond Ale	6.0%	330ml x 24
Maredsous Brune	Belgian Dubbel	8.0%	330ml x 24
Floris	www.baw.com.au		
Floris Apple	Fruit Witbier	3.4%	330ml
Floris Fraise Strawberry	Fruit Witbier	3.6%	330ml
Floris Framboise Raspberry	Fruit Witbier	3.6%	330ml
Floris Kriek Cherry	Fruit Witbier	3.6%	330ml
Floris Passie Passionfruit	Fruit Witbier	3.6%	330ml
Gouden Carolus	Www.baw.com.au		
Gouden Carolus Classic	Belgian Dark Strong Ale	8.0%	330ml
Gouden Carolus Tripple	Strong Ale	9.0%	330ml
Grimbourgen	Www.baw.com.au		
Grimbourgen Dubble	Specialty Beers	6.5%	330ml
Gulden Draak	www.baw.com.au		
Gulden Draak	Strong Ale	10.5%	330ml
Huyghe	www.hopandspirit.com.au		
Fruli Strawberry Fruit Beer	Fruit	4.1%	24x250ml
Huyghe Brewery	Beer Importers and Distributors		
Guillotine	Belgian Golden Strong Ale	9.3%	330ml x 24
Jupiler	www.baw.com.au		
Jupiler		5.2%	330ml
LA CHOUFFE	www.baw.com.au		
LA CHOUFFE		8.0%	750ml
MC CHOUFFE		9.0%	750ml
LA GUILLOTINE	www.baw.com.au		
LA GUILLOTINE		8.5%	330ml
Lindemans	www.phoenixbeers.com.au		
Lidnemans Kriek	Fruit Lambic	3.5%	12x375ml, Keg
Lidnemans Cassis	Fruit Lambic	3.5%	12x375ml, Keg
Lindemans Apple	Fruit Lambic	3.5%	24x330ml
Lindemans Faro	Sweetened Lambic	4.8%	12x375ml, Keg
Lindemans Framboise	Fruit Lambic	2.5%	12x375ml, Keg
Lindemans Gueuze	Lambic	4.5%	12x375ml, Keg
Lindemans Gueuze Cuvée René	Lambic	5.0%	12x375ml
Lindemans Kriek Cuvee Rene	Fruit Lambic	5.0%	12x750ml
Lindemans Pecheresse	Fruit Lambic	2.5%	12x375ml, Keg
Orval Brewery	Beer Importers and Distributors		
Orval	Belgian Blond Ale	6.2%	330ml x 24
Oud Beersel	www.australiantradepartners.com.au		
Bersalis Kadet	Ale	5.0%	24x330
Bersalis Triple	Abbey Tripel	9.0%	24x330
Framboise	Lambic	5.0%	12x375
Oud Geuze	Lambic	6.0%	12x375
Oud Kriek	Lambic	6.5%	12x375
PALM Breweries NV	www.htbeverages.com.au		
ESTAMINET	Belgian Premium Pilsner	5.20%	4x6x330mL
PALM Especiale	Belgian Amber Ale	5.40%	4x6x330mL
Rochefort Brewery	Beer Importers and Distributors		
Rochefort 10°	Belgian Dark Strong Ale	11.3%	330ml x 24
Rochefort 6°	Belgian Dubbel	7.5%	330ml x 24
Rochefort 8°	Belgian Dark Strong Ale	9.2%	330ml x 24
SCALDIS	www.baw.com.au		
SCALDIS AMBER	Strong Ale	12.0%	250ml
SCALDIS NOEL (Seasonal)	Strong Ale	13.0%	750ml
SEXY LAGER	www.baw.com.au		
SEXY LAGER	Lager	5.0%	330ml
Silly Brewery	Beer Importers and Distributors		
Abbaye de Forest	Belgian Blond Ale	6.5%	330ml x 24
Pink Killer		5.0%	330ml x 24
Real Belgian Pils	Belgian Pilsner	5.0%	330ml, 50L Keg
Saison Silly	Saison	5.0%	330ml x 24
Titje	Witbier	4.7%	330ml x 24
St Paul	www.fmliquor.com.au		
Blond	Ale	5.3%	330ml bottle
Double Crock	Ale	6.9%	500ml bottle
St Paul Double	Ale	6.9%	330ml bottle
St Paul Special	Ale	5.5%	330ml bottle
Triple Crock	Ale	7.6%	500ml bottle
St Sebastiaan	www.fmliquor.com.au		
Dark	Ale	6.9%	750ml bottle

Brand/Distributor/Name	Style	ABV	Unit
Dark Crock	Ale	6.9%	500ml bottle
Grand Cru	Ale	7.6%	750ml bottle
Grand Cru Crock	Ale	7.6%	500ml bottle Stella Artois
Sterkens	www.fmliquor.com.au		
Bokrijks Kruikenbier Crock	Ale	7.2%	750ml bottle
Hoogstraten Poorter Crock	Ale	6.5%	750ml bottle
Strubbe	www.australiantradepartners.com.au		
Dikke Mathile	Ale	6.0%	24x330
Ichtegems Oud Bruin	Sour Ale	5.0%	24x250
Ichtegems Oud Bruin Grand	Sour Ale	6.5%	24x330
Keyte	Abbey Tripel	7.7%	24x330
Witteon	Abbey Tripel	7.8%	24x330
Timmermans Brewery	Beer Importers and Distributors		
Bourgogne Des Flandres Blond	Flanders Blonde Lambic Infused	6.0%	330ml x 12
Bourgogne Des Flandres Brune	Flanders Brown Ale/Oud Bruin	5.0%	330ml x 12
Timmermans Framboise	Fruit Lambic	4.0%	330ml x 12
Timmermans Gueuze	Gueuze	5.0%	330ml x 12
Timmermans Kriek	Fruit Lambic	4.0%	330ml x 12
Timmermans Peche	Fruit Lambic	4.0%	330ml x 12
Timmermans Strawberry	Fruit Lambic	4.0%	330ml x 12
Van Eecke	www.australiantradepartners.com.au		
Hommelbier	Strong Ale	7.5%	24x330
Kapittel Abt	ABT	10.0%	24x330
Kapittel Blond	Ale	6.2%	24x330
Kapittel Dubbel	Dubbel	7.5%	24x330
Kapittel Pater	Dubbel		24x330
Kapittel Prior	Strong Ale	9.0%	24x330
Watou Wheat	Wheat	5.0%	24x330
Westmalle Brewery	Beer Importers and Distributors		
Westmalle Dubbel	Belgian Dubbel	7.0%	330ml x 24
Westmalle Tripel	Belgian Tripel	9.0%	330ml x 24

CANADA

Brand/Distributor/Name	Style	ABV	Unit
McAuslen	www.palaisimports.com.au		
St Ambroise Apricot Wheat Ale	Wheat Beer	5.0%	341 btl 4-pk
St Ambroise Oatmeal Stout	Oatmeal Stout	5.0%	341 btl 4-pk
St Ambroise Pale	Pale Ale	5.0%	341 btl 4-pk
Moosehead	www.australiantradepartners.com.au		
Moosehead	Pale Lager	5.5%	24x350
Moosehead Pale Ale	Golden Ale	5.0%	24x350
Whistler Brewery	Beer Importers and Distributors		
Whistler Premium Export Lager	Standard Lager	5.0%	330ml x 24

CHILE

Brand/Distributor/Name	Style	ABV	Unit
Kross	Wines of Chile		
Kross Golden	Amber Ale	5.0%	24x330
Kross Pilsner	Pilsner	4.9%	24x330
Kross Stout	Stout	5.2%	24x330

CHINA

Brand/Distributor/Name	Style	ABV	Unit
Tsingtao	Ettason		
Tsingtao	Lager		330ml

COSTA RICA

Brand/Distributor/Name	Style	ABV	Unit
Florida Bebidas	www.australiantradepartners.com.au		
Imperial	Pale Lager	4.6%	24x330

CROATIA

Brand/Distributor/Name	Style	ABV	Unit
Karlovacka	www.australiantradepartners.com.au		
Karlovacko	Pale Lager	5.4%	24x330

CUBA

Brand/Distributor/Name	Style	ABV	Unit
Bucanero	www.australiantradepartners.com.au		
Cubanero Fuerte	Pale Lager	5.4%	24x350
Palma Cristal	Pale Lager	4.9%	24x350

CZECH REPUBLIC

Brand/Distributor/Name	Style	ABV	Unit
BUDVAR BUDEJOVICKY	www.baw.com.au		
BUDVAR BUDEJOVICKY	Lager	5.0%	330ml, 50L
KRUSOVICE	www.baw.com.au		
KRUSOVICE CERNE (DARK)	Dark Lager	3.8%	330ml
KRUSOVICE IMPERIAL	Lager	5.0%	330ml, 30lt, 50lt
Plzensky Prazdoj	Coca-Cola Amati, 13 COKE (13 2653)		
Pilsner Urquell	European Lager	4.4%	330ml bottle

Brand/Distributor/Name	Style	ABV	Unit
Rohozec	www.australiantradepartners.com.au		
Skalak Dark	Dunkel	5.9%	20x500
Skalak Premier	Pilsener	5.3%	20x500
Skalak Special	Pilsener	6.0%	20x500

DENMARK

Brand/Distributor/Name	Style	ABV	Unit
Amager Bryghus	www.northdown.com.au		
3.Akt	Dunkelweizen	5.2%	500ml
Amager Fælled	Golden Ale	4.5%	500ml
Amager IPA	US IPA	7.0%	500ml
Black Nitro	Black IPA	7.6%	500ml
Bryggens Blond	Golden Ale	5.0%	500ml
Christianshavn Pale ale	Pale ale	5.5%	500ml
Citra Weiss	Hopfenweisse	5.2%	500ml
Dragoer Tripel	Abbey Tripel	9.0%	500ml
Forårsbryg	Biere De Garde	6.5%	500ml
Fru Frederiksen	Oatmeal stout	7.0%	500ml
Galanthus Nivalis	Oak-aged Barley Wine	11.2%	375ml
Hoestbryg	Belgian Strong Ale	8.5%	500ml
Hr. Frederiksen	Imperial Oatmeal Stout	10.5%	500ml
Hr. Frederiksen Port barrel	Oak-aged Imperial Stout	11.0%	375ml
Hr. Frederiksen Vaesel Brunch	Imperial Coffee Stout	10.6%	500ml
Imperial Stout	Imperial Stout	10.0%	500ml
Julebryg 2010	American Strong Ale	6.5%	500ml
Rugporter	Rye Porter	8.5%	500ml
Summer Fusion	Steam Beer	3.5%	500ml
Sundby Stout	Stout	6.2%	500ml
Beer Here	www.northdown.com.au		
Ammestout	Milk Stout	6.5%	500ml
Blackcat	Cascadian Dark Ale	4.7%	500ml
Dark Hops	Black IPA	8.5%	500ml
Fatcat	Red Ale	4.7%	500ml
Hopfix	IPA	6.5%	500ml
Hopticilus	Imperial IPA	9.0%	500ml
Infant øl	Dark Light-beer	2.7%	500ml
Jule IPA	American IPA	7.0%	500ml
Kama Citra	Indian Brown Ale	7.0%	500ml
Lupulis	US Pale Ale	4.7%	500ml
Malus Pater	Quadrupel Ale	10.0%	500ml
Mørke	Pumpernickel Porter	7.5%	500ml
Nordic Rye Ale	Traditional Ale	8.0%	30litre keg
Paske	Historic Ale	7.0%	500ml, 30litre keg
Tia Loca	Hybrid Wheat	4.5%	500ml
Weed	Smoked Wheat	5.5%	500ml
Yule Wine	Barley Wine (English style)	11.0%	500ml
Carlsberg	www.cub.com.au		
Carlsberg Elephant			
Fanø Bryghus	www.northdown.com.au		
Fanø Rav	Vienna Lager	4.6%	500ml
Fanø Vestkyst	IPA	5.7%	500ml
Mikkeller	www.hopandspirit.com.au		
Mikkeller 1000IBU	DIPA	9.6%	12 X 375ML
Mikkeller Green and Gold	IPA	5.0%	24x330ml
Mikkeller Single Hop Simcoe	IPA	7.0%	24x330ml
Nørrebro Bryghus	www.northdown.com.au		
Bombay Pale Ale	English IPA	6.5%	400ml
Ceske Bohmer	Czech Pilsner	5.2%	400ml
Forårs Bock	Doppelbock	7.5%	400ml
Fureso Framboise	Spiced Raspberry Wheat	5.0%	600ml
Globe Ale	Organic Ale	4.8%	400ml
Kings County Brown	Brown Ale	5.5%	400ml
Little Korkny Ale	Barley Wine	12.3%	600ml
New York Lager	Vienna Lager	5.2%	330ml Can
North Bridge Extreme	Imperial IPA	9.6%	600ml
Pacific Summer Ale	Summer Ale	5.6%	600ml
Paske Bock	Dark Bock	7.0%	600ml
Ravnsborg Rød	Irish Red Ale	5.5%	400ml
Stukyman Wit	Belgian Witbier	5.0%	400ml

ENGLAND

Brand/Distributor/Name	Style	ABV	Unit
Adnams	www.hopandspirit.com.au		
Adnams Broadside Ale	Old Ale	6.3%	12x500ml
Adnams English Bitter	Southern English Brown Ale	4.5%	12x500ml
Badger Brewery	www.beerandcider.com.au		
Blandford Fly (Ginger Beer)	Spice Beer (Ginger)	5.2%	8 x 500ml btl
England Gold	Blonde Ale	4.3%	8 x 500ml btl
First Gold	Standard Bitter	4.2%	8 x 500ml btl
Fursty Ferret	Standard Bitter	4.4%	500ml btl, 500ml can
Golden Champion	Blonde Ale	5.0%	8 x 500ml btl

Brand/Distributor/Name	Style	ABV	Unit
Golden Glory	Blonde Ale	4.5%	8 x 500ml btl
Hopping Hare	Premium Bitter	4.4%	8 x 500ml btl
Poachers Choice	English Strong Ale	5.7%	8 x 500ml btl
Tanglefoot	Premium Bitter	5.0%	8 x 500ml btl
Banks's Brewery	www.beerandcider.com.au		
Banks Bitter	Standard Bitter	3.8%	24 x 500ml can, 4 pack
Banks Mild	Mild Ale	3.5%	24 x 500ml can, 4 pack
Bateman's Brewery	www.beerandcider.com.au		
Dark Lord		5.0%	500ml can
Victory Ale		6.0%	500ml bottle
XXXB		4.8%	500ml bottle
Black Sheep	www.beerandcider.com.au		
Black Sheep Ale	Premium Bitter	4.4%	8 x 500ml btl
Golden Sheep	ESB	4.7%	8 x 500ml btl
Imperial Russian Stout	Imperial Stout	8.5%	24 x 330ml btl, 6 pack
Monty Python Holy Grail	ESB	4.7%	8 x 500ml btl
Riggwelter	Old Ale	5.7%	8 x 500ml btl
Brakspear Brewing Company	www.beerandcider.com.au		
Bitter	Standard Bitter	3.4%	12 x 500ml
Oxford Gold Organic	Premium Bitter	4.6%	8 x 500ml btl
Tripple	English Strong Ale	7.2%	8 x 500ml btl
Burtonwood Brewery	www.beerandcider.com.au		
Manns Brown Ale	Mild	2.8%	8 x 500ml btl
UshersFounders Ale	Premium Bitter	4.7%	12 x 500ml btl
Carling	www.australiantradepartners.com.au		
Carling Black	Lager	4.2%	24x500 can
Carlsberg AS	www.htbeverages.com.au		
Tetley's Smoothflow Ale	English Ale (Premium Bitter)	3.60%	6x4x440mL
Coniston			
Bluebird	Bitter	4.2%	12x500
Daleside	www.beerandcider.com.au		
Crackshot	Strong Ale	5.5%	12x500
Greengrass Old Rogue	Brown Ale	5.9%	12x500
Monkey Wrench	Strong Ale	5.3%	12x500
Morroco Ale	Traditional Ale	5.5%	12x500
Old Legover	bitter	4.1%	8x500
Pride of England	bitter	4.0%	8x500
Ripon Jewel	Strong Ale	5.8%	12x500
Duchy Originals	www.beerandcider.com.au		
Original Ale		5.0%	500ml bottle
Durham	www.australiantradepartners.com.au		
Bedes Chalice	Abbey Tripel	9.0%	12x500
Benedictus	Barley Wine	8.4%	12x500
St. Cuthbert	Pale Ale	6.5%	12x500
Temptation	Stout	10.0%	12x500
Fuller's	Lionel Samson		
1845 Celebration	Strong Ale	6.3%	12x500
Fullers E.S.B.	ESB	5.9%	12x500
Fuller's London Porter	Porter	5.4%	12x500
Fuller's London Pride	ESB	4.7%	12x500
Golden Pride	Strong Ale	8.5%	12x500
I.P.A.	IPA	5.3%	12x500
Organic Honeydew	Golden Ale	5%%	12x500
Greene King Brewery	Beer Importers and Distributors		
Greene King I.P.A.	India Pale Ale	3.6%	
Ruddles Country Premium Ale	Southern English Brown Ale	4.7%	
Old Speckled Hen	Extra Special/Strong Bitter (English Pale Ale)	5.2%	
Hardys and Hansons	www.fmliquor.com.au		
Olde Trip Ale	Ale	5.0%	500ml bottle
Hopback Brewery	www.beerandcider.com.au		
Crop Circle	Blonde Ale	4.2%	12 x 500ml btl
Entire Stout	Dry Stout	4.5%	12 x 500ml btl
Summer Lightning	Blonde Ale	5.0%	12 x 500ml btl
Taiphoon	Blonde Ale	4.2%	12 x 500ml btl
Jennings Brewery	www.beerandcider.com.au		
Cumberland Ale	Premium Bitter	4.7%	8 x 500ml btl
Sneck Lifter Ale	ESB	5.1%	8 x 500ml btl
John Smith	www.beerandcider.com.au		
John Smiths Extra Smooth	Standard Bitter	3.8%	24 x 500ml can, 4 pack
Newcastle Brown Ale	Northern English Brown Ale	4.7%	330ml btl, 30ltr
Marstons Brewery	www.beerandcider.com.au		
Burton Strong Ale	English Strong Ale	6.2%	8 x 500ml btl
Old Empire	English IPA	5.7%	12 x 500ml btl
Oyster Stout	Dry Stout	4.5%	12 x 500ml btl
Pedigree	Premium Bitter	4.5%	24 x 500ml can, 50ltr
Pedigree (Export)	Premium Bitter	5.0%	12 x 500ml btl
Moorhouse	www.australiantradepartners.com.au		
Black Cat	Dark Mild	3.4%	8x500
Blonde Witch	Golden Ale		8x500
Pendle Witches Brew	Strong Ale	5.1%	8x500
Morland	www.fmliquor.com.au		

Brand/Distributor/Name	Style	ABV	Unit
Excalibur Strong Lager	Lager	8.5%	500ml bottle
Nethergate	www.australiantradepartners.com.au		
Old Growler	Porter	5.5%	8x500
O'Hanlons	www.australiantradepartners.com.au		
O'Hanlon Port Stout	Stout	5.0%	12x500
Royal Oak	ESB	5.0%	12x500
Old Fart Brewing	www.australiantradepartners.com.au		
Old Fart	ESB	5.0%	12x500
Ridley's	www.fmliquor.com.au		
Old Bob Ale	Ale	5.1%	500ml bottle
Ringwood Brewery	www.beerandcider.com.au		
Fourty Niner		4.9%	500ml bottle
Old Thumper		5.6%	500ml bottle
Robinsons	www.phoenixbeers.com.au		
Chocolate Tom	Old Ale (Chocolate)	6.0%	12x330ml
Ginger Tom	Old Ale (Ginger)	6.0%	12x330ml
Old Tom	Old Ale	8.5%	12x330ml
Samuel Smith Brewery	Lionel Samson		
Samuel Smith Imperial Stout	Imperial Stout	7.0%	355ml x 24
Samuel Smith India Pale Ale	English IPA	5.0%	500ml x 12
Samuel Smith Nut Brown Ale	Northern English Brown Ale	5.0%	500ml x 12
Samuel Smith Oatmeal Stout	Oatmeal Stout	5.0%	500ml x 12
Samuel Smith Old Pale Ale	Standard/Ordinary Bitter	5.0%	500ml x 12
Samuel Smith Organic Best Ale	Special/Best/Premium Bitter	5.0%	500ml x 12
Samuel Smith Organic Lager	Munich Helles	5.0%	500ml x 12
Samuel Smith Taddy Porter	Brown Porter	5.0%	500ml x 12
Sharps	www.fmliquor.com.au		
Altantic IPA	Ale	4.6%	500ml bottle
Chalky's Bark Ale with Ginger	Ale	4.5%	330ml bottle
Chalky's Bite Ale with Fenel	Ale	6.5%	330ml bottle
Doom Bar	Ale	4.3%	500ml, 50L
Eden Ale	Ale	4.5%	500ml bottle
Single Brew Reserve Ale	Ale	5.0%	500ml bottle
Special Ale	Ale	5.0%	500ml bottle
Shepherds Neame	Lionel Samson		
Bishops Finger	ESB	5.4%	12x500
Masterbrew	Bitter	4.0%	12x500
Spitfire	Bitter	4.5%	12x500
Whitstable Bay Organic	Bitter	4.5%	12x500
St Peters	www.phoenixbeers.com.au		
St Peters Cream Stout	Cream Stout	6.5%	12x500ml
St Peters G-Free	Gluten Free	4.2%	12x500ml
St Peters Golden Ale	Golden Ale	4.7%	12x500ml
St Peters Honey Porter	Porter	4.5%	12x500ml
St Peters IPA	IPA	5.5%	12x500ml
St Peters Organic Best Bitter	Bitter	4.1%	12x500ml
St Peters Ruby Red Ale	Red Ale	4.9%	12x500ml
St Peters Suffolk Gold	Pale Ale	4.9%	12x500ml
Theakston	www.phoenixbeers.com.au		
Theakston Old Peculiar	Old Ale	5.7%	16x500ml
Theakston XB	Bitter	4.5%	16x500ml
Timothy Taylor	www.phoenixbeers.com.au		
Landlord	Bitter	4.1%	12x500
Wadworth	www.fmliquor.com.au		
Wadworths 6X Ale	Ale	5.0%	500ml can
Wells and Young	www.phoenixbeers.com.au		
Courage Directors	English Ale	4.8%	16x500ml
Kestral Super	Strong Lager	9.0%	24x500ml
Wells Banana Bread	Bitter / Fruit Beer	5.2%	16x500ml
Wells Bombardier	English Bitter	5.2%	16x500ml
Wells Waggle Dance	Honey Ale	5.0%	16x500ml
Youngs Bitter	English Bitter	4.5%	16x500ml
Youngs Double Chocolate Stout	Chocolate Stout	5.2%	16x500ml
Youngs Special London Ale	Strong Ale	6.4%	16x500ml
Wexford Irish Ale	www.fmliquor.com.au		
Cream Ale	Ale	5.0%	473ml bottle, 50L
Worthingtons	www.australiantradepartners.com.au		
White Shield	ESB	5.6%	8x500
Wychwood	www.beerandcider.com.au		
Duchy Original Old Ruby Ale (Organic)	ESB	5.0%	8 x 500ml btl
Ginger Beard (Ginger Beer)	Spice Beer (Ginger)	4.2%	8 x 500ml btl
Goliath Ale	Premium Bitter	4.2%	8 x 500ml btl
Hobgoblin Ale	ESB	5.2%	500ml btl, 50ml can, 50ltr
King Goblin	ESB	6.6%	8 x 500ml btl
Scarecrow (Organic Ale)	Premium Bitter	4.7%	12 x 500ml btl
Wychcraft Blonde Ale	Blond Ale	4.5%	8 x 500ml btl

FINLAND

Brand/Distributor/Name	Style	ABV	Unit
Lapin Kulta	www.australiantradepartners.com.au		
Lapin Kulta	Pale Lager	5.2%	24x330

FRANCE

Brand/Distributor/Name	Style	ABV	Unit
St Sylvstre	www.australiantradepartners.com.au		
Trois Monts	Biere de Garde	8.5%	6x750
Gavroche	French Amber Ale	8.5%	330ml x 24
rois Monts	Saison - Bière de Garde	8.5%	750ml x 6

GERMANY

Brand/Distributor/Name	Style	ABV	Unit
Aecht Schlenkerla	www.phoenixbeers.com.au		
Schlenkerla Marzen	Rauchbier	5.1%	20x500ml, Keg
Schlenkerla Urbock	Rauchbier	6.6%	20x500ml, Keg
Schlenkerla Weizen	Rauchbier	5.2%	20x500ml, Keg
Bitburger	www.baw.com.au		
Bitburger Premium	Lager		4x6x330ml, 50L
BITBURGER	Woolworths		
BITBURGER PREMIUM	Lager		4X6X330ML, 5L party kegs
Clausthaler Non-alc	www.baw.com.au		
Clausthaler Non-alc	Non-alc Beer:	0.5%	330ml
DAB Original	www.baw.com.au		
Dab Original	Lager	4.9%	Btl, Can, Kegs
Erdinger	www.baw.com.au		
Erdinger Alc Free	Non-alc Beer		330ml
Erdinger Champ	Weizen (Wheat) Beer:	4.8%	330ml
Erdinger Dunkel	Weizen (Wheat) Beer:	5.6%	500ml, 30lt
Erdinger Kristall	Weizen (Wheat) Beer:	5.3%	500ml
Erdinger Mit Feine Hefe	Weizen (Wheat) Beer:	5.3%	500ml
Erdinger Mit Feine Hefe	Weizen (Wheat) Beer:		
Erdinger Oktoberfest (Seasonal Availability)	Weizen (Wheat) Beer:		
Erdinger Pikantus	Weizen (Wheat) Beer:	7.3%	500ml
Fest Beer	Strong Lager Beer	5.8%	20 x 500ml btls Sold Out
FISCHER LAGER	www.baw.com.au		
FISCHER LAGER	Lager		
HANSA	www.baw.com.au		
HANSA PILS 6PK	Lager	4.8%	500ml
Hofbrau	WA - www.fmliquor.com.au		
Hofbrau Dunkel	Dark Lager	5.5%	330ml, 500ml btl, 50L
Hofbrau Hefeweizen	Wheat Beer	5.1%	330ml, 500ml btl, 50L
Hofbrau Original Lager	Lager	5.1%	330ml, 500ml btl, 50L
Maibock (Seasonal)	Bock	7.2%	500ml bottle, 50L
Oktoberfestbier (Seasonal)	Oktoberfest Lager	6.0%	330ml, 500ml btl, 50L
Schwarze Wiesse (Seasonal)	Wheat Beer	5.1%	500ml bottle
KOELSCH	www.baw.com.au		
KOELSCH	Kolsch		
Konig Ludwig Brewery	Beer Importers and Distributors		
Konig Ludwig Dunkel	Munich Dunkel	5.1%	500ml x 20
Konig Ludwig Weissbier	Weizen/Weissbier	5.5%	330ml x 24, 30L Keg
KOSTRITZER	www.baw.com.au		
KOSTRITZER DARK	Dark Lager		
LOWENBRAU	Woolworths		
LOWENBRAU 4X6X330ML			4x6x330ml
OETTINGER BEER	Woolworths		
OETTINGER BEER 4X6X330ML			330ML, 500ml can
Paulaner Brewery	www.samsmith.com		
Hefe-Weizen	Wheat Beer	5.5%	330ml
Munich Lager	Lager	4.9%	330ml
Pils	Pilsner	4.9%	330ml
RADEBERGER	www.baw.com.au		
RADEBERGER PILSNER 6PK	Pilsner	4.9%	330ml, 50L
SCHOFFERHOFER	www.baw.com.au		
SCHOFFERHOFER HEFE	WEIZEN (WHEAT) BEER	5.1%	500ml
SCHOFFERHOFER KRISTALL 6PK	WEIZEN (WHEAT) BEER	5.1%	500ml
SCHWELMER	www.baw.com.au		
SCHWELMER PILS	Pilsner	5.0%	500ml
Spaten	German Beverage Imports www.purebier.com		
Franziskaner Hefe Weissbier Dunkel	Dunkelweizen	5.0%	Bottle 500mL
Franziskaner Hefe Weissbier Hell	Weizen/Weissbier	5.0%	Bottle 500mL
Franziskaner Kristall	Weizen/Weissbier	5.0%	Bottle 500mL
Spaten Munich Lager	Munich Helles	5.2%	Bottle 500mL
Spaten Oktoberfestbier	Oktoberfest/Märzen	5.9%	Bottle 500mL
Staaliches Hofbräuhaus	German Beverage Imports www.purebier.com		
Hofbräu Dunkel	Munich Dunkel	5.5%	6 Pack
Hofbräu Hefe Weissbier Hell	Weizen/Weissbier	5.1%	6 Pack
Hofbräu Oktoberfestbier	Oktoberfest/Märzen	6.3%	6 Pack
Hofbräu Original	Munich Helles	5.1%	6 Pack
Sunner	www.phoenixbeers.com.au		
Sunner Kolsch	Kolsch	4.9%	24x330ml, 20x500ml,
Warsteiner Brewery	Beer Importers and Distributors		
Warsteiner	German Pilsner (Pils)	4.8%	330ml, 5L, 50L
Weihenstephan	www.phoenixbeers.com.au		
Weihenstephan Alc Free Hefeweiss	Alcohol Free Hefeweis	<0.5%	20x500ml
Weihenstephan Alc Free Original	Alcohol Free Lager	<0.5%	20x500ml
Weihenstephan Dunkel	Dunkelweiss	5.3%	20x500ml, Keg
Weihenstephan Fest Bier	Strong Lager	5.4%	20x500ml, Keg
Weihenstephan Hefeweiss	Hefeweiss	5.4%	500ml, 330ml, Keg
Weihenstephan Korbinian	Bock Lager	7.4%	20x500ml, Keg
Weihenstephan Kristall	Kristalweiss	5.4%	20x500ml, Keg
Weihenstephan Light Hefeweiss	Hefeweiss	3.5%	20x500ml
Weihenstephan Original	Lager	5.1%	20x500ml, Keg
Weihenstephan Pilsner	Pilsner	5.1%	500ml, 330ml, Keg
Weihenstephan Tradition	Dark Lager	5.2%	20x500ml, Keg
Weihenstephan Vitus	Bock Wheat	7.7%	20x500ml, Keg
Weihenstephan / Samuel Adams Infinium	Strong Lager	10.5%	6x750ml
Weltenburg Brewery	www.phoenixbeers.com.au		
Weltenburger Anno 1050	Vienna	5.5%	20x500ml, Keg
Weltenburger Asam-Bock	Bock Lager	6.9%	20x500ml, Keg
Weltenburger Barock Dunkel	Dark Lager	4.7%	20x500ml, Keg
Weltenburger Barock Hell	Dortmunder / Helles	5.6%	20x500ml, Keg
Weltenburger Hefeweiss Dunkel	Dunkelweiss	5.3%	20x500ml, Keg
Weltenburger Pilsner	Pilsner	4.9%	24x330ml, Keg
Weltenburger Urtyp Hell	Dortmunder / Helles	4.9%	20x500ml, Keg
Weltenburger Winter Traum	Vienna	5.2%	20x500ml, Keg
Weltnburger Hefeweiss Hell	Hefeweiss	5.4%	20x500ml, Keg

GREECE

Brand/Distributor/Name	Style	ABV	Unit
Mythos Brewery	www.samsmith.com, www.premiumbeverages.com.au		
Mythos	Lager	4.7%	330ml

HOLLAND

Brand/Distributor/Name	Style	ABV	Unit
Amstel	www.lion-nathan.com.au		
Amstel			
Amsterdam Mariner	Woolworths Liquor Brands		
Amsterdam Mariner			4x6x330ml, 4x6x500ml
Bouwerij De Molen	www.phoenixbeers.com.au		
Amarillo	Imperial / Double IPA	9.2%	24x330ml, 6x750ml
Bloed, Zweet & Tranen	Smoked	8.1%	24x330ml, 6x750ml
Bommen & Granaten	Barley Wine	15.0%	24x330ml, 6x750ml
Donder & Bliksem	Bohemian Pilsner	5.9%	24x330ml, 6x750ml
Hamer & Sikkel	Porter	5.1%	6x750ml
Heen & Weer	Abbey Tripel	9.5%	24x330ml, 6x750ml
Hel & Verdomenis	Imperial Stout	11.9%	24x330ml, 6x750ml
Hemel & Arde	Imperial Stout	9.5%	24x330ml, 6x750ml
Molen Engels	Bitter	4.5%	24x330ml, 6x750ml
Molenbier	English Strong Ale	9.2%	24x330ml, 6x750ml
Mooi & Meedogenloos	Imperial Stout	9.2%	24x330ml
Op & Top	Amber Ale	4.5%	24x330ml
Rasputin	Imperial Stout	10.7%	24x330ml, 6x750ml
Rijn & Veen	Hefeweizen	5.0%	24x330ml
Rook & Vuur	Smoked	8.2%	24x330ml, 6x750ml
Vuur & Vlam	IPA	6.2%	24x330ml, 6x750ml
Grolsch	Coca-Cola Amati, 13 COKE (13 2653)		
Grolsch Premium Lager	European Lager	5.0%	450ml / 1.5L swingtops
Heineken	www.lion-nathan.com.au		
Heineken	Lager	5.0%	5L party kegs
Oranjeboom	Woolworths Liquor Brands		
Oranjeboom Premium Beer			4 X 6 X 330ml

INDIA

Brand/Distributor/Name	Style	ABV	Unit
SKOL Brewery	Beer Importers and Distributors		
Royal Challenge Premium Lager	Standard Lager	5.0%	330ml x 24

IRELAND

Brand/Distributor/Name	Style	ABV	Unit
Coors	www.australiantradepartners.com.au		
Caffrey's Irish Ale	Bitter	4.2%	24x440 can
Murphy's Brewery	www.beerandcider.com.au		
Murphys Irish Stout	Dry Stout	4.0%	24 x 500ml can, 4 pack

ITALY

Brand/Distributor/Name	Style	ABV	Unit
Birra Moretti	www.lion-nathan.com.au		
Birra Moretti			
Birra Peroni	Coca-Cola Amati, 13 COKE (13 2653)		
Peroni Gran Riserva	Maibock	6.6%	330mL bottle
Birreria Ichnusa	www.arquilla.com		
Ichnusa	Lager	4.7%	Bottle 330 Ml
Ichnusa	Lager Anniversary	5.6%	Bottle 330 Ml
Birreria Messina	www.arquilla.com		
Messina Birra Di Sicilia	Lager	4.7%	Bottle 330 Ml
Birrificio Castello	www.arquilla.com		
CASTELLO	Lager	5.0%	bottle 330 ml
La Petrognola	Enoteca Sileno		
Farro White Beer (Bionda)	Specialty beer	5.5%	330ml
Le Baladin	Enoteca Sileno		
Elixir - Demi Sec with Whiskey Islay Yeast	Belgian Specialty Ale	10.0%	750ml
Isaac Wheat Beer	Witbier	5.0%	750ml
Isaac Wheat Beer	Witbier	5.0%	250ml
Noel Dark Double Malt	Spiced Beer	9.0%	750ml
Nora Biological Double Malt	Specialty beer	7.0%	750ml
Baladin Double Malt	Belgian Dubbel	8.0%	750ml
Xayuax Riserva 2006	English Barley Wine	13.5%	500ml
Magalotti 1845	Enoteca Sileno		
Birra Magalotti	Tradional Bock	7.1%	330ml
Theresianer	www.arquilla.com		
Theresianer	Lager	4.8%	bottle 330 ml
Theresianer	Pilsner	5.0%	bottle 330 ml
Theresianer	Vienna	5.3%	bottle 330 ml
Theresianer	Strong Ale	8.5%	bottle 330 ml
Theresianer	Pilsner Unfiltered	5.0%	bottle 750 ml
Theresianer	Wit Unfiltered	5.1%	bottle 750 ml
Theresianer	Bock Unfiltered	6.5%	bottle 750 ml

JAPAN

Brand/Distributor/Name	Style	ABV	Unit
Asahi	www.cub.com.au		
Asahi	Lager	5.0%	330ml, 30L
Baird Beer	www.northdown.com.au		
Angry Boy Brown Ale	Brown Ale	6.2%	360ml
Dark Sky Imperial Stout	Imperial Stout	9.0%	633ml
Ganko Oyaji	Barley Wine	9.5%	633ml
Kurofune Porter	Porter	6.0%	360ml
Numazu Lager	Unfiltered Lager	5.0%	360ml
Red Rose Amber Ale	Amber Ale	5.5%	360ml
Rising Sun Pale	US Pale Ale	4.2%	360ml
Saruga Bay Imperial IPA	Imperial IPA	7.5%	360ml
Shimaguni Stout	Stout	4.6%	360ml
Single-Take Session Ale	Belgian Ale	4.7%	360ml
Teikoku IPA	IPA	6.0%	360ml
Temple Garden Yuzu Ale	Citrus Ale	5.5%	633ml
The Carpenter's Mikan Ale	Citrus Ale	6.0%	633ml
Wheat King Ale	Wheat Beer	4.2%	360ml
COEDO Brewery	www.htbeverages.com.au		
COEDO Beniaka	Super Premium Lager brewed with		7.00%
24x330mL			
COEDO Kyara	Premium All Malt	5.0%	24x330mL
COEDO Ruri	German Pilsner (Pils)	5.0%	24x330mL
COEDO Shikkoku	Schwarzbier	5.0%	24x330mL
COEDO Shiro	Belgian Witbier	5.5%	24x330mL
Kiuchi	www.palaisimports.com.au		
Hitachino Nest Espresso Stout	Stout	7.5%	330 btl
Hitachino Nest Japanese Classic Ale	Classic Ale		
Hitachino Nest Real Ginger Brew	Ginger Beer		
Hitachino Nest Red Rice Ale	Red Rice Ale		
Hitachino Nest White Ale	Wit Bier	5.0%	330 btl
Sapporo	www.jfcaustralia.com.au		
Sapporo	Pale Lager	5.0%	12x650 can, 334ml

MEXICO

Brand/Distributor/Name	Style	ABV	Unit
DOS EQUIS	Woolworths Liquor Brands		
DOS EQUIS XX AMBAR			4 X 6 X 330ML
DOS EQUIS XX LAGER ESPECIAL			4 X 6 X 330ML
FEMSA	www.australiantradepartners.com.au		
Bohemia Classica	Pale Lager	4.6%	24x355
Tecate	Pale Lager	5.0%	24x355ml, 4x375 can
Grupo Modelo	www.cub.com.au		
Corona	Lager	5.0%	330mL
Mexicali	Unique Liquor		
Mexicali	Lager		
Sol	Woolworths		
SOL MEXICAN BEER			4X6X330ML

MOROCCO

Brand/Distributor/Name	Style	ABV	Unit
du Maroc	www.australiantradepartners.com.au		
Casablanca	Pale Lager	5.0%	24x330

NEPAL

Brand/Distributor/Name	Style	ABV	Unit
Mt Everest	www.australiantradepartners.com.au		
Gurkha	Pale Lager	5.0%	12x660

NORWAY

Brand/Distributor/Name	Style	ABV	Unit
Haand Bryggeriet	www.phoenixbeers.com.au		
Aquavit Porter	Barrel Aged Imperial Porter	10.0%	12x500ml
Ardenne Blonde	Saison	7.5%	12x500ml, Keg
Bavarian Weizen	Hefeweiss	5.5%	12x500ml, Keg
Bestefar	Traditional Ale	9.0%	12x500ml, Keg
Costa Rica	Coffee Porter	6.5%	12x500ml, Keg
Dark Force	Imperial Wheat Stout	9.0%	12x500ml
Dobbel Dose IPA	Double / Imperial Wheat	9.0%	12x500ml, Keg
Farewell Ale	Tradittional Ale	7.5%	12x500ml, Keg
Fyr & Flamme	IPA	6.5%	12x500ml, Keg
Good Force	Imperial Wheat	9.0%	12x500ml
Haandbakk	Sour / Wild Ale	8.5%	12x500ml
Haandbic	Lambic	4.5%	12x500ml
Hesjeol	Traditional Ale	6.5%	12x500ml, Keg
India Pale Ale	IPA	6.5%	12x500ml, Keg
Kreklingol	Fruit Beer	7.7%	12x500ml
London Porter	Porter	4.5%	12x500ml, Keg
Nissefar	Old Ale	7.0%	12x500ml, Keg
Nissemor	Old Ale	6.0%	12x500ml, Keg
Norweigian Wood	Traditional Ale	6.5%	12x500ml, Keg
Odins Tipple	Imperial Stout	11.0%	12x500ml
Pale Ale	American Pale Ale	4.5%	12x500ml, Keg
Royk Uten Ild	Rauchbier	8.5%	12x500ml, Keg
Nogne O	www.phoenixbeers.com.au		
Nogne O #100	Imperial / Double IPA	10.0%	12x500ml, Keg
Nogne O Bitter	Bitter	4.5%	12x500ml, Keg
Nogne O Blonde Ale	Blonde	4.5%	12x500ml, Keg
Nogne O Brown Ale	Brown Ale	4.5%	12x500ml, Keg
Nogne O Brun	Brun	6.0%	12x500ml, Keg
Nogne O Dark Horizon	Imperial Stout	15.5%	12x250ml
Nogne O God Jul / Winter Ale	Traditional Ale	8.5%	12x500ml, Keg
Nogne O Havrestout	Stout	4.5%	12x500ml, Keg
Nogne O Imperial Brown Ale	Imperial Brown Ale	7.5%	12x500ml, Keg
Nogne O Imperial IPA (#500)	Imperial / Double IPA	10.0%	12x500ml, Keg
Nogne O Imperial Stout	Imperial Stout	9.0%	12x500ml, Keg
Nogne O India Pale Ale	IPA	7.5%	12x500ml, Keg
Nogne O Julesnadder	Traditional Ale	4.5%	12x500ml, Keg
Nogne O Pale Ale	Pale	6.0%	12x500ml, Keg
Nogne O Porter	Porter	7.0%	12x500ml, Keg
Nogne O Red Horizon	American Strong Ale	17.0%	12x250ml
Nogne O Saison	Saison	6.5%	12x500ml, Keg
Nogne O Sunturnbrew	Smoked Barley Wine	11.0%	12x500ml, Keg
Nogne O Tiger Tripel	Belgian Tripel	9.0%	12x500ml, Keg
Nogne O Underlig Jul / Peculiar Yule	Traditonal Ale	6.5%	12x500ml, Keg
Nogne O Wit	Belgian Wit	4.5%	12x500ml, Keg

POLAND

Brand/Distributor/Name	Style	ABV	Unit
Brok	Qld - www.australiantradepartners.com.au		
Brok Export	Lager	5.2%	24x500
Poland			
Browar Amber	Qld - www.australiantradepartners.com.au		
Grand Imperial	Porter	8.0%	20x500
Zlote Lwy (Golden Lion)	Lager	5.7%	20x500
Okocim	Qld - www.australiantradepartners.com.au		
Okocim	Lager	5.5%	20x500
Okocim	Porter	8.3%	20x500
Zywiec	Negro International		
Zywiec	Porter	9.5%	24x330
Zywiec	Lager	5.6%	20x500
Zywiec	Lager	5.6%	24x500 can

PORTUGAL

Brand/Distributor/Name	Style	ABV	Unit
Uncier Bebidas SA	www.htbeverages.com.au		
Super Bock	Pale Lager	5.20%	4x6x330mL
Super Bock Green	Pale Lager infused with 1% Lemon Juice	4.00%	4x6x330mL

RUSSIA

Brand/Distributor/Name	Style	ABV	Unit
Baltika	www.australiantradepartners.com.au		
No.3 Classic	Pale Lager	4.8%	20x500
No.4 Original Dark	Dunkel	5.6%	20x500
No.5 Golden	Pale Lager	5.3%	20x500
No.6 Porter	Porter	7.0%	20x500
No.7 Export Lager	Pale Lager	5.4%	20x500
No.8 Wheat	Wheat	5.0%	20x500
No.9 Strong	Imperial Pils	8.0%	20x500

SCOTLAND

Brand/Distributor/Name	Style	ABV	Unit
Atlas	www.australiantradepartners.com.au		
Latitude	Pilsener	3.9%	12x500
Nimbus	Golden Ale	5.0%	12x500
Three Sisters	Bitter	4.2%	12x500
Belhaven	www.fmliquor.com.au		
Belhaven Best	Ale	3.5%	500ml,440ml can,50L
Belhaven Best Premium	Ale	4.8%	440ml can
Belhaven Fruit Beer	Fruit Ale	4.6%	500ml bottle
Belhaven Scottish Ale	Scottish Ale	5.2%	355ml btl,440ml can, 500ml btl
Belhaven Scottish Stout	Stout	7.0%	500ml bottle, 50L
Belhaven St Andrews Ale	Ale	4.6%	355ml btl, 500ml btl
Belhaven Twisted Thistle IPA	India Pale Ale	5.1%	500ml bottle, 50L
Belhaven Wee Heavy	Scotch Ale	8.0%	500ml bottle
BrewDog	www.hopandspirit.com.au		
BrewDog 5am Saint	Amber Ale	5.0%	6X4X330ML
BrewDog Hardcore IPA	Imperial American IPA	9.2%	6X4X330ML
BrewDog Punk IPA	IPA	5.6%	6X4X330ML
BrewDog Sink the Bismarck	Imperial American IPA	4.1%	330ml
BrewDog Tatical Nuclear Penguin	Imperial Stout	3.2%	330ml
BrewDog Trashy Blonde	IPA	4.1%	6X4X330ML
Cairngorm	www.australiantradepartners.com.au		
Black Gold	Stout	4.4%	12x500
Blessed Thistle	Bitter	4.5%	12x500
Sheepshaggers Gold	Golden Ale	4.5%	12x500
Trade Winds	Golden Ale	4.3%	12x500
Wild Cat	ESB	5.1%	12x500
80 Shillings	Golden Ale	4.1%	12x500
Deuchars IPA	Bitter	4.4%	12x500
Caledonian	www.australiantradepartners.com.au		
80 Shillings	Golden Ale	4.1%	12x500
Deuchars IPA	Bitter	4.4%	12x500
Harviestoun	www.northdown.com.au		
Bitter and Twisted	Golden Ale	4.2%	30litre keg
Mr. Sno'balls	English Bitter	4.5%	330ml
Ola Dubh 12	Imperial Porter (Oak Aged)	8.0%	330ml
Ola Dubh 16	Imperial Porter (Oak Aged)	8.0%	330ml
Ola Dubh 18	Imperial Porter (Oak Aged)	8.0%	330ml
Ola Dubh 30	Imperial Porter (Oak Aged)	8.0%	330ml
Ola Dubh 40	Imperial Porter (Oak Aged)	8.0%	330ml
Heather Ales	www.australiantradepartners.com.au		
Aqlba Scot Pine	Traditional Ale	7.5%	24x330
Ebulum	Traditional Ale	6.5%	24x330
Fraoch	Traditional Ale	5.0%	24x330
Grozet	Traditional Ale	5.0%	24x330
Kelpie	Traditional Ale	4.4%	24x330
Innis & Gunn	www.beerandcider.com.au		
Oak Aged Blonde	Wood Aged Beer (Blonde)	6.0%	12 x 330ml btl
Oak Aged Highland Cask	Wood Aged Beer (Scottish Strong Ale)	7.1%	330ml btl
Oak Aged Original	Wood Aged Beer (Scottish Strong Ale)	6.6%	330ml btl
Oak Aged Rum Cask	Wood Aged Beer (Scottish Strong Ale)	7.4%	330ml btl
Oak Aged Spiced Rum	Wood Aged Beer (Scottish Strong Ale)	6.9%	330ml btl
John Smiths	www.australiantradepartners		
McEwens Export	Bitter	4.5%	24x500 can
Orkney	www.australiantradepartners.com.au		
Dark Island	Old Ale	4.6%	12x500
Dark Island Reserve	Barley Wine	10.0%	6x750
Dragonhead	Stout	4.0%	12x500
Raven Ale	Bitter	3.8%	12x500
Red MacGregor	ESB	4.0%	12x500
Skull Splitter	Barley wine	8.5%	24x330

Brand/Distributor/Name	Style	ABV	Unit
Traquair	www.australiantradepartners.com.au		
House Ale	Strong Ale	7.2%	24x330
Jacobite Ale	Traditional Ale	8.0%	24x330
Wellpark	www.australiantradepartners.com.au		
Tennents	Pale Lager	4.0%	24x500 can
Tennents Super	Imperial Pils	9.0%	24x500 can

SOUTH AFRICA

Brand/Distributor/Name	Style	ABV	Unit
Windhoek	www.africapewines.com.au		
Windhoek	Lager	4.0%	24x330mL

SPAIN

Brand/Distributor/Name	Style	ABV	Unit
Grupo Mahou	www.australiantradepartners.com.au		
San Miguel	Pale Lager	5.0%	24x330
Hijos de Rivera	www.broadwayliquor.com.au		
Estrella De Galicia Reserva 1906	Lager	6.5%	330ml
Estrella De Galicia Special	Lager	4.7%	330ml
La Zaragozana	www.broadwayliquor.com.au		
Ambar Lager	Lager	5.2%	330ml
Ambar Pale Ale 1900	Pale Ale	4.8%	330ml

SRI LANKA

Brand/Distributor/Name	Style	ABV	Unit
Lion Brewery	Beer Importers and Distributors		
Sinha Lager	Standard Lager	4.8%	330ml x24
Sinha Stout	Foreign Extra Stout	8.0%	330ml x24

SWEDEN

Brand/Distributor/Name	Style	ABV	Unit
Kronleins	www.australiantradepartners.com.au		
Crocodile	Pale Lager	5.2%	24x330

SWITZERLAND

Brand/Distributor/Name	Style	ABV	Unit
Ninteen Thirty Six	www.australiantradepartners.com.au		
1936	Pale Lager	4.8%	24x330

THAILAND

Brand/Distributor/Name	Style	ABV	Unit
Chang	Woolworths Liquor Brands		
Chang Beer Bottles 4x6x330ml	Pilsner		

TURKEY

Brand/Distributor/Name	Style	ABV	Unit
Anadolu Efes	www.australiantradepartners.com.au		
Efes	Pilsener	5.0%	24x330

USA

Brand/Distributor/Name	Style	ABV	Unit
Boston Beer Company	Beer Importers and Distributors		
Samuel Adams Boston Lager	Premium American Lager	4.8%	355ml x24
Samuel Adams Noble Pils (Seasonal)	Classic American Pilsner	4.9%	355ml x24
Samuel Adams Summer Ale (Seasonal)	American Wheat or Rye Beer	5.5%	355ml x 24
Brooklyn Brewery	www.palaisimports.com.au		
Brooklyn Lager	Lager	5.2%	355 btl 6-pk
Brooklyn Local 1	Belgian Tripel	9.0%	750 btl
Budweiser	www.lion-nathan.com.au		
Budweiser			
Genesee	www.australiantradepartners.com.au		
Dundee Honey Brown	Dark Lager	4.5%	24x355
Minhas Craft	www.australiantradepartners.com.au		
Dixie	Pale Lager	4.5%	24x330
Moylan's	www.northdown.com.au		
Chelsea's Porter	Porter	5.0%	650ml
Chelsea's Porter	Porter	5.0%	50L keg
Dragoon Dry Irish Stout	Stout	5.0%	650ml, 50L keg
Hopsickle Imperial IPA	Imperial IPA	9.2%	650ml
Hopsickle Imperial IPA	Imperial IPA	9.2%	50L keg
Kilt Lifter Scotch Ale	Scotch Ale	8.0%	650ml, 50L keg
Moylander Double IPA	Double IPA	8.5%	650ml, 50L keg
NorCal IPA	US IPA	6.8%	650ml, 50L keg
Old Blarney barleywine	Barley Wine	10.0%	650ml, 50L keg
Ryan Sullivan's imperial stout	Imperial Stout	10.0%	650ml
Ryan Sullivan's imperial stout	Imperial Stout	10.0%	50L keg
North Coast	www.palaisimports.com.au		
Acme California IPA	IPA	6.5%	355 btl 6-pk
Acme California Pale Ale	Pale Ale		
Blue Star			
Brother Thelonius			

Brand/Distributor/Name	Style	ABV	Unit
Le Merle			
Old No.38 Stout	Stout		
Old Rasputin Imperial Stout	Imperial Stout	9.0%	355 btl 4-pk
PranQster			
Red Seal	Amber Ale	5.5%	355 btl 6-pk
Scrimshaw			
Pabst	www.australiantradepartners.com.au		
Blue Ribbon	Pale Lager	5.0%	24x355
Lone Star	Pale Lager	4.7%	24x355
Sierra Nevada	www.phoenixbeers.com.au		
Sierra Nevada Hoptimum	Double / Imperial IPA	10.4%	12x710ml
Sierra Nevada Autumn Tumbler	Brown Ale	5.6%	24x355ml
Sierra Nevada Bigfoot	Barleywine	9.6%	24x355ml
Sierra Nevada Celebration Ale	American IPA	6.8%	24x355ml
Sierra Nevada Glissade	Golden Bock	6.4%	24x355ml
Sierra Nevada Harvest Ale (Northern Hemisphere)	American IPA	6.7%	12x710ml
Sierra Nevada Harvest Ale (Southern Hemisphere)	American IPA	6.7%	12x710ml
Sierra Nevada Kellerweiss	Hefeweiss	4.8%	24x355ml
Sierra Nevada Pale Ale	American Pale Ale	5.6%	24x355ml
Sierra Nevada Porter	Porter	5.6%	24x355ml
Sierra Nevada Stout	Stout	5.8%	24x355ml
Sierra Nevada Summerfest	Lager	5.0%	24x355ml
Sierra Nevada Torpedo	American IPA	7.2%	12x710ml

VIETNAM

Brand/Distributor/Name	Style	ABV	Unit
South East Asia Brewery Ltd.	www.htbeverages.com.au		
Halida Premium Lager	Pale Lager	4.50%	2x6x330mL

WALES

Brand/Distributor/Name	Style	ABV	Unit
Brains	www.australiantradepartners.com.au		
Bitter	Bitter	3.5%	24x440 can
Dark	Dark Mild	4.1%	8x500
Reverand James	Old Ale	4.5%	8x500
SA	Bitter	4.2%	8x500
SA Gold	Golden Ale	4.7%	8x500
SA Premium	Bitter	4.2%	24x440 can

CIDER & PERRY
BELGIUM

Brand/Distributor/Name	Style	ABV	Unit
Anthony Martin Brewery	Beer Importers and Distributors		
Douglas Celtic Cider	Common Cider	4.5%	500ml x 20
Stassen	www.phoenixbeers.com.au		
Stassen 'Over Ice' Apple	Cider	5.4%	24x330ml
Stassen 'Over Ice' Apple	Perry	5.4%	24x330ml

ENGLAND

Brand/Distributor/Name	Style	ABV	Unit
Aspall Cyder	www.aspall.co.uk www.littlecreatures.com.au		
Aspall Suffolk Cyder	Apple Cider	5.5%	12 x 500ml bottles
Aston Manor Brewery	www.beerandcider.com.au		
Crumpton Oaks Farmhouse	English Cider	5.0%	24 x 500ml can, 4 pack
Crumpton Oaks Farmhouse	English Cider	5.0%	6 x 2ltr PET
Frosty Jacks White Dry	English Cider	7.5%	500ml can, 2ltr PET, 3ltr PET
Kingstone Press Dry	English Cider	5.3%	12 x 660ml btl
Knights Malvern Gold Medium	English Cider	6.0%	12 x 750ml btl
Knights Malvern Oak Dry	English Cider	6.0%	12 x 750ml btl
Badger Brewery	www.beerandcider.com.au		
Applewood Oak Aged	English Cider	6	8 x 500ml btl
Chardolini	www.beerandcider.com.au		
Sparkling	Perry	7.5%	750ml bottle
Cornish Orchards	www.fmliquor.com.au		
Cornish Orchards Cider	Cider	5.0%	500ml bottle
Henneys Cider Co	www.phoenixbeers.com.au		
Fromme Apple Sweet Cider	Sweet Cider	5.7%	16x500ml
Fromme Dry Cider	Dry Cider	6.0%	16x500ml
Vintage Cider	Still Cider	6.5%	16x500ml
Moles	www.australiantradepartners.com.au		
Black Rat		4.7%	24x500 can
Samuel Smith Brewery	Beer Importers and Distributors		
Samuel Smith Organic Apple Cider	Common Cider	5.0%	500ml x 12
Thatchers	www.beerandcider.com.au		
Gold Cider	English Cider	4.8	6 x 500ml btl
Green Goblin Oak Aged	English Cider	6	12 x 500ml btl
Westons	www.wbaustralia.com.au		

Brand/Distributor/Name	Style	ABV	Unit
Westons	Cider		

FRANCE

Brand/Distributor/Name	Style	ABV	Unit
Domaine Dupont	www.phoenixbeers.com.au		
Cidre Bio	Farmhouse Cider	5.5%	6x750ml
Cidre Bouche Fermier	Farmhouse Cider	5.0%	12x750ml
Cidre Cuvee Colette	Farmhouse Cider	6.9%	6x750ml
Cidre Dupont Reserve	Farmhouse Cider	7.5%	6x750ml
Givre	Ice Cider	6.9%	6x375ml
Normandy Cider	Farmhouse Cider	5.5%	6x750ml

IRELAND

Brand/Distributor/Name	Style	ABV	Unit
Magners Brewery	www.suntory.com.au		
Magners Irish Pear Cider	Cider	4.5%	568ml Pint Bottle Case: 12 units
Magners Irish Pear Cider	Cider	4.5%	330ml 4-pack Case: 24 units
Magners Original Irish Cider	Cider	4.5%	568ml Pint Bottle Case: 12 units
Magners Original Irish Cider	Cider	4.5%	330ml 4-pack Case: 24 units

SOUTH AFRICA

Brand/Distributor/Name	Style	ABV	Unit
Savanna	www.africapewines.com.au		
Savanna	Dry Cider	6.0%	24x330mL

SPAIN

Brand/Distributor/Name	Style	ABV	Unit
Champanera de villaviciosa	www.broadwayliquor.com.au		
Escanciador ES	Sparkling Cider	5.0%	330ml
Escanciador Extra Original	Sparkling Cider	4.0%	700ml
Escanciador Sidra	Cider	5.0%	250ml
Riera Natural Cider	Cider	5.0%	700ml

SWEDEN

Brand/Distributor/Name	Style	ABV	Unit
Kopparberg	Woolworths		
Kopparberg Apple Cider 15x500ml	Cider		
Kopparberg E/flower And Lime 15x500ml	Cider		
Kopparberg Elderflwr/lime Cidr 4x6x330ml	Cider		
Kopparberg Mixed Fruit Cider 15x500ml	Cider		
Kopparberg Mixed Fruitcider 4x6x330ml	Cider		
Kopparberg Pear Cider 15x500ml	Cider		
Kopparberg Strwbery & Lime Cdr 24x330ml	Cider		
KOPPARBERG STRWBERY AND LIME 15X500ML	Cider		

GLUTEN FREE BEER
ENGLAND

Brand/Distributor/Name	Style	ABV	Unit
G-Free	www.phoenixbeers.com.au		
G-Free	Gluten Free Beer		
Wold Top	www.australiantradepartners.com.au		
Against the Grain	Gluten Free Ale	4.5%	12x500

GERMANY

Brand/Distributor/Name	Style	ABV	Unit
Lammsbraue	www.phoenixbeers.com.au		
Lammsbraue Gluten Free	Gluten Free Beer		
Schnitzerbrau	www.blackwoodlane.com.au		
Premium	Gluten Free Lager	5.0%	330mL
Lemon	Gluten Free Lager	2.6%	330mL

JUST TASTED A GREAT BEER OR CIDER?

Share your own tasting note on the Beer & Brewer forums at www.beerandbrewer.com

Index

AUSTRALIA

ACT

- **BREWERIES/BEER COMPANIES**
  1. Stricklands Beer Group — 17
  2. Wig & Pen Tavern & Brewery — 17
  3. Zierholz Premium Brewery — 17

- **BEER BARS (Incl. Brew Bars/Pubs)**
  1. All Bar Nun — 17
  2. Belgian Beer Café — 17
  3. Debacle — 17
  4. King O'Malleys — 17
  5. O'Neills — 17
  6. PJ O'Reilly's — 17
  7. The Durham Castle Inn — 17
  8. The George Harcourt Inn — 17
  9. Tongue and Groove — 17
  10. Wig & Pen Tavern & Brewery — 17
  11. Zierholz Premium Brewery — 17

- **BOTTLESHOPS**
  1. Dan Murphy's — 17
  2. Plonk Beer Store — 17

- **VENUE PROFILES**
  1. Dan Murphy's — 18
  2. Plonk Beer Store — 19
  3. Wig & Pen Tavern & Brewery — 18
  4. Zierholz Brewery — 18

NSW

- **BREWERIES/BEER COMPANIES**
  1. 4 Pines Brewing Company — 49
  2. Australian Hotel & Brewery — 49
  3. Badlands — 25
  4. Balmain Brewing Company — 49
  5. Barons Brewing — 49
  6. Black Duck Brewery — 33
  7. Bluetongue Brewery Café — 29
  8. Brewtopia — 49
  9. Brothers Ink — 49
  10. Byron Bay Premium Brewery and Buddha Bar — 33
  11. Casella Wines — 37
  12. Central Ranges Brewing Co. — 25
  13. Doctor's Orders Brewing — 49
  14. Ekim Brewing Co — 49
  15. Endeavour True Vintage Beer — 33
  16. Federal Hotel — 33
  17. Five Islands Brewery — 41
  18. Fusion Brewing — 49
  19. Happy Goblin Brewery — 49
  20. HopDog BeerWorks — 41
  21. Hunter Beer Company — 29
  22. Infusion Bar and Brewery — 41
  23. John Boston Premium Beverages — 49
  24. King St Brewhouse & Restaurant — 47
  25. Koala Beer — 29
  26. Kosciuszko Brewing Company — 41
  27. Longboard Beer — 41
  28. Malt Shovel Brewery — 49
  29. Mountain Ridge Brewery — 41
  30. Mudgee Brewing Co — 25
  31. Murray's Craft Brewing Co — 29
  32. Paddy's Brewery — 49
  33. Redoak Boutique Beer — 49
  34. Rocks Brewing Co. — 49
  35. Scharer's Brewery at George IV Inn — 41
  36. Schwartz Brewery Hotel — 49
  37. Snowy Mountains Brewery — 41
  38. St Arnou — 49
  39. St Peters Brewery — 49
  40. Steel River Brewery — 29
  41. Stone & Wood — 33
  42. The Dalgety Brewing Company (Snowy Vineyard Estate) — 41
  43. The Little Brewing Company — 33
  44. The Lord Nelson Brewery Hotel — 49
  45. The Old Goulburn Brewery — 41
  46. Thirsty Crow Brewery — 37
  47. Tooheys Brewery — 49
  48. Underground Brewing — 49
  49. William Bull Brewery — 37

- **BEER BARS (Incl. Brew Bars/Pubs)**
  1. 3 Weeds — 47
  2. 4 Pines Brewing Company — 49
  3. Australian Hotel & Brewery — 49
  4. Badlands Brewery Bar — 25
  5. Banjo Patterson Inn (Kosciuszko Brewing Company) — 41
  6. Bavarian Bier Café's — 47
  7. Bazaar Beer Café — 47
  8. Belgian Beer Café's — 47
  9. Bluetongue Brewery Café — 29
  10. Byron Bay Premium Brewery and Buddha Bar — 33
  11. Coogee Cafe After Dark — 47
  12. Doma Bohemian Beer Café — 47
  13. Essen Restaurant — 47
  14. Five Islands Brewery (Illawarra Brewing Co) — 41
  15. George IV Inn (Scharer's Brewery) — 41
  16. Harts Pub (Rocks Brewing Co.) — 49
  17. Hotel Delany — 29
  18. Potters Hotel Brewery Resort (Hunter Beer Company) — 29
  19. Infusion Bar and Brewery — 41
  20. Jackson's on George — 47
  21. King St Brewhouse & Restaurant — 47
  22. La Boheme Restaurant & Café — 47
  23. Löwenbräu Keller — 47
  24. Mary Ellen Hotel — 29
  25. Mudgee Brewing Co — 25
  26. MuMu Grill — 47
  27. Murray's at Manly — 47
  28. Murray's Craft Brewing Co — 29
  29. Opera Bar — 47
  30. Pizza e Birra's — 47
  31. Prague Beer Restaurant — 47
  32. Pumphouse Bar — 47
  33. Redoak Boutique Beer Café — 49
  34. Royal Oak Hotel — 47
  35. Schwartz Brewery Hotel — 49
  36. Silo Restaurant & Lounge — 29
  37. The Albion Hotel — 29
  38. The Australian Hotel — 47
  39. The Clarendon Hotel — 29
  40. The Local Taphouse — 47
  41. The London Hotel — 47
  42. The Lord Nelson Brewery Hotel — 49
  43. The Riverview Hotel — 47
  44. The Town Hall Hotel — 47
  45. The Welcome Hotel — 47
  46. Thirsty Crow Brewery — 37
  47. Tommy's European Beer Café — 47
  48. Underground Brewing — 49
  49. Union Hotel — 47
  50. Woolloomooloo Bay Hotel — 47
  51. Yulli's — 47

- **BOTTLESHOPS**
  1. 1st Choice — 48
  2. Amato's Liquor Mart — 48
  3. Balmain Village Cellars — 48
  4. Broadway Liquor (Little Bottler) — 48
  5. Dan Murphy's — 25, 41, 48
  6. Harrigan's Cellars — 29
  7. Hotel Delany — 29
  8. IGA Plus Liquor — 48
  9. Liquor Stax (Unique Liquor) — 48
  10. Little Bottler — 48
  11. Northmead Cellars (Little Bottler) — 48
  12. Platinum Liquor Store's — 48
  13. Porter's Liquor Store's — 48
  14. The Australian Hotel — 47
  15. The Oak Barrel — 48
  16. The Sackville Hotel — 48
  17. Warners at the Bay (Pub Mart) — 29

- **CIDER PRODUCERS**
  1. Small Acres Cyder — 25

- **DISTILLERIES**
  1. Brumby Schnapps Distillery (Thredbo Valley Distillery) — 41
  2. Red Dirt Distillery — 33
  3. Stone Pine Distillery — 25

- **VENUE PROFILES**
  1. 4 Pines — 55
  2. Australian Hotel & Brewery — 56
  3. Badlands Brewery Bar — 50
  4. Bitter & Twisted International Boutique Beer Festival — 52
  5. Bluetongue Brewery Cafe — 51
  6. Dan Murphy's — 52
  7. Harts Pub — 57
  8. Hunter Beer Co. — 53
  9. Mudgee Brewing Co. — 50
  10. Murray's Craft Brewing Co — 52
  11. Platinum Liquor — 55
  12. Redoak Boutique Beer — 59
  13. Schwartz Brewery Hotel — 56
  14. Silo Restaurant Lounge — 55
  15. The Albion Hotel — 53
  16. The Australian Hotel — 58
  17. The Clarendon Hotel — 55
  18. Warners at the Bay — 54

NT

- **Drinking Holes**
  1. Adelaide River Inn — 63
  2. Crab Claw Island — 63
  3. Daly Waters Historic Pub — 63
  4. Darwin Sailing Club — 63
  5. Darwin Ski Club — 63
  6. Darwin Trailer Boat Club — 63
  7. Goat Island Lodge — 63
  8. Humpty Doo Hotel — 63
  9. Mandorah Beach Hotel — 63
  10. The Lazy Lizard Tavern — 63

QLD

- **BREWERIES/BEER COMPANIES**
  1. XXXX Ale House & Brewery Tours — 69
  2. Bacchus Brewing Co — 69
  3. Blue Sky Brewery — 73
  4. Brewhouse Brisbane — 69
  5. Brews Brothers — 69
  6. Burleigh Brewing Co. — 77
  7. Carlton BrewHouse — 77
  8. International Hotel — 69
  9. MT Brewery — 77
  10. Sunshine Coast Brewery — 77
  11. Townsville Brewing Company — 73

- **BEER BARS (Incl. Brew Bars/Pubs)**
  1. 5th Element — 69
  2. Archive Beer Boutique & Bistro — 69
  3. Bavarian Bier Café — 69
  4. Belgian Beer Café Brussels — 69
  5. Black Forest German Café — 69
  6. Blue Sky Brewery — 73
  7. Breakfast Creek Hotel — 69
  8. Brewhouse Brisbane — 69
  9. Brisbane German Club — 69
  10. Burleigh Brewing Co. — 77
  11. Carlton BrewHouse — 77
  12. Cru Bar & Cellars — 69
  13. Fox & Hounds Country Inn — 77
  14. International Hotel — 69
  15. King Ludwig's German Restaurant & Bar — 77
  16. Laguna Jacks Cellar & Bar — 77
  17. MT Brewery — 77
  18. Scales & Ales — 69

244

19. The Bowery	69	
20. The Gunshop Café	69	
21. The PA, Jupiters Hotel & Casino	77	
22. The Spotted Cow	77	
23. Townsville Brewing Company	73	

- **BOTTLESHOPS**
  1. Dan Murphy's — 69
  2. Drinx — 69
  3. Era Bistro & Wine Store — 69
  4. Festival Cellars — 69
  5. Grand Central Hotel & Cellars — 69
  6. Nectar Beer & Wine Specialists — 69

- **DISTILLERIES**
  1. Bundaberg istilling Co — 77
  2. Castle Glen Liqueurs — 77
  3. Mt Uncle Distillery — 73
  4. Tamborine Mountain Distillery — 77

- **VENUE PROFILES**
  1. Archive Beer Boutique — 79
  2. Blue Sky Brewery — 80
  3. Brewhouse Brisbane — 78
  4. Burleigh Brewing Company — 80
  5. Mt Tamborine Brewery — 81
  6. Sunshine Coast Brewery — 78
  7. XXXX Ale House & Brewery Tours — 78

■ SA

- **BREWERIES/BEER COMPANIES**
  1. Barossa Valley Brewing — 93
  2. Barossa Brewing Company — 93
  3. Beard and Brau Brewery — 89
  4. Boar's Rock Beer — 97
  5. Brewboys Tasting Room — 89
  6. Coopers Brewery — 89
  7. Goodieson Brewery — 97
  8. Grumpy's Brewhaus — 89
  9. Holdfast Bay Brewing Company — 89
  10. Knappstein Enterprise — 93
  11. Lobethal Bierhaus — 89
  12. Lovely Valley Beverage Factory — 97
  13. McLaren Vale Beer Company — 97
  14. Pikes Oakbank Beer — 93
  15. Port Dock Brewery Hotel — 89
  16. TAFE Regency Campus — 89
  17. Thorogoods — 93
  18. Saltram — 93
  19. Swanky — 93
  20. Swell Brewing Co — 97
  21. The Steam Exchange Brewery — 97
  22. West End Brewery — 89
  23. Woolshed Brewery — 93
  24. Yorke Brewing — 93

- **BEER BARS (Incl. Brew Bars/Pubs)**
  1. Barossa Valley Brewing — 93
  2. Barossa Brewing Company — 93
  3. Belgian Beer Café – Oostende — 89
  4. Coopers Alehouse at the Earl — 89
  5. Gilbert St Hotel — 89
  6. Grumpy's Brewhaus — 89
  7. Hahndorf Inn — 89
  8. Holdfast Bay Brewing Company — 89
  9. Lobethal Bierhaus — 89
  10. McLaren Vale Beer Company — 97
  11. Port Dock Brewery Hotel — 89
  12. The Austral Hotel — 89
  13. The Colonist — 89
  14. The Crown & Sceptre — 89
  15. The Earl of Leicester Hotel — 89
  16. The Kings — 89
  17. The Lion Hotel — 89
  18. The Steam Exchange Brewery — 97
  19. The Wheatsheaf Hotel — 89
  20. Woolshed Brewery — 93

- **BOTTLESHOPS**
  1. Bar on Gouger — 88
  2. Belair Fine Wines — 88
  3. Dan Murphy's — 88
  4. Edinburgh Hotel — 88
  5. Goodwood Cellars — 88
  6. Melbourne Street Fine Wine Cellars — 88

- **VENUE PROFILES**
  1. Beard and Brau Brewery — 100
  2. Coopers Brewery — 99
  3. Dan Murphy's — 98
  4. Goodwood Cellars — 100
  5. McLaren Vale Beer Company — 101
  6. Pike's Oakbank Beer — 100

■ TAS

- **BREWERIES/BEER COMPANIES**
  1. Boag's Centre for Beer Lovers — 107
  2. Cascade Brewery — 113
  3. IronHouse Brewery — 107
  4. Moo Brew — 113
  5. Seven Sheds — 107
  6. Taverner's Brewery — 107
  7. The Tasmanian Chilli Beer Company — 113
  8. The Two Metre Tall Company — 113
  9. Van Dieman Brewing — 107
  10. Wineglass Bay Brewing — 113

- **BEER BARS (Incl. Brew Bars/Pubs)**
  1. Bar Celona — 112
  2. Blue Café Bar — 107
  3. Cock 'N' Bull — 107
  4. Customs House Hotel — 112
  5. Kings Meadows Hotel — 107
  6. Knopwoods Retreat — 112
  7. Mobius Lounge Bar — 112
  8. MONA Wine Bar — 112
  9. Mud Bar & Restaurant — 107
  10. Pub in the Paddock — 107
  11. Republic Bar — 112
  12. Shipwright's Arms — 112
  13. The Alley Cat — 112
  14. The Brisbane Hotel — 112
  15. The IXL Long Bar — 112
  16. The New Sydney Hotel — 112
  17. The Squires Bounty — 112

- **BOTTLESHOPS**
  1. 9/11 — 112
  2. Big Bargain Bottleshop — 112
  3. Channel Court Cellars — 112
  4. Club Hotel Bottleshop (Big Bargain) — 107
  5. Cool Wine — 112
  6. Crown Cellars (Thirsty Camel) — 107
  7. Grape Bar & Bottleshop — 112
  8. Original Pizza Pub Bottleshop (Big Bargain) — 107
  9. Thirsty Camel — 112
  10. Wursthaus Kitchen — 112

- **CIDER PRODUCERS**
  1. Tasmanian Inn Cider (North West Bay Cider) — 113

- **DISTILLERIES**
  1. Hellyers Road Distillery — 107
  2. Lark Distillery — 113
  3. Nant Distillery — 113
  4. Small Concern Whisky Distillery — 107
  5. The Tasmania Distillery — 113

- **HOMEBREW SHOPS**
  1. Northern Home Brewing — 107
  2. Tasmanian Home Brewing — 113

For more Homebrew Shop listings please go to www.brewcellar.com.au

- **VENUE PROFILES**
  1. Australian Honey Products — 114
  2. Moo Brew — 115
  3. Van Dieman Brewing — 114

■ VIC

- **BREWERIES/BEER COMPANIES**
  1. 2 Brothers Brewery — 127
  2. 3 Ravens Brewery — 127
  3. Arctic Fox Brewery — 141
  4. Avonmore Estate Biodynamic Wines — 137
  5. Beacon Brewing Co. — 145
  6. Bellarine Estate and Bellarine Brewing Co — 145
  7. Bitch Brewing — 127
  8. Boat Rocker Brewing Company — 127
  9. Boyntons Feathertop Winery — 133
  10. Bridge Road Brewers — 133
  11. Bright Brewery — 133
  12. Buckley's Beer — 149
  13. Buffalo Brewery — 133
  14. BROO Beer — 127
  15. Bullant Brewery — 141
  16. Carlton Brewhouse & CUB Brewery — 127
  17. Coldstream Brewery — 149
  18. Coldwater Creek Tavern & Microbrewery — 141
  19. Echuca Brewing Company Brewery Bar & Grill — 137
  20. Dolphin Brewery — 137
  21. Effen Enterprises — 127
  22. Forrest Brewing Co — 145
  23. Grand Ridge Brewery — 141
  24. Harcourt Valley Vineyard — 137
  25. Hargreaves Hill Brewing Company — 149
  26. Hawthorn Brewing — 127
  27. Hickinbotham Winery & Brewery — 129
  28. Holgate Brewhouse — 137
  29. Independent Distillers — 145
  30. James Squire Brewhouse Portland Hotel — 127
  31. Jamieson Brewery — 133
  32. Kooinda Brewery — 127
  33. Matilda Bay Garage Brewery — 141
  34. Mt Markey Winery & Lone Hand BrewHouse — 141
  35. Mildura Brewery — 137
  36. Moon Dog Craft Brewery — 127
  37. Mornington Peninsula Brewery — 129
  38. Mountain Goat Brewery — 127
  39. O'Brien Brewing — 137
  40. Otway Estate Winery & Brewery — 145
  41. Piss Beer Co — 127
  42. Port Pier Café — 145
  43. Red Duck Provedore — 145
  44. Red Hill Brewery — 129
  45. Rusty Water Brewery — 29
  46. Savaraln Brewery — 141
  47. Scottish Chief's Tavern Brewery*
  *Check if operating prior visit. — 145
  48. Southern Bay Brewing Company — 145
  49. Sundance Brewing International — 127
  50. Sweetwater Brewing Company — 133
  51. Temple Brewing Company — 127
  52. The Flying Horse Bar & Brewery — 145
  53. Three Troupers Brewery — 137
  54. Thunder Road Brewing Company — 127
  55. Tooborac Hotel & Brewery — 137
  56. True South Brewery — 127
  57. University of Ballarat — 137
  58. White Rabbit Brewer — 149

Brewery Tours
Take a guided tour of the breweries in Melbourne, the Yarra Valley, Mornington Peninsula or Macedon Ranges with Aussie Brewery Tours; 1300 787 039 or www.aussiebrewerytours.com.au

- **BEER BARS (Incl. Brew Bars/Pubs)**
  1. 2 Brothers Brewery — 127
  2. 3 Ravens Brewery — 127
  3. Bar Fred — 125
  4. Beer DeLuxe — 125
  5. Belgian Beer Café Bluestone — 125

6. Belgian Bier Café Eureka	125	
7. Bertha Brown's	125	
8. Biero Bar	125	
9. Big Mouth	125	
10. Bimbo Deluxe	125	
11. Breakfast & Beer	137	
12. Bridge Road Brewers	133	
13. Bright Brewery	133	
14. Buffalo Brewery	133	
15. Campari House	125	
16. Carlton Brewhouse and CUB Brewery	127	
17. Chapel St Cellars	126	
18. Charlie's Bar	125	
19. Coldstream Brewery	149	

- **BEER BARS (Incl. Brew Bars/Pubs) CONT'D**

20. Collins Quarter	125
21. Cocoon Bar, Swanston Hotel	125
22. Echuca Brewing Company Brewery Bar & Grill	137
23. European Bier Café	125
24. Great Northern Hotel	126
25. Hargreaves Hill Brewing Company	149
26. Hell's Kitchen	125
27. Hickinbotham Winery & Brewery	129
28. Hofbräuhaus	125
29. Holgate Brewhouse	137
30. Jamieson Brewery	133
31. Josie Bones	125
32. Little Creatures Dining Hall	126
33. Lucky Coq	125
34. Mildura Brewery	137
35. Mitre Tavern	125
36. Mornington Peninsula Brewery	129
37. Mountain Goat Brewery	127
38. Mrs Parma's	126
39. Napier Hotel	126
40. Oscar's Ale House	125
41. Otway Estate Winery & Brewery	145
42. Scottish Chief's Tavern Brewery*	
*Check if operating prior visit.	145
43. Penny Blue	125
44. Phoenix Brewery Restaurant	137
45. Port Pier Café	145
46. Portland Hotel (James Squire Brewhouse)	127
47. Rainbow Hotel	125
48. Red Duck Provedore	145
49. Red Hill Brewery	129
50. Rusty Water Brewery	129
51. Saint & Rogue	125
52. Sweetwater Brewing Company	133
53. Tazio Birraria, Pizzeria	125
54. The Albert Park Hotel	125
55. The Aviary	125
56. The Cherry Tree Hotel	125
57. The Courthouse	126
58. The Dispensary Enoteca	137
59. The Flying Horse Bar & Brewery	145
60. The Fox Hotel	125
61. The Local Taphouse	125
62. The Retreat Hotel	125
63. The Rifle Brigade Hotel	137
64. The Royston	125
65. The Shamrock Hotel	137
66. The Terminus Hotel	125
67. Three Degrees Bar	125
68. Tooborac Hotel & Brewery	137
69. Transport Hotel	125
70. True South Brewery	127
71. White Rabbit Brewery	149
72. Wine Bank on View	137
73. World Restaurant & Bar	125
74. Young & Jackson Hotel	125

- **BOTTLESHOPS**

1. 1st Choice	126
2. Acland Cellars	126
3. Australian Wine Clearance Centre	126
4. Blackhearts & Sparrows	126
5. Carwyn Cellars	126
6. Chapel St Cellars	126
7. Cloudwine	126
8. Dan Murphy's	126
9. Prince Wine Store	126
10. Purvis Beer	126
11. Purvis Cellars	126
12. Slowbeer	126
13. Smith Street Cellars	126
14. Speakeasy Cellars	126
15. Swords Select	126
16. The Local Bottle Store & Provisions	26
17. Yarragon Ale House	141

- **DISTILLERIES**

1. Bacchus Distillery	141
2. Bakery Hill Distillery	127
3. Timboon Railway Shed Distillery	145
4. Victoria Valley Distillery	127

- **HOMEBREW SHOPS**

1. Brewer's Choice	149
2. Grain & Grape	126

For more Homebrew Shop listings please go to www.brewcellar.com.au

- **CIDER PRODUCERS**

1. Beechworth Cider	133
2. Kellybrook Winery and Kelly Brothers Cider Co.	149
3. Punt Road Wines and Napoleone & Co Cider	149

- **VENUE PROFILES**

1. 2 Brothers Brewery & Beerhall	150
2. Aussie Brewery Tours	150
3. BREW Cellar Distribution	152
4. Brewer's Choice	157
5. Bridge Road Brewers	154
6. Bright Brewery	154
7. Bullant Brewery	156
8. Coldwater Creek Microbrewery	156
9. Grain and Grape	152
10. Grand Ridge Brewery	155
11. Hargreaves Hill Brewing Company	157
12. Hickinbotham Winery & Brewery	154
13. James Squire Brewhouse	152
14. Mountain Goat Brewery	150
15. Napoleone & Co Cider	157
16. Savara in Brewery	156
17. Sweetwater Brewing Company	154
18. The Fox Hotel	153
19. Young & Jackson Hotel	151

WA

- **BREWERIES/BEER COMPANIES**

1. Billabong Brewing	173
2. Blacksalt Brewery	173
3. Blackwood Valley Brewing – The Cidery	177
4. Bootleg Brewery	163
5. Brew42 Brewery	177
6. Bush Shack Brewery	163
7. Cheeky Monkey Brewery & Cidery	163
8. Colonial Brewing Company	163
9. Cowaramup Brewing Company	163
10. Denmark Brew & Ales	177
11. Duckstein Brewery	163, 181
12. Eagle Bay Brewing Co	163
13. Edith Cowan University	173
14. Elmar's In The Valley	181
15. Feral Brewing Company	181
16. Gage Roads Brewing Co	173
17. Indian Ocean Brewing Company	173
18. Ironbark Brewery	181
19. Last Drop Brewery & Restaurant	173
20. Little Creatures Brewery	173
21. Mash Brewing	172, 177, 181
22. Matso's Broome Brewery	165
23. Moody Cow Brewery	177
24. Nail Brewing	173
25. Occy's Brewery	163
26. Old Coast Rd Brewery	177
27. Swan Brewery	173
28. Tanglehead Brewing Company	177
29. The Grove Vineyard (Liqueur Factory, Distillery, Nano Brewery and Cafe)	163
30. The Monk Brewery & Kitchen	173
31. The Old Brewery	173
32. Wild Bull Brewery	177

WA Brewery Tours
0423 976 116, tours@thebrewersdray.com.au

- **BEER BARS (Incl. Brew Bars/Pubs)**

1. Belgian Beer Cafe Westende	172
2. Bootleg Brewery	163
3. Brew42 Brewery	177
4. Bush Shack Brewery	163
5. Cheeky Monkey Brewery & Cidery	163
6. Clancy's Fish Pub's	163, 172
7. Clancy's Fishbar City Beach	172
8. Colonial Brewing Company	163
9. Cottesloe Beach Hotel	172
10. Cowaramup Brewing Company	163
11. Duckstein Brewery	163, 181
12. Eagle Bay Brewing Co	163
13. Elizabethan Village Pub	172
14. Elmar's In The Valley	181
15. Feral Brewing Company	181
16. Five Bar	172
17. Indian Ocean Brewing Company	173
18. Ironbark Brewery	181
19. J.B. O'Reilly's	172
20. Last Drop Brewery & Restaurant	173
21. Little Creatures Brewery	173
22. Malt Market Bar & Kitchen	163
23. Mash Brasserie Rockingham	172
24. Mash Brewing	177, 181
25. Matso's Broome Brewery	165
26. Moody Cow Brewery	177
27. Moondyne Joe's	172
28. Occy's Brewery	163
29. Ocean Beach Hotel	172
30. Old Coast Rd Brewery	177
31. Queens Tavern	172
32. Sail & Anchor Hotel	172
33. Settlers Tavern	163
34. Tanglehead Brewing Company	177
35. The Best Drop Tavern	172
36. The Brass Monkey Hotel	172
37. The Generous Squire	172
38. The Grove Vineyard (Liqueur Factory, Distillery, Nano Brewery and Cafe)	163
39. The Last Drop Tavern	172
40. The Monk Brewery & Kitchen	173
41. The Norfolk Hotel	172
42. The Old Brewery	173
43. The Paddo	172
44. The Roebuck Bay Hotel	165
45. Wild Bull Brewery	177
46. Zeebar	165

- **BOTTLESHOPS**

1. Big Brews Liquor	172
2. Cellarbrations Carlisle	172
3. Dan Murphy's	172
4. Greenmount Liquor	172
5. International Beer Shop	172
6. Liquor Barons Mt Lawley	172
7. Mane Liquor	172
8. The Beer Store	172
9. The Freo Doctor Liquor Store	172

- **DISTILLERIES**

1. Great Northern Distillery (The Kimberley Rum Company)	181
2. Great Southern Distilling Company	177
3. The Grove Vineyard (Liqueur Factory, Distillery, Nano Brewery and Cafe)	163
4. Wild Swan Distilling Co	181

- **CIDER PRODUCERS**

1. Blackwood Valley Brewing – The Cidery	177
2. Cheeky Monkey Brewery & Cidery	163
3. Mountford Wines (Tangletoe Cider)	177

- **VENUE PROFILES**
  1. Belgian Bier Café Westende — 188
  2. Billabong Brewing — 190
  3. Bootleg Brewery — 183
  4. Bush Shack Brewery — 184
  5. Cellarbrations Carlisle — 188
  6. Cowaramup Brewing Company — 182
  7. Eagle Bay Brewing Co — 183
  8. Edith Cowan University (ECU) — 187
  9. Elmar's in the Valley — 190
  10. Feral Brewing Company — 191
  11. Liquor Barons Mt Lawley — 188
  12. Maltmarket Bar & Kitchen — 182
  13. Mane Liquor Beer Specialists — 189
  14. Mash Brewing Company — 190
  15. Matso's Broome Brewery — 186
  16. Moody Cow Brewery — 184
  17. Sail & Anchor Hotel — 185
  18. The Brewers Dray — 190
  19. The Freo Doctor Liquor Store — 184
  20. The Grove Vineyard, Liqueur Factory, Distillery and Nano Brewery & Cafe — 182
  21. The Monk Brewery & Kitchen — 184

- **NEW VENUES?**
To nominate a new beer venue, please go to www.beerandbrewer.com and vote for them in the Beer & Brewer Awards, or feature them in the Forums.

NEW ZEALAND (NZ)

NORTH ISLAND

- **BREWERIES/BEER COMPANIES**
  1. 666 Brewing Co — 207
  2. Aotearoa Breweries — 199
  3. Boundary Road Brewery — 207
  4. Brauhaus Frings — 207
  5. BREW — 199
  6. Croucher Brewing Co — 199
  7. Epic Beer — 207
  8. DB - Tui — 203
  9. DB - Waitemata Brewery — 207
  10. Hallertau Brewbar — 207
  11. Hawkes Bay Independent Brewery — 199
  12. Independent Liquor — 207
  13. Island Bay Brewing — 203
  14. Kaimai Brewing Company — 199
  15. Kiwi Breweries — 199
  16. Liberty Brewing Company — 199
  17. Lion Breweries — 207
  18. Mike's — 199
  19. Peak Brewery — 203
  20. Roosters Brew House — 199
  21. Saratoga Estate — 207
  22. Shunters Yard Brewery — 207
  23. Sunshine Brewery — 199
  24. Steam Brewing Company — 207
  25. The Coromandel Brewing Company — 207
  26. The Leigh Sawmill Café — 207
  27. Tuatara Brewing Co — 203
  28. Waiheke Island Brewery — 207
  29. Waipa Brewery — 199
  30. Waituna Brewing — 203
  31. Wassail Brauhaus — 199
  32. Yeastie Boys — 203

- **BEER BARS**
  1. Andrew Andrew — 207
  2. Bar Edward — 203
  3. Brew on Quay — 207
  4. Brewers Bar — 199
  5. Cock & Bull — 207
  6. Fort Street Union — 207
  7. Galbraith's Alehouse — 207
  8. Golden Dawn — 207
  9. Gothenburg — 207
  10. Great Kiwi Ale House — 199
  11. Hashigo Zake — 203
  12. House on Hood — 207
  13. O'Carrolls — 207
  14. Malthouse — 203
  15. Tahi Bar — 207
  16. The Bluestone Room — 207
  17. The Brühaus — 203
  18. The Duke of Marlborough Hotel — 207
  19. The Hop Garden — 203
  20. The Occidental Belgian Beer Café — 207
  21. The Pear Tree — 207

- **BOTTLESHOPS**
  1. Moore Wilson's — 203
  2. New World — 203
  3. Regional Wines & Spirits — 203

- **HOMEBREW SHOP**
  1. Brewers Coop — 207

SOUTH ISLAND

- **BREWERIES/BEER COMPANIES**
  1. 8 Wired Brewing — 219
  2. Arrow Brewing Co — 211
  3. Brew Moon Brewery — 211
  4. Cassels & Sons — 211
  5. Dead Good Beers — 219
  6. DB Mainland Brewery — 211
  7. Dux de Lux — 211
  8. The Emerson Brewing — 211
  9. Founders Brewery — 219
  10. Golden Bear Brewing — 219
  11. Green Man Brewery — 211
  12. Harrington's Breweries — 211
  13. Invercargill Brewery — 211
  14. Lighthouse Brewery — 219
  15. Lion Nathan — 211
  16. Matson's Brewery — 211
  17. McCashin's Brewery Bar — 219
  18. McDuff's Brewery — 211
  19. Moa Brewing — 219
  20. Monkey Wizard Brewery — 219
  21. Monteith's Brewing Co. — 219
  22. Nelson Bays Brewery — 219
  23. Pink Elephant Brewing — 219
  24. Renaissance Brewing — 219
  25. Speight's Brewery — 211
  26. Sprig & Fern Brewery — 219
  27. The Mussel Inn — 219
  28. The Twisted Hop — 211
  29. Three Boys Brewery — 211
  30. Totara Breweries — 219
  31. Townshend Brewery — 219
  32. Wanaka Beerworks — 211
  33. West Coast Brewing — 219
  34. Wigram Brewing Co — 211

- **BEER BARS**
  1. Albar — 211
  2. Atlas Beer Café — 211
  3. Cardrona Hotel — 211
  4. Metro Cafe and Bar — 211
  5. Minibar — 211
  6. Pomeroy's Old Brewery Inn — 211
  7. Roots Bar — 218
  8. Scotch Wine Bar — 218
  9. Sprig & Fern Tavern's — 218
  10. The Abbey Ale House — 218
  11. The Free House — 218
  12. The Malthouse on Dodson — 218
  13. The Moutere Inn — 218
  14. The Old Bank — 218
  15. The Secret Garde Ale — 218
  16. Tonic — 211
  17. Traveller's Rest — 218

- **CIDER PRODUCERS**
  1. Redwood Cellars

- **VENUE PROFILES**
  1. Brewers Coop — 220
  2. Kaimai Brewing Company — 221
  3. Malthouse — 220
  4. McCashin's Brewery — 222
  5. Mussel Inn Café Bar and Brewery — 222
  6. Regional Wines & Spirits — 222
  7. Renaissance Brewing Company — 222
  8. St Katherine's Brewing Co. — 220
  9. Sprig & Fern Brewery — 223
  10. The Free House — 223

- **NEW VENUES?**
To nominate a new beer venue, please go to www.beerandbrewer.com and vote for them in the Beer & Brewer Awards, or feature them in the Forums.